The Archaeology of Liberty
in an American Capital

The publisher gratefully acknowledges the
generous contribution to this book provided
by the General Endowment Fund of the
University of California Press Foundation.

The Archaeology of Liberty in an American Capital

Excavations in Annapolis

Mark P. Leone

UNIVERSITY OF CALIFORNIA PRESS
Berkeley • *Los Angeles* • *London*

University of California Press, one of the most
distinguished university presses in the United States,
enriches lives around the world by advancing
scholarship in the humanities, social sciences, and
natural sciences. Its activities are supported by the UC
Press Foundation and by philanthropic contributions
from individuals and institutions. For more information, visit www.ucpress.edu.

University of California Press
Berkeley and Los Angeles, California

University of California Press, Ltd.
London, England

Library of Congress Cataloging-in-Publication Data

Leone, Mark P.
    The archaeology of liberty in an American capital :
excavations in Annapolis / Mark P. Leone.
        p.   cm.
    Includes bibliographical references and index.
    ISBN 0-520-24450-8 (alk. paper)
    1. Annapolis (Md.)—Antiquities.   2. Excavations
(Archaeology)—Maryland—Annapolis.   3. Annapolis
(Md.)—Social conditions—18th century.   4. Annapolis
(Md.)—Social conditions—19th century.   5. Elite
(Social sciences)—Maryland—Annapolis—History.
6. Power (Social sciences)—Maryland—Annapolis—
History.   I. Title.

F189.A647L46   2005
975.2'5502—dc22   2005005761

Manufactured in the United States of America
13 12 11 10 09 08 07 06 05
10 9 8 7 6 5 4 3 2 1

This book is printed on Natures Book, containing
50% post-consumer waste and meets the minimum
requirements of ANSI/NISO Z39.48–1992 (R 1997)
(Permanence of Paper).

Contents

List of Illustrations and Tables   vii

Preface   xi

1. The Importance of Knowing Annapolis   1

2. The Research Design   34

3. Landscapes of Power   63

4. The Rise of Popular Opinion   111

5. Time and Work Discipline   152

6. From Althusser and Lukács to Habermas:
   Archaeology in Public in Annapolis   179

7. African America   192

8. What Do We Know?   245

Appendix   267

Works Cited   281

Index   307

Illustrations and Tables

ILLUSTRATIONS

1. Aerial view of the central part of Annapolis — 5
2. Façade of Chase-Lloyd House — 6
3. William Paca House mantel — 9
4. St. Anne's Church and the Maryland State House — 10
5. The Maryland State House — 13
6. Death's head excavated from Jonas Green's print shop — 28
7. Large holster boss with spread eagle, excavated from Brice House — 32
8. Looking up the double stair of the Chase Lloyd House — 39
9. Charles Willson Peale's museum — 40
10. The Calvert House hypocaust — 43
11. View down the main path in the William Paca Garden — 44
12. Scientific instruments from Annapolis — 46
13. Individual pieces of printer's type with impressions — 49
14. Floor plan of the Hammond Harwood House, showing the façade — 50
15. Desk with many compartments — 54
16. Excavated toothbrush handles from Annapolis — 56
17. Cache from the kitchen, Slayton House — 59

18. Map of the William Paca Garden 65
19. Map of the 1771 Charles Carroll of Carrollton Garden showing geometric subdivisions 74
20. Map of the Ridout Garden showing its terraces, falls, and beds 76
21. 1990 Map of State Circle 86
22. Archaeological units dating from c. 1700 around State Circle 88
23. Archaeological units dating from c. 1800 around State Circle 89
24. 1885 Map of State Circle 90
25. 1882 Map of the front of the Maryland State House with its immediate landscaping 91
26. The 1718 Stoddert plan with a geometric egg 92
27. Lines of sight into State and Church Circles 95
28. Individual pieces of printer's type with printer's ruler 112
29. Large O and J against a printer's ruler 121
30. *Maryland Gazette*, December 3–10, 1728 125
31. *Maryland Gazette*, January 13, 1748 126
32. *Maryland Gazette*, January 28, 1768 128
33. *Maryland Gazette*, January 10, 1788 130
34. *Maryland Gazette*, February 4, 1808 131
35. *Maryland Gazette*, January 7, 1813 136
36. Charles Willson Peale supervising the excavation of a mammoth skeleton in New York 146
37. Creamware dishes, teacups, and filigreed ceramic basket 158
38. The Charles Carroll House in Annapolis, where the first cache of spirit materials was discovered 201
39. The room in the Charles Carroll House where the main cache of spirit materials was found 202
40. Artifacts in the main Cache of spirit materials in the Charles Carroll House 204
41. Slayton House, street façade, 1920s 206
42. Slayton House, cache from the kitchen 208
43. Slayton House, cache from the kitchen hearth, 209
44. Slayton House, cache from the kitchen 211

45. The Brice House cosmogram   217
46. Black mirror and black and white beads, Brice House
    cosmogram   219
47. Pins from the Brice House cosmogram   220
48. Red flannel from the Brice House cosmogram   222
49. Button with inlaid bits of mother of pearl from the
    Brice House cosmogram   233

TABLES

1. Percentages of wealth by social group (class) in Annapolis,
   1688–1777   16
2. The population of Annapolis, 1699–1980   19
3. Census information on whites and blacks in Anne Arundel
   County and Annapolis, 1755–1860   20
4. Possession of clocks and scientific instruments by wealth
   group in Annapolis, 1688–1777   47
5. Percentage relative error for the fit of an egg and a circle 93
6. Percentages of the typefaces used in the *Maryland Gazette*
   from the early eighteenth to the late nineteenth centuries
   by stratigraphic context   133
7. Percentages of spaces used by typeface in the *Maryland
   Gazette* from the early eighteenth to the late nineteenth
   centuries by stratigraphic context   134
8. Percentages of the typefaces and spaces used in the early
   eighteenth- to late nineteenth-century *Maryland Gazette*
   based on the total number of pieces found   135
9. Variety of tableware shapes from nine archaeological sites
   in Annapolis, 1700–1900   156
10. Variety of tableware decoration from four archaeological
    sites in Annapolis, 1700–1900   160
11. Caches of artifacts from the Slayton House in Annapolis
    tied to African spirit traditions   210
12. Caches of artifacts from archaeological sites in Virginia
    tied to African spirit traditions, 1702–1920   225
13. Textual references in the Federal Writers' Project composite
    autobiographies listing purposes and placement of artifacts
    tied to African spirit traditions   226

Preface

Although the idea in this book is my own, and I am responsible for how it is played out and the possibilities for a view of history that it creates, my former students and current colleagues contributed in important ways to the project of making Annapolis archaeology contribute to understanding the history of our country. Paul A. Shackel, Barbara J. Little, Parker B. Potter Jr., and Elizabeth B. Kryder-Reid wrote big and groundbreaking dissertations on Annapolis through Archaeology in Annapolis. Paul R. Mullins, Mark S. Warner, Eric Larsen and Hannah Jopling explored African America. Christopher N. Matthews made the nineteenth century a problem by showing how Annapolis modernized behind the mark of historic preservation. And Matthew Palus made understanding the twentieth century into a problem by studying the use of public utilities to create a dependent suburb out of a freestanding town and also archaeology as an activity that could be regulated by government to control property value. Jennifer Babiarz took us out of Annapolis and onto Wye Island to follow William Paca, as has Lisa Kraus. I borrowed heavily from all of them.

There were two recruiting environments from which students came to Archaeology in Annapolis. The Department of Anthropology runs an annual archaeological field school in Annapolis and has since the summer of 1982. For six weeks each summer since, with one exception, between ten and twenty-two students, mostly undergraduates and mostly from the University of Maryland, College Park, came to learn archaeology in Maryland's capital city through our field school. We became a welcomed neighborhood fixture in the city. Over the years, about 330 students learned archaeology, contributed to the project, became better educated scientists and more articulate citizens, and earned the gratitude of their teachers, of whom I was one. From this field school has come part of the younger generation of American and British historical archaeologists. To all of them, I am grateful. Each is listed by name in this preface.

The second environment from which students were recruited is the Masters of Applied Anthropology program at the University of Maryland, College Park. This program requires an internship, not a thesis, and many internships were taken through Archaeology in Annapolis, with many MAAs making substantial contributions to our project. Michael Lucas, Kristopher Beadenkopf, Jason Shellenhamer, Amelia Chisholm, Matthew Cochran, and Robert Chidester have made the project better and more accessible to the public and to the scientific communities.

Lysbeth Acuff, Gilda Anroman, Stephen Austin, Alecia Parker, Tara Tetrault (Goodrich), and Kirsti Uunila participated, learned, and gave back energy, intelligence, and dedication. Each of our MAAs has founded proud careers.

Archaeology in Annapolis began as the idea of St. Clair Wright, one of the founders and, certainly, the visionary behind Historic Annapolis's success. Much of the success of the archaeological program came from the administrative steadiness of Pringle Symonds and her senior staff members, Judith Sweeny, Lynell Bowen, Patricia Kohlhepp, and Dorothy Callahan, to all of whom I am in debt for guidance and help as Archaeology in Annapolis developed.

Ann Fligsten has always provided support and advice for Archaeology in Annapolis, both while she was president of Historic Annapolis Foundation and subsequently. Joseph M. Coale III and Brian Alexander, presidents of the Historic Annapolis Foundation appreciated the role of archaeology in their organization. Gregory Stiverson also led the organization. Julie Fife, Mary Corey, Heather Ersts, and Glenn Campbell have been important contributors in archaeology's success in the Historic Annapolis Foundation. Lucy Dos Passos Coggin, former garden director, and Richard Shaw, when chief gardener in the William Paca garden, were always welcoming and helpful. Ruffin Wright, longtime gardener, was always willing to help.

The project maintained two laboratories simultaneously, one in Annapolis and one in College Park. Beth Ford and then Bob Sonderman

ran the laboratory in Annapolis. Both laboratories were then run hero-
ically by Julie Ernstein, Elizabeth Kryder-Reid, Marian Creveling, Lynn D.
Jones, Laura Galke, Jessica Neuwirth, and Thomas Cuddy, who were always, it seemed, in two places at once. They made all the site reports
possible.

People who volunteered to process the artifacts excavated throughout the city enabled Archaeology in Annapolis to work. Nancy Stein gave
her time and organizational skills for many years. Karen Dicke, Syd
Gaardner, John Quinan, Jennifer Stapleton, and Bill Turpin made so much
archaeology happen, helped to make the project participation available
to people in the city, and were of such good will that they made archaeology an almost inevitable part of daily life for many city residents.

Early on in the creation of Archaeology in Annapolis, St. Clair Wright
and Pringle Symonds turned to the city of Annapolis for financial help in
supporting the necessary laboratory activities for a citywide project that
was operated mainly through the University of Maryland. Mayor Richard
Hillman agreed to consider a grant for a laboratory supervisor. The members of the City Council agreed. Successive mayors have agreed to put
funding proposals into their budgets and these have been approved by
City Councils since about 1983. Such funding by the Annapolis City Council made Archaeology in Annapolis possible. The funding paid for the laboratory supervisors, while many dedicated Annapolis citizens worked in
the laboratory in Annapolis, signaling to everybody that both the university and archaeology were welcome in the city. I am particularly grateful to Mayors Richard Hillman, Dennis Callahan, Alfred Hopkins, Dean
Johnson, and Ellen Moyer. Mayors Johnson and Moyer each understood
that the archaeology was a university research project run by students
and teachers who were scientists. The mayors showed everyone that they
and the city could sponsor long-term scientific projects. My gratitude to
the Mayor's Office and to the members of the City Council is deep.
Mayor Ellen Mayer has been particularly helpful, as has Robert Agee,
city manager.

Barbara Jackson Nash of the Banneker-Douglass Museum made
possible our initiative to understand the archaeology of the city's African
American communities. The initiative and questions belong to her. Our
joint successes belong to the museum. Lawrence Hurst, Maisha Washington, Elizabeth Stewart, and Wendy Perry sustained much of the archaeological work we did together. The Stanton Center under the director of Kirby McKinney was welcoming. Many African American churches
welcomed the work of Archaeology in Annapolis, as did the leaders of

the city's Kunte Kinte Festival, Leonard Blackshear, the late Bertina Nick, and Judith Cabral. Professors Robert Hall and William Hall were pilots, beacons, and never-failing friends.

We excavated for four years at St. Mary's Church and worked in and around the Charles Carroll House at the invitation, under the direction, and with the close collaboration of Robert Worden. I owe him a great deal. He read the final manuscript of this book and improved it.

Paul Pearson, who owned and developed the Calvert House Hotel and State House Inn was the first commercial property owner to support Archeology in Annapolis. He did so generously with access to his properties, his funding, and his patience.

We also excavated for four years at the Jonas Green print shop and I am particularly grateful to Captain and Mrs. Randall Brown for providing access to their property and for their support. Philip and Susan Dodds allowed us to excavate throughout the Bordley Randall House property. They were great to work with. Margaret Dowsett allowed us to excavate at the Sands House and Anne Jensen, its current owner, has been welcoming. Stewart Knower of King and Cornwall on 22 West Street, whose gifts to Archaeology in Annapolis have been substantial, provided access and funding for our extensive excavation there, led by Julie H. Ernstein.

The civilian and military staff of the United States Naval Academy allowed us to sample the heart of their beloved institution. Without their help, we could not have been the first archaeologists to explore their land and marine resources. The Navy's preservation staff was particularly helpful.

Our extensive work at the site of the Anne Arundel County Courthouse site was made possible by Al Luckenbach. Tony Lindauer made important discoveries there and was helpful at other sites in Annapolis.

The International Masonry Institute enabled our work at the Brice House.

Many professional archaeologists worked with, in, and through Archaeology in Annapolis. Foremost is Anne E. Yentsch with whom I established an early partnership in directing the project. Her book on Annapolis is justly well known. Richard J. Dent, also an early partner in directing the project, oversaw the years of important excavations at Reynolds Tavern. Joseph W. Hopkins III, Esther Doyle Reed, and Jennifer Stabler took important leads in major archaeological excavations, as did Donald Creveling, Constance Crosby, Laura Galke, C. Jane Cox, Thomas Bodor, and Elizabeth Seidel.

John Seidel established our competence in GIS at College Park. He also led our excavations at the main campus of the Naval Academy. John Seidel's lead on GIS was followed by John Buckler's, Joseph Mueller's, and Daniel Reyes's. The Maryland Historical Trust provided funding for the GIS of the city started by John Seidel and completed by John Buckler.

When Archaeology in Annapolis began, I sought advice from prominent archaeologists whom I knew and admired. I modeled our excavations on the care and dedication long shown to historical archaeology by Stanley South. Only with persistence could we bring off a semblance of his scientific skill. When we did approximate it, it was because of the skill and understanding of my own students who had a profound ability to combine problem and methods.

Readers will be able to judge Jim Deetz's central importance to my thought from this book. He didn't agree with this analysis, but he never failed to respect the seriousness of this effort.

Kathleen Deagan and Stuart Streuver were more than kind in giving me guidance when this project began. I don't need or want to repeat their warnings or advice here. They were correct. I never forgot what they told me and I remain grateful a quarter century later. I hope I have done the same for my students.

The Maryland Historical Trust's archaeologists have played a role in sustaining Archaeology in Annapolis. Richard Hughes has provided balance and guidance on our archaeology, and funding for our GIS development. Wayne Clark has explained to many people that an archaeological project in the state capital is of benefit to all. I have certainly tried to make it that way, more so after hearing Wayne's reflections. He has also explained that the use of theory in archaeology—especially Marxist theory—is not in itself an indictment of an archaeologist. Charles Hall has always been an encouraging and steady colleague.

The Maryland Humanities Council virtually caused Archaeology in Annapolis to be Archaeology in Public in Annapolis. While open, accessible interpretations were a goal, only Mary Blair and the whole staff over many years provided the know-how and funding to design and effect public education through archaeology.

The Maryland Humanities Council provided ten or eleven grants for public performance based on archaeology. The council connected me to Philip Arnoult, founder of the Theatre Project of Baltimore, who, with John Strausbaugh designed, mounted, and trained us in public archaeology. He allowed us to teach successfully outside a university setting, and this has been an unusual accomplishment.

Our first large grant to establish a public, free teaching program for visitors to Annapolis based on archaeology came from the National Endowment for the Humanities. I am grateful to George Fahr and Steven Mansbach for their help at NEH. In addition, in 1990, I received an NEH Fellowship for Independent Study and Research and wrote the first version of this book. It took me an additional decade to finish the task. The financial and moral support of the NEH and especially its local arm, the Maryland Humanities Council, have been pivotal to the success of using archaeology to found and maintain a factually based alternative approach to the history of Annapolis.

Equally strong support has come from the University of Maryland. William (Brit) E. Kirwan, now chancellor of the University System of Maryland, visited Archaeology in Annapolis four times and encouraged support while he was campus vice chancellor and then campus president. I responded to his presence and smile with a flow of positive science and news out of Annapolis that was good for the city, campus, and state. President John Toll, Vice President Robert Smith, and current campus President Daniel Mote have understood the role of an archaeological project for the public good in the state capital. The deans, chairs of anthropology, and vice presidents of research at the University of Maryland, College Park, have provided a constant flow of funding for the field school, laboratories, equipment, computer (IT) development, graduate student funding, undergraduate support, faculty development, travel, conferences, and publication support for the growth and development of Archaeology in Annapolis. No one person in a position of financial leadership has been more crucial in this role than Cynthia Hale in our dean's office. Dean Irwin Goldstein and Associate Dean Stewart Edelstein have been supportive of the growth and development of this project. Terrence Roach and Susan Bayly have been helpful and protective.

Bill Stuart, my colleague of many years, said to me once as I was trying to understand hoodoo or conjure, and causing myself more trouble than I should have, that African religions practiced in villages, as traditionally described by anthropologists, were often a means of social control. At that moment I understood the interpersonal nature of what I had been seeing in Annapolis—a small town—and reading in the Federal Writers' Project composite autobiographies. At that moment and at many others I appreciated his collegiality. My colleagues Tony Whitehead and Fatimah Jackson always appreciated the role archaeology could play in anthropology. Both tried to be supportive and were. I am also grateful to Erve Chambers, Aubrey Williams, Judith Freidenberg, Janet Chernela, and Michael Paolisso.

Julie H. Ernstein's persistence in our field probably matches my own. She is a good archaeologist, thorough scholar, dedicated and superior teacher, and loyal friend. We have traveled together down the long, not easy road to understanding eastern Maryland's past through historical archaeology. Ernstein indexed this volume.

James M. Harmon directed the excavations of Willam Paca's Wye Island landscape and made the important discoveries there. The owners of Wye Hall have been very generous in their support of archaeology.

Barbara Wells Sarudy introduced me to Maryland gardens beyond Annapolis and broadened my understanding of them. She has always been helpful.

Christopher Nagle gave invaluable help on statistics.

Marlys Pearson read the *Maryland Gazette* for me and found the citations illustrating precision, use of scientific methods and techniques, and the material on the formation of women's lives in the eighteenth century. Her choices were excellent and have taught me more and more as my understanding of Annapolis has expanded. Kimberly Schmidt, William Fennie, and Jeffrey Snider helped make and enforce decisions that had far-reaching impacts on my department, project, and books. Each was an important moral influence on how I did what I did. They did not make mistakes and tried to keep me from making them too.

Lisa Royce, Heather Austin, and Richelle Patterson made much of my administrative life possible and were partners in much of the success needed before a book like this was possible.

Jennifer Babiarz, Stanley Herman, and Sarah Waring, all three University of Maryland graduate students, have organized for me while I wrote, thought about, worried over, fussed about, and thought out loud about this book. They have been my companions during this process, and my debt to them can only be repaid through whatever they learned from seeing book-writing up as close as it gets without doing it yourself.

People who read this book made all the difference. Jean Russo, whose historical judgment I respect, read for historical detail and for intellectual accessibility. I am grateful for her willing and patient direction on many parts of this writing and research. Randall McGuire and Thomas Patterson read the manuscript and suggested many improvements in many ways. They both made a big difference.

Nan Wells, my wife, has always been willing to listen and keep faith that this book's problems could be solved and that it would be done. She got us to South Africa and into African and Asian communities there. In turn, our friends in those communities taught me why I had to return to Annapolis and offer to begin research and action, based on our African experience, with my colleagues of African descent in Annapolis. I found light in archaeology in South Africa and hope for the future of a socially aware or progressive historical archaeology in African America in Annapolis. This would not have happened without my wife.

Nan and I adopted Veronika in 1993, and Vika has formed this book by causing me to put it first and then second in a continuous oscillation of personal debate about who and what come first for me. I never did find an answer, but now she's grown up and successful and the book's out. My sister, Joanne Leone, has always offered encouragement and admiration, and Sayra and Neil Meyerhoff have always been supportive. Elizabeth Anderson, Joan Davenport, Jim Green, Matthew Daley, and Edward Dulaney have always been encouraging and given their long-term support.

Joseph Antonellis and Irving Zaretsky, friends who are family members, have sustained me through this process of writing. Stephen Kwass has been an important guide.

Timothy Malone provided most of the names of the students who took our archaeological field school. I am very grateful to him. Photographs for many of the illustrations in this book were taken by Howard Erenfeld and Steven M. Cummings. To these professionals whose artistry is so clear, I am in debt. I am in debt to Blake Edgar, Cynthia Fulton, and Peter Dreyer for making the production of this book so professional and delightful. Stanley Holwitz has been a colleague since he encouraged me to write my first book.

In writing this book, I have relied on many, many colleagues who are accomplished scholars and who, even though they may often disagree with the explanations I advance, have written the foundations on which I operate. Charles Orser (1988a, 1988b, 1996, 2004; Orser and Fagan 1995), Robert Paynter (1985, 1988, 1990), Tom Patterson (1986, 1989, 1999, 2003), Terrence Epperson (1990, 1999), and Randall McGuire (1988, 1992a, 1992b) have worked for years to conceptualize archaeological theory within a Marxist and Marxian framework, as have others. These authors have brought a productive theoretical framework to historical archaeology that emphasizes class, ideology, race, resistance, capital's role, consumption, workers, factory conditions, and, in general, an orientation to relations between owners and workers, owners and consumers, and dominant and subordinate groups. I include here Alison Wylie

(2002), who helped clarify my archaeological thinking, and Carmel Schrire (1988, 1995), who showed me how to write about problems in historical archaeology. These scholars do not see identity, nation build-ing, colonial institutions, or trade as neutral or as smoothly functioning ways in which Europe extended itself to virtually all places around the globe. We have tended to act as mutually reinforcing scholars who wanted to ease archaeology to the left and, in the case of the people I cite here, particularly to move historical archaeology to an inclusion of political considerations and political action on behalf of greater democracy for excluded groups. The lead these scholars provided can be seen through-out the arguments I make.

I am beholden to early founders of historical archaeology like J. C. Harrington (1955) who labored to make room for the existence of the field. We all owe a big debt to Ivor Noël Hume (1963, 1969, 1974, 1982) for many reasons. He inspired me because he wrote for everyone. His is a gift that few can equal: the ability to reach beyond the scientific lan-guage of the field—a necessary language to be sure—to all readers of American history. He saw that Americans wanted to read about our past through excavation and linked access to the discoveries made that way and the surprises that came from digging historic ground. He took method and made it drama, made it comprehensive, and of national importance. He did something else that no other leader in the field did in the 1980s. He acknowledged that others interpreted archaeological findings for their own purposes. Even though he would not have gone my route, through our conversations, he helped me see that living needs shaped archaeol-ogy, as much as archaeology's discoveries shaped final interpretations in a place like Colonial Williamsburg. In acknowledging his large role in historical archaeology and in my own intellectual development, I recog-nize his discoveries and his enormous scholarship.

When we were students together at the University of Arizona, Robert Schuyler (1970, 1978) began his definitions of historical archaeology. Later, when we were graduate students together, and then early profes-sionals, I saw him work out the scope of the field, its early expressions in the Society for Historical Archaeology, and his determination that it should be neither an arm of prehistoric archaeology nor the weak and dominated offshoot of the Society for American Archaeology. Robert Schuyler was determined that the field be anthropological and not be tied either to colonial North America or the U.S. East Coast. He has trained many excellent students in this field, but his greatest impact on me was his introduction to Leslie White and the idea of cultural evolution and economic determinism. Throughout this book, I have used Marx's descendents, Althusser, Lukács, and Habermas, people who learned as much from Marx as White did, but people who aimed for modern society in a way that did not occur to or interest Leslie White.

Although my work on materialist theory has been developing for three decades, I am new to understanding the African Diaspora and its materials. My introduction to African American culture happened in Annapolis by working with African Americans there who had a use for archaeology. And then my own colleagues began to introduce me to how to think about analyzing what we had been discovering. Frederick Lamp and Gladys-Marie Fry explained interpretations and scholarly opinions. Fry introduced me to the Federal Writers' Project composite autobiographies and the impact of these on her thinking and on African Americans. Timothy Ruppel became a senior partner of whom I could ask help, meaning, sense, history, and even how to shape questions when I had only gut responses and feelings. Jessica Neuwirth (Ruppel et al. 2003) made important discoveries out of what we were excavating in Annapolis through her extensive reading on African diasporic religions. A little earlier, Lynn Jones (1999) had bravely looked at spirit bundles and connected them to Africa. Laura Galke (2000) did the same and made connections I had not guessed at.

I recognize that I am reporting findings that are part of a big, long effort to study, ground, formulate, and rationalize what has come to be known as African diasporic studies. Because I am less familiar with its scholarship than with landscape studies, or with theory in historical archaeology, my own context is less grounded. But the discoveries and interpretations we are responsible for through Annapolis fit into, expand, and are proudly offered to this tradition, one central to the heightened success of American historical archaeology.

Two of my first teachers were Frederick Lamp and John Vlach, both of whom generously offered support and direction about our discoveries when local scholars were dismissing them. Simultaneously, friends like Teresa Singleton (1985, 1988, 1995), Jerome Handler (1974, 1978), and Michael Blakey (1983, 1989) and his colleague Warren Perry influenced me by showing how to think about the problems, their evidence, historical depth, and political importance to people of African descent. This includes Douglas Armstrong (1990). Charles Fairbanks (1972, 1984) is credited within historical archaeology with the earliest excavations of a slave cabin. Robert Schulyer (1980) excavated Sandy Ground on Staten Island, also an African American site and connected to a living community.

Kathleen Deagan, David Hurst Thomas, and Stewart Streuever, who have mounted large archaeological projects on which I modeled Archaeology in Annapolis, were parallel influences on my approach in Annapolis. The true roots of this model for me are the expeditions in Arizona mounted by my teachers Emil Haury, Paul S. Martin, Raymond H. Thompson, and William Longacre. All had institutional projects that were famous, operated over long periods, required constant fundraising, and sustained both scientific and popular publications. Kathleen Deagan (1983, 1995) created the famous Saint Augustine archaeology project, which along with Pamela Cressey's (1985a, 1985b, 1989) in Alexandria, was a model of how to work in a historic urban core. Kathleen Deagan and Pamela Cressey both worked on African American material, at Fort Mose and in a series of African American houses in Alexandria, respectively. From Alexandria, Stephen Shephard's (1987) work on domestic ceramics from the nineteenth century helped define issues on African American foodways and identity.

One of the largest tasks I have undertaken in Annapolis has been the proper identification of spirit bundles whose origins were in West Central Africa. There are two problems within these, one scholarly and one political. The scholarly problem is how to identify the way the spirit traditions worked and in doing so to discover their African origins. There are many scholars whose work on the issue well before mine made it possible—even easy—for my colleagues to succeed at some of our tasks. The second problem—a place of respect and acceptance for Africa's history in Annapolis—was facilitated by other scholars like Michael Blakey, Robert Paynter, and David Hurst Thomas, whose work with descendent communities became an essential model.

Much of this book's message is about how dominant a dominant ideology is. My initial conclusion was that a dominant ideology governed life in eighteenth-century Annapolis, but I reached it by assuming that all or most people who came across the apparatus of the ideology accepted it because it gave them a sense of privilege and turned out to be part of earning a living.

I realized that African religious traditions—their secrecy, wide acceptance, and profound difference—might have placed believers outside the dominant ideology. Because the bundles we excavated were dismissed locally as the result of bad housekeeping, I owe a large debt to those many archaeologists before me who had excavated, understood, and published materials on African spirit bundles. Such bundles had been found in Maryland by Eric Klingelhofer (1987), by Ken Brown and Doreen Cooper (1990) in Texas, and in other places by Larry McKee (1992, 1995), and Charles Orser (1998a, 1998b, 1992, 1994, 2004). Other materials that spoke of African traditions kept alive were published by Ywonne Edwards (1990, 2001), Maria Franklin (1997, 2001), Laurie Wilkie (2000, 2001), and Patricia Samford (1996, 2000). The work of these scholars and that of other archaeologists (Adams 1980, 1987; Adams and Boling 1989; Reeves 2004; Young 1996) working on parallel aspects of African American culture predates mine and has made it easier to build an appropriate meaning for the discoveries in Annapolis. Even earlier, scholars and field archaeologists discovered caches of magical bundles before there was a widespread scholarly tradition to rely on and understood that archaeological practice required careful excavation and full reporting. These archaeologists are the ones I relied on most when C. Jane Cox in Virginia and Matthew Cochran in North and South Carolina assembled the corpus of parallel materials that prove beyond doubt what the caches are.

FIELD SCHOOL

1982

Robert W. Douglas, Amy M. Maurer, Sandra L. Wilson, Edward A. Simmons, Mark C. Cramer

1983

Edward J. Bush, Nancy Jo Chabot, Mark A. Donaghy, Julie H. Ernstein, Tara L. Goodrich, Stacia G. Gregory, Pamela L. Henderson, Aileen R. Hughes, Lawrence J. Konefal, Brenda A. Kooken, Pauline L. Nolan, Lillian F. Shaffer, Matthew R. Virta, Pamela L. Whetstone, Johnston M. Zell, Patricia B. Mitzel, Kay K. Spruell

1984

Barbara I. Bowen, Vincent G. Chick Jr., Theresa A. Churchill, Joyce L. Harrison, Patricia A. Lockeman, David B. Sachs, Helen L. Schindler, Deborah A. Sickle, Charles W. Stearns, Cynthia S. Walker, Patricia Seitz, Jack Pearson, Naomi E. Leach

1985

Stephen P. Austin, Robin L. Burke, Kathleen D. Doherty, Heidi L. Hoffmann, Rukshan A. Jayewardene, James R. Kirchner, Barbara A. Ray,

Ellen C. Saintonge, Patricia A. Secreto, Larry N. Stillwell, Helen A. Sydavar, Raymond E. Tubby, Patsy S. Walker, Susan L. Weidner, Ann Curtin, Henry S. Cone, Phillip J. Hill, Barbara Ann Lichok, Angeline K. Petrucci

1986

Raylene A. Jonason, Marie C. Preusse, Michael W. Chakwin, William L. Helton, Rosanna P. Farrell, Karla Y. Rahman-Schneider, Emily L. Ramones de Berrizbeitia, Samuel T. Brainerd

1987

Hettie Lou Boyce, Parker B. Potter, John M. Dalto, Walter A. Ewing, Robert E. Fernandez, Michele L. Feutz, Judy R. Hankin, Elizabeth Ann Hughes, Carey A. O'Reilly, Karie E. Peterson, Etta M. Saunders, Eileen L. Simms, Jennifer A. Stabler, Pamela M. Wilhelm, Mary Anne Woods, William L. Helton, Dagmar J. Nika

1988

Janice T. Bailey, Michele M. Beavan, William R. Carter, Martin Gallivan, Frankland M. Gorham, George R. Guess, Miriam Ann Heppe, Patricia Lapasset, Justin S. Lev-Tov, Sarah E. Mitchell, Thomas F. Mueller, Dwayne W. Pickett, Paul A. Popernack, Jonathan L. Rones, Darcey D. Schoeninger, Elizabeth Anne Schuck, Monica E. Vondrasek

1989

Laura A. Beattie, Patrick D. Callahan, Alan M. Green, Lynn D. Jones, Lisa J. Kingham, Sheryl E. Kuttar, Simon J. Lewthwaite, Thomas A. Offit, Tia M. Ristaino, Doris M. Yochum, Cameron Haires

1990

Teresa L. Aquino, Robert E. Bomback, Briece R. Edwards, Rachel T. Finlay, Gary R. Giuffrida, Katherine W. Hitch, Marcey L. Jastrab, Jeffery D. Maybaum, Nicole R. Nejelski, Amy E. Nicols, Yvonne M. Parker, Ali Rad, Robert W. Thornett, Christine A. Vom Saal, John J. Wilkinson, Alberto Woginiack, Dana K. Yeck, Anna S. Yellin, Marjorie I. Ingle, Dana G. Holland, Patricia M. Parkinson, Marlys J. Pearson, Kimberly M. Wanda

1991

Michael P. Cruz, David A. Darby, Vidya Dorai, John D. Graminski, Mara R. Greengrass, Victoria L. Gruber, Dennis H. Gryder, Paula J. Lewis, Lisa

Ann Maday, Helen S. McKean, Tracy L. Shiflett, Charemon E. Watkins, Jessica P. Weinberg, Lori Ann White

1992

John J. Buckler, James E. Christian, Christina E. Clagett, Kevin M. Etherton, Mark B. Goleb, Carolyn Lee Kibbe, John M. Kieser, Keith I. Kobin, Steven B. MacLean, Cassandra M. Michaud, Stephanie G. Millard, Steven J. Moore, Abdul K. Mustapha, Kerry L. Ogata, Timothy M. Pugh, Sonja R. Samsoondar, Eladio J. Sendi, Megan Ann Wehrstedt, Elizabeth C. Winstead, Jason Shapiro, Linda J. Greatorex, Kirsti Uunila

1993

Aaron W. Aumiller, Valerie K. Banko, Bryan Berjansky, Nancy R. Broderick, Anna Marie Burlaga, Bridget E. Butler, Elizabeth A. Cherry, C. Jane Cox, Hannibal A. Guerrero, Lori J. Hudson, Simone D. Key, Lisa Ann Kovatch, Darby S. Laspa, Erika K. Martin, Eric P. Skolnick, Christopher Sperling-Gonzalez, Helaine D. Suskin, Jeffrey N. Weiss, Gilda Anroman

1994

Zoe A. Burkholder, Catherine E. Smyrski, Shirley M. Frisbee, Julia Ann Harrison, Tracy D. Perreton, Joni Jefferson, Michele N. Schwartz, Michael R. Clark, Katharine Rae Rieman, Margaret E. Noonan, Nicole B. Robbins, Sondra G. Silver, Brooke Courtney, Patricia R. Lisle, Caryn R. DiStefano, Jeffrey M. Leone, Luke A. Bertorelli, Francesca J. Tadle, Kathleen L. Wilmering

1995

Jennifer E. Falkinburg, Brian R. Bartel, Gary J. Melancon, Walter L. Graves, Brian P. Miller, Joel J. Tyberg, Cheryl Ann Criswell, Amanda Principe, Eleni G. Kambanis

1996

John A. Donahue, Gregory S. Clarke, Poorvee A. Vyas, Melissa S. Larson, Grant E. Capes, Catherine L. Stevens, Diana E. Corley, Christopher M. Bolton, Nathaniel S. Patch, Bonnie Bernstein

1997

Geoffrey H. Frost, Ireti M. Akinola, Christopher H. Gordon, Jason B. Rust, Kathryn M. Cavanaugh, Joshua E. Cogan, Theresa E. Solury, Todd E. Yocum, Melinda R. Vazzana, Colin F. Beaven, Scott D. Wilhelm,

Melissa K. Hawes, Jason B. Haller, Catherine T. Downes, Brandon L. Grodnitzky, Prashant Kaw, Veronica V. Parcan, Leo D. Berman, Bonnie K. Scranton, Debra A. Stoe, Marilyn J. Sklar, Josephine A. Boyd, Timothy J. Ruthemeyer, Kathleen M. Aiken, Stephanie L. Havsler, MaryAnne T. Seman, Deborah F. Gayle, Donna A. Williams, Paul L. Gieser, Matthew L. A. Moyer, Brett E. Edwards, Karen E. Getzinger, Richard H. Levine

1998

Patricia M. Griffin, Emily J. Harbo, Michael C. Byrns, Arielle K. Fishman, Carol M. Bushar, Virginia E. Hutton, Barbara Ann Thompson, Lauren P. Best, Wu-Lung Chin, Rayanne E. Harris, Richard Kantrowitz, Kai E. Frick, Dae Cho, Jennifer J. Babiarz, Margaret E. Ortzman, Sara Ann Kalish, Stephanie D. Smith, Kimberly Ann Holmes, Daniel J. Schlueter, Kelly Ann Arford

1999

Linda M. MacKey, Michelle L. Niedzwiadek, Sarah Beth Nachlas, Teresa R. Cabanilla, Meaghan P. Massella, Regina M. Shaw, Kareen K. Morrison, Jessica E. Paupeck, Robi M. Rawl, Jennifer L. Robles

2001

Sarah-Anne L. Bastien, Jennifer L. Friend, Shannon M. Hemming, Carrie E. Todd, Ashton S. Phillips, Laura M. Figueroa, Caroline T. Wrightson, Ana B. Cabrera-Peralta, September Smith, Michelle A. Clements, Mary T. Vittum, Ian S. Rogers, Jamie Ann Betts, Emily Brown, Heidemarie K. Gauss, Angela M. Arias, Anna B. Hill, Bradley R. Wilhelm, Robert C. Whetsell

2002

Daniel S. Smith, Charlotte C. King, Heather M. Lindsay, Kelly C. Raschka, Kristen A. Hill, Robert E. King, Megan M. Crandall, Kristen M. Corbin, Michael L. Sanderson, Ryan F. Austin, Whitney A. Sprague

2003

Gwynneth M. Anderson, R. Victor Boniface, Jessica M. Shamoo, Matthew P. Liu, Claudia Rossel, Ana S. Barrenechea, David R. Piper, Milagros A. Ruiz, Natalie A. Cooper, Colleen G. Pritchard, Michael J. Thalmann, Melissa N. Gribble, Michael R. McAndrew, Tonika D. Berkley, Laura Hoffman

2004

Jenna Armitage, Kelley Barr, Jan Brodeur, Kelsey Creech, Matthew Coogan, Kristin Deily, Jessie Grow, Michelle Klinefelter, Erica Marrari, Peter Matranga, Stephen Merkel, Brian Ostahowski, Nellie Pang, Serenity Purcell, Margaret Randall, Karen Reichardt, Derrick Scott

CHAPTER 1

The Importance
of Knowing Annapolis

Annapolis is and always has been a small city. It is important because of
what happened in it—and what was designed to happen in it. It has tall
historical stature because it is vividly connected to the American Revolution, the events of which remain so important to us. It remains famous
because the United States Naval Academy, the embodiment of American
naval excellence and ingenuity, occupies a significant and beautiful piece
of the city. Indeed, for most Americans, Annapolis means the Naval Academy, its traditions, midshipmen and women, and football against Army
(Fleming 1988).

Annapolis also means holidays sailing on the Chesapeake Bay. To
some, it is an old, distinguished state capital. To others, it is a historic
destination. If we limit ourselves to a rehearsal of what we know as out-
siders, then Annapolis has an identity made up of its role in American
independence, naval history, boating and sailing, and a historic place to
visit. Most people either know or are willing to guess that it is Maryland's capital.

I shall examine these identities briefly so that there is some context
for the details I provide that explain what can be learned from the archaeology of this old city that came, long ago, to call itself "the Ancient
City." Before I wander into familiar and comfortable identities for Annapolis, I want to be fairly clear that I do not think that they are the only
reasons for the city's importance. It is the planned, deliberately created
nature of the city's identity and operation, from which its famous side

is derived, that I hope to draw out. Annapolis may appear durable but small, important but not paramount, and historic but not crucial; however, it is also clear that it epitomizes a part of America that we tend to ignore. Annapolis and its way of life were planned, thought out, and then created. It is of great importance because it was not spontaneous, opportunistic, or dependent on the success of capital or entrepreneurial activity. Historically, it combined southern, patriotic, upper-class conceptions of right government with ways of social planning for an affluent, slave-owning hierarchical society that minimized conflict (Riley 1887, 1897, 1901; Stevens 1937; Taylor 1872).

This is a good time in American history to learn about Annapolis. It has never been more beautiful or more accessible. We have also just finished a quarter century of archaeological excavation there (see Appendix), so there is a lot to show. Moreover, we are also living in a time of very steeply distributed wealth and social quiet, and Annapolis can also show us how that is sustained.

Before I report on the archaeology, here is the impressive surface that should prompt a closer look at the city. Today, 35,000 people live in Annapolis. At the time of the American Revolution, about 1,300 did. But only in the demographic sense is it small. Historically, Annapolis was a place where the Revolution was argued and played out, and as a port on Chesapeake Bay, where some of its dangerous consequences during the War of 1812 occurred. Washington and Jefferson visited it—Washington often. Annapolis was on the land route from Virginia's Northern Neck and Williamsburg, where Virginia's leaders sat, to Philadelphia, New York, and Boston, where the North's wealth, population, and leaders were. For a brief period after the success of the first phase of the Revolution, Annapolis became the capital of the new United States and the new legislature met in the still new Maryland State House. In fact, the formally organized and widely attended ceremony where Washington resigned his congressional charge to lead the army against the British occurred in this building. Every once in a while, as with the Watergate crisis, we remember how significant it is that the military forces are constitutionally subordinate to elected civilian officials. This carefully choreographed act in Annapolis established that subordination. This act may not be as important as the Declaration of Independence and the Constitution, but it quashed the notion of government by king, hero, general, or acclamation.

All four of Maryland's signers of the Declaration of Independence lived in Annapolis. Their houses are still there, and two of them are open to the public. The William Paca House was restored and opened to visitors in 1976, with its gardens opened in 1973, by the Historic Annapolis Foundation, the city's—indeed the state's—premier preservation organization. The most famous, or at least most effective, Annapolis signer was Charles Carrollton of Carrollton (Hoffman 2000), whose big house and large property were given to the Roman Catholic Church twenty years after his death for the founding of the permanent parish and as a seat for an order of missionary priests and brothers. Carroll broke the colonial-era law against Catholics voting. He played the role that exemplified what Jefferson meant by not legislating to establish religion. Carroll was wealthy and he contributed to the industrial revolution in America by financing the Baltimore and Ohio Railroad, the country's first, the Chesapeake and Ohio Canal, and the iron mines and foundries (worked by slaves in some cases) that were the origins of the steel industry in Baltimore. The Carrolls also patronized Benjamin Latrobe, who, with his colleagues, designed the most important new buildings in Baltimore, making it an example to the new nation of how to build a republican city in an independent country.

As you walk around Annapolis, the Naval Academy is both more and less noticeable than you supposed it would be. The occasional midshipmen and women (the latter are officially called midshipmen) are self-evidently nice American kids about to undergo a substantial transformation. You rarely see a naval officer. The Academy is behind a tall yellow and red brick wall, and although open to the public, it is still physically removed from the level of access and intimacy that characterizes the rest of the city. The Academy is big and has big buildings that emphasize grandeur, reminiscent of the New York Public Library and Grand Central Station, built between 1899 and 1907. It is an engineering school for unusually talented students and is both accessible the way a college is and as remote, because you cannot see its purpose happening, any more than a visitor walking through Harvard Yard can see learning and fame.

Annapolis is on a small peninsula, and at its waterfront, you can see far enough to imagine the expanse of Chesapeake Bay. You know this is a port city, a water-oriented city, and you can see plenty of water as you walk around. Its buildings frame water views. But there are no large boats, ships, steamers, or cargo vessels. There is nothing really big at the dock. And historically there never was much that was big either. Annapolis is an administrative city masquerading as a port. But the real port is all of Chesapeake Bay and its 150 rivers. And then after the Revolution, Baltimore grew up and became the match for Charleston, Philadelphia, New

York, and Boston. But even so, Annapolis today is the self-named boating capital of America in popular lore and, perhaps, commercial fact. Its
waterfront is crowded as completely as you could imagine with the masts
of all kinds and sizes of pleasure boats. There are many hundreds of them
on view and thousands of them around the Bay.

Throughout the nineteenth century and the first half of the twentieth,
Annapolis was one of the many Chesapeake Bay ports where watermen,
black and white, formed the base of the oyster industry. Many African
American oystermen worked out of Annapolis and supplied the city's
packing houses, where African American women worked, processing tons
of oysters annually.

Boating, as it is now called, is done for pleasure; it is not a livelihood,
although it is a very big business. It is a weekend activity that occasionally becomes a sport. In the fall in Annapolis, there are two large boat
shows, one for sailboats and one for motor boats. These are very large
sales fairs that show off models, machinery, and improvements in all the
many ways that make leisure boating more attractive. Annapolis is a place
to see boats, store and maintain boats, build them, and berth them. Although visitors normally approach Annapolis by land, many have arrived
and continue to arrive by water. For the city is not only a port, it is also
a destination and a node on a string of settlements to be visited around
Chesapeake Bay.

With the publication of Alex Haley's *Roots* (1976), Annapolis became
famous because Kunte Kinte arrived there from Africa and became a slave.
Annapolis suddenly became known for its slave past, something that is
still being defined as a subject. The city's African American past and
present (its population is one-third African American) are still being negotiated, and archaeology has played an important part in this. Annapolis
has a large, vibrant, and historically old African American population
that is certain of its own past. The facts, traditions, patterns, African origins, and American records of that past are now being winnowed and
assembled.

The final prominent reason to learn about Annapolis is historic preservation. Preservation in Annapolis has deliberately transformed the city,
using an idea for the city's identity that first appeared in the 1880s. You
don't go to Annapolis to see the results of historic preservation. Yet that
is what you do see. Annapolis is full of fine old, beautiful buildings. It
has fifty-five eighteenth-century buildings, including the wonderful State
House. It has several of the finest houses built in eighteenth-century America, among them the Hammond-Harwood, Chase-Lloyd, Brice, Upton

FIGURE 1. Aerial view of the central part of Annapolis, showing the oldest part of the city. Courtesy of the Historic Annapolis Foundation.

Scott, and Adams-Kilty houses. It has others that are even more famous because of their owners: the Charles Carroll House and the William Paca House. It has a thousand nineteenth-century buildings, mostly vernacular houses. It has more than all these however; it has their urban context, which is made up of the intact seventeenth-century city plan and its subsequent use as a footprint for the growth of the city. As you walk through Annapolis today, you see a seventeenth-century street pattern, a scatter of large, beautifully placed eighteenth-century homes, a homogeneous set of nineteenth-century houses and stores, and a hundred and twenty years of effort to keep them all intact. All this appears as a set, without anything inauthentic, and none of it is the result of happenstance (Fleming 1988; R. J. Wright 1977; St. C. Wright 1977c; Kearns 1977a; Tatum 1977).

On the surface, Annapolis gives the appearance of always having been the way you see it today, as though it were a marvelous serendipitous survival. There is a little truth to that, however, because Annapolis never industrialized the way its eighteenth-century peers did, and it had lost its investment capital to Baltimore by the 1790s. Baltimore became the industrial urban giant of the Chesapeake and remains one. But it is what lies below the appearance of accidental survival that makes Annapolis

FIGURE 2. The façade of the Chase-Lloyd House, one of eleven or twelve
large Georgian mansions built in Annapolis from the 1760s on, most of which
survive and remain in use. All of these houses are highly compartmentalized
internally, and most have extensive archaeological records. They represent the
architectural and aesthetic acme of the city's prerevolutionary achievement.
Photograph by Howard Erenfeld.

important for us. Annapolis was and is no accident. It was designed, held
a clear view of itself, hosted carefully scripted political events, and remains highly controlled, all of which constitute the real basis for our
scholarly attention, and beyond that, our attention as citizens of the country whose founding republic was thought out and created in Annapolis
by men who went there often. The history to learn in Annapolis is neither in the mannequins and sales room reproductions nor in the furniture and often scant explanations in the historic houses. It is in the views,
glimpses, and archaeology (Kryder-Reid 1991; Little 1987; Matthews
2002; Matthews and Palus 2005; Palus 2005; Mullins 1999; Potter 1994;
Shackel 1993; Warner 1998; Yentsch 1993) of the town, and this is much
harder to understand but conveys a deeper lesson, one that makes Annapolis stand for the American universe.

    You go to Annapolis because you hear it is special, a unique survival.
You discover, as I did, that it illustrates how the country came to be as
it is. In this sense, it is a place to learn a general lesson, one nowhere on
display explicitly, but visible everywhere if you know where to look. My

approach turns Annapolis around. It takes a place that presents itself as unique and makes it serve a general educational purpose.

Annapolis is worth understanding, indeed, is historical in the first place, because it was an environment for what planning actually means, which is social control. The work I report here is both a part of the process and a deliberate effort to make the control visible and conscious.

There are two quite obvious and living elements to understanding Annapolis as a planned city, and a third that is much less obvious, but far more important and special to this study. Obvious is the fact that Annapolis was drawn up and laid out as a city by Maryland's second royal governor, Francis Nicholson, in 1695. It is not a happenstance city like Boston or early New York, nor is it organic: it didn't just happen the way early cities arose as trading centers (Reps 1965, 1972). The second is that since 1952, there has been a planned, politically powerful, and successful effort to preserve the city against unwanted development: big, modern, poorly designed buildings scattered anywhere. This is a kind of planning, although it is diametrically opposed to the urban renewal that began with tearing down large, old urban cores, and replacing them with bigger, denser, up-to-date buildings.

The third way that Annapolis is planned is seen in the social fashioning of people into a homogeneous whole, in their own eyes, if not in economic and political reality. Annapolis made itself into a community, and similar phenomena occurred all over the new republic. The topic of this book is the many ways this happened. Not all the ways in which homogeneity was achieved are still visible, but one is and can still be appreciated today quite directly: the three-dimensional look of the city, which is the result of its baroque street plan, the principles of which were also used to build its formal gardens.

A BAROQUE CITY

People go to visit Annapolis today to see a survival, and they go to Williamsburg to see a re-creation. Although both have been heavily altered, the two cities appear the same because of their size, the number of eighteenth-century buildings left, and the sense of order that both communicate. Even though Annapolis has many intact eighteenth-century buildings surrounded by nineteenth-century urban fabric, and Williamsburg is a twentieth-century creation around a core of eighteenth-century buildings, both were and are baroque, and they were both designed within a few years of each other by Francis Nicholson, who was governor of

Maryland first and then governor of Virginia. The term "baroque" implies spatial and thus visual order and comes from Counter-Reformation Rome, which created an architectural and urban style that put hierarchy in place on the ground, as well as in social life. Pope Julius II (1503–13) and his successors redesigned and rebuilt Rome to articulate power through art, urban planning, and architecture. The Rome we see today, the Rome of enormous churches, prominent places for them, the Rome of vistas to the Cross and to the papal arms, the Rome where the popes are ever present, and the institutional church is everywhere is a product of the use of baroque built forms and their intent to establish the authority of those at the top of the social pyramid and the hoped for subordination of those not so placed. Art historians, architectural historians, and urban historians will also recognize that there is a theory that accompanies all built baroque forms. The theory involves mathematical proportions, optical illusions, and the creation and maintenance of social order.

That order was one with steep sides and a potentate on top. Fernand Braudel, the French historian of the early modern European world's economic and social structures, points out, however, that baroque design was based on a wish for a monopoly on power rather than being an expression of power already achieved (1979, 489–91). When Louis XIV was refounding royal authority in France and Christopher Wren was bolstering monarchial authority in London, Nicholson was displacing the Catholic Calverts, who had owned Maryland outright as lords proprietor since Maryland's founding in 1634, by establishing the authority of the new Protestant king of England, William II. These are the circumstances under which authority was sought by employing baroque forms in urban design, landscape design, architecture, and the decorative arts.

Baroque urban design employed lines of sight, usually along principal streets, ending in a symbol of monarchical authority at the focal point. Thus any pedestrian in such an urban setting confronted objects of papal or royal authority everywhere throughout the day. The symbols of authority thus appeared to be unavoidable. This physical and thus psychological inevitability was a way of achieving power. It is much cheaper than maintaining an army, although it is not a substitute for doing so.

Annapolis is a true baroque city. Its streets were and remain organized to lead the viewer to the seats of civil and religious power. In the center of the city, on its highest points, Nicholson placed two circles, in baroque fashion, one for the state house to sit in, the other for the state church to stand in. Circular roads were designed to ring each building

FIGURE 3. William Paca House mantel. The baroque scrollwork in this 1760s mantel shows that Renaissance design interpreted as Georgian aesthetics is actually better connected to later ideas of order and power. Annapolis's great houses and the Georgian order are baroque, not Renaissance, in theoretical derivation. Photograph by Howard Erenfeld.

the way the very large public squares of Rome, and later Paris, served to highlight large public monuments, which were either in their center or appeared as the centerpiece.

Nicholson was ingenious in that he combined the idea of a public square focused on a civic monument and the Roman idea of an amphitheater where the inclined sides of an oval focused all eyes down on an object, the action in the arena. Nicholson wrapped his public buildings with perimeters that functioned like public squares and then took the natural hillsides and sculpted them so that all views led up to the seat of public action. He took the amphitheater and turned it inside out; he made people's eyes climb the hill to look at the centers of political and ecclesiastical action.

Part of Nicholson's late seventeenth-century plan drew the main streets and paths of the city into the two circles. Often this sort of baroque urban design is called a wheel or sunburst, having the effect of putting the monarch's seat in the hub of a wheel or in the face of the sun, with the spokes or rays leading to or radiating out from the central place. A wheel

FIGURE 4. St. Anne's Church and the Maryland State House. A period painting of the central buildings in Annapolis, which also shows vernacular houses.
Photograph by Howard Erenfeld.

cannot operate without a hub, and the sun radiates warmth and power.
These are the images and concrete effects behind baroque design, including Nicholson's Annapolis. One can see its operation today as one
walks around the city. It is one of the reasons Annapolis feels so inti-
mate. You can see and be seen by those who wish to be in authority. And
it was so intended.

Eight streets and paths lead into State Circle and seven lead into Church
Circle. Some are long, some short; all direct the view to the two centers
of power. Because their operation is still clear, Annapolis is worth a visit.
Because my project in Annapolis worked extensively on State Circle, its
visual design and structure are better known than they were before our
extensive archaeology.

One of the reasons to see and appreciate Annapolis is to see how it
is part of Maryland, a state that was and remains—at least in its built
form—a product of the Enlightenment. The Enlightenment is characterized by rationality, the idea that the universe was governed by knowable laws or rules, and so was the whole of human society. This set of
optimistic assumptions began in the Renaissance of the fifteenth century,
but it was influenced by Lutheranism and Calvinism in the sixteenth and

seventeenth centuries and combined with the growth of the sciences. By the time Maryland was founded in the 1630s, it exhibited a well-worked-out idea that you could combine practices like town planning and social reform like widespread landownership and an owner's political independence as expressed in his right to vote in his own governance.

Maryland was founded as a society in which one could worship freely, own property, and vote, provided one was a male Christian (Brugger 1988). This excluded women and Jews, but it covered both Puritans and Catholics and later included Quakers and Methodists. Such Enlightenment liberty existed to weaken war and struggle, was utopian, and was an experiment in social change. This is one way, among many, in which Maryland can be seen as a planned society.

In Maryland, the social organization of the Enlightenment was first projected in a small baroque settlement called St. Mary's City (H. M. Miller 1988, 57–73), today an important archaeological park in southern Maryland. In every way, we now know, thanks to the work of Henry Miller (1986, 1988), Garry Wheeler Stone (1974), Silas Hurry (Leone and Hurry 1998), and Timothy Riordan (Riordan, Hurry, and Miller 1995), that St. Mary's City was the planned predecessor to Annapolis. It was organized using lines of sight that combined roads and focal points at their ends that consisted of the chief seventeenth-century public buildings, the church and state house. At the center of the town, where the major roads met, was the large house of the proprietary Calvert family, where the colonial governor lived.

Once Henry Miller figured out how St. Mary's City was organized on the ground, it made far more sense to archaeologists and tourists. It was not a medieval holdover from rural England. It was an early modern effort put together by people educated in Europe, familiar with Rome and influenced by the Counter-Reformation through the Jesuits, among others. The houses were crudely built because English technology was being applied to new American materials, but neither their spatial arrangement nor the aims of the colony were in any sense crude.

Centralized, modern planning using baroque principles, as carefully expressed in St. Mary's City, was also available to Francis Nicholson fifty to sixty years later when he laid out a new capital, Annapolis, over Arundel Town, a very small port on the Chesapeake Bay to the north of St. Mary's City. But whether Nicholson needed St. Mary's City as a model or not, is moot, given the baroque rebuilding of London as designed by John Evelyn and Christopher Wren.

One of my messages, conveyed through archaeology in this book, is the planned quality of Annapolis. Although for some historical reason, the use of such centralizing and controlling ideas is not widely celebrated now as a part of Maryland's history, the trajectory is quite obvious and runs from the seventeenth-century founding city to Annapolis to late eighteenth-century Washington in the District of Columbia, which was part of Maryland when created, to nineteenth-century Baltimore, to the Levittowns of the 1940s and 50s, and to James Rouse's Columbia of the 1960s. Much of Maryland is not planned, at least visually, but there is a strong civic tradition (Ernstein 2004) behind the examples I cite.

I want to develop this idea further because there are abundant data on landscapes in Annapolis. I argue that urban planning embodies a tension experienced as a desire for social control because the plan is based on the idea of citizens with sufficient individual freedom to recognize and respond to a summons by the monarch or the state. You have to think you have some freedom if you are to answer a call to be organized. Therefore, Annapolis is a place to see how individual liberty and central planning work together.

If I am to explain why Annapolis is worth knowing, I inevitably have to explain its relation to Baltimore, a city unlike Annapolis that needs no introduction. Baltimore is a nineteenth-century city, not an eighteenth-century one. It was small and unimportant before the American Revolution but grew rapidly. By the 1790s, it had become the hub of industrialization in the Chesapeake area, and it was important enough by the War of 1812 for the British to try to capture it, a fight that produced the American national anthem.

Baltimore not only led the industrialization of the state, but many of those who led the Revolution founded important institutions there based on the same ideas of deliberate social planning they fostered in Annapolis (Frey 1893; McDougall 1993; Olson 1997; Stover 1987). Baltimore is every bit as thought-out as Annapolis was, but with a different theory. Baltimore is a federal city; it flourished during the Federal Era (roughly 1788–1830), was designed and built then, and housed serious intellectuals like Charles Carroll of Carrollton and Benjamin Latrobe. These men may not be seen as intellectuals as we use the term of Thomas Jefferson and Alexander Hamilton, but they read and wrote widely and thought in public about the founding of the new American republic.

Baltimore was a series of separate towns that grew toward one another around a set of novel domed public buildings placed on the city's hills and squares. The greatest and most famous of these are Latrobe's cathedral, the first monumental Catholic church in America and one of

FIGURE 5. The Maryland State House. This late eighteenth-century print shows the height of the new dome, its ranks of windows, and the public grounds around the capital, which contained a treasury, eight-sided public privy, school, and public market. Photograph by Howard Erenfeld.

the great buildings of Western architecture, and Robert Mills's early monument to George Washington. The domed lecture halls of the first University of Maryland building, the stock exchange, the prison, the public library (never built), and the Unitarian, Baptist, and Episcopal churches were all designed by Latrobe or his students and protégés. They were to form a skyline or horizon, with the monument to Washington watching over the whole. Yet the skyline is not what's important: The interior of each of these buildings is a domed room, often with good acoustics, derived from the then new science of acoustics. These rooms were often well lighted by large windows with clear glass. The rooms had two qualities: people could both see and hear and be seen and be heard. The explicit reason for this design was that it gave citizens democratic access to those in elected authority. Also important, however, the new republic based much of its power on teaching people to watch both one another and themselves, based on the notion, elaborated by the English utilitarian thinker Jeremy Bentham (1748–1832), that if individuals were confronted with the fact that they could actually be watched—as from a perch or a lectern—they would respond by watching themselves, making it less likely that they would need to be cited for civic misbehavior. Such a notion of surveillance was fostered by buildings Bentham called panopticons. Baltimore is an ideal place to see such buildings.

The 1780s dome of the Maryland State House in Annapolis, which could be seen all over the city and still can be today, is an early example of socially motivated panoptic architecture (the term I prefer to "Federal," a name for the architectural style that tends to deny information about social intent). Subsequently, the urban format still so evident in Annapolis was perpetuated in Baltimore, but the planning there was panoptic rather than baroque. Anyone studying Annapolis thus needs a guide to understanding Baltimore, because although the two cities seem so different, their intellectual origins were quite closely linked. This is in part because men like Charles Carroll of Carrollton played so big a role in both, thus creating a real continuity.

WEALTH AND CLASS

The way in which the wealthy and the poor, the powerful and the powerless, were managed without substantial violence is another reason to seek to understand planning in Annapolis. It teaches us much about America's history. The relevant material was gathered by Lois Green Carr and her colleagues, and I have been guided in my attempts to understand its importance by Jean Russo's study of changing wealth in the eighteenth-century city.

Annapolis did not produce a school of historians that focused on itself until the 1960s, when Carr brought together a group of American scholars who examined the primary documents (Walsh 1983) of the seventeenth and eighteenth centuries to better understand the founding generations and subsequent colonial history of Tidewater Maryland, from St. Mary's City to Annapolis. Although Dr. Alexander Hamilton, a local physician who founded the Tuesday Club in 1745, produced a social commentary on many aspects of political life at the time (Hamilton 1948 [1744], 1988, 1990), he had no intellectual descendents until Carr and her associates began their lifelong study of rural and urban Maryland. Edward C. Papenfuse's study of Annapolis is foundational to this effort (Papenfuse 1975).

I use the material on wealth in Annapolis to show the change from a very small city, where there was substantial equality in wealth from one family to the next, to one with a steep hierarchy with very wide ranges of wealth among families. Once the trends in wealth holding are clear, questions arise that become the reasons for my analyses in this book. These questions make Annapolis worth understanding and remain relevant in this country today.

In the late seventeenth century in Annapolis, there are only a few records to indicate how rich people were at the time of their death, which is when a written inventory and estimate of the wealth of the head of a household was made. The numbers in table 1 combine inventories of wealth at time of death, from the decedent population, and of course give only a partial view of the distribution of wealth in Annapolis. The base lines are the periods 1689–99 and 1700–1709. In 1689–99, 28 percent of the wealth was held by the poorer 75 percent of population, and 72 percent by the 25 percent who were moderately richer. The former possessed less than £50 each and the latter between £226 and £1,000 each. This was not egalitarian, but neither were the moderately well off equivalent to the truly rich who soon emerged. In the first decade of the eighteenth century, when Annapolis was still being organized as a capital city, there was more evenly spread wealth within the middle wealth groups, representing 69 percent of the population, than soon came to be the case.

Then the trend to great differences in wealth becomes clear by the period ending in 1722. The trend to consolidating wealth in a few hands that was in place by 1730 continued through the Revolution. By 1770, 85 percent of the wealth recorded by probate inventories in Annapolis was held by 20 percent of the population. Thirty percent of the people had 2 percent, and they were the poorest. The middle wealth groups, or 56 percent of the population, held 13 percent of the wealth. By the Revolution, there was a lot more wealth in Annapolis to be sure, but it was concentrated in very few hands. Moreover, a very large percentage of the population had very little of it. Inventories of the decedent population represent neither all the wealth nor all the people; they are, in fact, a skewed sample. They do not represent women, slaves, long-term residents who died elsewhere, children, and the very poor or the propertyless. But decedent inventories do show wealth and its concentration in fewer and fewer hands through its passage into the possession of the richest. The trend to concentrated wealth holding intensified throughout the eighteenth century.

The early distribution of wealth was both reflected in and fostered by the street plan with its many small, inexpensive lots intended for artisans and small business owners. Possession of these many pieces of city land passed into the hands of a very few rich men whose wealth was

TABLE 1. Percentages of wealth by social group (class) in Annapolis, 1688–1777

| | | | | Estate values | | | | | Total wealth and number of those inventoried | |
| | £0–£50 | | £51–£225 | | £226–£1,000 | | >£1,000 | | | |
Year	Wealth	Population	Wealth	Population	Wealth	Population	Wealth	Population	Wealth	Population
1688–99	28	75	0	0	72	25	0	0	£321	4[a]
1700–1709	8	46	14	23	53	23	26	8	£2,221	13
1710–22	4	38	17	42	21	13	56	8	£8,480	40
1723–32	1	30	7	30	14	21	78	18	£42,009	33
1733–44	2	37	9	27	12	16	76	20	£20,946	51
1745–54	2	48	3	13	7	13	88	26	£16,647	31
1755–67	1	26	6	34	7	15	86	25	£32,982	53
1768–77	1	30	8	43	4	7	87	20	£18,345	30

SOURCES: Russo 1983; Leone and Shackel 1987, 1990.
[a] Not a statistically valid sample but the only data available.

founded, in part, on aggregating these as the base for even more wealth in a process yet inadequately described.

> The original plan was to have as many landowners as there were lots, but in actuality, a small number of men were acquiring large numbers of lots in the town, contrary to the intent of the legislature and Governor Francis Nicholson. In 1707, the General Assembly moved to curb the ownership of large tracts of land within the city. Because the greatest part of the lots within the same Town and Port [have come] into very few hands to the great discouragement of several neighbors and others who would build and live there.
>
> Lindauer 1997, 20

The process was not reversed.

I have long wanted to know how this could have happened peacefully, with civic cooperation, and at a time of social and political revolution. Revolutionary leaders like William Paca and Charles Carroll were among the richest men in the city. After independence, Paca was elected governor and was reelected twice, although there was as yet no popular vote. Carroll was simultaneously elected a state senator and a U.S. senator. Where did their popular support come from among a population that was getting poorer and poorer, not necessarily in absolute terms of amounts of money, but in sheer numbers? Even though there was a property qualification for holding office, I want to know the source of their support and the absence of opposition to them and their peers among the still disfranchised. Look at the last horizontal line in table 1. Thirty percent held 2 percent of the wealth and 43 percent held 8 percent of wealth around 1775. These people were poor, and they were three-quarters of all the people in the city. Why were they revolutionaries? Even more, why did they elect the very men to office who were making money off them by collecting their rents and interest payments? These are among the questions that make Annapolis worth bothering with.

I do not know the difference in terms we would all understand today between how a family lived on £50 a year as opposed to £1,000. In some ways, it does not matter. But among such people, the man, who was legally the head of the household, would have rented both his house and the lot it was on, paying separate rents. He would have been a craftsman who owned his tools, a few dishes, some furniture. He employed no slave labor and probably died early.

These ordinary people often paid their land rent and sometimes their house rent to Charles Carroll or to one of the other three very wealthy men who owned much of the land in the city. These men had invested in city lots and some of the property on them and made some of their money by loans, the resulting interest payments, and the rents they collected from their neighbors throughout the small town.

Table 1 shows that over three or four generations, a hierarchy of wealth was created in Annapolis. It does not matter to my argument whether that hierarchy was imported from the original capital in southern Maryland or grew locally. It could have been created both ways, because the Carrolls, for example, were given a great deal of land by the Calverts when they arrived in Maryland and thus had considerable capital to begin with. I am interested in how the substantial differences in wealth were sustained without violent protest, without police, without an army of the colonial elite's own, and in an environment of social and economic tension with Great Britain from at least 1750 on, which led to violent revolution.

The American Revolution was a long time coming in a town like Annapolis. It was not an overnight affair at all. Where did its support come from when those who led it and those who fought it came from the same town, and where the leaders had been making some of their money out of the rent and interest payments of those who became their followers?

This is not a fundamentally different question from Edmund Morgan's in his controversial 1975 book *American Slavery, American Freedom,* which points out that the southern leaders of the American Revolution sought their independence and political liberty on the backs of their slaves, furthered that relationship through the Civil War and Emancipation, and then continued it in other forms. Conservative historians were uncomfortable with Morgan's analysis because he strongly implied that this country's love of personal liberty was supported—indeed, was made possible—by the labor of an unfree slave population and then an exploited working class. My own analysis here asks the same question of life in Annapolis, which became highly stratified in terms of wealth in the course of the eighteenth century and remained that way after the Revolution.

POPULATION

Although I have established why Annapolis is important to write about, the historical fact to be overcome is that the city was small in terms of its permanent population (tables 2 and 3). The total population of Annapolis in 1783, ninety years after it was made the capital of Maryland, was 1,280. In 1800, it was 2,212, and in 1810, 2,188. In 1820, the total

TABLE 2. The population of Annapolis,
1699–1980

Year	Population
1684	"the towne land at Proctors" consisted of a handful of houses and one tavern
1699	about 250
1760	about 1,000
1775	1,326
1783	1,280
1790	2,170
1800	2,212
1830	2,623
1860	4,658
1870	5,744
1880	6,642
1950	10,047
1960	23,385
1970	29,592
1980	30,000

SOURCE: Papenfuse 1975, 14.

population was 2,292. We are thus dealing with a small, highly stratified population.

Annapolis was the capital, and the legislature met there annually for ninety days, during which time the populace was much larger. The added population was transient, as were the students at St. John's College in Annapolis, which was chartered in 1784, then the much larger U.S. Naval Academy, founded in 1845. These populations, not normally counted in a census, make the town more like a city in its diversity. They also make it bigger, richer, and more stable. A fluctuating population of legislators and students also characterized Williamsburg. These were not natural cities with multiple economic or market functions; they were in fact planned, artificial towns, surrounded by much larger rural populations only loosely connected to the center.

Annapolis is the seat of Anne Arundel County, which had a total population in 1755 of 13,150. However, the county had no other city, so these people were scattered in small settlements, large plantations, and smaller homesteads. There is no separate figure for people living in Annapolis in 1755, although it is likely that there were fewer than the 1,280

TABLE 3. Census information on whites and blacks
in Anne Arundel county and Annapolis, 1755–1860

Year	Location	Group	Population	Percentage group population	Percentage total population	Total population
1755	Anne	white	7,648		58	
	Arundel	mulatto	210		2	
	County	free	105	50		
		slave	105	50		
		black	5,292		40	
		free	33	1		
		slave	5,259	99		
						13,150
1783	Annapolis[a]	white	822		64	
		slave	453		36	
						1,275
1800	Annapolis	white	1,294		58	
		black	919		42	
		free	273	30		
		slave	646	70		
						2,213
1810	Annapolis	white	1,296		59	
		black	892		41	
		free	328	37		
		slave	564	63		
						2,188
1820	Annapolis	white	1,374		60	
		black	917		40	
		free	391	43		
		slave	526	57		
						2,292
1830	Annapolis	white	1,587		61	
		black	1,036		39	
		free	458	44		
		slave	578	56		2,623
1840	Annapolis	white	1,707		61	
		black	1,085		39	
		free	586	54		
		slave	499	46		2,792

TABLE 3 *continued*

Year	Location	Group	Population	Percentage group population	Percentage total population	Total population
1850	Annapolis	white	1,826		61	
		black	1,185		39	
		free	533	45		
		slave	652	55		3,011
1860	Annapolis	white	3,228		71	
		black	1,301		29	
		free	826	63		
		slave	475	37		4,529

SOURCES: For 1755, see "The Population of Maryland, 1755," *Gentleman's Magazine* 34 (1764), in Papenfuse and Coale 1982, 37; for 1783, see Maryland 1783; for 1800, 1810, and 1820, see U.S. Bureau of the Census 1800–1820. Figures for 1755 to 1820 supplied by Jean Russo. For 1830, see U.S. Bureau of the Census 1832; for 1840, 1850 and 1860, see id. 1841, 1853, and 1864. See also Maryland State Planning Commission 1934–35.
[a] Data from tax assessment records. No free blacks were enumerated.

of 1783. No independent demographic dynamic that I know of was operating to create a larger city population, and the county's population remained far larger than that of Annapolis until well into the nineteenth century.

Much is known about town development in early Maryland and the difficulty of establishing cities in the area of Chesapeake Bay in the seventeenth century. Baltimore was Maryland's first large city, with a population of 90,000 by 1800. In 1752, Baltimore had about 200 residents, and it did not begin to grow until the time of the Revolution, after which it grew rapidly. Many efforts were made by the colonial government to found and sustain towns along the Bay and its many rivers, but these did not work out well. Tobacco farming, Maryland's major crop and business throughout the colonial period, required large amounts of land and resulted in a thinly spread population. Tobacco exhausted the nutrients in the soil, which required constant clearing of new ground and moving houses. Originally, the Bay's rivers were navigable to areas far further inland than later silting allowed, so tobacco could be put aboard ships more easily. This meant that no transshipment points in the form of towns were needed. While this set of facts is universally used to explain the absence of towns in Maryland in the seventeenth century and for much of the eighteenth, it does not explain adequately how the scattered plantations were provisioned, governed, or sold indentured labor and, later, slaves. These, for the most part, are town-based activities, and we know they did occur in towns like Londontown and Providence (Gibb 1999; Luckenbach 1995; Luckenbach, Cox, and Kille 2002; Gadsby 2002), but these were small.

Annapolis was not just a town, however; it was a city. It had power, wealth, highly specialized workers, producing industries, a steeply hi-erarchical social order, civic monuments, and the written records re-quired to make all these work. Notably, too, Annapolis was a slave city. A large proportion of its people was from Africa or of African descent. The 1783 tax assessment shows a total population of 1,275, of whom 822 (64 percent) were white and 453 (36 percent) black (table 3). Slaves were held in 116 households, or 53 percent. Censuses recorded 2,213 Annapolis residents—1,294 (58 percent) white and 919 (42 percent) black—in 1800; 2,188—1,296 (59 percent) white and 892 (41 percent) black—in 1810; and 2,292—1,374 (60 percent) white and 917 (40 per-cent) black—in 1820.

So, by the end of the Revolution and throughout the era of the early republic, Annapolis was roughly a third black and two-thirds white. To-day, about a quarter of the population of Annapolis is of African descent and about three-quarters of northwest European, Latin, and Asian de-scent. It has been a diverse town since the eighteenth century, and its cul-ture should be expected to be as diverse as well. Archaeologically, it has certainly turned out to be.

Many people in Annapolis of African descent were free, not slaves. This is a particularly important part of the city's history, because free-dom was neither easily obtained nor kept. In 1800, the total black pop-ulation was 919, with 273 free and 646 slaves, or 30 percent free and 70 percent slave. It is not clear how long so many people had been free, but we must see freedom as a condition based on earning capacity, some emancipation, the availability of jobs, and a general social willingness to support freedom. We must also see an African American population deeply committed to freeing its members and to advertising their liberty.

In 1810, the total black population was 892, with 564 slaves and 328 free, or 63 percent slave and 37 percent free people of African descent. By 1820, the total black population was 917, with 526 slave and 391 free, or 57 percent enslaved and 43 percent free. Such figures go up to Emancipation and show (1) an expanding number of free people of African descent, (2) a decreasing number of slaves in the city, and (3) that about a third of the total population was of African descent, more and more of whom were free. They depict a demographically small but politically important American capital city, fully in the slave South, but one of the more northern such cities, with a large African and African American population.

These figures are quite surprising for the slave-holding South. If we flash back to the first population figures for Anne Arundel County, which includes Annapolis, but in which figures for Annapolis were not broken out, the total population in 1755 was 13,150 (table 3). The total black and mulatto population was 5,502, or over 40 percent. But 5,364 of the black and mulatto population were enslaved. That is 99 percent of all people from Africa, or of mainly African descent, were thus slaves in 1755. There were only 138 free people of African descent. This changed substantially by 1800 in Annapolis, as opposed to Anne Arundel County, when free and enslaved people of color were enumerated separately. By then, a third of the black people of Annapolis were free, and one can begin to see the difference between the city and the plantation countryside in terms of promoting freedom.

Population figures for Annapolis are not evenly available. But if we set the figures for the distribution of wealth from 1688 to 1777 alongside the fact that about a third of all Annapolitans were black, a few of whom were free wage earners, it is clear that the city's wealth spanned a wide range, from the rich to middling property owners, to wage workers, to the poor, to those who were slaves, which is to say other people's property. This hierarchy became fixed and permanent by about 1720 and did not change with the Revolution.

Why did this pyramidal society last? What made it stable? This is a significant question when asked of Annapolis society in the period from 1690 to 1770, which was not a time of substantial internal conflict. There were strains, yes, but not violence. The economy of both the city and the surrounding countryside was based on slavery. Annapolis was not a major slave market, but William Paca owned a hundred slaves and the Carrolls over a thousand in the course of the family's history. Despite these differences in wealth, freedom, and opportunity, there was support for the American Revolution among some of the members of these different groups. Many among the rich and those with property, and even among those with only some, helped rationalize, promote, finance, and fight for American independence. When it was over, the rich became the newly powerful, and slavery and poverty still existed, albeit now surrounded by the new ideals of personal liberty, freedom, and voting rights for property holders. The Revolution was a big risk for all who supported it. It also was a risk, in retrospect, for those who did not support it. The rich who supported it got new power. The poorer who supported it got a new idea but not political or economic change.

IDEOLOGY AND THEORY

My explanation involves ideology and its critiques. The concept of ideology I use here is Marx's and was defined most usefully for me by the French theorist Louis Althusser (1918–90). It was taught to me by Steve Barnett and Martin Silverman (Barnett and Silverman 1979, 39–81) and their former students Janet Dolgin and JoAnn Magdoff (Dolgin 1977; Magdoff 1977). The critiques of my use of this idea that I respond to come from Nicholas Abercrombie, Stephen Hill, and Brian Turner (1980) but enter archaeology through Ian Hodder and Lauren Cook, and Stephen and Mary Beaudry. In light of the empirical work I describe from Annapolis, I tend to see Althusser as being more correct than his critics when all is said and done, albeit with some room for modification.

Without too much scholarly apparatus on my part, the argument begins by asking the large version of the question I have asked. Why don't people rebel against the conditions capitalist economies put them in, namely, exploitation? You either see slavery, racism, sexism, poverty, and joblessness as exploitation, or you see America as the land of limitless opportunity. I see more of the first than of the second, and I want to understand how it works, as well as how to change it. The second condition also exists, and I believe that making opportunity more widely available is not only healthy for democracies but also can be done by getting at the origins of the first set of conditions through scholarship and social action based on it. I have tried to do this through Archaeology in Annapolis, conceptualized in 1981 by St. Clair Wright as a citywide project to excavate sites for the purpose of understanding the city as well as preserving its below-ground remains. I brought the University of Maryland into partnership with the Historic Annapolis Foundation on the basis of using the resulting archaeological research to educate students, residents, and visitors.

Althusser defines ideology as the given, the obvious, and our ideas about things taken to be natural (Althusser 1971, 127–86). Ideology is what we say we take for granted. It is neither formal religion, philosophy, nor civic religion. Ideology is hard to spot, but once spotted, it appears to surround us. Ideology is notions of cause, person, gender, nature, time, life's reasons for being, opportunity, hope, and so on. Althusser's contribution to

Marx was to allow us to see an example of ideology in the concept of the person, one we call the individual, whom we normally define as the basic unit of social life, explored throughout this book.

The purpose of ideology is neither to motivate nor to teach but to hide and mask. Within capitalism's classes, social divisions such as those I have described for Annapolis, are antagonisms based on substantial differences of wealth and on the exploitation among neighbors that created those divisions: slavery, rents, manipulated interest rates, monopolies on land-ownership, differential access to power, racism, an inferior place for women, and religious bigotry. Marxist scholars see these as the political and economic facts of daily life in a capitalist society. The function of ideology, depending on the stage of capitalism that a society is in, is either to justify these conditions as given in nature and ordained by God or to mask them behind notions like personal freedom, liberty, and opportunity that blind people to the realities of everyday life.

Ideology hides the conditions of daily life, so that they appear to be beyond discussion. There are two ways this can happen. Realities like uneven wealth and unjust working conditions can be explained in ordinary but universally used language that tells people that the hierarchy of nature—its measured qualities and its law-like forms—includes society, which is naturally a social pyramid with those at the top being all-powerful. Thus, ideology takes a historically accidental circumstance and explains it as inevitable, making it seem unchallengeable, or unwise, treasonous, or sacrilegious to challenge. So, ideology can place cultural forms in nature and make them seem natural, and thus given. Marx and Althusser point out that the reverse is actually the case. Nature or the divine is made to look hierarchically ordered and social life is declared to be natural and an emanation of the natural or divine, or both. This mixes up the explanation for order by pointing people to the heavens or the woods, rather than to local circumstances and the immediate motivations of the rich. This is called a transparent or naturalizing ideology. Transparency comes because one hierarchy produces the other and they are both scaled; natural because cause is placed outside human control and, to some degree, beyond human understanding, but not beyond human admiration.

The other kind of ideology is one that masks. If a person believes that he is an individual with rights and opportunities, believes that hard work and talent will produce equity because he (or she eventually) is guaranteed equal access by law or nature, then that person sees himself as having free will or as an active agent of his own life. This is a very powerful cultural convention and serves to mask the social reality that surrounds many people who believe this. It is not so much that people deny poverty or injustice as that they see themselves as exempted from them by their rights, opportunities, and will.

The first kind of ideology, one that naturalized social inequality, characterized life in Annapolis through the time just before the American Revolution and certainly lasted until the early 1770s. It depended on people seeing themselves as individuals who could, as a result of their being in possession of themselves and their freedom or personal liberty, be called successfully to take a place in a natural hierarchy. The second kind, which can be illustrated by the notion of a watchful citizenship, can be found in Annapolis by the 1750s and became ascendant after the Revolution. This version of ideology also depended on defining a person as an individual, but one whose personal vote gave life to the state. I hope to trace the forms of the ideology of individualism, whether placed in nature or hidden in watchful citizenship, through our archaeological work.

The problem with using the Marxian concept of ideology is that it does not adequately support democracy (McGuire 1992b, 93–144; Miller 1972, 432–47), to which I and the vast majority of all American scholars who are interested in class are dedicated. The reason to use the idea of ideology is its explanatory productivity and its capacity to reverse tired and uninteresting explanations of American liberty, which have come close to bankrupting themselves.

The major critique of Althusser's work on ideology has two components to it. The most global critique argues that if ideology masks social reality so completely as to be virtually impenetrable, then democratic processes, which are based on universal participation and majority rule, are not enough to cure or address the inequities created by capitalism. If Althusser's hypothesis is correct, workers and most others who are exploited not only do not see the truth of their condition but also are virtually powerless to change what they are subjected to. It also denies any substantial analytical ability among those who are rich and powerful to moderate the conditions within society, even in self-interest. Althusser's is a pessimistic view.

The second part of the critique of ideology asserts that Althusser is in fact empirically incorrect, and that only the rich and powerful are usually taken in by ideology, whereas the exploited often see right through it, but are subjected to violence and threats to such an extent that they can do little to moderate their own circumstances. Thus, ideology is pierced frequently, but such clarity leads nowhere, because political change is either very slow or constantly aborted.

The concept of alternate or other voices derives from the second part of this critique and, at least as articulated in historical archaeology, is a source of hope for democratic action. In my opinion, this argument is best made by Jürgen Habermas (1984–87), who contends that despite the absorptive capability of capitalism, which seeks to homogenize and to reproduce people in conditions useful to producing, buying, and consuming, capitalism is resisted successfully by some groups. These include many Native Americans, the Amish, radical Mormons who live communally, monastic communities, and others with explicitly conscious rationales of social equality, socialized wealth, consensus as a governing principle, or divine revelation in the context of a deep concern about avoiding the world's goods. These goods are those produced in abundance by the consumer revolution that began in the eighteenth century, when plenty and frequent replacement came to dominate buying. Habermas allows us to see the importance of some American groups, whose significance we may not have seen before. But there are many, many others, often known as first peoples, indigenous people, religious minorities, radical Muslim groups, ethnic groups, and in general those who have not yet been incorporated into capitalism, or who have rejected it, as in the case of both Fidel Castro's Cuba and aspects of Ayatollah Khomeini's Iran.

Normally, within American historical archaeology, the purpose of finding and highlighting other voices, sometimes called muted groups (Little 1994, 196–204), is to extend the cultural franchise to these speakers. If such people found their past, celebrated, and learned about it, or if their past, long ignored, denied, held in contempt, or regarded as anonymous, was dug up and called heritage, then they would be equally proud Americans. There is, no doubt, some effectiveness to this hope, especially through pride and catharsis. The aim of this rationale for American historical archaeology is twofold. It is, first, to enfranchise those thought to be without a history and, second, to protect democracy by bringing more participants to it.

But there is much more to Habermas. He points out that there are those who successfully exempted themselves from such disfranchisement. He wants to move that process into democratic capitalist societies. He wants to change the consciousness of the majority about their own circumstances by showing them how others have perceived capitalist conditions and created a way around them. For Habermas, the alternatives

FIGURE 6. Death's head, protesting the Stamp
Act, excavated from Jonas Green's print shop. In
1765, this piece of type was used to accompany
a *Maryland Gazette* headline announcing the
"expiration of free speech." Photograph by
Howard Erenfeld.

are already saved; they don't need archaeology. It is the increasingly wide
bottom of the mainline that needs those outside it. My interpretation of
this is that the job of historical archaeologists is to understand how some
groups ameliorated capitalist practices, and then to explain both that fact,
and the means by which they did so, to those who are aware that they
need an alternative, but do not have one, so that they can do so too. Our
job is to translate to our own needy peers, which has been the main goal
of anthropology since its founding.

When the goal of consciousness for the majority becomes the goal of
historical archaeology, there is a secondary problem that is immediately
evident. The main goal is to explain to ourselves the lives of others who
kept themselves free or freer. This may provide an alternative for the reading, attentive, needy parts of society. It may also enhance the democratic
process for those excluded because they were neither appreciated nor noticed. But then, because we can actually see the results of the operation
of ideology on past peoples and on their present descendants, we can
hope to know whether its impact can be moderated.

One of my goals in this book is to ask whether groups have escaped the enveloping role of ideology. Who saw through it, and what is the evidence? If there is a positive answer, then Althusser needs to be modified so that the concept of ideology provides for a less dense and hard-to-pierce mask. A big piece of the reason to understand Annapolis is to see the long struggle for freedom by people of African descent and by poor people of European descent that took place there. Annapolis is a long-term site of struggle for freedom and liberty, and it is worth seeing that struggle. The struggle was not only against the British, it was with one another.

Annapolis is an arena for viewing the struggle, because it has made itself into a museum town. You can not see much of that struggle when you look today at Boston, Philadelphia, or New York. You can see parts—and famous ones at that—but they are often so altered that they look like stage sets. I am thinking of the strange setting of Faneuil Hall in Boston. And the odd, garden-like setting of Independence Hall in Philadelphia. Although quite different now from the way it looked in the eighteenth century, Annapolis imparts an authenticity that combines both the reality of a densely lived in place and one with a lot of fairly old buildings. It is a Williamsburg that works, a Williamsburg without the need for the prefix colonial.

HISTORIC PRESERVATION IN ANNAPOLIS

The final reason why Annapolis is worth paying attention to is its authenticity and how that quality was created. Even though the first house was designated as historic in the 1880s, probably to help preserve it, and a group of citizens tried to preserve the town in the 1920s, the current appearance of the city dates to a preservation effort started in 1952 and organized by a group of women and men known originally as Historic Annapolis Incorporated and more recently as the Historic Annapolis Foundation. Annapolis is not simply old and historic. Nothing is. It was made that way.

Nobody rebuilt Annapolis the way that John D. Rockefeller Jr. sponsored the complete redesign, rearrangement, and rebuilding of Williamsburg to produce Colonial Williamsburg. Rather, the buildings and the city plan that were there were protected by laws and by the placement of new, well-designed adjacent buildings, the removal of numerous storefront signs, overhead utility lines, 1950s aluminum streetlight poles, and buildings that blocked vistas to the water, and the use of sympathetic materials and proportions for pavements, home additions, and controlled height and width for the larger commercial and public buildings in the city. Annapolis looks quite different in 1950s photographs, even though it was neither rebuilt nor renewed the way many other large cities were in the 1950s and 1960s.

The story of Annapolis's preservation is famous, and the heritage tourism it generates for the city is the measure of its success. St. Clair Wright, who helped found the modern Annapolis preservation movement, envisaged the city as a museum without walls, as she put it, and saw the context of the buildings as just as important as any one of them individually. This idea gave great significance to vernacular buildings, those of no particular historical importance, worker housing, African American churches, the street pattern and its focus on vistas, and nineteenth- and early twentieth-century domestic structures. The concept was remarkably advanced for its day, has turned out to be impressively democratic in an aesthetic sense, and produced what many call a remarkably livable town. However, in the past decade or so, it has become a fossil, which was never the intent of those who saw the need and use for a resuscitated urban, historic core.

So that the new Annapolis, one that appeared to be both modern and historic would not be a fantasy—and long before Disneyworld and Disneyland made such a policy necessary—Historic Annapolis Incorporated stressed the need to assemble all the city's historic documentary records, plus surveys of standing buildings, most of which had never been catalogued in any way. Historic Annapolis began a collaboration with many scholars, particularly in the period 1960–80. A photographic archive was created. Surveys of the ownership of all the lots in the historic area were done. There were analyses of the tax records, censuses, probate inventories, court records, and ads in the *Maryland Gazette*. There are about 1,900 buildings in the core of the city, and they were all classified by style and period. They were then connected to their own lot histories and some specifics of who had owned them (Papenfuse and McWilliams 1971). All this too, makes Annapolis a planned city, but in the sense of a determination to keep the past alive and of use. My problem was how to use this past for public, democratic purposes.

I began to study the archaeology of the city in 1981 and 1982, at the invitation of St. Clair Wright, and in turn invited Anne E. Yentsch (1993) and then Richard J. Dent to join me as partners. Archaeology in Annapolis was sponsored by the University of Maryland, College Park; Historic Annapolis Incorporated; and the City of Annapolis, all of which consistently and generously funded the project.

Between 1981, when we began to excavate, and the early twenty-first century, we dug several dozen sites (see Appendix), some big, some small,

and came to know the city's archaeology very well. The area was settled in the early 1650s, and the earliest remains, which date from the
late seventeenth century, are quite scarce, but the stratigraphy is intact
in most places.

The research design for Archaeology in Annapolis was the examination of the structure of power based on changing wealth. We initially
used critical theory that combined Marxian concern with economics and
politics to make a commitment to explaining in public how modern conditions came to be. Subsequently, we combined critical theory with
Habermas and eventually with postcolonial theory. We took the archaeology and tried to show, not just George Washington and the great houses,
but class structure. Then, work with African America changed my use
of theory.

Some Marxists in the early twentieth century envisaged raising the consciousness of ordinary working-class people by explaining how society
worked, either publicly, in settings like museums, or privately through
books about social conditions. Certainly, by the mid-twentieth century,
this hope was gone, crushed and completely destroyed by the success of
Nazi propaganda—the very opposite of self-reflective consciousness—
and of the equally lie-filled totalitarianism of Stalin's era.

Out of this failed hope, one generated in Europe as much by Freud as
by Marx, came Althusser, who argued, convincingly I believe, for the extreme difficulty of creating a popular class-based consciousness. This entire book is about showing Althusser to be incorrect. Nobody could want
him to be correct, after all. Nonetheless, his argument remains quite powerful when one looks at modern society.

One early effort to prove ideology to be changed through popular consciousness was made by the Hungarian Marxist Georg Lukács, who
spelled out Marx's role for historical activity, namely, how historians—
and I hoped people like me and my students—could work honestly and
productively in a public setting like Maryland's capital city.

Lukács argued that popularly available historical narratives would
create consciousness of people's actual conditions. He was wrong, and
it's a pity that he was, for we still do not have a way to show how divisions of wealth, power, and the divisions in society that they cause are
created and maintained. Our best cures are still charity, philanthropy,
and prayer. These are good but regularly prove incomplete. Democratic
action through voting and other means of nonviolent action were what
I hoped for when I used Lukács's idea of explaining the origins of the
modern conditions that lead to inequality.

FIGURE 7. Large holster boss with spread eagle,
excavated from the John Brice House. The image of
the eagle with wings and feathers probably represents
flight in an African American context of spirit use.
Courtesy of the Anacostia Museum and Center for
African American History and Culture, Smithsonian
Institution. Photograph by Steven M. Cummings.

When I felt that my use of Lukács failed, I turned to a later twentieth-century idea based on understanding the same problem. Habermas, a German social philosopher writing in the aftermath of World War II and Stalinism, felt that enhancement of democratic processes was the only solution to the inequality inherent in capitalism. His major work is devoted to promoting equality through the use of language modeled in such a way that the settings of its use and its content promote both mutual understanding among all users and equal opportunity to speak and be heard. This is one of the origins of notions like equal voices, muted voices, hidden voices, and hidden transcripts.

My use of Habermas, however, comes from his idea that critiques of capitalist society exist and were made by those at its bottom and margins, by those who saw its actions and found ways to survive it. These critiques and alternative social actions—cultures—may be of use in mainline capitalism to promote a discussion of alternatives to some of capitalism's excesses.

Lukács (1971, 83–222) generated the way I chose to explain ideology in public. Because that tie did not produce a critical self-awareness, I turned to Habermas, first, by extending history making to others and second, by seeing others who were outside of the blindness of ideology and had alternatives to capitalism within democracy.

Habermas has led to postcolonial ideas like those of Homi Bhabha (1994, 236–56), who helped me rationalize novel changes in critical theory. These changes involved placing archaeology in the hands of others, who then produced different critiques and different archaeological results.

The following chapters on landscape, printing, ceramics, and spirit bundles derived from Africa make the case not only for the power of ideology but also for who modified it.

CHAPTER 2

The Research Design

This book is about the ideology that a person is an individual, and this hypothesis unifies the book and its data. I get the idea of individualism from the Scots political philosopher C. B. Macpherson (1962), whose work I learned about from Richard Handler's useful adaptation of it in anthropology (Handler 1988; Handler and Saxton 1988). The idea of individualism is important because it was the single most motivating concept in the American quest for freedom and then independence. It guided the American Revolution long before people coupled personal freedom and individual liberty with national independence. That coupling was a long time coming, but was probably inevitable, just as parliamentary democracy was itself probably inevitable in Britain and all its colonies.

Individualism's central characteristic is the freedom of the self, which is freedom from dependence on the will of others. Macpherson argues that ties between people are voluntary and based on the individual's own interests, as he sees them (1962, 263–77). A person owns himself and his capacities and cannot alienate the whole of himself, although he can sell, that is, alienate, his labor. All relationships are contractual and an individual, by definition, owes the state nothing; indeed, it is the task of the state to protect the free relations between the individuals.

Because people owe none of their freedom or possessions to the state, individuals are the proprietors of their own property and capacities. Macpherson, who derives this nest of propositions from Hobbes and Locke, calls this possessive individualism (1962, 263–64).

This is the definitional foundation behind James Deetz's work on New England archaeology that was so productive, and it is behind my argument here. There are three or four keys to possessive individualism so far: people own themselves and are solely responsible for themselves (this also applied to women, at least from their own viewpoint). "Possessions" means not only material goods but talents, traits, and anything learned, as well as the belief that the state was subordinate to the individual's interests. The idea is anti-monarchical, anti-authoritarian, anti-hierarchical, and eventually anti-slavery. In other words, it was potentially leveling and democratic. However, it was also quite conservative, because it equated property with success and the right to govern, and property's absence with failure and the possibility that those without it might make claims on those with it. Thus, while possessive individualism was historically anti-monarchical, it was not anti-hierarchical in American democratic hands. Its only stopping point until the nineteenth century was that the theory defined those who were capable of governing as those owning real property.

Possessive individualism is an unusually powerful idea. It is so powerful that we tend to think that it is not a social construction but inevitably true. My position in this book is that it is not only a social construction but also a mask that hides something far more real: the steep hierarchy of wealth, power, possessions, slavery, poverty, oppression, and exploitation. The reality of these in Annapolitan society and the potential conflict arising from them was hidden by a wider and wider social absorption into the notion of possessive individualism, or what people saw as the right of personal freedom and liberty.

Possessive individualism is thus what Marx—and I use Althusser as his definitional descendant—calls ideology. It is not reality, although it is very real and material. It is a mask that hides reality. People either cannot see through it, or they may, but not for long, because the result is so unsettling, or they may see through it clearly but may not want to do anything about it, either because it benefits them or because they are so surrounded by potential sources of violence, like slaves, that they can do almost nothing about it.

Possessive individualism is an ideology. It is brought into being and sustained by techniques like seeing/watching, reading/talking, and eating/etiquette. These techniques create and maintain the self. Michel Foucault calls them technologies of the self. They are my data and take the archaeological forms of landscapes, print and reading, and dishes and etiquette. These are technologies, not the ideology itself, but rather the archaeological remains of ideology. Not only are these remains material and visible, but they also show how absorptive ideology is: how convincing, how utterly personal, and how disciplining.

There is nothing mysterious about the use of terms like "disciplines" or "technologies of the self." They invite us to see the rules of daily life as recent and as ways of making our bodies and minds productive for others. The person who argued that reading, penmanship, and calculation were about disciplining the body for use in the modern state was Foucault. While not a Marxist, he was concerned with how the modern democratic state got its power to maintain control of its citizens without a huge police-like apparatus. He focused on self-control and found that its basis was—and is—how we are taught that we are individuals, and that our responsibilities are to learn, internalize, and constantly subject ourselves to the combination of rules tied to mechanisms (like toothbrushes, glasses, knives, forks, clothing, deodorants, driving tests, rules for politeness, anger control, voice modulation, anticipating the reaction of others, and punctuality). Foucault argued that this is how modern citizens are made, because this is how a state founded on democracy actually exercises power.

Foucault is important in my book because so many of his technologies have archaeological reality. His work is doubly useful because of how weak government was in Annapolis and Maryland throughout the eighteenth and early nineteenth centuries. Thus, I raise the question of how a relatively peaceful society could exist with both relatively weak central authority and a steeply ranked hierarchy based on great differences in wealth and condition.

Marxists do not like Foucault because he does not focus on the state and the power of its institutions and economy. But Foucault can be made to show that his technologies train mass-produced people, called individuals, who are the working middle and lower classes of any capitalist society. Moreover, Foucault provides an important means of spotting how workers are reproduced, as well as how ideas of self-improvement, using ideas of the self, are adopted by people outside capitalism through modernization, nongovernmental organizations, self-help philanthropies, Christian missionary activity, and radio and television, acting on a worldwide basis.

Finally, there is the issue, always there, of freedom. Possessive individualism was enunciated by Hobbes in the seventeenth century as a foundation for a free people. Marx argued that capitalism within democracies and other forms of government produced substantial conditions of unfreedom. But let us not forget that Marx wanted freedom, not oppression.

Once we see the play or tension in Annapolis between the quest for freedom before and after the American Revolution and the steep hierarchy of wealth and power in the city both before and after the Revolution, we can also see how the American struggle for freedom continued and how it works. We can also see that it was never finished, and that we ourselves are not spectators but participants in it.

Neither Macpherson nor Marx and most of his descendants dealt adequately with the notion of consciousness as a means of liberation, that is, they did not deal with the social means of producing consciousness as a way of promoting social change. If Macpherson is correct, and possessive individualism is the basis for society today in liberal democracies, there may not need to be a theory of consciousness. If the Marxists are correct in their late twentieth-century form, then such a theory is needed, and it is necessary to show how to learn from the experiences of peoples struggling for freedom and with its absence. The struggle for freedom with the idea of consciousness is illustrated here both by the mid eighteenth-century Tuesday Club in Annapolis and, more powerfully, by the struggle for freedom by African Americans, which takes up much of this book. Possessive individualism existed long before the American Revolution and has certainly continued long after it. Under the monarchy, the theory was that individuals were free and governed themselves by having equally propertied people represent them in Parliament. There was a natural hierarchy, and the propertied were its pinnacle. The technologies (Foucault 1979) of the self actually revealed the hierarchy of nature and society and taught people how to acquire more possessions and develop their capabilities. This set of ties and assumptions broke down around the 1750s in Annapolis and collapsed in the 1770s.

After the Revolution, possessive individualism remained the dominant ideology, but instead of being transparent in supporting and explaining the hierarchy that was a monarchy and a set of colonial relations, the ideology of personal liberty was proclaimed, hiding the fact that the steep pyramid of wealth and slavery remained unchanged. So the ideology of possessive individualism did not itself change, but its role went from being a lie plainly in sight to a lie far more difficult to see through, unless you were black. I have described the archaeology of techniques of the self that supported possessive individualism both before and after the Revolution. I have also included the technique of panoptic citizenship for the way citizens were to maintain one another in a newly democratic society after the Revolution. The first set of technologies dealt with transparent hierarchy and the second with an actual hierarchy disguised as a republic.

At the time Annapolis was founded, people in Europe believed that they could look at nature and learn from it (see, e.g., Philip Miller 1733, "Vegetable Staticks"; Castañeda 1996, 1–30). Those lessons were part of taming or domesticating nature. Domestication meant, not just taming the wild, the potentially useful, and the dangerous, but people applying lessons to themselves so that they would be able to be synchronized with natural law. In the eighteenth century, this meant being more productive by being more harmonious with the natural order. In this sense, Annapolis was planned. It was to be orderly, and so were the individuals in it. This was achieved by watching, talking, reading, and performing. Such looking was done with categories used to make observations, often of people who saw themselves as individuals, by people observing society as though it were a part of the natural world. This was so both before and after the American Revolution.

In order to learn, which was to acquire a part of the rules of nature for yourself, it was necessary to systematize, or create categories of knowledge. This meant measuring, counting, locating, dividing, arranging, classifying, and then being sure that those typologies accurately reflected nature. These sets of activities were thought to exhibit natural laws, and Annapolis was meant to be a city designed according to these natural principals. However, Annapolis was also to be a place for using natural laws to allow people to make themselves into subjects and, after 1776, into citizens. This hypothesis meant that the city's people were to be a model for nation building all along, and that the city was to be built as an active place for this to happen, both as a colonial city in an imperial state and as a capital city in a newly independent nation.

Annapolis has been a planned place since 1695. But it is not just a planned space. Its planning is based on the Enlightenment idea of collecting all observable knowledge rationally (Castañeda 1996, 100–103). Libraries, laboratories, and gardens were places to collect and study all knowledge, as were museums. Libraries included encyclopedias, laboratories included observatories and lists of observations, gardens included both plants and animals. Zoological gardens and museums—until recently called "cabinets of curiosities"—included hierarchical rankings of everything on earth and the earth itself. Libraries, laboratories, or laboratory-like observations, and many gardens existed in the city.

My hope in this book's array of materials is to show how Annapolis put the subject, and later the citizen, in an observable environment (Ba-

FIGURE 8. Looking up the double stair of the Chase-Lloyd House. The divisions and subdivisions of interior space are all represented in this photograph. The balance, symmetry, and compartmentalization used in the English-speaking colonies from about 1740 on served to control levels of society and the quality of interaction between individuals. Photograph by Howard Erenfeld.

con 1968; Bentham 1962; Foucault 1979; Mukerji 1997) and taught subjects and citizens the rules for behaving both as proper subjects and, later, as citizens. People were taught what to expect of one another by being observers and models of natural behavior. They were to be the objects in the lessons to be learned and to learn from seeing their fellows as models. In Annapolis, some, like Dr. Alexander Hamilton (1990), saw this and some did not. But whether they saw it or not, the Enlightenment assumed human beings and their behavior to be natural and nature to be systematic and knowable, and it believed that by reflecting knowledge of it back on people, one could create a more workable society. Its ideas could not cure poverty but could rationalize it as a natural transitional state in any individual's condition. The only thing the Enlightenment did not discover was that its assumptions were inventions.

My point about poverty comes from Annapolis, from conditions beginning in Europe by the middle of the eighteenth century tied to the early Industrial Revolution, and from the reform movement that began in Britain and that took root in the early United States during the earliest

FIGURE 9. Charles Willson Peale's museum. Peale's museum embodied virtually all of the elements of the Enlightenment project. It contained plants, animals, Native Americans, his portraits of revolutionary heroes, the results of his excavations, and even a device for having an evocative silhouette of a visitor cut out by one of Peale's slaves. Photograph by Howard Erenfeld.

part of the Federal Era. Enlightenment philosophers certainly understood social hierarchy. They also attempted to deal with slavery, eventually almost all condemning it as unnatural or unworkable. Poverty was quite another matter. I suspect, based on my understanding of mid eighteenth-century Annapolis, that widespread poverty was seen as a permanent social condition, over which not much control could be exercised.

Examples of poverty are easy enough to enumerate in eighteenth century Annapolis, and they include the condition of women, children, single young adults, and men who died owning less than £50, but these people are difficult to find archaeologically, except for slaves and free Africans or people of African descent. Anne Yentsch (1991a, 1991b) and Barbara Little (1994) have made the best efforts in Annapolis archaeology regarding women. The free poor are not part of my analysis, however, because I and my present and former students have not successfully argued the archaeological evidence for them in the eighteenth and early nineteenth centuries. The evidence for the proletariat is missing from the archaeology in this book, except for free African Americans. Even though the poor are visible in the lowest rank of probate inventories, a glimpse from Alexander Hamilton, and the Federal Writers' Project composite autobiographies (see p. 224 below), evidence for them is archaeologically hard to detect. In the glimpses we have, they are outside liberty, individualism, and freedom of opportunity for the most part. They were outside these ideological constructions for many reasons. Some, like Hamilton's (1948) country bumpkin, were outside because they had not been included yet. Others, like slaves, were excluded and eventually were ambivalent about being included. Many of the poorest tried to be included, and by the mid-nineteenth century, they were if they stayed in town. So some of the poorest were within and some were outside the ideology of individualism at the same time.

Because this is a study of power and how it was maintained, I want to frame my analyses in three different ways. I use Annapolis history from the late seventeenth century to today, but for some eras in the city I have little material, and some data may not appear chronologically commensurate with others. Second, this book is built on an array of work by other scholars, who have informed my work, directed it, and provided context. Their work has been indispensable to the questions I have posed and the methods I have used. Third, my work on Althusser's dominant ideology thesis is well known. Even so, some scholars (e.g., McGuire 1992b, 106–15, 138–42) have argued that I should use a more subtle view of ideology than the view I began with in the 1980s. As a result, I have come to see that power and ideology have a more complex relationship than I first saw, particularly for those in the economic middle and for those at the bottom of society's hierarchy of money and tolerance.

LANDSCAPES

National cities (Anderson [1983] 1991) were important to nation building because they created subjects and citizens through the use and enforcement of rules. National cities created nations, and this idea included new colonial capital cities as well. As conceived of by Europeans, such cities were usually designed and built according to baroque principles, which meant the use of avenues, façades, focal points, and lines of sight, all constructed to focus on views or vanishing points directed at seats of power. Such displays of sight and vistas usually involved the explicit use of the principles of perspective to create optical illusions (Langley 1726).

My first case for such discipline comes from walking in Annapolis. In the series library, laboratory, garden, and museum, there is the understanding that a garden was an array of living plants in a planned landscape from which one learned through active observation. Lost today, but very much part of the conscious intent of virtually all the literature on how and why to build gardens and urban settings derived from their principles, was how they affected the builder of a garden and the visitor to one.

There is a series of nested claims that I want to make on urban planning and landscape architecture. First, such landscapes were planned. They were built according to a series of printed, widely available, and widely understood rules (Langley 1726; Dézallier d'Argenville 1722 [1709]; Philip Miller 1731–39). The landscapes were comparable, and there were many of them. In fact, there were hundreds, maybe even a few thousand, formal, planned landscapes laid out in British North America in the eighteenth and early nineteenth centuries, from New Hampshire to Georgia (Lockwood 1934).

The formal landscapes were intended to illustrate the principles of optics, hydrology, the engineering of slopes, the heat and light supplies needed by plants, and, of course, the variety of plant life. At a minimum, gardens were to have an array of plants, but it was not this array that was supposed to be encyclopedic. The encyclopedic array was to be the knowledge the gardener was to exhibit, which allowed him, and occasionally her, to show the principles of nature required to create and maintain the landscape itself. The encyclopedia was to be in the builder's head, in the names and effects of the flowers, not under his or her feet.

The planned landscape was a proposition in geometry and therefore in spatial harmony, aimed at producing emotional reactions like awe, satisfaction, and calmness. There was an enumerated array of emotions that an individual was to cultivate and produce. Much of this was also true of city planning, whose rules were the same.

The planned landscape was built of living elements, from which one learned, with the gardener as the teacher. Since the gardener required a class as the recipient of instruction, the subject had a set and predetermined place. The gardener and those he or she instructed were entirely within the garden and were its actual purpose. But because illusion and harmony, and not the political and economic circumstances surrounding landscape construction, were the central lessons, gardens and street plans only implicitly communicated an orderly means for resolving the conflicting issues they were created around, like colonial subordination and slavery.

Annapolis shows us how a century of landscape design and its ar-

FIGURE 10. The Calvert House hypocaust. Remnant of the firebox and
below-floor channel for conveying heat beneath an early eighteenth-century
greenhouse attached to the Annapolis home of the Calverts, Maryland's
proprietary family in the seventeenth century. Excavated by Anne E. Yentsch.

chaeology has managed a way to present its coherence. Annapolis features the reconstructed William Paca Garden of 1763 as the preservation masterpiece of the Historic Annapolis Foundation (St. C. Wright
1977a, b, 160–73). A visitor of any background is immediately involved
in the extraordinary beauty, interest, and satisfaction of the garden. But
there were at least ten other similar gardens, two of which still survive
and whose archaeology I shall describe in detail. They all date to the
time just before the beginning of the American Revolution. We as archaeologists were both the first to compare these gardens and the first
to puzzle out the tie between the gardens and the city plan, for they were
all baroque landscapes.

The Nicholson plan for the city, designed in 1695, survives intact (Reps
1972). The gardens and the city plan have never been unified through
scholarly study. The city street plan has consistently been called baroque,
but it had never been connected in modern times to baroque political
theory. The gardens, laid out seventy years later than the town plan, have
usually been characterized as the product of slightly behind-the-times English taste. They have not been seen as baroque, as operating according

FIGURE 11. View down the main path in the William Paca Garden. The geometry evident in this photograph is an attempt to show the principles of order that can be found in plants, waterworks, and optics. Photograph by Howard Erenfeld.

to the same set of planning principles as the town plan, or as having been built to serve essentially the same set of political circumstances.

The core of the city plan is State Circle, originally called Public Circle. We excavated all around the circle in 1990 and spent several years understanding the stratigraphy and shape of the circle (Read et al. 1990). Based on that work, my students and I analyzed the heart of the Nicholson Plan and found that State Circle was meant to be an egg, a geometric shape that could be used to unify irregular points into a visually harmonious whole, while also producing the appearance of being circular (Leone, Stabler, and Burlaga 1998). We also found that the streets entering both State and Church Circles had sides that converged or diverged as they reached the Maryland State House and State Church, depending on whether the streets were long or short. The Nicholson Plan, when built, used principles of optics as exhibited through geometry to create the appearance of harmony as well as to enforce hierarchy. The geometry of the plan and that of the city's gardens all placed the teaching of natural law in the hands of those who could exhibit their mastery of it through their own creations in gardens and open spaces. These were the baroque leaders, some of whom aspired to be at the apex of the natural social hierarchy as well.

Because the core of the city and the focal point of each garden was a planned vista, my analysis took these into consideration. My argument is that the function of the central pavilion in the Paca Garden was to serve as a focal point, the element that makes point perspective work. The pavilion was not about tea, after dinner escapes, or games. In fact, being in it was probably only an afterthought. The purpose of the Enlightenment garden was to house knowledge that was universal so that it could serve as the basis for instruction in the laws of nature, as well as to subject people to its author, owner, and planner. Planned landscapes were intended to take people and show them the natural sources of power and authority and to convince them that the sources were authentic. Subjects were needed by the monarchical state, and citizens by the new republic. These were created by walking in the new landscapes. At least some subjects were.

One of the lessons I have learned from the critiques of my work that have been published over the years is that I have not grappled adequately with the notion of ideology as I have used it (Beaudry, Cook, and Mrozowski 1991; Hodder 1986). Who saw through its apparatuses? Initially, I did not believe many people did. Now, I present a range of data that show a more balanced and comprehensive, as well as a more hopeful, picture for challenge and change. The issue is that if people saw through ideology, there was the possibility of resistance, which could take many forms. With resistance could come change in Annapolis and thus some leveling of the city's wealth and more democratic access to its power. So who saw and what did they see? Who, besides the rich and powerful, bought into the ideology? There are a lot of data showing that different people were inside and outside the ideology of individualism.

My worst mistakes regarding the use of Althusser's definition of ideology occurred when I analyzed William Paca's 1763 formal garden, which had been carefully excavated and rebuilt by Historic Annapolis Foundation. I never asked who would not agree to the ideology of natural hierarchy behind its plan. Since then, I have asked, and through two colleagues, Barbara Sarudy (1989) and Jean Russo (Faris 2003), I gained access to a detailed analysis of a contemporary vernacular garden laid out in Annapolis by William Faris, a watchmaker, silversmith, and tavern keeper (see J. S. Brown 1977), who kept a diary of his work on it from 1792 to 1804. Faris was an artisan, not a wealthy man, but quite prosperous, and he describes his gardening activities and garden well.

FIGURE 12. Scientific Instruments from Annapolis. Inventories from Annapolis show that musical instruments, scientific instruments, and other devices for measuring nature, like clocks, were widely available and often quite inexpensive. The inexpensive ones have disappeared. Those pictured here would not have been in common use. Photograph by Howard Erenfeld.

He also describes the social contacts he made through plant exchanges in the town, and thus part of the social function of his garden. He owned at least one slave, who worked with him to maintain his garden. Faris thus offers an opportunity to see how a petit bourgeois owner handled gardening and how independent of the owning class he may have been. Because he offers insights into some of the rest of the city, he provides a larger view of the ideology of individualism.

Gardening was connected to telling time and surveying in the eighteenth century. Sundials were used in Annapolis, as were all the usual instruments for measuring space: telescopes, globes, sextants, and quadrants. These items were not necessarily used in a garden, but some were essential to land surveying, making maps, and finding the way around Chesapeake Bay and at sea. I have gathered these as a category and called them scientific instruments (see table 4).

I argue that there was a secondary, ideological role for these instruments and that they functioned like the gardens, that is, were the objects by which nature was seen as rule-abiding and hierarchical. Like gardens, these handheld instruments individually convinced a viewer or reader of a map

TABLE 4. Possession of clocks and scientific instruments by wealth group in Annapolis, 1688–1777

	1688–1709			1710–32			1733–54			1755–77		
Estate value	cases	n	%	cases	n	%	cases	n	%	cases	n	%
						Clocks						
0–£49	0	9	0	1	24	4	3	33	9	5	23	22
£50–£225	0	3	0	7	27	26	10	18	56	12	30	40
£226–£490	1	4	25	7	12	58	9	11	82	5	9	56
£491+	0	1	0	5	9	56	10	15	67	16	17	94
						Surveying instruments, telescopes, barometers, thermometers, globes, etc.						
0–£49	0	9	0	0	24	0	3	33	9	0	23	0
£50–£225	1	3	33	2	27	7	3	18	17	2	30	7
£226–£490	0	4	0	1	12	8	2	11	18	2	9	22
£491+	1	1	100	3	9	33	4	15	27	6	17	35

SOURCE: Computer Analyses of Anne Arundel County probate inventories, with a breakout for Annapolis. Done through Historic St. Mary's City Inventory Files, courtesy of Lois Green Carr. Annapolis: Maryland State Archives. Also published in Leone and Shackel 1987 and Shackel 1993, 97–98. Note: *n* is total probates; cases are probates with clocks or scientific instruments, etc.

that he was seeing the laws that nature had to offer when carefully observed. These instruments were in the hands of people in the middle and lower classes at a fairly early date, and I have argued that the ideology of individualism they taught at a personal level spread well beyond the elite.

Throughout, I have argued that landscapes of the Chesapeake region were oriented toward seeing, but that after the Revolution, reciprocal watching, or panopticism, went hand in hand with the ideology of individualism, and that the voting individual was the core of the republic's power (Foucault 1979, 170–94; Leone and Hurry 1998). I think this pattern is most obvious in Federal Era Baltimore. But before the construction of Baltimore's domes as a technology of the panoptic state exemplifying watching in both directions—being seen and being watched—the dome of the Annapolis State house already constituted a panopticon. There is evidence, moreover, that it was used that way. It is self-evident that it was universally visible in Annapolis; it still is and is so depicted in prints of the era and in the nineteenth century. We need, however, to consider who used the ideology of individualism to persuade themselves that people had to watch over both themselves and others, because that was a citizen's job, and the citizen was key to the new republic's existence.

READING, PRINTING, AND WATCHING

Subjects were also created by reading, particularly the dominant language (Anderson [1983] 1991, 67–82). Although some of my primary ideas about the disciplines of reading and writing come directly from Benedict Anderson, and many of his come from Foucault, it is the idea of publicly trained, and observed behavior that I want to pursue here. I shall concentrate on reading, and particularly on newspaper reading, because in Annapolis we excavated (Cox and Buckler 1995) the print shop where the *Maryland Gazette* was produced from 1745 to 1830 (B. Little 1987; Thomas 1975, 531–56). We recovered 11,000 pieces of printer's type and analyzed about 6,000 of them. This is evidently the largest analyzed collection of printer's type ever found archaeologically in North America. Furthermore, the *Maryland Gazette* was one of the most famous of all American colonial newspapers because of the quality of its printing. It played an important role in the city, especially during the years leading to the American Revolution. There are three elements about printing in Annapolis that I want to draw out here from the *Maryland Gazette*. One is the layout of the paper. The second is the shape of the printed words. The third is content.

I am interested in three separate but interrelated developments in the *Gazette,* because print played such a large role in shaping people's thoughts and lives. One was the changes that operated to alter the visual appearance of the newspaper so that it looked more regular by 1750 and became so by using rules to sort categories of information and to arrange them into predictable spaces.

As a part of this first inquiry, I wanted to know if the layout of the newspaper began to resemble that of the new table setting that James Deetz (1977) has described in the context of New England. If, as Deetz says they did, eighteenth-century dining tables came to show regular separation between the diners, regular separation on the plate between foods eaten, and regular courses, all with appropriate dividers like serving dishes and silverware, did the faces of newspapers change too? When did the changes occur, and what did they actually look like? When people are individuals, they are separate from one another, and they each have separate parts too, which are treated like possessions. To learn this, there were many technologies of the self.

My students found over many years of study that the newspaper's content was progressively subdivided onto different pages and their margins were straightened (B. Little 1987, 1988, 1992). More columns were added,

FIGURE 13. Individual pieces of printer's type with impressions. Photograph courtesy of Thomas W. Cuddy.

and horizontal dividers were used to break them up. Political news from London was separated from political news in Annapolis. Letters were separated from advertisements.

The rearrangement of the printed page and the rearrangement of the lines of type on any page were all described by my students who studied the *Maryland Gazette.* Changes in grammar were noticed this way too, through comparison with the manuals that were used by printers throughout the English-speaking world for page composition. Our surface conclusion, while assembling these observations, was that the appearance of the newspaper page was being affected by the same ideas of separation and segmentation that Deetz has observed so fruitfully with respect to eating and living habits in seventeenth- and eighteenth-century New England.

After tracing the changing organization of information on the page of the *Maryland Gazette,* the second element of printing in Annapolis that interested me was the shape of its words. Here is the problem addressed by the shape of words. With the American Revolution, the individual who was already entitled to possessions, including property and liberty, became a citizen whose vote empowered the state. The monarch was gone. How did people at very different levels of wealth, including those who were impoverished, some of whom were overworked, loyalists, people

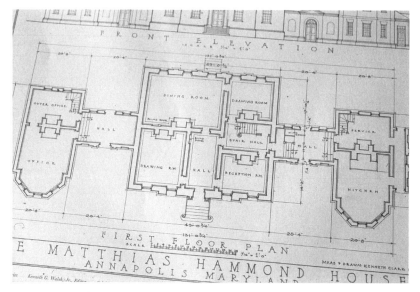

FIGURE 14. Floor plan of the Hammond-Harwood House, showing the façade. Often celebrated as the most beautifully designed of the city's mansions, the Hammond-Harwood House demonstrates the architectural order used to copy and reinforce the divisions of social and intellectual life that accompanied the Enlightenment's understanding of orderly nature. Photograph by Howard Erenfeld.

on every margin conceivable, and many others who did not know—or want to know—one another, become fellow citizens?

Benedict Anderson and Jacques Derrida suggest that one important way citizenship was actually created so that people saw themselves as having the same ideas in common was through the creation of popular opinion. Popular opinion was brought about, in part, by reading the newspaper, with any reader supposing that many others were reading and absorbing the same news (Anderson [1983] 1991, 61–65; Derrida 1986).

Newspapers were widely available in Europe and all its colonies. They were created by printers who were often also postmasters, thus the newspaper was the funnel for the flow of shared information. Printers in the American colonies often received state subsidies for printing government forms and copies of current laws. The newspapers in turn reported the arrival and departure of ships, providing free or paid notice of shipments of all kinds of goods and their amounts and prices. This included slaves, and their country of origin was often named. Newspapers carried news, obituaries, and a little editorial opinion. Each issue of the *Maryland Gazette* was four pages long, and complete runs survive from 1745 on.

Jonas Green, later Anne Catherine Green, and then their sons printed the *Maryland Gazette* in Annapolis from 1745 on (B. Little 1987). The newspaper was signed on the bottom of the back page of each issue. Their editorship was always acknowledged, although the form varied until it switched to anonymity. Much of Annapolis was illiterate in the eighteenth and early nineteenth centuries, but the *Gazette* was read out loud in taverns. So we were dealing with a visual and aural document, but one increasingly meant for the eyes only. The *Gazette* was also read far from Annapolis, so it was not just local, notably because it reported so much material from Europe. But it was often quite opinionated, didactic, and dramatic. The material is captivating now and may have been then too. The *Gazette* was not a substitute for news or daily gossip in town, but it was much more than a newsletter or almanac. While it did not report many of the details of people's daily lives, it must have helped shape them. Certainly, almost all the ads were local. In any case, it was read and shared and was a part of daily life and a mirror of and for daily life—maybe mostly for—and thus constitutes an imagined description of it.

Popular opinion has two qualities: it is authorless, and it appears to be widely held. Anderson cites the large audiences who read newspapers or heard them read, an audience linked in no other way ([1983] 1991). Derrida (1986) cites the advent of documents during the American Revolution that appeared authorless because their ideas had to be seen as belonging to those who subscribed to them: individuals who owned their own opinions like all their other possessions. Popular opinion looked authorless and had to appear to be widely accepted and held by distant strangers, who saw themselves as linked through these shared opinions. While a citizen had to be an individual possessing liberty and freedom, the content of citizenship became shared opinions. This could only occur through texts written by people whose authorship appeared anonymous and that were read at a physical distance from the authors by people who had never met, had hitherto had nothing in common, and who came to think they had something in common through reading. This is what Anderson calls an imagined community. Derrida calls it the United States.

We can see this second process in the *Maryland Gazette*. How did a newspaper come to be designed so as to display popular opinion? Such opinion could only exist if people saw themselves as individuals with the liberty—even the responsibility—to have opinions on political matters, and my second question about the *Gazette's* page organization is thus, how did it come to appear so homogeneous that it looked undesigned, or authorless? The prediction was that in order to produce a printed page that appeared homogeneous, printer's type would have had to become more and more uniform. Type is distinguished by typeface, like Caslon or Baskerville, style of print, like roman or italics, and size, now measured in points. In the 1980s, when I first thought about type and when Barbara Little was analyzing Jonas and Anne Catherine Green's work for her dissertation, we predicted that type would become more and more homogeneous, that is, that there would be fewer and fewer styles and sizes. This prediction, in the form of a hypothesis, led to our (Harris 1986) early discovery that repeating quotation marks at the beginning of each line, use of big capital letters, capitalizing all the letters in nouns, and distinguishing between *s* and *f* (the long, or medial, form of the letter *s* used when it fell within or at the beginning of a word) all disappeared by the middle of the eighteenth century. These changes made any page appear more uniform.

Although this was where we began, it was not where we ended. My later question, one associated more with the founding of the nation than with the rise of the individual, was how could the paper be designed so that individuals believed that the printed opinions of others spoke for them as its readers? How could this happen when they never met? How were people to be fellow citizens when they had little in common except the idea that they were fellow citizens? How were the imaginary and unprecedented to be made real? The reality of nationhood occurred because people imagined that they had opinions in common because they were reading the same paper at the same time. For this to happen, the signs of authorship had to disappear, which did in fact happen. Further, the paper became mechanically homogeneous in appearance. It all began to look produced, or prearranged in some inevitable nonartistic sense. We discovered the elimination of authorial presence through an analysis of type (Austin and Brainerd n.d.; Coleman and Johnson 1985; Harris 1986; Arias, Hill, and Figueroa 2002). After mid-century, capital letters for all the letters in a noun disappeared and initial capital letters became much smaller. With these changes, individual lines became much more uniform in appearance. Lines became much less idiosyncratic visually. The surprise is that the authorless page required not only a greater range of sizes but, more particularly, the use of many more very small sizes of print. Analysis thus showed the very reverse of the hypothesis that there would be more and more homogeneous type. We discovered more and more heterogeneity. And, most important, we discovered this element of the imagined community through archaeology.

The third element of printing in the *Maryland Gazette* that interested me was its content. I wanted to know the rules for eating, gardening, and seeing, and instead I found the rules for calculating, measuring, and farming. These amounted to the same process of defining individual behavior and etiquette. These were the technologies of the individual, the technologies of ideology. I was also interested in James Deetz's notion that people were beginning to see themselves as individuals, and I wanted to know what the rules and disciplines actually looked like for these in Annapolis.

Behind changes to orderliness at the table lay the idea that people were individuals, which was the Renaissance definition of a human being as separate and distinct from all others, with rights, a history, and property. Each person was worthy in and of himself or herself. At the heart of *In Small Things Forgotten* (Deetz 1977), which was the initial inspiration for my research in Annapolis, was the idea that people in New England came to see themselves, not primarily as family members or as community members, but as free-standing individuals. English North America adopted a modernizing identity from Europe that sponsored ideas of individual rights, personal liberty, private property, privacy for many functions, and separate chairs and place settings at a dining table.

Deetz points out that functions of daily life like cooking, eating, waste disposal, and elimination became separately demarcated and located apart from each other. This followed from seeing people as individuals who performed varied activities, with each given a separate setting or room. Certainly, the separation of activities occurred. However, there is another practice that I want to rely on in order to build to an understanding of the changed content of the *Maryland Gazette*. The individual was supposed to be able to learn and absorb new practices throughout life, thus possessing them (Macpherson 1962) and in turn exemplifying them for others to observe. This occurred through a constant process of reading, learning, showing, and then acquiring more knowledge. This was how a person was to make himself into an individual. The content of the *Gazette* shows the process. Because I take the idea of the individual as an ideology, I want to know how the process worked through reading.

I argue in my analysis of printing and the *Maryland Gazette* that the creation and use of popular opinion is a technology that sustains the ideology of individualism within the dream of republican government. A

FIGURE 15. Desk with many compartments in Annapolis. The Enlightenment project of systematically discovering ordered nature included compartmentalizing that knowledge in inventories, principles, rules, and record books. All of these devices were held in writing instruments like this. Photograph by Howard Erenfeld.

single author or a small number of them created newspapers with opinions and conveyed these in such a way that printed opinion acted the way Marshall McLuhan ([1964] 1994) said of newspapers. People "wash" themselves—immerse themselves—in print and select in such a way that they think that what they read is for them and of them; that it is theirs. Benedict Anderson argued that when people saw each other informed by the same materials, singular opinions became plural and thus widely held. Did anyone see written opinion as just that, and see it as a social construct? Did anyone see it cynically or see it with a knowing smile? Did anyone pierce the ideology of popular opinion?

In the 1740s and early 1750s, Annapolis produced its single most remarkable text, *The History of the Ancient and Honorable Tuesday Club*, written by Dr. Alexander Hamilton (Hamilton 1990; see also Breslaw 1988), who founded a discussion and social group. The book is a mock history of the Tuesday Club's eleven-year history. It is an explicitly self-aggrandizing parody of rational histories, filled with satiric commentaries on contemporary society, particularly monarchical government and proprietary authority. It is a self-mocking description of a group's opinions of itself that satirizes popular opinion and the way that such opinion makes itself important by making its origins seem inevitable. It is a critique, in other words.

The dozen or so members of the Tuesday Club owned some property, some slaves, no inherited wealth, ran businesses, were largely dependent on money they made themselves, did not have sumptuary appointments that gave them a subsidized living, and, in short, were middle-class or petit bourgeois. They should be within ideology if Althusser is correct, and thus they constitute an important reflection on his hypothesis. I include the Tuesday Club in the chapter on printing and reading because of the importance to the club of texts performed out loud, written, and read, and because the printer Jonas Green was a member. The club is important because its members used parody to reveal the artificiality of popular opinion.

DISHES AND DINING

Ceramics, tableware, and dishes are my third set of materials (Leone 1999; Beadenkopf et al. 2002). Deetz puts forward a set of arguments that caught the attention of all historical archaeologists, and this is where his work, specifically with regard to dishes, becomes relevant again. Citizens were made through the routines of daily life in which habits of mind became habits in action, and where ideas that contradicted economic reality came to be believed and thus, in some sense, real (Foucault 1979, 195–228, 257–92).

Deetz's argument is that table settings became modular after the beginning of the eighteenth century in New England (Deetz 1977, 46–61). Most people ate from a separate dish, with accompanying utensils. Big central dishes for stews eaten partially by hand were replaced by sets of equal-looking dishes, with sets of forks, individual chairs, and mugs or glasses. On the table's surface, everything was modular, but behind the uniformity of shape and style was the conception that people were not modular at all, but uniquely individual. They should therefore have separate, hierarchically ordered private spaces. In this way, the individual became the building block of society. But it took a very long time for this to happen in Annapolis, which may mean that the ideology of individualism did not penetrate all at once, evenly, or completely.

Deetz points out that just as food was separated on a plate into portions and courses, so were sleeping, eating, and cooking. These separa-

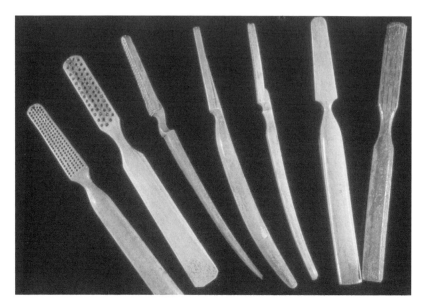

FIGURE 16. Excavated toothbrushes from Annapolis. These represent the early phase of American hygiene and rules for personal cleanliness, which simply extends dining etiquette to body etiquette. Among users of African American spirit traditions, the web of holes could serve as a device for catching and trapping the spirit when the toothbrush handle was buried in a place where spirits traveled. Photograph by Howard Erenfeld.

tions also meant that personal elimination was more private and that garbage disposal occurred in well-defined pits. These separations are easy to see archaeologically. However, it is also the case that the rules of etiquette adhered to by an individual made the user an inspector of others. It is that process, not really a cognitive pattern, but a conscious exercise in power among fellow and sister individuals, that linked material culture and made the diner an observer of himself and others.

Deetz argues for New England. Could I find the pattern in Annapolis? As any historical archaeologist knows, Deetz was correct, in general. Therefore, if one were going to look for sets of dishes, how could you verify Deetz's idea? When did the segmentation of the dinner table occur? How did one measure uniformity of forms and uniformity of decoration, because both variables characterized a set?

In Annapolis, we found a way to measure these uniformities for the ceramics of ten dwellings over about a hundred and fifty years. There was a lot of variation, and African Americans, whether slave or free, poor or middle-class, always remained different. In addition to finding that the pattern that characterized New England also characterized Annapolis, we created a chronology for Deetz's patterns and measured the variation in the pattern. I argued that eating was a discipline, taught at home as rules and observed widely as a mark of individualism. Individualism, or a person's capacity to self-inspect, signaled readiness to learn other rules, to observe portions, be punctual, accept being observed by others, and be subject to working for wages, carrying debt, and being responsive to market pressures. I argued that the Georgian Order was the order of capitalism (Leone 1988), because it produced both workers and consumers. We found that the process of ceramic change began in Annapolis before it began in New England. Moreover, it occurred among the rich and the poor at the same time, but in different degrees. African Americans, completely modern and sophisticated in the ways of the world that they were in, and entirely capable of eating any way they chose, put together a dining table different from that of other households.

THE RESULT IN TERMS OF FREEDOM

Nowhere in this book have I chosen to see society as functional. It functions, to be sure, but it is not harmonious, kind, or charitable. People try to be harmonious, kind, and loving, and they may succeed. But my portrayal of Annapolis as a capital city is based on seeing how people worked and were governed without the use of excessive external force. People made themselves into loyal subjects and patriotic, freedom-loving citizens through use of the environments that were present in Annapolis.

What did people see when they watched one another? I argue that they saw each other from their position as individuals. They also saw themselves acquiring more possessions, including learned technologies, in a process of fulfillment and completion, but never getting there completely (R. Handler 1986, 1988, 1991). Many people did not react when they saw the widening gulf between owners and renters, owners and wage earners, or the decline of widely distributed, moderate wealth. They may have noticed the loss of property and independence among people from whom wealth had been extracted through interest rates and rents, but had no way to analyze it. Many people certainly knew of land speculation in Annapolis (Lindauer 1997, 20), but they had no abstraction available through which they could act on that knowledge. But they could see that they were living as individuals, and then as citizens, and hoped that they personally could do better or blamed themselves for not having done better. These became believable abstractions through the daily practice of the disciplines I have outlined: walking, reading, and eating. We must also ask who did see and try to escape these processes, because that is key to challenging capitalist economies.

Once the setting I am describing is connected to the world of making a profit through the use of the technologies of the ideology of individualism (Leone and Hurry 1998), two questions are left. What other areas of life should be included? And was escape possible (Habermas 1984–87)? My analysis of landscapes, print, and dishes is limited to the eighteenth and nineteenth centuries and describes the origins of the ideology and its ties to the American Revolution, with whose notion of liberty for the individual we still struggle. My presentation of African spirit practices, a religion derived from West Central Africa that began in the eighteenth century, comes up to the present, because it is still practiced in Annapolis.

In a self-conscious archaeology (Leone, Potter, and Shackel 1987), I thought there could be ways to moderate modern conditions, and eventually I saw the search for those leading to African America. Its basic critique is important, because it is old, large, and different. If the archaeology of landscapes and printing shows beginnings, then African America shows a historical critique and modern alternatives.

Did the notions of personal liberty and of the citizen with voting rights seem convincing to African Americans in Annapolis? Once I ask the question and confine the answer to it from 1790 to about 1920, there are two results. One comes from Paul Mullins and Mark Warner's work on free African Americans. The other comes from my project's work on bundles for spirit management. The answers are summed up by W. E. B. Du Bois's famous phrase "the two souls of black folks" (1969 [1903], 4, 16–17). Our analysis of free African American life before and after Emancipation shows strong efforts by African Americans to incorporate themselves into mainstream life through property ownership, consumption of popular goods and brands, building conventional housing, and furnishing homes in a completely conventional way, in other words, of being within the values of the dominant ideology. But because of slavery and racism, there was always a struggle for these goals.

African religion was another matter. It was a struggle for freedom in another way, one that was built on an explicit understanding of the existence of an alternative world to European rationality. The spirit tradition derived from West Central Africa that I present is the opposite of Enlightenment rationality. It not only denied the rationality that produced possessive individualism and its later form the panoptic citizen, it also only worked if there was a believing community joined to its African roots

FIGURE 17. Cache from the kitchen, Slayton House. A set of common pins plus a crab claw fragment and button with four holes distinguish this cache. Courtesy of the Anacostia Museum and Center for African American History and Culture, Smithsonian Institution. Photograph by Steven M. Cummings.

to support it. The material on spirit use seems to be the strongest evidence of a whole group outside the dominant ideology.

There were two roads into African American forms in Annapolis, and they led to different results. The first came from scholars who were offended (Beaudry, Cook, and Mrozowski 1991; Hodder 1986, 164–70) by my use of Louis Althusser (1971) to analyze eighteenth-century material culture as a vehicle of ideology. Because Althusser conceptualizes ideology as virtually impenetrable, I did not ask who might have seen through a naturalistic ideology. That was clearly a mistake. The question was a good one: Who saw exploitation behind the self-promoting images that the rich and powerful used? Then, who saw through the ideology of personal liberty? Did these same people produce a critique of their treatment? Or an alternative way of leading life? But the central question will always remain: Was there an alternative from which people learned? Could they modify daily life, and could they teach the rest of us to modify how we are treated?

The second road to African America in Annapolis ran through South Africa. When I taught at the University of Cape Town in 1988, a man of Indian descent explained to me that in South Africa, archaeology was a site of struggle. I had never heard the term before, nor had I ever heard of anyone seeing archaeology as having that kind of potential. He held archaeology to be as central to life as access to good medicine, good schools, and equality. Indeed, in South Africa, access to archaeology and its potential was the equivalent to having hold of a decent past. Archaeology was a way to have a proper identity. It was part of a wholesome life and was to be fought for.

When I returned to Annapolis with this experience in Africa, after having met many, many Africans who had a far fuller appreciation of and use for archaeology than anyone in or out of the archaeological profession in the United States, I decided to approach the leaders of the Banneker-Douglass Museum in Annapolis. The museum was then the State of Maryland's Center for African-American History and Culture. There I met Barbara Jackson Nash who, as can happen in some inspired moments, gave me my assignment and every opportunity to realize it. "We want to know what is left from Africa," she said. "Do we have archaeology? We're tired of hearing about slavery. Tell us about freedom." There were many, many free black people in Annapolis and Maryland before 1865, but I did not know their archaeology or the evidence for their African origins.

There turns out to be a lot of African American archaeology in Annapolis, and much of it describes free blacks. Archaeology in Annapolis has worked on this initiative since about 1990. But it is with the answer from African origins that I can construct the possibility of escape from the disciplines and little imprisoning habitual technologies of capitalism and from surveillance. This escape is venerable, articulate, and, insofar as religion is effective, viable.

I spend a lot of time in this book describing spirit traditions represented by buried bundles that were used to control the spirits of the dead. We have excavated at least seven sites in Annapolis where we knew in advance that Africans or people of African descent had lived. We found ritual bundles in three of the seven.

I was led to many of the data I report by Gladys-Marie Fry, a colleague of mine, now emerita, in the English Department at the University of Maryland (Leone and Fry 1999), and by Timothy Ruppel, now teaching at Howard University (Leone, Fry, and Ruppel 2001; Ruppel, Neuwirth, Leone, and Fry 2003). We compared the material in Annapolis bundles to material from excavated archaeological sites in Virginia where African Americans had lived and predicted where such materials were likely to be found. During all this work, we integrated the narratives of former slaves collected in the 1930s as part of the Federal Writers' Project into our work. Originally and still sometimes referred to as the composite autobiographies (Hyatt 1970; Rawick 1972, 1977, 1979), these autobiographies are compelling, systematic descriptions of life in slavery. What came across to us in these narratives was the cultural and psychic autonomy people of African descent preserved. They knew what slavery was, and they hated it, and in this was a critique of the business of capitalism. While they were slaves legally, they were not slaves to themselves.

My colleagues and I combined the archaeology of African spirit traditions with the world described in the composite autobiographies to see a culture partially outside capitalism. Such traditions, which were not whole from Africa, but originated there, were widely shared in communities of African descent in the New World, where they were widely practiced. In no way was Annapolis isolated from the lives that Africans made. Behind the Georgian façades, Annapolis was also an African city.

Because I am writing about surveillance and about both willingness and inevitability in the process, I focus on consciousness and resistance to the way that capitalist labor reproduces itself. West Central African spirit traditions were a form of resistance with three characteristics that I want to invoke. They were practiced in secret and kept secret from the white world. They were not just bits and fragments of spirit practices but a religion, or possibly the foundational elements of one or more religions. Third, they were utterly foreign and often about death. The hope, forgiveness, and love in Christianity were not at their core, although these were possibly at their periphery. This religion was not familiar, and it could be frightening. It is important in this context because it helped preserve an African identity and a coherent sense of community, even though not everybody who knew about it used it. It is another culture within ours.

We know through archaeology that the tradition of invoking the spirit of dead ancestors had been in Annapolis at least since 1790 (Logan et al. 1992). Expressions of these traditions are found today in the greater Washington area, along with other religions from Latin America's African diasporic communities: Santeria, Condomblé, Voodoo, and Palo Mayombe (Ruppel 2003). These are all practiced more or less underground and by many people who also practice Christianity.

The 1930s composite autobiographies of former slaves give the lie to capitalist practices. So did the consumption practices of free people of African descent in the city. They frequently led lives outside the market and, as Paul Mullins (1999) shows, they quoted Du Bois and Frederick Douglass and often knew what they were doing and why. The white world read Douglass and Du Bois and largely rejected them, just as it initially and largely rejected all the other Americans who found capitalism wanting, such as Joseph Smith, Mary Baker Eddy, Mother Ann Lee, and the other utopian socialists.

This critique and rejection of modern conditions is half of the twin souls of black folk. The other half is the life led in public by people of African descent, of trying to get along, trying to be like everyone else, of making do and of asking for full membership and doubting it will ever come. Paul Mullins and Mark Warner have also described this half of the black world well. It is inside the ideology of individualism, opportunity, equality, and self-sufficiency. But the conscious doubts of black people leave us all room to see the unconvincing nature of the dominant ideology.

CHAPTER 3

Landscapes of Power

The William Paca Garden is the most beautiful place in Annapolis. Even though its beauty is not an illusion, it contains one. Furthermore, the arrangement of the garden exists to make the illusion possible. Once this arrangement is accepted as planned and deliberate, and even as its basic reason for being, then the garden and its beauty cannot be taken as is. The garden was not incidental to the life of Annapolis in the eighteenth century and is not today. It is not the product of leisure, money, or taste, although all three are related—even central—to it. It is a function of power, particularly its absence. That is how it worked and how, in its authentically recreated state, it still works. Because the reconstruction by the Historic Annapolis Foundation is so faithful to the original (Shellenhamer 2004), we can understand the garden's purpose both then and now.

I want to walk you through the garden. As you stand at the garden door of the William Paca House and see the garden, perhaps for the first time, or for the first time in a long time, you look down on a green space filled with plants placed or clipped into geometric shapes. You can see both the garden's depth and its plan. Virtually any eighteenth-century garden works this way. Because these gardens are exhibits of natural law—particularly solid geometry—you need a preface to volumes in the sense of geometric space. The overview you get from the entry platform provides just that visual preface. But you only get it once. From this elevation, you also see the paths through the garden and the ways though the geometry. In fact, if you are aware, you see that you will be walking the geometry. Then, because at this point you have no choice, you go down the stairs and are at eye level with the garden.

At eye level, at the top of the central path of the garden, or grand allée, you are far more a captive of the garden than you are the person in charge. I did not realize this at first. And it is difficult from the distance of twenty years to recreate my first impression. But that impression led eventually to this chapter and, indeed, to this whole analysis of how a baroque capital city working its way toward democracy—or at least to the idea of personal liberty—operated. I think that when you stand at the head of this descent garden, not on the staircase looking down into it, you cannot realistically judge just how far you are from the object you are invited to reach. I could not estimate how far I was from the Summer House, or Pavilion, the focal point. For some reason, that bothered me.

There were some attendant issues that I picked up in a secondary way, but that were presented as unresolved problems in why the garden had been built as it was. Out of these, I built a case against which I placed my own analysis of both the garden and the baroque uses of space in the city as a whole.

There are three issues here. There was no explanation available, St. Clair Wright thought, for why the flats in the garden, or terraces, were of unequal width. The actual flat spaces where the beds were placed were of very different dimensions, becoming narrower as they become more distant from the viewer. They were roughly 60 feet, 45 feet, and 15 feet wide. All were the same length. Second, the map of the garden derived from its rebuilding in 1970 was a major descriptive and explanatory tool for understanding Paca's reborn garden. The map was drawn by Laurence S. Brigham (Paca 1983) when he designed the parts of the garden that could not be known via archaeology. The map shows the parterres where flowers, rose bushes, holly trees, and shaped boxwoods are planted in geometric shapes. It is quite beautiful and the garden is seen from above, as is the case with almost any map. It used to be displayed prominently in the garden's visitor center. Its concept as a plan viewed from above was reproduced in the numberless tours given in the garden. The garden's depth was irrelevant in the tours, including the many given by Mrs. Wright herself. She was the guiding force behind the garden, the visionary who enabled it, and the author of its actual authenticity. I was walked through the garden by her many times over at least ten years. She knew it was a falling, or descent, garden. She subsequently sponsored the research that showed that the whole space was an exercise in plane geometry. But as you walked through the garden with her, or by yourself with

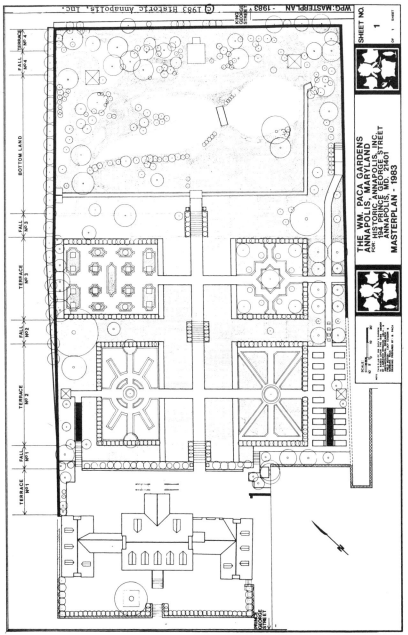

FIGURE 18. Map of the William Paca Garden showing terraces, falls, and modern surface features. Courtesy of the Historic Annapolis Foundation.

a pamphlet, or with a gardener/guide, the space was flat (Wright 1977a; Russo 1990). The stairs were there, but not their reason; the falls were there, but no explanation for their angle or visual effect. Your nose, love of flowers, rare plants, and shapeable shrubs were satisfied, but not the connection between your eyes and brain. You had to use your eyes, but there was no connection between them and how the space was playing on them. Depth as a concept was missing and still is.

Taste was the third and, in some ways, the most productive issue. William Paca's education in Philadelphia made him explicitly knowledgeable in eighteenth-century classical information (Stiverson and Jacobsen 1976). He had to know Latin, the classics, some architecture, lots of law and legal precedent, and philosophy tied to the Enlightenment. Taste was presented by Mrs. Wright as a function of education. Paca had married a woman of wealth, and therefore taste in his case was also a function of marriage and money. And as Mrs. Wright and others explained to me, his good taste was peculiar to him. Many contemporaries of similar education, marriage status, wealth and standing lacked it. According to Mrs. Wright, in a now lost citation, Thomas Jefferson called Paca's garden the most elegant in Annapolis. It was thus presented as unique, even though Mrs. Wright was actively involved in the protection of other gardens and encouraged the study of other eighteenth-century Annapolis gardens. She introduced me to all of them quite deliberately and encouraged my plan to map them topographically.

Although never intended or foreseen, her conclusion about the Paca garden's uniqueness meant that it was not systematically compared to the other eighteenth-century gardens in the city. Two gardens remained intact; others survived as fragments. Moreover, Paca's garden design was never systematically evaluated in relation to the eighteenth-century garden manuals printed in London that told how to create planned landscapes. Paca and others like him in Annapolis possessed copies of such manuals, including three or four very popular and often reprinted books with large amounts of practical and scientific information on every aspect of gardening. While these had been collected by Historic Annapolis, they had not been compared systematically with the archaeology of the garden or with other remaining gardens.

When I began my work on Paca's garden in 1983, I did not know the literature on garden history. There was at the time no work on the social science of such planned spaces that I knew of. Garden history was concerned with the historical evolution of gardens, dominated by horticultural concerns, energized by love of rare and difficult-to-raise plants, and focused on one garden at a time. It was not a developed scholarly area that encouraged comparison. This meant that gardens were taken as a given. The first task I faced was how to make gardens into a problem. This was before Chandra Mukerji did the same using the gardens at Versailles, and did a much better, but not a fundamentally different, job (Mukerji 1993, 1997).

I took disparate elements to build a problem. In the first place, I thought the garden's depth was much more important than its interpretation communicated. Secondly, although Paca had been wealthy, he was not one of the very rich; furthermore, he was not a self-made man—he had married money, not once but twice in the course of his life. I also had my doubts about the comforts of such wealth and the leisure it was supposed to produce. Paca had owned slaves, initially only a few, but over a hundred by the time of his death, and for any intelligent person, such ownership was an enormous burden. Moreover, he had signed the Declaration of Independence and would not support the Constitution until the Bill of Rights was attached to it. I surmised that he either had not been rich enough to satisfy himself or had not thought that he had enough power to protect his property.

The third element I added to these two was my strong interest in the role of ideology in capitalist societies as hypothesized by Louis Althusser (1971). The elements of Althusser that moved me intellectually were that ideology hid the origin of exploitative relationships, and that it was material. Out of these elements I quite quickly formulated the idea that the Paca Garden layout was a technology of ideology. It was built to naturalize the conflict between slaveholding , diminishing power, and Paca's strong desire to be better able to control the political influences on his own wealth. I have argued (Leone 1984, 1987; Leone, Ernstein, et al. 1989; Leone and Shackel 1990) that his was a garden about power, not plants. It was a garden not to demonstrate power but to accrue adequate amounts of it to protect his wealth.

Our first and most lasting archaeological discovery was only one element in this argument. It takes the most time to describe, because it was original, empirical, and unexpected. That is, the Paca Garden contained an optical illusion that had been quite deliberately built into it and was the key to understanding that the garden materialized ideology. Furthermore, we eventually found that the same was true of similar contemporary landscapes.

Soon after seeing the Paca Garden, I was introduced by my Annapolis mentor, St. Clair Wright, to two gardens in Annapolis that were supposed

to be survivors from the eighteenth century. Although enclosed and removed from public view, the Ridout and Carroll gardens were not at all
beautiful. They were terraced lawns with shrubs, not very orderly, and
no better maintained than anyone else's yard. They did not look like the
Paca Garden, but I was told that they were original. They were. I also
was introduced to the historic garden literature. I read a great deal of
Batty Langley (1726) and also A. B. Lockwood's *Gardens of Colony and
State* (1934).

It was not hard to discover the rules for placing houses and for laying out gardens as a part of a house's landscape. Even though these were
very well known (Martin 1984) and were almost invariably followed in
their day, and even though I have quoted them before, they are worth
summarizing here, because there is now more illustrative material from
our archaeological project to show how the literature was used.

From about 1750 on, in Maryland, the rule was that a great house,
that is, the core of a plantation, which was not necessarily very large,
should be put on the edge of a rise, so that the land could fall off to a
vista on one side and opened onto flat land on the other (Langley 1726,
1967 [1740]; Miller 1731–39). Then, depending on whether the house
was in a town or out in the countryside, the landscape was to be altered
to make the vista appear shorter or longer than it actually was (Dézallier d'Argenville 1722 [1709], 138, plate 6). The rules of perspective distance were to be employed to alter the perception of the view (Miller
1731–39, "Garden"; Langley 1726, 196, 201).

The books on gardening use at least three ideas to create impressions
of distance. The one of greatest importance in improving my understanding
of Paca's garden involved how to build the bottom plane, the ground level
itself (Dézallier d'Argenville 1728 [1712], 117, fig. 3). If a descent garden
were to be laid out in a small space, then the builder's desire was supposed to be to make the garden appear larger than it actually was by making the object of view appear further away. This could be achieved by creating terraces that decreased in width as they receded from the viewer.
So, at the Paca Garden, the visitor stood at the top of a relatively narrow
upper terrace. Then the broad terraces stretched out roughly 60 feet, 45
feet, and 15 feet respectively to the garden's lowest point. This formula
for gradation helped create the illusion of greater distance than existed in
fact. The fit with these procedures in Paca's garden was remarkable and
explains the uneven dimensions of the terraces. Since the garden books
are specific on diminishing terrace width, the issue then became to discover whether they were employed on other gardens besides Paca's.

The garden books were just as clear about lines of sight. Most people were familiar with this obvious way of creating the appearance of distance when not much existed. A small city garden was to be made to look bigger than it was by using lines that converged on a focal point, thus appearing to drive the focal point further away from the viewer. These lines could be the sides of the path that led to the focal point. Instead of making the sides parallel, they could be made to converge gradually and to complement the eye's natural inclination to draw lines together as a person looked into the distance.

To build a terrace, the gardener might employ Batty Langley's principle "XXVII. The proportion that the base of a slope ought to have to its perpendicular, is a three to one, that is, if that perpendicular height be ten feet, its base must be thirty feet; and the like of all others" (1726, 201).

The manipulation of space in order to create perspective is made precise in principle:

> XV. That all walks whose lengths are short, and lead away from any point of view, be made narrower at their further ends than at the hither part; for by inclination of their sides, they appear to be of a much greater length than they really are; and the further end of every long walk, avenue, etc. appears to be much narrower than the end where you stand.
>
> And the reason is, that notwithstanding the sides of such walks are parallel to each other, yet as the breadth of the further end is seen under a lesser angle than the breadth of that part where you stand, it will therefore appear as if contracted, altho' the sides are actually parallel; for equal objects always appear under equal angles, Q.E.D.
>
> Langley 1726, 196

As we were to discover, there were several ways to make lines converge (Leone and Shackel 1990; Roulette and Williams 1986; Hopkins 1984). Nonparallel rows of hedges on the way to a focal point could be planted or clipped so as to begin to converge. The edges of the garden, built or grown, could be altered to converge. The angle of the flower beds could be set to converge, and so could lines of trees whose shapes were then altered to enhance the impression made by their trunks. Lines of sight could be created on the ground, as well as above it. Suddenly, it began to be clear that this was not a map that was being created in these gardens; it was a volume.

The third way of creating a sense of distance was by using color. I found this idea in a now lost garden magazine and in an eighteenth-century garden dictionary (Langley 1726, 193–96). If green, the desired color in a garden, were graduated from yellow to black-green, in other words from light green that is yellowish to very dark green that has a blackish tone to it, the light green was to be at the viewer's feet and the dark green at the greater distances in the garden. This added to the appearance of space and could be created by clipping grass close at the viewing station and by planting very dark evergreens and oaks on the outer limits of the garden. Some of this knowledge had never fallen out of use among well-trained garden designers, but it was widely shared in the later eighteenth century and certainly through the Federal Era.

It did not appear possible to pursue use of color in eighteenth-century garden archaeology, and I never invested in palynology because too much garden research was focused on specific plants without any adequate understanding of what impression a hue, as opposed to a species of plant, was supposed to make. I focused on bottom or ground planes and lines of sight.

Here is what I inherited from St. Clair Wright and the Historic Annapolis Foundation, then Incorporated, to do my work. When the Paca House had been bought by Historic Annapolis Incorporated in 1967 (Wright 1977b), it was the foyer and front for a 1906 hotel, the Carvel Hall Hotel, that had been built over William Paca's garden. It is likely that only a long-term garden advocate would have realized that such a house would not only have had a formal garden but could not have existed without one. They went together indispensably in eighteenth-century European terms. But those terms had been lost, except in the fairly arcane circles of garden historians, circles that had yet to gain credibility and acceptance among other historical scholars. However, St. Clair Wright was a garden enthusiast and knew the relationship between a house and its garden (Lockwood 1934, 5–7).

She had the Paca Garden excavated in at least three, close-together phases (Powell 1966; G. Little 1967–68; Orr and Orr 1975a; Shellenhamer 2004). The first phase, in the late 1960s, found the base of the garden wall in several places. Because the hotel had been built within the boundaries of the land owned by Paca, the wall's foundations had remained in place. The discovery of a garden wall was not a minor matter, because no one had known the wall had existed, and it certainly was not clear that city gardens had to be surrounded by walls.

The garden wall's foundations were found in several places. Because substantial lengths of it were found, the descents or falls were also found in shadow form, because the wall's foundation was built as a slope where the ground was a descent. The foundation of the wall was actually laid at an angle where the ground fell for the descent. Because of this, the height and angles of the terraces and slopes were available. When found on both sides of the garden, this set of archaeological discoveries provided justification for the bottom plane for the whole upper two-thirds of the garden.

The hotel had been built over the main part of the upper garden, and the lower part of the garden was buried under the hotel's parking lot. The lower third was excavated by Glenn Little, who did a careful and compelling job on the part of the garden that was intact under fill, using trenches to find the stratigraphy and other features (G. Little 1967–68, n.d.). Little made several major finds, including a brick-lined canal that had channeled water through the garden. As I understand it, water began to fill the lowest part of the garden once the overlying fill was removed, and this led to his discovering the pond. To be sure, where there is a bridge, as in Charles Willson Peale's portrait of Paca, there is likely to be water. The modern shape of the pond, a fish, is conjectural. But there had to have been a basin of water, given the depth of the garden and the canal, and Little found it.

The topography of the lower garden undulated, rising to a mound, where there was a Summer House. The ground then fell off to the pond, which stretched across two-thirds of the center of the lower garden, with the bridge at an angle to the upper path, and then rose to the back wall. There was no central path in this part of the garden. This absence of rectilinear geometry was and is thought to be evidence of a wilderness garden, a place of curvilinear geometry. Glenn Little's profiles of the stratigraphy within the trenches that were used to figure out the undulations, suffice to convince me of the likelihood of this. At a minimum, the bottom of the garden was not laid out using the principles of rectilinear geometry. As a result, Laurence Brigham and St. Clair Wright (personal communication) used curvilinear geometry for this section of the garden. All the unpublished original archaeology is reported and summarized by Jason Shellenhamer (2004).

From Philip Miller (1731–39, "Wilderness"), we can see the plans and elements that could be used to make a wilderness garden. The generic rules advised that a wilderness was to be designed on paper first and had many parts, some open, some closed, some tall, and some at ground level. A wilderness had considerable life in it, which was introduced through running water, active food-producing areas, and animals and birds in cages and warrens. Above all, it was not to be a series of quadrants, that is, areas constructed using rectilinear geometry.

Langley indicates how the paths and colors were to be managed, a set of rules not fundamentally different from those used in the rectilinear part of the garden. I quote all this to show how clear laying out a precise garden was if the rules were followed:

> To draw a beautiful regular draught, is not to the purpose, for although it makes a handsome figure on the paper, yet is has a quite different effect when executed on the ground: nor is there anything more ridiculous and forbidding than a garden which is regular, which instead of entertaining the eye with fresh objects, after you have seen a quarter part, you only see the very same part repeated again without any variety.
>
> That the several parts of a beautiful rural garden, are walks, slopes, borders, open plains, plain parterres, avenues, groves, wilderness, labyrinths, fruit-gardens, flower-gardens, vineyards, hop-gardens, nurseries, coppiced quarters (thicket of bushes), green openings like meadows; small enclosures of corn, cones of evergreens, of flowering shrubs, of fruit-trees, of forest-trees, and mixed together: mounds, terraces, winding valleys, dales, purling (rippling) streams, basins, canals, fountains, cascades, grottos, rocks, ruins, serpentine meanders, hay-stacks, wood-piles, rabbit and hare-warrens, cold baths, aviaries, statues, obelisks, menageries, pheasant and partridge-grounds, orangeries, melon-grounds, kitchen gardens, herb-garden, orchard, bowling green, dials, precipices, amphitheatres, etc.
>
> In order to achieve some of these:
>
> That grand avenues be planted from such large open plains, with a breadth proportionate to the building, as well as to its length of view.
>
> XIV. That the walks leading up the slope of a mount, have their breadth contracted at the top, full one half part, and if that contracted part be enclosed on the sides with a hedge whose leaves are of a light green, 'twill seemingly add a great addition to the length of the walk, when viewed from the other end.
>
> XVI. That the walks of a wilderness be never narrower than ten feet, or wider than twenty-five feet.
>
> Langley 1726, 193–96

There is an additional source for the garden's geometrical authenticity, also something I inherited. In the 1980s, Barbara Paca (Paca-Steele and Wright 1987), a descendent of the builder and a person familiar with the garden literature, showed that plane geometry formed one of the main elements of the garden, based on the geometry of the surviving house.

Barbara Paca became familiar with one of the initial recommendations for building a formal garden in the period literature. She found the solution to the problem of relating the house to its garden, called a net of squares. Using a common dimension of the house derived from the façade or some principal room, the garden planner was to lay out on paper—or on the ground—a grid of squares over the whole space that was to become the garden. It was the same as taking a sheet of graph paper and laying out the whole garden within the grid. With this technique, the gardener could be sure that all the basic divisions and design elements of the garden were multiples of each other, thus creating a visual harmony that was more felt than mathematically apparent.

Barbara Paca took a map of the garden as it had been rebuilt and, following a hunch that a measure taken from the original house was the base measure of the garden, overlaid it with a set of rectangles that when divided by a diagonal produced 3–4–5 triangles (Paca-Steele and Wright 1987, 314, 316) . Her result encompassed the whole garden. A "net of squares" 49½ feet by 66 feet covered the garden as defined by its original walls. Not only did major elements of the garden fall evenly on the lines of the grid, but so did visual punctuations like small buildings and the tree that had been replanted on the spot where Peale shows one in his contemporary painting of William Paca.

Barbara Paca's work showed that in any grid, it was possible, indeed inevitable, that squares, when subdivided, could be triangles and that large right triangles created diagonals throughout the space being planned. It was then visible that such a possibility led to crosscutting alignments in space that could be marked by objects, including plants. Paca demonstrated the truth of this in her ancestor's garden.

This exercise showed that Paca's garden was planned out in advance through the use of plane geometry, which showed that the garden had been conceptualized from above. Thus, a bird's-eye view was essential to building and understanding the garden and presumably any other garden like it.

OTHER GARDENS

I did not lead myself to the other gardens in Annapolis; St. Clair Wright led me to them. After she showed me the Charles Carroll of Carrollton Garden and the Ridout Garden, I realized that the key to using them to understand Paca's garden was mapping them, not digging them. In the early 1980s, my team made topographic maps of both and began one of Tulip Hill outside the city as well. These maps served two purposes. They provided a much-needed descriptive comparative base for comprehending Paca's garden. Second, the analysis of his garden could be moved to an emphasis on depth and perspective as seen by the viewer and away

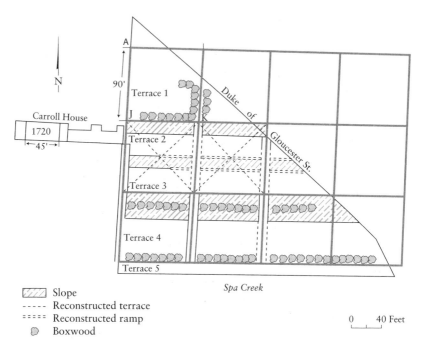

FIGURE 19. Map of the 1771 Charles Carroll of Carrollton Garden showing
geometric subdivisions.

from an emphasis on the garden as a map, seen from above, which was
appropriate in planning a garden, but not when viewing one on a daily
basis or as a visitor.

A topographic map records three dimensions visually and therefore
shows height and depth. Such maps had never been made of planned landscapes in Annapolis before, including Paca's garden itself. We made one
of the Ridout Garden in 1984 (Hopkins 1984) and our first one of the
Carroll Garden in 1986 (Roulette and Williams 1986), and Barbara Paca
(1983) made a new one of her ancestor's garden (1983) at about the same
time (see fig. 18). With these maps, the Paca Garden lost any uniqueness
it might have had, apart from its modern manicured appearance. There
was now a comparative base for looking at all of them. The maps also
provided evidence of the forms needed to use perspectives to create vistas.

Our maps were not at first revolutionary and were sometimes difficult
to understand, because we ourselves did not understand the rules for
building these gardens. Just as you can excavate without knowing in advance the features you will find, so you can also map with a good sense

of accurate procedure but not know in advance what you are going to see when you are done. The map of the Carroll Garden had inaccuracies, because the garden was so big and we were inexperienced. The resulting map nonetheless showed all the space around the house and recorded the terraces and falls and stood as convincing evidence of the garden's size and likely authenticity.

The map of the Ridout Garden (Hopkins 1984) showed the terraces but left one wondering where any vista could have been. By the time we made this map, we knew garden beds were important to making the solid geometry of a garden work to create perspective, but we did not know how. In the Ridout Garden, there were beds left as depressions on two of the biggest terraces in the garden. There were also beds along the central ramp, which still held shrubs. We mapped all these.

In the Ridout Garden, the beds lining the sides of the grass-covered central ramp were living. We did no digging in the garden, and I assumed that these beds either were original or replaced originals. I stress that this is an assumption, because there is no documentation that I know of on the history of the garden between the 1760s, when it was laid out and now, except for the fact that the house is still in the hands of the family that built it and the garden and house have not been altered. Mrs. Wright told me that she had had an archaeologist dig in the central ramp to see whether the slopes had been joined by sets of stairs, as she had discovered was likely the case in Paca's garden. There were none evident in the Ridout Garden. This archaeology was not recorded, so the micro history of alterations is not recorded, and thus the age of these beds was not either.

The beds along the central ramp in the Ridout garden were in pairs, with three sets of them descending the main terraces. The inner edges of the beds nearest the ramp were all equidistant from each other. The back edges of the sets of beds have diminished width as the sets descend. The upper beds were three feet wide, the middle were two and a half feet wide, and the lowest about two feet wide (Hopkins 1984, figs. 1 and 2). This made the beds look like trapezoids from above, even though each was actually a rectangle. The effect, however, was to create converging lines of sight on the focal point by narrowing the outer edges of the central axis of the garden. Although the shrubs and other plants now in the beds no longer make a major contribution to creating a narrowing visual funnel down the garden, a little shaping with clipped shrubs could fix that and originally would have supplied the precision necessary to create the vista for the garden.

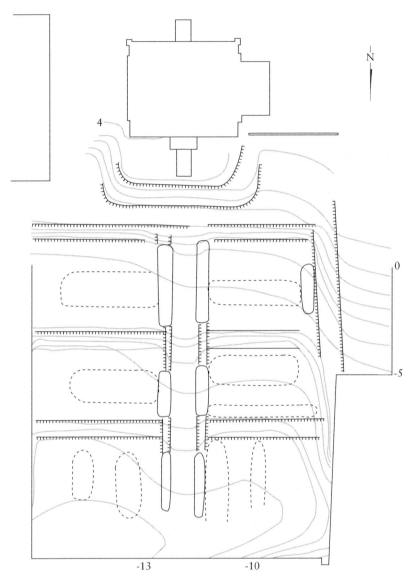

FIGURE 20. Map of the Ridout Garden showing its terraces, falls, and beds.

After my team had mapped the Ridout Garden and begun to absorb the rules of perspective, as well as Barbara Paca's work on the net of squares, we also began to comprehend our own earlier map of the Carroll Garden. This took a while, and we finally linked our map to an aerial photograph of Annapolis that included the Carroll garden in a very clear exposure.

Unlike the Paca and Ridout gardens, the Carroll Garden appeared enormous and had 400 feet of shoreline on a wide creek that enters the Severn River, which flows into the Chesapeake Bay. It had an extensive water view, while the others had a limited view at best. In the Carroll Garden, we discovered that the terraces broadened as they descended, which was the opposite of what they did in the Paca and Ridout gardens. Then we discovered that the sides of the one remaining intact ramp in the Carroll Garden broadened a few inches as it reached the water. The back edges of the central beds in the Ridout Garden did not narrow a lot, but they did indeed narrow. We would never have noticed these variations, although we certainly included them on the topographic map, if we had not been attempting to understand how space was to be managed to create vistas using the rules of perspective. By the mid 1980s, we were thus creating a comparative base using topographic maps to see whether depth in falling gardens had been systematically built to create optical illusions of distance.

The key to my understanding of baroque landscapes in Annapolis was to understand them in general. At the very least, that meant challenging the unique status accorded to the Paca Garden. But at an even more general level, it meant equating the design of the 1760s gardens with the 1690s design for the new capital city. But there had to be a tie to London and Rome too, because London was where the colonial administrators learned their lessons in urban design, and Rome is where baroque theories of power and urban and landscape design originated (Bacon 1968). So there was a large body of material to play with, especially because the Annapolis designers were both well educated and experienced.

Annapolis leaders were not provincial, and what they did was not usually a direct copy of what was available in the design books or what was to be seen when visiting Europe. There were significant differences. Often, in modern Annapolis, these differences have been attributed to being out of touch with, or stylistically behind, the mainstream, but I disagree.

To substantiate this disagreement, my first task as a scientist was to find a foil. I did so by opposing primary sources to each other. The sources were archaeology, period literature, aerial photography, other photo-

graphs, and living opinion. I emphasized the differences among all these
and did not dismiss any source as unworthy. The point was not to use
one to corroborate the other; differences and variation were hidden that
way. The point was to highlight discrepancies and then to explain them.
A bigger and more accurate picture was built up that way (Binford 1982,
1983a, 1983b, 1987).

I assumed that eighteenth-century garden books and the archaeology
of gardens were epistemologically distinct. They had been created by different people for different purposes, and any differences between them
needed to be noted carefully. My analysis has been built on creating systems of differences and then, to contrast the differences, highlighting
them. Normally, historical archaeology proceeds by finding something,
searching the literature for an identification, and then saying that there
was a match and thus certain knowledge.

This common approach in historical archaeology had two enormous
weaknesses. It marginalized virtually all differences between things excavated and the written sources used to identify them. There was either
a match or there was a weak analogy. Second, by epistemologically priv-
ileging any written source, the value of virtually anything found archaeologically inevitably became less significant. Digging was treated, even
by archaeologists, as an expensive way of knowing, and often as an inferior one at that.

My assumption was both simple and complex. Anything written had
an author with an audience in mind and a fairly narrow purpose. The
things that were excavated had been made, used, and discarded by different people, under varied circumstances, for a variety of purposes. So
I attempted to take the ensemble of our excavated findings and the ensemble of written sources and contrast them with each other drawing
from Binford's elaboration of middle range theory.

I contrasted what was thought of as a flat, excavated place that had
originally been laid out as a garden, by a future patriot using his own
taste, that was accompanied by an interpretation that never mentioned
wealth and slaves, and I doubted these aspects of the garden's description. To build the contrast, I took my own failure to estimate the length
of the garden as a problem. I added other, equally old gardens, and the
assumption that slaves and wealth must have been tied to garden design
through politics. I built two separate grids of real data, the results of archaeology and details from the period garden books, to explore my doubts
about the garden and contrasted them with each other.

The first of the independent grids was archaeology. This included the archaeology of the Paca Garden and the two typographic maps of the Ridout and Carroll gardens. The second grid came from the period garden books used in Annapolis. Because these were dictionaries of directions with very clear language about how to build and cultivate gardens, and an explanation of what a garden was meant to accomplish, it was easy to see how interrelated all the parts of a garden were to be.

The archaeological grid contained data on three dimensions, water control, placement of buildings, chronology, and some plant remains. The dictionary grid described lines of sight, parterres, historical themes enacted by plant choice and distribution, geometrical shapes, the frames of mind to be evoked by gardening, how to observe and reproduce the laws of nature as Isaac Newton did, and what a visitor was to see as he or she went through the garden.

This second grid of data showed that the garden was for the purpose of reproducing the laws of optics, hydrology, horticulture, the physics of heat and light, and the evocation of classical mythology. These were explicit. Gardens were places to give and learn lessons. They were places for watching nature and modeling one's actions on it.

The setting of the house was specified in a landscape, the very necessity for a landscape was specified, as were the views, plants, groves, pots, a greenhouse, walks, shapes, and everything else. It was an object for use in horticulture, animal husbandry, social standing, and the owner's personal intellectual and psychic life. All this was from the grid of data derived from the garden books.

When the archaeological grid and the grid from contemporary sources were juxtaposed, there were substantial discrepancies. The archaeology produced no reasons for uneven dimensions in the gardens; the garden books could not explain why all the gardens in Annapolis were built at once. To comment on these discrepancies, I chose to focus on the deliberate building of vistas using the rules of perspective to create the illusion of distance.

While walking people through the garden, the owner was to be like Isaac Newton, observing and recording the laws of nature and explaining them. But because the owner had actually created an environment using these laws, there was an element of reproducing nature that used Newton as a model. All these actions were to impress a visitor, but never exempted the builder from being the most impressed of all.

Running parallel to all this reading was an older idea from art history that I had read and had contrasted with James Deetz's use of the idea of the Renaissance in his book about Puritan New England. I was never happy with the idea that Deetz's Georgian mindset in the New England of the 1680s was the same as that of the Italian Renaissance in 1450. Some of the shapes and proportions, yes, but not the decoration. It was baroque to me. Despite the eternally close link between Renaissance and Reformation, the style and, more important, the politics were baroque. Baroque was not merely a style. Baroque style is the result of a theory of power (Bacon 1968; Braudel 1979), and I wondered whether it was practiced in the politics and thus the landscapes of Annapolis.

Baroque acts of show, often quite expensive, were used to demonstrate power and position when these were desired rather than achieved (Braudel 1979, 488–93). That was the basis for the deliberate, conscious use of illusion. Enormous sea battles mounted in public squares flooded for the occasion, theater performances, banquets, and house and palace façades were designed as extraordinary—and even unnatural—feats, where nature was supposed to be so well understood that it was brought under control and exhibited to show off the majestic abilities of the owner and patron.

The show was designed to impress and was used at the ebb of power, not when power was achieved. It was not the result of wealth, even though show was obviously expensive. Wealth was supposed to be the result of power achieved through show. Baroque style embodied a theory of power when there was not enough of it. So, put another way, show based on illusions, themselves thought to be based on natural or divine law, was a substitute for force and money. To work, it had to be all-encompassing.

If one grid on gardens had ideas and practices about baroque performance, then the other grid, when compared, had the terraces, plane geometry, and a famous quest for power within it. Suddenly, for me, these gardens were never supposed to be flat maps, equal spaces, places for lovely flowers, or products of leisure, taste, or money. They were not exhibits; they were quests. They looked stable but were quite unstable, just as baroque decoration was.

To me, the problem arose from the dates when the gardens were built and the careers of the families who built them. Once I began to understand that the Paca Garden, the Ridout and Carroll gardens, and the garden dictionaries used to build them had been used to create optical illusions, I realized that illusion might be a metaphor for all later eighteenth-century Annapolis, not just a study for the principles of optics. But why an illusion of any kind, metaphorical or optical?

The explanation came in the clustering of the dates when the gardens were built. Paca built his in 1763, Ridout in the same or next year, and

Charles Carroll of Carrollton began his in 1771 and continued building it into the 1770s. The earliest falling garden I could find in Maryland was built in the 1750s; Paca built his second and last garden on Wye Island in 1792 (Leone, Harmon, Neuwirth 2005). The end of such gardens was during the Federal Era (Sarudy 1989, 125), but in Annapolis, they ended with the start of the Revolution. These were the general dates for Maryland: 1750–1820, or a period of political instability and rapid change.

The garden books used to design and tend the landscapes of Annapolis date from the 1720s. There is some sense that they were used to build environments that were stylistically outmoded by the time of their construction. Certainly wilderness landscapes of the kind associated with Capability Brown were popular in England when Annapolis was preferring forms familiar since the seventeenth century and even earlier. Not only was there a discrepancy between the dates of the direction books used for garden building, but there was also a discrepancy in the styles used in Annapolis and those preferred in England at the same time. Annapolis was laying out English 1720s gardens in the 1760s and 1770s.

It never made sense to me to explain the lag in style between up-to-date London and the provincial American colonies in terms of distance. There was constant, frequent traffic, and people like Paca and Carroll were actually educated in England and France. Why should there be a lag in style if there was no lag in communication?

If style was part of the illusion, and illusion is a part of reality, then style was not superficial. I mounted the argument that when it was built, the garden was a rationale for power desired, not held. I argued that a garden builder in the 1760s in Annapolis, or anywhere else in the American colonies, was demonstrating a conscious command of natural law that saw hierarchy in nature and society as natural. Those who could demonstrate such knowledge and act on it should also lead. They were using baroque theory because it solved a particular problem and was so widely known.

Because Paca was mounting an argument about natural law (Miller 1731–39, "Garden") and his place in the hierarchy that was not true but rather was illusory, the garden too was an untrue claim. It was a wish. It was to produce an ostentatious display built to convince viewers with vistas of power that did not yet exist. This is what Louis XIV had done at Versailles 130 years earlier (Mukerji 1997), and what the popes did when they began a new, and eventually baroque, St. Peter's in the 1450s and redesigned Rome.

The final element of the grid about planned landscapes is politics. The juxtapositioning of gardening manuals and the archaeology caused me to open up Paca's heroic status as a signer of the Declaration of Independence. What was his patriotism based on? My turn on the facts focused on his not being very wealthy initially, although his wife was, and on their owning slaves, at least 100 by his death late in the eighteenth century. Paca, Carroll, and other more famous revolutionaries from Virginia were increasingly losing authority over the politics of their own lives, property, and wealth. As the colonies got richer, more populous, more independent economically of Britain, and more self-confident, Britain imposed more taxes and laws, sterner courts, and less military protection, with, as we all know, no political representation. The richer Paca, Carroll, and the others got, the less power they saw they had. We know what they eventually did.

I argued that these families used a different strategy first, and that it failed. The strategy was derived from using show, flamboyance, or ostentation to show people how impressive they were. It was rule through ostentation. A baroque theory of power was at its core a wish for power (Braudel 1979, 489–91), not an adjunct to power already held and exercised. Sometimes it worked, as with Louis XIV and, earlier, with the papacy's building programs. The financial basis of show was, however, the economic engine that can be created by both public works projects and the public indebtedness needed to get the projects going.

Because the kind of show used by the American provincial elite did not create the level of power they wanted to achieve, the strategy did not work very well here. It did not matter whether slaves, free African Americans, or poor white people believed in the ideas on display, but it did matter whether middle- and upper-class people were impressed. I think these garden schemes clustered at a time of needed power, which was the 1760s to the 1790s in Chesapeake politics, or the wider period from the 1750s and to the 1820s, when authority was still weak. The case is clearer for the coincidence between baroque gardens and their proposed hierarchy and weak authority in the 1760s to the 1790s. This is why the falling gardens were not built gradually, but in spurts.

If my explanation of the planned landscapes makes sense, it highlights the use of contrasting descriptive grids of these landscapes to generate questions. It also highlights one essential procedure. No source of information can be declared privileged or be made to seem inferior. Traditional opinion has to have a respected place, respected in the sense of being worth exploration. And then ask why the different sources of information do not fit together. They obviously never will fit perfectly, and where they do not, the reasons for discrepancies must be asked about aggressively. How can gardens be described as flat when they fall? Why call them maps when they were meant to surprise? Why call them unique when there were hundreds of them, perhaps even a thousand? Why focus on patriotism as post hoc social achievement when it was an act of long-thought-out and reluctantly felt frustration?

The builder and observer, or teacher and instructed, in the landscapes, including the one on whom the laws of optics were supposed to work, was the individual; it was he who was to place himself in the hierarchy of knowledge and ownership. Because the Renaissance rules of perspective operating here were all based on portraying reality as one could observe it, including the differences between one person and another, a garden was meant to impart ownership of knowledge to individuals who would see such knowledge as a possession. For such landscapes to be effective, each viewer had to see him- or herself as having the freedom to learn new knowledge and to act on it.

THE CITY PLAN

If this method of discovery works, and if it produces a plausible explanation for Annapolis landscapes, then does it work at any other time? The other time is the late seventeenth-century Annapolis town plan itself. We have excavated extensively in the city's heart, Public or State Circle, and thus understand much of the city's design of 1695. I would like to balance our work on the circle against the main argument of this chapter by comparing the idea that uses flat space understood by way of maps to the idea that manuals of landscape architecture and the results of archaeology describe depth to create illusions, all acting on the eyes of individuals through the laws of perspective.

State Circle is the center of Annapolis and was laid out by Francis Nicholson, the second royal governor, to hold the State House on the highest rise in the city. Nicholson moved Maryland's capital seat from Catholic St. Mary's City, founded by the proprietary Calvert family in 1634 and dominated by them. The Calverts were the Lords Baltimore. After the installation of William and Mary in England, the numerically greater Protestant population of Maryland supported the new monarchs, ousted the Calverts, and made the Church of England the established church in Maryland.

The initially weak royal government sought friendlier areas and transformed Arundelton, established in 1669, into Annapolis in 1695 (Brugger 1988, 3–83). Nicholson, a seasoned British administrator, redesigned the city using baroque principles that were well understood and had already been used in the 1660s at St. Mary's City itself. The main element of baroque landscapes was the use of vistas with objects of state power at the center of a view. When I began work in Annapolis in 1981, the city plan was called baroque, and it was recognized that the two circles in the city were deliberately designed to hold the State House and state church. A series of streets and alleyways led directly into them, so that the main buildings held a prominent position.

I inherited four ideas about Nicholson's plan that I have worked with, just as was the case with Paca's garden. Out of these, I built a problem and contrasted it to published principles of planned landscapes from the seventeenth and eighteenth centuries as I had for the falling gardens. I also contrasted traditional historical ideas to archaeology. In the case of State Circle, we had the chance to conduct an extensive excavation that we could use to develop an explanation of the city plan.

State Circle, and, indeed, all of Nicholson's plan for Annapolis, is usually understood and explained through a 1718 rendition of the original plan. This plan is called the Stoddert map and is the oldest surviving rendition of what Nicholson created. It shows a large circle, a smaller circle, and streets radiating from both in all directions, including to views of the Chesapeake Bay. The Stoddert survey is a record of what was on the ground; it was not imaginary. Virtually all attempts to understand central Annapolis take this map as a starting point.

John Reps (1965, 1972) who is one of this country's premier urban historians, sees Nicholson's plan through the Stoddert rendition. Because the streets radiating out from State Circle leave it at odd and irregular angles, and not at regular intervals, Reps concluded that Nicholson did not fully understand baroque urban planning and that his plan was inept (Reps 1965, 108; 1972, 123–24, 127).

When you look at State Circle itself today, it appears circular enough. You cannot see the whole thing, because it is like a necklace around a neck. It appears to rise and in some places to droop, because it encompasses an undulating slope. You cannot see it all at once, but you can see that it is not level. There is, in fact, no place to stand on the ground to tell whether or not it is circular. But it looks circular. Furthermore, because it is not a true circle today, one assumes it must have taken on its current shape over time when people failed to realize that it was supposed to be a circle. Was it therefore altered over time from the circle it was called in 1718 to the shape one could see now if one stood above it? If we add what Reps thought about Nicholson's inexact use of baroque ideas to the notion that the circle might have been altered over time, the result is a provincial effort at design, the exactness of whose execution wandered over time. We do not have anything precise, in other words.

This was the set of interpretations I found beginning in 1981, which anyone visiting the city could have picked up as well, but there was an angle that was interesting because of what it did not lead to. The Historic Annapolis Foundation had been explicitly and publicly committed to opening the views, which it called vistas, to and from the State House, especially to the water (Kearns 1977a, 1977b). Its leaders, St. Clair Wright and Pringle Symonds, urged removal of commercial signs mounted perpendicularly on buildings, telephone poles, overhead wires, and buildings at the ends of vistas that closed off views. Eventually, these visual eyesores or impediments were virtually all removed, and, as one can tell from photographs, the change that this clearance created was remarkable. Instead of commercial strips, streets once again became the visual funnels to public monuments that they had been designed to be. There was, therefore, an understanding that baroque planning included clear views to public seats of power but not the use of perspective to create illustions.

I inherited the void between the late seventeenth-century street plan and the late eighteenth-century gardens. The street plan was an imposition by the British colonial administration. Preservationists thought it was a marvelous survival. But no one connected it to the gardens.

My team was awarded the contract to dig the Circle before the road around it was rebuilt. The public works project for State Circle was to replace the roadbed and surface, which had deteriorated. The project was to replace all the underground water, sewage, and gas lines, and to place the telephone and electric lines underground for the first time. Before this work was done, we were to excavate.

We obtained a 1990 existing conditions map that accurately described the location of everything on the surface, including the inner and outer curbs of the road, the sidewalks, and the low wall around the park in which the State House sits. We picked twenty-two spots to excavate and placed units that were either 5 feet by 5 feet or 2½ feet by 5 feet. We dug all of these stratigraphically, and all of our archaeological data were derived from them (Read et al. 1990).

We picked our pits to recover the stratigraphy of the Circle. We wanted to know how old the Circle was, whether any buildings around it predated it, and how and when its edges had shifted. If it had been altered,

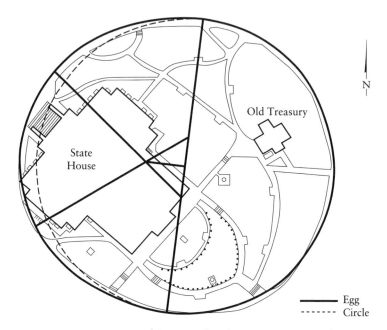

FIGURE 21. 1990 map of State Circle. This is a survey map drawn
in 1990 of the outline and buildings on State Circle. An egg shape and
its triangles and a circle are superimposed.

when and how had this been done? These were our main questions as
archaeologists.

Before we began, we had three independent pieces of evidence that the
Circle's perimeter had not always been what it was in 1990. Two of these
were from our own earlier archaeological excavations at sites on the Circle's periphery. During the 1980s, we had excavated the front yard of the
State House Inn, a building of Victorian appearance but that had been there
since the eighteenth century (Shackel 1988). We found three eighteenth-
century soil stains from fence palings in a curved row three feet in from
the sidewalk around the Circle, or about ten feet closer to the building
than the modern curb. The location of the fence showed that at least on
this side, the Circle had been much wider in the eighteenth century.

On the opposite side of the Circle, at the Calvert House site, we excavated the front yard and found a public well fifteen feet in from the
modern curb, as well as the end of an oyster shell–covered walk well inside the modern yard (Yentsch 1993, 97–128). Both indicated that in the
eighteenth century, the perimeter of the Circle had been greater in this
direction than it was now.

We also chose to dig near the intersection of the Circle and Francis Street, where there is a house placed at an odd angle to the Circle. It faces neither the Circle nor Francis Street, but is askew, yielding the standard interpretation that it was there before the Nicholson plan was implemented.

These three historical items provided some basis for exploring origins, changes, and dates for events in the alteration of the Circle. Beyond these, we picked places where we could tie the archaeology to known historic buildings so that we had reference points we could play off.

The archaeology took about three months; the analysis and report about another six (Read et al. 1990). We made a set of simple discoveries. The stratigraphy of the Circle was intact for a continuous two-thirds to three-quarters of its entire perimeter. About a third had been lost, probably in the first half of the twentieth century when a big addition to the State House was placed on its west side. We found many points on the Circle's outer perimeter that could be dated stratigraphically. These included posts, a public well, public paths, edges of fences, and edges of pavements. Because these locales were beyond the perimeter of the present Circle, we concluded that there was a difference between an earlier perimeter and the present one. However, when we plotted the dated points from previous perimeters on the current master map, we realized two things. There never was a true circle, because no compass could link what we found. And the Circle's perimeter had changed frequently. We could date the changes at least broadly.

These discoveries showed the absence of a true circle around State Circle and constant tinkering with the shape, but they did not contribute to our understanding of either the circle's plane or its solid geometry. Then came an intuitive link. One day, I asked Jennifer Stabler, who was working on a modern map of the Circle that also had our archaeologically dated spots on it (Leone, Stabler, and Burlaga 1998), if the Circle looked like an egg. Was State Circle an egg shape? I got the idea about the shape and of how to draw one from Alexander Thom's analysis of henge monuments in Northwestern Europe. In his old movie *Cracking the Stone Age Code,* Thom showed how to draw an egg shape by using four circles drawn from four centers that were formed from two triangles back to back. It is a simple idea and Jennifer Stabler went and viewed the film, got Thom's book (1978) out of the university library, and started to draw eggs by hand on our master map. In a short while, she showed that the modern 1990 Circle was not just an egg shape, but a perfect one, one so perfect that it used two adjacent 3–4–5 right triangles as its center, thus

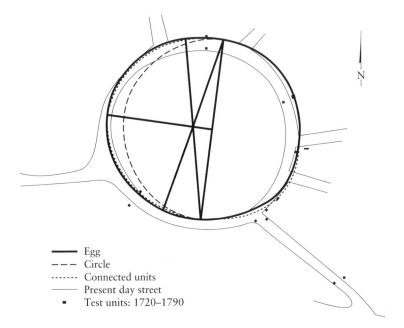

FIGURE 22. Archaeological units dating 1720–1780 around State Circle. The units are connected with arcs calculated to link as many of the dated points as possible, and a perfect egg shape and circle are superimposed.

guaranteeing that the short leg of the triangle divided evenly into the perimeter of the Circle, leaving no fragment.

It was very hard to do a similar analysis of the archaeological spots by hand. We were not at all sure we could find out whether the circle had been egg-shaped in the past just because it was now. Nonetheless, that was the direction in which our discovery led.

A couple of years later, an undergraduate major in our department, Amy Burlaga, used Geographic Information Systems (GIS), a technology introduced to us by John Seidel, to solve the problem of how old the egg shape was. Burlaga learned GIS and began to digitize the early maps of State Circle. Here is what she did and what she found.

Because GIS operates so that points on a map can be added or removed at will, it allows a very large number of points to be entered all at once without creating visual clutter. A GIS program draws lines and arcs on command as vectors, and it will try to use true circles and other geometric shapes as directed. It will also compare the differences between shapes.

Our archaeologically dated locales on the perimeter of State Circle

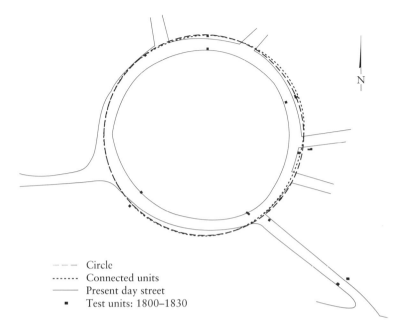

--- Circle
······· Connected units
——— Present day street
▪ Test units: 1800–1830

FIGURE 23. Archaeological units dating from c. 1800 around State
Circle. This shows archaeological test units dating from 1800–1830 and
the edges of State Circle. The units are connected with arcs calculated to
link as many of the dated points as possible and a circle is superimposed.
An egg shape did not fit this figure.

fell into chronological clumps. We lumped together all the eighteenth-
century dates, then all the early nineteenth-century dates, and then all
those from the late nineteenth century. I admit that lumping all the dates
from the eighteenth century together is crude, but was necessary to provide adequate material. The earliest date was about 1720; the latest was
about 1780. All the dated points were digitized, and then arcs were drawn
through the chronologically clumped locales. The program imposed a
true circle, an ellipse, and an egg shape on the same three sets of points.

Burlaga found that the points most closely approximated an egg shape
in the eighteenth century (Leone, Stabler, and Burlaga 1998). Around
1800 and in the early nineteenth century, the points most nearly approximated a circle. And from 1880 to today, the Circle was egg-shaped. If
an egg can be described as having a peak at one end and a butt end at
the other, then the Circle pointed south in the eighteenth century and
north from the 1880s on. The Circle was also almost 100 feet greater in
diameter today than in the eighteenth century.

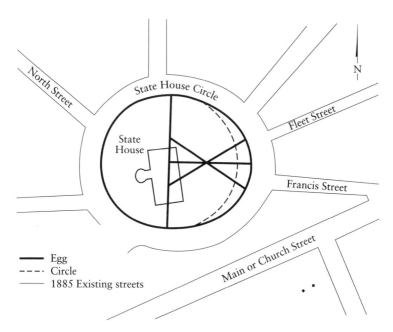

FIGURE 24. 1885 map of State Circle. This figure is taken from the 1885 Sanborn Fire Insurance map. An egg shape and circle are superimposed.

Then Burlaga turned to historical maps of the Circle, a process begun earlier by Stabler. Burlaga found a map of the interior of State Circle that showed that the 1880s rebuilding of the terraces leading up to the State House had been designed so that the highest was shaped as a perfect egg, with the peak beginning right below the State House dome and the butt end extending onto the lawn overlooking the city.

Our final move was to digitize a good reproduction of the Circle as drawn on the Stoddert map of 1718. If the Circle had actually been an egg shape in the eighteenth century, as the archaeology showed was possible, then the map could provide the evidence to prove it. Everybody had always believed that because the center of the map of the city is labeled a circle, it was one. But when you look at the map and ask whether it is a circle, you discover that the picture is not so clear. When the GIS program was used to overlay circles and egg shapes on them, it turned out that both Public and Church Circles had been egg-shaped in 1718. The GIS program automatically draws a perfect circle, multiple ellipses, and various eggs over any space. It tries for goodness of fit. The difference is visible, of course, but the spaces between a true

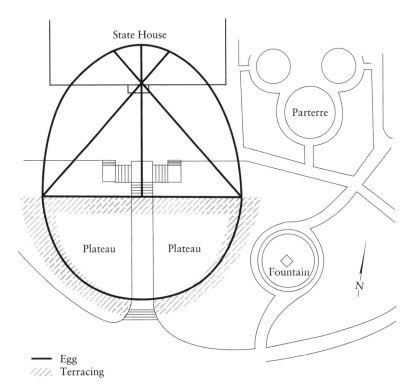

FIGURE 25. 1882 map of the front of the Maryland State House with its immediate landscaping. This is a fragment of Gray's 1882 plan for the redesign of State Circle. It shows the plateau in front of the Maryland State House. An egg shape is superimposed.

circle and what was on the Stoddert plan can also be quantified, as seen in table 5.

The GIS program experiments with arcs until the best fit is achieved and the fit is measured. The process of fitting is achieved quickly with the program, far faster than would ever have been possible by hand. And the conclusion that Public Circle was originally designed and laid out as an egg shape is conclusive, as a result.

Why should an egg shape be used in urban design? There are two answers, one given in terms of plane geometry, the other in terms of solid geometry. These come from the period books on large planned landscapes. If one is presented with the need to join a series of irregularly spaced spots or locales into a harmonious design, it was possible to do so using an egg shape. If constructed using plane geometry, which is probably how

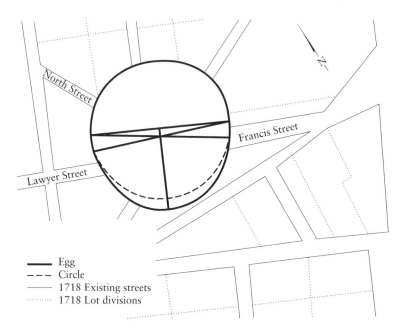

FIGURE 26. The 1718 Stoddert plan with a geometric egg shape. This is
a plot of the 1718 Stoddert map. An egg shape and circle are superimposed.
The street called State Circle almost entirely coincides with the egg and
is thus not visible here.

one would have been mapped in the seventeenth or eighteenth centuries,
an egg shape is four joined arcs. It is also actually one continuous arc,
which can be described using calculus, and the formula for that was also
available at the time. However, it was simpler to use the much earlier
but more primitive method.

Therefore, because Francis Nicholson founded and imposed the new
capital city on a preexisting town, with property and houses already scattered about the spaces he intended to make into a new city, he not only
had to deal with these, but also to incorporate some of them into his
plan. He bought some properties and had to incorporate others near his
new circles (Lindauer 1997, 12–18). One way to create a harmonious
space out of what was already there was to draw an egg. This could be
done an infinite number of times by adjusting the lengths of the legs of
the two triangles used to make the centers of circles, and then their intersecting arcs. Whenever a leg of a triangle is lengthened or shortened, the
center of the circle moves accordingly and so does its arc. But the arc
will still intersect with the other three arcs composing the egg shape. When

TABLE 5. Percentage relative
error for the fit of an egg and a circle

	Circle	Egg
Figure 21: topographic map, 1990	1.8	0.6
Figure 22: test units, c. 1700	1.6	0.5
Figure 23: test units, c. 1800	0.5	no fit
Figure 24: Sanborn map, 1885	2.0	0.4
Figure 26: Stoddert plan, 1743	1.0	0.6

NOTE: The data in this table show that in the eighteenth, late nineteenth, and twentieth centuries, State Circle was shaped like an egg, and that between about 1800, ending by 1885, it was shaped more like a circle. The data were calculated by Leonard F. Burlaga (used here with permission), father of Anna-Marie Burlaga, the University of Maryland undergraduate who made the original AutoCAD maps of State Circle (Burlaga 1995, 35), from which I cite their work.

The original formula for this table can be found in Burlaga 1995 and is summarized by L. F. Burlaga as follows: "A measurement point along the true periphery of State Circle (taken from the maps) was recorded every ten degrees. The distance between the point and the model egg/circle was computed and entered into a formula to determine the relative error of each. The distance is a positive number measured along a line perpendicular to the egg/circle that passes through the data point" (Leone, Stabler, and Burlaga 1998, 306 n.13)

done on paper, the disparate points can be toyed with until the largest possible number of them can be incorporated into the perimeter of the new design. Thus, an egg shape is flexible when used in urban design.

The second answer to why use an egg shape is the appearance. The period books on planned landscapes make the point that, when viewed on the ground, a true circle appears to be a lozenge, not a circle at all. To fix this appearance, an ellipse, oval, or occasionally, an egg shape may be drawn that will, when built, provide the appearance of a circle. Given the shape of the Annapolis hilltop that holds the Maryland State House, which is actually more like a geological bench, State Circle acts like a necklace around a neck. It appears to be harmonious, in that it looks circular; it slopes without angles or obvious changes in its arc, and it disappears from view behind rises like the State House and trees, so that its actual shape cannot be viewed from any one spot on the ground. This is just the way the bottom of the falls is arranged in descent gardens designed to provide no visual clue to actual distance. The disappearance of the curve of the Circle created the illusion that its arc was continuous. Actually, the curve of the arc shifts regularly. Nonetheless, the appearance of harmonious continuity was created and maintained.

The appearance of harmony was and remains created through the illusion of building one thing in space and calling it another, like building an egg and calling it a circle, and building a small landscape and making it look big. However, the locale of the State House within the Circle is not the only view to be considered. The Circle is approached by roads and an alley that entered from eight points and led into the Circle, all with straight, unobstructed views of the State House itself.

Once we started analyzing the Circle as an egg shape whose reason for being was to create the illusion of harmony, we realized that we were likely to have access to the same baroque ideas for creating illusions that were to work seventy years later in the Paca, Ridout, and Carroll gardens and other great planned landscapes in the city. Therefore, we asked whether any of the eight entries into the Circle was created using lines of sight. Did any have converging or diverging sides? Jennifer Stabler measured the widths on maps of all eight entry streets, Francis, Cornhill, East, Maryland Avenue, Northeast, and School Streets and Lawyer's Alley (Read et al. 1990, v, 32, 213–15). She found that if a street was short and had a close-up view of the State House, the lines of the street converged as they approached the State House. When the view was long, the sides of the street diverged as the sides approached the State House. Maryland Avenue had parallel sides, as did all the other streets of the old city, except for those entering Church Circle, which also had lines that converged or diverged, depending on length. This was about as conclusive a set of corroborating evidence as one could wish for in order to demonstrate that the circles had been constructed like the hub and spokes of a wheel, or the rays of a baroque sunburst. They created illusions about the positions of power. This was the connection between the city plan of 1695 and the gardens of the 1760s to the 1770s. They were intended to establish power through built illusions of control over its source in a hierarchically organized natural world. They were not markers of power achieved.

Stabler found the converging and diverging street sides that we attribute to Nicholson. Burlaga extended these same lines into State Circle on the Stoddert plan and found that, just as Reps had seen (1965, 108; 1972, 123–24, 127), they converged at a place well off the Circle's center, making it look as though Nicholson had missed the point somehow. But the Stoddard plan does not show the location of the State House, even though the first one had been built by the time the Stoddert plan was drawn in 1718. The top of the hill is on one side of the Circle's interior, and the State House sits there, not in the Circle's true geometric center, used by Reps. All the sightlines of Nicholson's roads converge on this off-center hilltop and exactly on the State House itself. All views lead

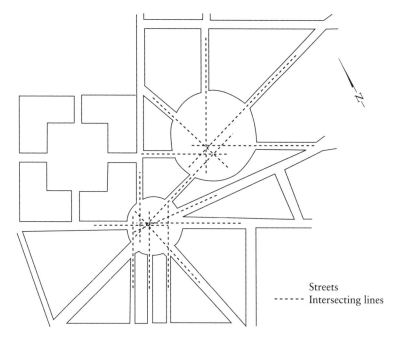

Streets
------ Intersecting lines

FIGURE 27. Lines of sight into State and Church Circles. John Reps's (1972) rendition of the Stoddert plan of 1718 (digitized), with Reps's center lines of the streets intersecting on State and Church Circles. State Circle is the larger of the two. The State House is the locus of the intersection.

directly up to the State House, from all over the town. Nothing inept about that.

Come forward now, about a hundred years to 1789 and the newly independent United States, struggling with a failed confederation and with a new federal Constitution. Annapolis had briefly been the new federal capital city. And its leaders would have liked it to have had the role permanently. During the 1780s, a new dome was built on top of the State House, the one we see there today. When the new top was built, no other part of the exterior of the building was changed that I know of. Our archaeology has shown that the surface of the Circle was also flattened, given a curb, possibly extended to the east, and its surrounding slopes smoothed. Nothing was done that would suggest that lines of sight or the egg shape were altered. This suggested that the illusions of size and distance as one approached were still important to the design. The concept that the individual was to do the viewing was still behind the design.

By the alteration of 1789, the monarch was gone, the individual was a citizen with representatives he elected, and the new government was as weak as Nicholson's had been in 1695, and as Paca's and Carroll's statutes had been in the 1760s and early 1770s. Now they were in power, but they could not exercise much. I believe the new top on the Maryland State House reflected this and was meant as an experiment to deal with it.

Here is how I think the new top was to work as an exercise in the solid geometry of vision (Leone and Hurry 1998). My description is balanced against Jeremy Bentham's (1962) idea for a new correctional system that used the reform of conscience as a way to change people. The new top of the Maryland State House is called a dome, and from within, it does look like one; structurally, it is one too, because the inner shell, made of wood and covered with decorated plaster, is suspended from the outer shell, the way almost all domes were made from the Renaissance on.

But the top does not look like a dome; it looks like a cross between a small dome and a pagoda-like, Chinese Chippendale tower. It does not look bad, but it has few, if any direct precedents. It never became the model for anything else, and I think it can usefully be seen as an experiment. It has four vertical ranks of stacked, ranked windows on all eight sides. Therefore, it looks as though you can see anywhere in town or to the horizon from almost any height. There is a walk all around the topmost element.

This description led me to Jeremy Bentham's panopticon, or inspection station (Foucault 1979, 200–228). Bentham intended his panopticon as a prison, but particularly in the American Federal Era, the design was used for schools, hospitals, libraries, churches, and even houses, as well as prisons (Van Horne 1986; Van Horne and Formwalt 1984). A panopticon is a round or octagonal building with rooms around its outer edges and a thin outer wall pierced by windows that light all the rooms, with each cell holding only one person. Under a dome-like roof in the center was a raised platform with a station for a guard, teacher, doctor, master, or anybody with authority or a lesson to teach. The station was enclosed, so that the watcher could not always be seen. Every peripheral backlit room had a transparent opening to the center so that the inspector could easily see the watched. Constant visibility was called inspection, and Bentham's idea was that those watched would learn to internalize the new, proper rules for good behavior rather than be subject to constant reminders from the watcher to reform. That's how the panopticon was supposed to work, and it required that the watched see themselves as individuals with possessions, including a conscience.

The concept was widely translated into many social forms in the new United States. I cannot demonstrate that Bentham's design was fitted to the new top of the Maryland State House, although I have shown that Bentham had considerable influence on Benjamin Latrobe and his colleagues when they designed and built most of the important public buildings in Baltimore in the early nineteenth century, which were often sponsored by the very same men and families who lived with the construction of the new State House dome in Annapolis (Leone and Hurry 1998).

The perception that a panopticon design was used in Annapolis, and just a short time later on many public buildings in Baltimore, comes from my reading of Michel Foucault and emphasizes the idea of government based on the notion of individuals as citizens. Foucault calls surveillance, or watching, a discipline, and he itemizes the disciplines, which he calls technologies of the self. They include manners, reading, speaking, and all the patterns associated with Deetz's Georgian mind-set. Foucault identifies these internalized technologies as the sources of power in the brand new forms of government created in the United States and France: republics whose foundation was the citizen (Foucault 1979, 135–69). Because the citizen who votes appeared to be the basis of governmental legitimacy, Foucault asks where force was in the new state. Where was the actual power to keep people in line? Some of it was in the heads of people who believed that it was their task to learn the rules of governance and to enforce these on others, as well as on themselves. Foucault calls this situation mutual inspection and moves Bentham's ideas out of his prison and into the schools, churches, libraries, hospitals, and homes that Americans actually built for panoptic inspection.

Both Bentham and Foucault understood that there need not be an actual inspector in the station; people would quickly imagine one there anyway and adjust their behavior as though they were being watched. This is how Foucault got to self-inspection, an idea that was enhanced when an individual saw that the technologies he or she was learning—like gardening, reading, or writing—were acquired possessions like property, could be bought, and increased one's social worth.

There is no question that late eighteenth-century Annapolis had such etiquettes, which were advertised and available through the *Maryland Gazette*. I raise this whole possibility now because of the similarity of the newly redesigned Maryland State House dome, set high above Annapolis— briefly the national capital—looking down over the whole city through the many streets radiating out from it, to Bentham's panopticon. Why all the windows, rank upon rank of them? Why did Charles Willson Peale paint the view from the top and bring it down to the ground, so that the houses so visible from the top could also be seen from below (Matthews

2002, 85, fig. 15, and 86, fig. 16; Bellion 2004, 529)? Why the novel shape that looks more like the central inspection platform inside Bentham's panopticon than either a conventional dome or a tower?

If a community was to be created out of people who were newly allied to one another, and some whom had previously been strangers or even potential antagonists, it could be done through imagining that citizens elected those who governed, watched them govern in public, and watched the governors watch them. This mutual watching is caught in the many windows of the new dome. This, then, was my idea that linked citizenship with the dome's form and with Benedict Anderson's (1991) imagined community.

The Annapolis dome is accessible by foot all the way up to the top, and there is a viewing platform all around the top. The plaster inside the internal stairs and ladders is covered with the graffiti of its many visitors, thus showing that people did climb up and look out. We certainly know that Charles Willson Peale did and tried to paint the whole view (Radoff 1972; Bellion 2004). I recite these known facts only to show that people could be seen from below looking out from above. But this is only the most literal reading of the viewing platform in a panopticon. One only has to notice that the flagpole perched on top is and was used daily, and required some minor official to mount the dome every day, in order to establish the actuality of constant inspection.

The sights from the dome and its use for inspection are all visible in a period quotation from an Annapolis resident:

> The dome which Clark designed and built for the State House has been the defining landmark of the Annapolis skyline for 208 years. It was also, for many years, a popular spot from which to observe the city and the Chesapeake Bay beyond. Charles Willson Peale planned a dramatic cyclorama of Annapolis with eight views from the dome and a centerpiece drawing of State Circle from Cornhill Street. Only the drawing of the State House was completed and published in 1789. Thomas Jefferson spent a most enjoyable three hours in September 1790 on the balcony of the dome with James Madison, Thomas Lee Shippen and an Annapolis friend who entertained them with the gossip related to each of the houses they could see from their perch above the town.
>
>   www.mdarchives.state.md.us/msa/stagser/s1259/121
>   /5847/html/story.html (accessed October 20, 2004)

Because we know that Bentham's ideas influenced Latrobe, and that Latrobe and his colleagues created a new Federal style of building best seen in Baltimore, I want to insert here my sense of these new buildings before returning to Annapolis. Latrobe, Robert Mills, and Maximilian Godefroy designed a dozen of the most important new buildings in Baltimore between 1807 and 1820 (Trollope 1997; Beirne 1957). These include the Catholic cathedral, the Episcopal, Baptist, and Unitarian churches, the public library (never built), stock exchange, the operating theater of the new University of Maryland, and the first monument ever built to George Washington. They all contain central-lighted domed rooms; many have semi-circular rows of seats, many windows, and few pillars. They are all like panopticons, but without cells. Everybody inside could be seen by everybody else, and in the center, or at the central point, was the leader, teacher, or model, as in the case of the Washington Monument. I offer the hypothesis that many panoptic buildings were built in Baltimore and one large monument using the first citizen to watch over all.

There is no question that the new Annapolis dome and the many rotundas in public buildings in Baltimore acted to facilitate the qualities that were to be cultivated in citizenship: equal access, equal hearing, equal instruction, and equal visibility. When reversed, each such quality included mutual observation by people as to who was observing the rules. Within all this was the self-discipline required by a citizen in a democracy. These are the buildings in which various disciplines were taught (De Cunzo 1995), and where the results were often assessed in public and extended. Thus, the panopticon utilized the solid geometry of the city's plan with the rules of vision and inspection that constituted one way to create citizens in a new republic.

SUMMARY

I want to summarize where Annapolis causes you to walk and what the walk might cause you to see, depending on who you are or were. My thesis is that from 1695 to after the American Revolution, urban planning throughout the city aimed at impressing each individual with natural order expressed through geometry built as spaces to impress viewers with the builders' command of order. Subjects were made by making individuals see that they were subjected to an authority so impressive that nature could be commanded into harmonious forms built all around. This is when and why the marvelous vistas of Annapolis were made. This is why they were designed and built in the late seventeenth century, when royal authority was weak, and in the 1760s, when local elites were feeling particularly threatened. It is also why Nicholson's plan and the later formal gardens were built using the same rules.

The new republic was also weak. Its base of power was not the monarch on top of the hierarchy in formal terms, but rather the colonial elite, who remained in virtually complete charge until the 1820s. The problem was how to get citizens to govern themselves and to support the state when it was being founded and did not possess much power, and when power was still hierarchically controlled. How could a new republic work when those in charge were much richer than most of the newly enfranchised? The result was the construction of a previously nonexistent community by many minor daily acts that convinced some people they were one by their watching one another. Bentham, Foucault, and Benedict Anderson have been my guides to this hypothesis. Drawing on their ideas, I saw a new set of relationships emerge through the uses of common procedures like seeing and reading. Seeing occurred in landscapes and included watching, while supposing you were in turn being watched by your fellows, some of whom were actually elected to do so. This was mutual inspection.

By the Federal Era, the Constitution said that those within were the same as those without. This was made to happen by the technology of panoptic citizenship, which itself was dependent on the ideology of personal liberty, and liberty was the basis of the franchise for citizens. The newly powerful included the former colonial elite, who had led the Revolution, allied to lower- and middle-class whites with a little property and much to fear from the poorer and the enslaved, who were not included in power, but who were subject to the ideology that rationalized the new source of power, that is, the possibility of eventual citizenship. The newly powerful built a suitable environment to bring about the republic they all imagined together. The panoptic environment is most clearly seen as it was developed in Baltimore. In these two sets of illustrations, Annapolis and Balitmore, there really was no privacy.

It is easy enough to confuse the panopticon's superintendent with governors, legislators, preachers, teachers, fathers, doctors, and with authoritative men and their texts. But that is not the point. Rather, these men and their texts operated in a built environment where they and their newly willing fellow citizens watched and evaluated one another while they all learned the new rules of citizenship in the new nation.

EXEMPTIONS

These ideal planned environments were supposed to create people who saw themselves as individuals and who did not see the many above them in the economic hierarchy as fundamentally different from themselves, but did they? There is some evidence of what gardening in planned landscapes did accomplish. Garden dictionaries and manuals provided ideas and plans, although these were not necessarily followed. Certainly, we know such works were used much later than when they were printed and very far from where they were written and published.

In Annapolis and in Baltimore, there is substantial information on gardening in planned landscapes by the middle class gathered by Barbara Sarudy (1989), who was interested not only in upper-class planned landscapes of the kind I have described so far but also in gardens built and maintained by artisans and people of much less wealth and power. How did these individuals think about individualism and liberty?

The best example from Annapolis of an artisan gardener who built and maintained a whole landscape like those of Paca and Carroll was the silversmith, clockmaker, and tavern keeper William Faris (J. S. Brown 1977; Faris 2003), whose diary tells us about his gardening. Faris leased a city lot fronting on West Street, which was the main land entrance to the city, so people could see his tavern and his garden display (Sarudy 1989, 142). We know something about how many such gardens there were in Annapolis at this time, and we dug a similar one on Main Street (Shackel 1986) that, like Faris's, was bordered by a picket fence and divided into beds, with paths between them. Sarudy records at least sixty-seven gardens in eighteenth-century Baltimore owned by members of the elite, merchants, artisans, and others whose wealth was much more limited. The best impression I can appeal to in order to explain how frequently small, formal gardens were built and maintained is the look of Colonial Williamsburg today, where many houses, no matter how ordinary, had an ordered garden—no lawn, but rectangular beds, often centered on a well or tree, sheds, outhouses, and stables. Williamsburg's array of vernacular gardens is not a fantasy, given what Sarudy found in Baltimore and the picture of order and diligence William Faris paints of his garden and those of others in Annapolis. It is also clear that these gardens were ornamental and for pleasure. Faris grew thousands of tulips and sold the bulbs, and he was not alone in doing so. Almost all gardens were used to grow vegetables for home use. But even though gardens produced food and profit, neither was their primary function. They were pleasure gardens, and although practical, they were modeled on the geometry of those of their wealthier neighbors (Sarudy 1989, 142–43).

This modeling made the gardens an adjunct to eighteenth-century concerns with scientific botany, farming, plant improvement, and husbandry. Faris experimented with grafting and cross-pollination of boxwood, cab bages, and tulips (Sarudy 1989, 143). He not only recorded the weather, but also conditions favorable for plant propagation.

Faris arranged his garden (Faris 2003, 81) with rectangles, circles, straight paths, and vistas, the way the great gardens of Annapolis did, although he did not incorporate the use of falls, because his land was flat. He edged his beds and trimmed them, thus continuing the plane geometry found in much of the rest of the town.

Sarudy notes that Faris delighted in growing and propagating tulips. He grew tulips named for republican and classical heroes named by Alexander Contee Hanson, chancellor of Maryland, and one of Faris's most active gardening partners (Faris 2003, 311). These included "General Washington," "Lady Washington," "Adams," "Hamilton," "Dr. Franklin," "Archimedes," "Cato," "Cicero," and "Cincinnatus" (Sarudy 1989, 142). He chose to press some named for American Revolutionary War generals (Faris 2003, 88).

Given the geometry of Faris's garden, given his daily work in it, his commitment to writing about it, and the sentiment expressed in his names for the tulip specimens he planted and whose names he cited, it is fair to say that his garden was like those of Paca and Carroll insofar as it expressed the belief that nature was lawlike and that those who could live out those laws were the natural leaders of society. For him, this occurred after the Revolution, given the dates of his diary, but his record nonetheless shows that he saw in his gardening what the other gardeners saw in it as well. I would argue that he was inside the ideology of possessive individualism because he regarded himself as an individual and nature as lawlike, duplicated the republican practice of being viewed, treated his elected leaders as models, and saw their shared republican ideas as responsible for his own success.

Faris and many other middle-class gardeners in Annapolis and Baltimore before and after the Revolution worked in public behind fences and gates right off the city's streets and maintained ordered spaces and plants in them. Hence we might conclude that they saw themselves subject to panoptic inspection. Whatever the case, the process served to cover up the steeply hierarchical divisions of wealth and power in the city.

Here is a specimen of Faris's gardening notes:

> 1801 Tuesday 29th a fine morning. Sylve's [his slave] diging the Flower Beds and I have planted 115 Parrot tail Tulips that ware sown in 1798 on the Border next to Snow Ball Bushes . . . next 83 Dutch Tulip off setts from Doctor Scott—a fine day.

Thursday Octr 11th finished planting the four nursseery Beds. the first Bed 170. second 175, the 3 Beded 210 the 4th Bed 207. in the whole 762 Tulips besides Hyacinth, wing'd Hyacinths & John Quills in the evening came on to rain.

Fryday 2th a cloudy morning. Finished planting two of the circel. Beds and How'd the other. A fine day.

Faris 2003, 369

From this we can see that he perceived nature as orderly and understandable and worked within the known elements of it. He likewise worked within the local hierarchy, because Dr. Upton Scott, mentioned in his diary, who built and ran an enormous house and gardens, both flat and falling, belonged to one of the upper levels of society.

Faris showed little emotion about his garden, his present editors say (Faris 2003, 29). But to anyone reading about it, its lived out order is its pleasure. And the living out is not with tulips, but with those who give him them, buy bulbs from him, and otherwise interact with him. He lived within the new democratic but ranked society (Faris 2003, 368n52; 258n69).

In the following heated exchange, Faris shows us how and why panopticism worked.

Finished planting ye parsnips and finished the assparagrass Beds. While at work at the assparagrass Bed two people I took to be girls climed up on the fence (I declare I did not know who thay ware). I desired them to get off the fence. The Biggest reply'd shee would not. She would sett there as long as she pleas, I told her she should get down. She replyd she would not get down for me. I told her she was an impudent slut and get down or I would make her and went to wards whare she was on the fence. As I lifte my hand to put her hand off the fence she said you Impedant scoundrele tuch me if you Dare. I pushed her hand off the fence. She stept down and call'd me an Old Dog Old Dog, I told her she was a strumpit. How dare you to call me so, she reply'd, as you are an Old Dog, . . . I curs'd her & her Husband and I told she was an Impudent Bitch . . . the girl call[ed] me several approbious names.

Faris 2003, 110–11

This is how discipline worked in the new republic. It used fences, eyesight, scolding, name-calling, some force, and a lot of hailing by name and epithet. Of course, this event of March 20, 1792, could have occurred earlier, but its elements show how citizens who owned property and those who felt so empowered that they could take some of its owner's rights, maintained one another's place in a hierarchy, and without force.

Here was panoptic inspection with an inspector, a would-be challenger who reversed the gaze, and the emotional result. So there was plenty of passion and meaning in the geometry and botany of gardening.

There are several sorts of evidence for gardens, gardening, and gardeners in Annapolis beyond William Faris. Paul Popernack (1989), while an undergraduate with us in the Department of Anthropology, surveyed Annapolis deeds, leases, and mortgages from 1694 to 1800, totaling 644 properties, with a few listed more than once. He found that of the properties listed through deeds, between 20–25 percent had gardens. Because not all recorded properties had structures on them when sold or leased, the percentage of properties with gardens is likely to have been much higher. Gardening was thus common but not always recorded. Despite all these data, I cannot argue that all home owners gardened. In fact, based on Popernack's figures, only about one house in three or four had a garden.

Sarudy counted and describes the books available for gardens, and plants and seeds advertised for sale, and lists eighteenth-century Maryland gardeners (Sarudy 1989, 154–55). All her data demonstrate that gardening was a skill that was catered to by frequent publication, a craft that people could learn and be hired to do, and that enslaved people were trained to be skilled at and hired out by their owners to do. She collected information on sixty-seven eighteenth-century Baltimore gardens, showing them to be a mix of flat and terraced gardens, belonging to people who had from no slaves up to 226 slaves. Twenty-five percent of the owners held no slaves. While gardening cost money, it was not necessarily expensive. The gardeners included tailors, druggists, millwrights, storekeepers, clerks, and glaziers, as well as merchants and gentlemen.

The final piece of evidence showing the spread of the ideology of possessive individualism through the world of gardening well beyond and below the elite is the number of people who owned scientific instruments and clocks tied to gardening. These numbers came from Annapolis inventories and included sundials, quadrants, telescopes, thermometers, barometers, globes, and similar devices for measuring temperature, space, and time. By 1710, over a quarter of the poorer population owned some kind of clock and a few of the poorer owned a scientific instrument, thus showing the presence of the tools through which measurements of nature could be achieved by using gradations, hierarchy, and precision, all with the intention of observing order in human society and in plant life. By 1760, among the poorest, about 20 percent owned some instrument for telling time and half of the middling groups did. Virtually all the richest did. Among the upper middling wealth group, as well as among the richest part of the population by 1760, 22 percent and 35 percent respectively owned scientific instruments; the next poorest owned 7 percent. Therefore, by the 1760s almost everyone owned a watch or clock, and many owned a scientific instrument.

My argument here is that using such instruments indicated being absorbed into the ideology of possessive individualism, because people saw themselves as either learning or controlling some external element for their own possession. Part of my argument is also that all these instruments measure hierarchical order, and when people believed that that was what was happening, they reproduced it as well. In other words, these instruments blended the users with the actual circumstances of their lives and helped them to reproduce society intact. Aside from this possibility, the important fact is the penetration of the use of all these techniques of the ideology of possessive individualism so far down the economic hierarchy at such an early date.

Who else was within ideology? We know that slaves built and maintained many of these gardens in Annapolis and Baltimore because of Sarudy's research and because the labor required in some was considerable. If formal gardens realized an ideology of individualism, did that ideology have an impact on the slaves, or on free people of African descent, thus more fully incorporating them into a society homogenized by personal liberty, while separated by ever greater divisions of wealth? If so, the ideology was very effective; if not, then it was less so. The best data I have come not from the eighteenth century but from autobiographies of former slaves collected as part of the Federal Writers' Project in the 1930s that contain descriptions of gardening before 1864 and Emancipation.

Timothy Ruppel, Jessica Neuwirth, Gladys-Marie Fry, and I (2003) have described slaves in their landscapes. The FWP slave autobiographies cover all states where slavery was found, and we selected data from all, which was originally gathered and written up by Ruppel (Ruppel et al. 2003, 330–31). Gardening was common among plantation slaves and provided food for them and their families. Some plots were large, and they were farmed at night, after work, or on Saturdays and Sundays. The master did not provide time. Crops belonged in whole or in part to the slave and could thus sometimes be sold, with the money being kept by the slaves. Some narratives relate that cash from gardening was used to buy food, coffee and sugar, Christmas presents, and, sometimes freedom. Such gardening, along with other kinds of work for wages could provide a way to save enough to pay an owner for freedom, the epitome of possessive individualism in the American context.

Ruppel and Neuwirth have also found that gardens and yards maintained by people of African descent were often thought to be populated by spirits, making them profoundly different from all the gardens described so far that feature Enlightenment rationality. Grey Gundaker (1993) has helped lead the way to recognizing the materials and practices involved. According to the slave autobiographies and Caribbean ethnography (Price 1990; Price and Price 1999), spirits—aiming for or aimed at a house and its occupants—entered through gates, doors, and chimneys. Because the spirits of dead people could be controlled to provide health, protection, and other wishes, they could be brought from streams and woods, where they traveled, into human control through yards by way of their openings. Their entrance to and presence in yards was controlled in many ways, including by sweeping, the activity responsible for the unplanted and ungrassed appearance of some African American yards.

I have been very sketchy about yard work here, because the point has been to show that people of African descent often kept gardens, sometimes called yards, and that these provided food, cash, and a place to express African and diasporic religious meanings. They do not seem on the surface to have directly expressed or embodied the otherwise infectious dominant ideology of individualism. But we cannot know that until we find out how they operated.

The composite autobiographies or narratives are quite clear about how commonly slaves grew their own food on their own lots, although they did not own the land. Individuals gained some independence this way. Some sustained distant family members or bought their own freedom and that of their own relatives this way. Neuwirth has pointed out that gardening for freedom produced a major break in the ideology behind slavery: utter unsuitability for personal freedom or individualism. I would add that the break was accompanied by a belief in the ideology of personal liberty and freedom. Free former slaves showed that the ideology of a natural hierarchy was unworkable. But by the late nineteenth century, they had begun a debate among themselves over whether personal liberty was a condition to be sought by believing in it or was an ideology itself to be overcome through collective action.

We know from Timothy Ruppel's (2003) work that: Henry Gibbs farmed his plot and garden patches on Saturday afternoons. Charlotte Beverly identified "moonlight" as the available time for raising cotton (Rawick 1977, 8: 823; 1: 40). Hector Smith of South Carolina declared: "Oh, dey work dey garden by de moonshine en fore light good in de morning cause dey had to turn dey hand to dey Massa work when day-light come here" (Rawick 1972, 13, pt. 4: 101).

Ishrael Massie, a former Virginia slave, said that working the garden depended on how you saw yourself: "ef dey didn't have anything fer ya to do ya could do dis work fer yoself at night ime ef ya wuz a smart fel-low" (Perdue 1976, 210). Massie's father raised tobacco at night to buy clothes for his family.

Cash crops raised in slave gardens bought fiddles, clothes and pies, horses and saddles; marbles, candy, and toys for the children; coffee and tea for the household; chairs, beds, and bedsteads for the cabin; and, finally, Christmas presents. Sam Anderson, a former Mississippi slave, described a man named Dollie who raised cotton on Saturday nights. Eventually, Dollie saved $500 and purchased his wife's freedom. Linda Thornton's father bought a horse with the work he did during "extra time." Prince Johnson's grandmother sold enough corn to buy two feather beds (Rawick 1977, 12: 5; Rawick 1972, 10, pt. 6: 328: Rawick 1977, 8: 1168).

Frederick Douglass (1986, 114) said that "thinking and industrious" slaves employed their holiday time in making "corn-brooms, mats, horse-collars, and baskets," which would generate cash. As many for-mer slaves indicated, industry and work beyond the requirements of the slaveowners were valued in the slave quarters, because they promoted the interests of the community. Cora Carroll Gillam's mother had an acre of ground adjacent to her house in the slave quarters, and she used the patch to raise vegetables, chickens, and hogs, taking advantage of the clandestine networks that existed between slaves and whites. Gillam's mother sold her goods to buyers on the trading boats going down the river. Her market negotiations and purchases, involving both trading boats and itinerant peddlers, occurred because she was "smart enough" to raise commodities to sell and exploited the opportunities to market.

Caroline Ates, a former Georgia slave, saw the same kind of self-possessed initiative as Gillam: "If we wuz smart an' made a good crop, we had mo' money than the lazy ones did." Laura Thornton employed similar distinctions when she compared her father's industry to that of others: "Many folks too lazy to git theirselves somethin' when they have the chance to do it. But my daddy wasn't that kind. His old master gave him the ground and he made it give him the money" (Rawick 1979, 1 [Arkansas]: 84; Rawick 1977, 3, pt. 1: 26; Rawick 1972, 10: pt. 6: 328).

The dominant ideology produced by capitalism existed in the economic matrix of plantation slavery that typified all of southern Maryland, in-

cluding Anne Arundel County and thus Annapolis. In a place like Annapolis in the late eighteenth century, about a third of all African Americans had become free, mostly through manumission but some by having earned enough cash to purchase their freedom. Thus slaves, legally
defined as human property like houses, cows, and iron pots, were people
deprived of virtually all legal rights but could earn enough money to be
free, just like all other free individuals. Slaves used capitalism to buy freedom, but in order to do so they had to see themselves as having the right
to be free: they possessed freedom by selling the products of their labor.
They acted like C. B. Macpherson's possessive individuals (Macpherson
1962). Some slaves used the economy to achieve a place in the dominant
ideology of the elite and middle class. Eventually, they exposed the dominant ideology as a mask. This was neither ridicule nor parody; it was a
functioning reality, visible to everybody and produced a major contradiction within a hierarchical society. They showed that the ideology could
not hide economic and political reality.

I conclude that in a slave society like Annapolis, the dominant ideology of possessive individualism penetrated all the way down from the
richest to the enslaved, but by the time it got to the bottom, it was not
an ideology. It was a lie. As we shall see in chapter 4, the prerevolutionary colonial elite used parody to signal to the governing elite that they
saw the cracks in ideology that coupled monarchical hierarchy with individual liberty. However, before and after the Revolution, Africans managing their own freedom did not just challenge the ruling ideology, they
actively exposed it by redefining whom it included. It included the least
and transformed slaves into people who could claim to be equally free
and property-owning. Thus, the dominant ideology not only masked capitalism's internal contradiction at the top but also was used against the
ideology of individualism to produce a substantial challenge to hierarchy
on the ground. Possessive individualism was turned around and was made
revolutionary. But only for a few moments, and only for some.

All around an ideology like possessive individualism is culture, which
creates consciousness through language, and all the means of thought
and action that we normally include in learned behavior. Before and
after the Revolution, people saw both hierarchy and the idea of individualism. Based on my data, only some at the top saw that hierarchy pre-
cluded individualism for the propertyless and those of African descent.
It is likely, however, if I can project African American gardening back
into the late eighteenth century, that some slaves saw possessive individualism and wanted it and actually possessed it for themselves. This

not only provoked a challenge to the ideological basis for hierarchy, but also led to the revolutionary era debate about who could and could not be a citizen with rights. Some slaves and former slaves agreed with the ideology of individualism and turned it into a living critique; others kept African traditions of community and kinship alive, thus rejecting an ideology of possessive individualism.

My argument is based on seeing formal landscapes as places where people worked daily, and where people walked and watched every day. Virtually everyone—or certainly most people—gardened in one way or another, because this was a planned and a largely agricultural society. My conclusion based on gardening as a technology of the self is that it supported an ideology that ran through society and that saw a person as an individual with rights, including possessions like liberty, but that attempted to exclude those without property, namely, poor whites and those of African descent. While the exclusion was attempted, it did not work, and the resulting contradiction produced a view that may have allowed the ideology to be seen as an artificial construct. Given the relatively large numbers of people in Annapolis of African descent who were free but outside the enfranchised elite, I argue that no ideology could go on for long presenting itself as being for the common good of all people when it was in fact quite partial. This test of Althusser's hypothesis thus shows him to have had a powerful idea that needs to be modified. Hence there is a chance for reform within capitalism.

Ideology avoids violence while allowing the social order of capitalism to reproduce itself. This is an order of inequality that was sustained by the notion of personal freedom or liberty that stemmed from the ideology of possessive individualism. Possessive individualism meant owning property, which took the on-the-ground form of hierarchical degrees of wealth. When wealth was argued to be a natural possession, the justification for hierarchy was apparent to all. The instability in this arrangement came when the American wealthy realized they were never going to be able to defend the property that was "naturally" theirs. Thus, because the British state violated its purpose, the Americans founded their own.

In the United States, the ideology remained possessive individualism, with panoptic citizenship as a technology making it work. All this hid a hierarchy that was just as unstable, if not more so, as that hidden by a naturalizing ideology. Stability came because gardeners like Faris and others like him made and maintained gardens that had the same meanings as those of the elite. But Africans and African Americans made gardens that looked different, were used for a very different purpose, and were sustained by utterly foreign religions. And with these gardens they duplicated the ideology of possessive individualism because with them they sometimes bought their freedom. They weakened the ideology severely by becoming possessive individuals with freedom and then by exercising that freedom. Free African American men with property qualifications could vote until the early nineteenth century, when the practice was made illegal (Faris 2004, 8). This weakened the hierarchy's hold on power by exploiting the dominant ideology. Such a practice breached the mask hiding differential power. Such an event allows us to see that some did not believe in the ideology embedded in landscapes of power but rather made their own landscapes, used them to challenge the dominant ideology, and began a reform. Thus, landscapes were a powerful tool of ideology; most people gardened within ideology, but some saw through the ideology and used their lives to resist it.

CHAPTER 4

The Rise of Popular Opinion

This chapter analyzes printer's type dating from about 1750 to about 1820 or 1830 that was used in the *Maryland Gazette,* published in Annapolis. But because the type was used to print words, and these words survive (the *Gazette* is in the Maryland State Archives), it is also about the printed material available for public consumption wherever the *Gazette* was read. The *Gazette* was printed at the Jonas Green print shop, which we excavated. The printer's type from the shop was used to print more than the newspaper, of course, but the paper was its most important, widely used, and widely known product.

You don't write essays about type and its use in newspapers without wanting to do more than make sense of the excavated remains of printing. Printing has, after all, been the hallmark of Western civilized life since the late fifteenth century. It is both an adjunct of our memory and the cause of some of our common life, insofar as printing unifies us in its universal availability.

I present the type and the printed *Maryland Gazette* as material vehicles, or technologies, of the ideology of individualism. They existed to create and reinforce the notion that a person was the most important element in society. He or she, and neither the family nor the community, was at the core of society's functioning. This central social element became ever more visible and significant after 1750 through printing.

The printed page, with its design, layout, decoration, and general look, is my first consideration. My colleague Barbara Little has made sense of

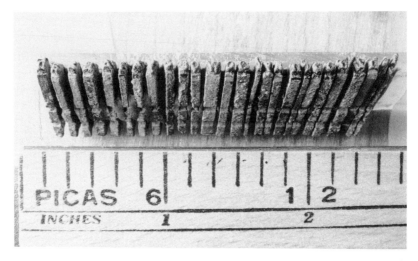

FIGURE 28. Individual pieces of printer's type with printer's ruler. Photograph courtesy of Thomas W. Cuddy.

a very large and complex corpus of excavated printer's type and established the basic analysis that the *Gazette* became progressively more segmented (B. Little 1987). Over time, the pages of the newspaper came to seem modern: mass-produced, mechanical, predictable, and rule-guided. I have chosen to call this the appearance of being without an author, or authorless. Authorial power was missing because the printer's craft came to be defined as producing regularity on the page, not a signature style. The form of the page allowed readers to entertain the fantasy that the newspaper represented what they thought, and that it was produced for them. It appeared to be a classless document in which readers and listeners could see their own desires, thoughts, arguments, conditions, and futures.

The newspaper was printed for a set of eyes, and its voice was directed at an individual reader, not at a community of hearers acting in concert. Its increasing mechanical smoothness facilitated the illusion that the reader could see him- or herself in and on its pages and never worry about why the Greens were saying and selecting what they were printing. In fact, the Greens and other upper- and middle-class citizens wrote for the newspaper and had their say in its pages. But the appearance of individual authorship was separated from its pages. And it had to be in order for readers to see themselves in what they read. This process began around 1750 and can be seen in the type.

There was a second process operating as well, which can be seen in the paper's content. The first process masked the author and allowed the reader to see himself as the creator of the news rather than as its subject. The truth was that opinion was always authored and was often class-centered. The mask was that the rules of printing, grammar, and language were impartial and that anyone who participated was equal to anyone else who could read and comprehend.

The content I have chosen to emphasize shows how individuals were shaped and, more important, how they were meant to reproduce themselves through training. By individuals, I mean people who worked in a hierarchical society, whether power was based in politics or wealth, and who produced themselves as reliable labor. The *Gazette* contains many essays about shaping and training people for roles as productive individuals, including belonging to a gender.

Finally, since I am writing about ideology, I ask whether people used and believed what they read and were taught? Who realized that the process was an ideology, or mask, for a hierarchy of power? The best answer comes from the *Records* (Hamilton 1988) and *History of the Ancient and Honorable Tuesday Club* (Hamilton 1990), produced in the mid-eighteenth century by a group of middle- and upper-middle-class white men who met regularly and put on parodies of contemporary monarchical politics. They satirized much of contemporary society. While the *History* was not printed until recently, it is important in this context both because the printer Jonas Green was a club member and because the members clearly saw through the political rationale of monarchy and the formality of the disciplines then coming into middle- and upper-class use that defined individuals as rule-abiding, predictable people. The club members parodied both, performed the parody in public, and thus showed that the techniques of ideology were visible to them and unacceptable.

Just as the William Paca Garden is the most beautiful spot in Annapolis today, and may have been in the eighteenth century as well, the remains of the Jonas and Anne Catherine Green print shop are one of the archaeological treasures of the city. My colleagues and I excavated a collection of 11,000 pieces of printer's type from the shop (B. Little 1987; Cox and Buckler 1995). What to do with them? How did printing work then? In fact, why is this a treasure?

In order to deal with this huge and unprecedented collection of printer's type, a problem had to be articulated. This took years, but under the leadership of Barbara Little (1987, 1988, 1992, 1994, 1998) and with the work of many students, it was finally achieved. The larger problem, to which the print shop is tied, remains: understanding how a planned, baroque capital city brought itself into existence as a colonial capital and then transformed itself into the capital of a new republic with newly minted, reading citizens.

The newspaper printed for decades by the Greens, the *Maryland Gazette,* was one of the main instruments by means of which people in Annapolis watched and interacted with one another in order to learn and internalize society's lessons. How did that observing frame of mind get established using print? What persuaded individuals to watch themselves willingly? The American republic achieved this goal fairly peacefully. As Benedict Anderson has suggested (1991, 62–63), and as I would like to elaborate here, postrevolutionary self-watching occurred through something called popular opinion, the idea that virtually perfect strangers come to believe that they agree with one another because they read the same widely available material and are mutually informed. But the process of creating popular opinion began well before the Revolution and can be seen in the type used to print the newspaper.

Popular opinion could exist, however, only because people were not merely a crowd. The whole process was dependent on the strong cultivation of the idea that a person was an individual, the basic building block of society, and the ultimate unit of social value and social control. Popular opinion was the result of having a society of individuals each of whom believed that he or she had rights. After the Revolution, citizens by law had rights, one of which, albeit for propertied men only, was the right to vote for elected officials. But citizens did not come ready-made; they had to be created in some image. This could be done through mass printing and reading, whether out loud or silently. This was the process called popular opinion, and I argue that an examination of the process of printing the *Maryland Gazette* shows how it happened, and that it originated in the 1750s.

Annapolis was a city made up of people who linked themselves together in the performance of being something new. In order for popular opinion to be created, people had to be public. They had to be seen, to show off, to appear to be willing to learn, listen, perform, inspect and report, and reform once reported or called upon. In this way, first the new colonial capital and then a new nation in a transformed capital city were created.

These were the questions that Little and I gradually came to ask about printer's type after the scope of the sample became visible. Before the type was discovered, however, James Deetz had identified the process of defining individuals in dining patterns, floor plans, and personal attributes engraved on tombstones in the mid-eighteenth century (Deetz 1977, 43). By the later eighteenth century, for example, formal dining tables required separate place settings and an elaborate array of specialized serving dishes. There was substantial heterogeneity in form but homogeneity in decoration, or style, with dishes of many different sizes and shapes all painted (or glazed) in the same pattern and colors. In short, there were equal dishes for equal individuals, equally spaced, with equal utensils, and a chair for each diner.

Could this same process also be seen on the contemporary printed page? And if it could, what would the page look like? If a newspaper was like a table top or a house floor plan, then how would it be organized visually and in terms of spatial spread of information? How did a page printed explicitly for popular use get organized? And how was printer's type used to do the job? In other words, how did the advent of the individual influence the organization of the printed page?

Our predictions, given a commitment to using a form of scientific method that would enhance making discoveries, as opposed to appearing to verify what anyone could guess, were simple. Drawing on Deetz's work, and based on very little actual initial knowledge of printing, type, or the *Gazette* itself, Little and I predicted a more and more homogeneous set of typefaces, which would have the effect of making the printed page appear more and more uniform stylistically, like a late eighteenth-century dining table. We also predicted more and more segmentation of the pages, like courses dividing a meal and food within a course, with more boxes for specific purposes. The look would be uniform as well as segregated. I suggested too that there would be fewer and fewer different typefaces and styles used, so that a less varied-looking printed page resulted. These predictions served as a way to get started on an analysis of the type and the pages of the *Gazette*.

No one, it seemed, had ever looked at printer's type archaeologically. There was little literature on the subject. This is because not much type has been recovered and no one had spent much time figuring out what to do with the type itself. There was a literature on printing, including colonial printing, but it focused on the orderliness of the printing process, the successful use of printer's rules, the aesthetics of the page, and printing technology. It did not focus on type. The history of printing literature told us that there was very little change in the way type was made and used from about 1650 to about 1830 (B. Little 1988, 276; 1992, 9). This implied that the type used to produce the *Maryland Gazette* was not going to show much change for most of its history, 1728 to 1830 (B. Little 1987, 219–20). So what would the type look like if it did not change?

Little summarized the increasing number of columns, the increase of printed lines between them, between sections of the newspaper, between stories, and between advertisements between 1745 and 1814 (Coleman and Johnson 1985) as showing the segmentation of the newspaper (B. Little 1988, 277–80). She interprets these changes and the use of segments as increasing consistency in the use of rules that produced consistency in layout. She observes that Parks, the first printer in Annapolis, used no lines between advertisements in the 1720s and builds the argument that changes like the introduction of lines show a change in patterning of format toward both standardization and segmentation (ibid., 280). "This created a more segmented façade" (ibid., 284).

Little connects this change in appearance to a false symmetry between people and goods. She sees the trend toward defining individuals as equal as contemporaneous with the mass production of artifacts, which by definition are identical. She notes that the appearance of equality among people is only an appearance. The political environment for a connection comes from the dramatic increase in "demand for newspapers as they became vehicles of controversy and propaganda," and as they produced "news" more frequently as the Revolution approached (ibid., 286). So, is there a connection between mass produced things, a segmented and standardized page, and the printing of controversial news and opinions about equality? What is the connection between equality and mass production? This introduces the need for the notion of ideology.

We were also interested in contrasting findings made by analyzing type against the findings made by analyzing the pages of the *Gazette*, which has survived complete from 1745 on, making it an amazing source of information. But the type has likewise survived, at least 11,000 excavated pieces of it. Because the *Gazette* was so rich in information and because there were no suggestions in the literature about how to analyze printer's type, I faced the danger of making the type look ancillary to the paper in the overall investigation. I had to avoid the accusation that any question I might ask of printing type could be answered faster, more cheaply, and more reliably by looking at the paper itself. After all, wouldn't every piece of type at the shop have appeared sooner or later on the printed page? Probably, but you could never tell, because type pieces were made to look alike, even though manufacturers did not always succeed (B. Little 1992, 90–91), and there was no way of knowing how much type it took to print the *Gazette*. And you could also never tell from the printed page how much small or large type was being used to make boxes, columns, or large and small print—or rather you could for any one is-sue, but not overall, because there was no complete collection of type left. You could also never tell whether a printer had type choices on hand long before he multiplied his uses of them. Even if you could tell from the printed page that type was becoming more and more uniform in style and height, you would never know how many fonts were required to achieve this. Only excavation could reveal the quantities used. Moreover, I would not have asked the questions in the first place without the type. The type generated some of the questions.

As part of the work on type, Little noted that printing had promoted the duplication of identical copies (B. Little 1992, 88). Printing democ-ratized texts by disseminating them widely, thus giving popularity and power to printed ideas. Printing spread and reinforced vernacular lan-guages, and in some cases spread and planted stereotypes. Standardized texts also lead to the improvement of texts through correction of errors. Little notes the connections between the improvement of the accuracy of texts and the spread of copies, which, when read, produced notice of errors that could be corrected in subsequent editions. Behind this, she observes, lay a search for certainty that arose when some saw the "irre-concilable inconsistencies" that appear when there are many texts to read (ibid.). Thus, standardization leads to highlighting that which cannot be standardized and may produce a view of the world in which there are inevitable conflicts.

This insight was preceded by her demonstration of standardization among elements of printer's type, such as type heights to paper through-out the period 1750 to 1830. Height to paper is the length of the piece of type, and uniformity of length aids in assuring that each letter will hit the paper (ibid., 90–91).

From her analysis, Little deduces two key points. First, the news-paper's content was segmented by type that was standardized. Second, such production connected readers with the expectations of everyday life. Little—citing Elizabeth Eisenstein (1979, 1983)—asked how inconsis-tencies revealed by the use of printing between the realities of what people were reading, experiencing, and reporting were dealt with as newspa-pers became vehicles for controversy, propaganda, and "news" and dou-bled in number in the decade or so before the Revolution (B. Little 1988: 286). Given that inconsistencies were revealed by the standardization of the printing process, and segmentation of information was, or could be, complementary to the production processes of capitalism, what occurred to relieve the inconsistencies and simultaneously facilitate profit making and wage labor production?

Ideology functions to mask inconsistencies. It masks contradictions between observations, experiences, and people's talk and behavior particularly when the contradictions are produced by differences in wealth and power. For example, printing multiplied the reported inconsistencies throughout the English-speaking world. But it also showed how inconsistent a liberty-loving people was, with some being very rich and others, neighbors and debtors, being poor. The segmentation of the newspaper hid these through physical and conceptual separations. Our job was to discover how. In 1983, my archaeological field school began excavating at the site of the Green family print shop. In those days and until her departure from the Historic Annapolis Foundation (then Incorporated), St. Clair Wright suggested sites for excavation, often based on a combination of historical importance and danger from some form of development. The home owned by the Greens still stands and is still owned by their descendants. The house was closed for renovation while we dug there and remained unoccupied for a long time, allowing us access to all its below-floor spaces. We dug an enormous amount over four summers.

My graduate and undergraduate students began in the backyard, which was available and was presumed to be the locale of the lost print shop. We found the shallow, 18-inch-wide brick foundation of the print shop within the first week of digging, and, indeed, found pieces of printer's type on the first day or two. We were very happy and felt quite privileged to be so lucky. Many years later, I realized that such luck has characterized Archaeology in Annapolis in good part because the city of Annapolis is so well preserved.

The excavation was run by Constance Crosby and Donald Creveling for the first two years. Little took over for the last two years and drew her 1987 dissertation, *Ideology and Media: Historical Archaeology of Printing in Eighteenth-Century Annapolis, Maryland,* from the work. She undertook the analysis of all aspects of the site, but particularly focused on printing and the Green family (B. Little 1988, 1992, 1994, 1998). Indeed, she changed the focus of attention from Jonas Green, who was seen as the famous colonial printer, to the whole family, including Anne Catherine Green and her sons who were printers, into the nineteenth century. Little also undertook the task of cataloguing the type. This was a monumental job, whose dimensions will only become clear as others use her work (B. Little 1992). Unlike with virtually any

other class of historic artifacts, there was no established way of cataloguing printer's type until she created one.

Little studied the literature on type and printing and categorized the
type using three key variables. The basic definition of a font was a set of
pieces of individual items cast all at once, from several hundred to 10,000.
On the sides of each piece of type was a set of grooves, called nicks, which
identify each piece with all others in the font. This was like a bar code. It
was never visible on the page. She identified 160 separate fonts at the
Greens' shop for the time it was used (B. Little 1987, 195–232; 1992) .
There were twenty-three possible typefaces, and these were sometimes
called fonts also. Then, there was the type size, which meant height of the
letter. Diamond was smallest; French Canon largest; and Long Primer,
English, and Pica were the most common sizes used. This was one of the
key variables that controlled how much print can occur on a printed page.
There were also fonts of spaces, the type that made the white space between words and lines, columns, and sentences. Little classified about
4,000 pieces of type this way, which was the basis for any analysis. Later,
Matthew Moyer, taught by Little, classified another 2,000 pieces using
the same system in order to create a larger sample for further analysis.

Because the type did not come with dates, its chronology had to be
established by comparison with the pages of the *Gazette.* This was difficult to do, because the printed image of the type was not at all easily
matched with the impression made from an archaeological piece of type.
There was also no way to establish the range of years through which a
piece was used. Stratigraphy was an alternative way of creating a chronological ordering. This too was established carefully by Little (1987; Cox
and Buckler 1995), who built on the initial and equally careful work at
the Green site by Constance Crosby.

The stratigraphy of the Jonas Green site was complicated and not uniform across the site. While everything was intact below the ground, the
shop foundation and its successive articulations to the house were just
below the modern surface and had been trampled, bruised by many oc-
cupations, and abraded here and there. When the shop, which was a
wooden structure with two rooms, had been taken down around 1830,
the shallow foundation had been covered over only with a couple inches
of soil. So everything was still there, but not deeply buried or protected.
Fortunately, the backyard had not been used for much after the print shop
was taken down.

There were several layers to the shop, and these showed how it had
been connected to the main house and then was freestanding. Garry

Wheeler Stone, then from Historic St. Mary's City, figured out the building phases of the house itself for us (B. Little 1987, 178). It had begun
as two small 20 × 20 foot rooms with an alley between them, and became the current large gambrel-roofed structure by 1790. In phases, the
alley had been made into the central hallway of the house, leading to the
work yard and print shop. The one-and-a-half-story house had become
a full two stories, with a set of upstairs rooms, by late in the century,
with the kitchen connected directly to the back of the house and parallel to the print shop. All the units formed a U, with a narrow yard between shop and kitchen.

The print shop had a wood-lined cellar, which contained the most complex stratigraphy of the shop. Jonas Green's shop caught fire in 1765
and was badly damaged, but the blaze was contained before the house
burned down. We could still see the charred clapboards of the house when
we worked there. It must have been a very dangerous situation. The shop
was devastated, and in the rebuilding, much of the debris, including lost
type, was dumped into the cellar hole, leaving it deeply and cleanly
stratified. We used this deposit to date some of the type, and Little used
the stratigraphy across the site to create contexts for dating the fonts.
This was a key accomplishment, because it allowed her to say when a
font was in use, which could not be done using the pages of the *Gazette,*
because all fonts of the same face appear nearly the same. The stratigraphy provided a chronology of font frequency. It told us how many fonts
of which styles and sizes were used at once.

Little identified nine stratigraphic contexts, beginning in the 1750s and
ending in the 1890s. These were established by excavation in natural layers, whose contents were screened, and then by using dated ceramics.
These levels gave temporal parameters to the excavated printer's type.
The dated contexts were reexamined and made more precise over time
and took final form in the completed site report on the Green family print
shop, which was written and assembled by Jane Cox and John Buckler
(1995), in close collaboration with Little. This work was finished in 1995,
but the analysis of type and the pages of the *Gazette* remained ongoing.

Because the stratigraphy for activity areas, which Little called contexts, was not continuous across the print shop site, she listed them separately, with their stratigraphy dated by historic ceramics, as follows:

Context 9   Early eighteenth century

Context 8   Middle eighteenth century

Context 7   Late eighteenth century

FIGURE 29. Large O and J against a printer's ruler. Photograph courtesy of Thomas W. Cuddy.

Context 6   Late eighteenth century

Context 5   Late eighteenth to early nineteenth century

Context 4   Late eighteenth to early nineteenth century

Context 3   Middle to late nineteenth century

Little undertook to understand the Greens and succeeded. Many undergraduate and graduate students worked on the *Gazette* using an adaptation of Jim Deetz's ideas and charted the changing organization of the layout of the *Gazette* statistically. Some looked at the organization of content, one worked on the content itself. One student worked on the distribution of type size over time on the page. When these results are assembled, we see that the *Gazette* changed between 1750 and 1785 so that it appeared visually homogeneous—less decorated—and with its material sorted by subject, with different subjects segregated. Content became less about magic and Europe, and more about rules for doing things and about Maryland.

How was visual homogeneity achieved? The initial work to answer this question was done by Teresa D. Harris (1986) in a class research project. She examined the newspaper itself and discovered major changes in visual appearance beginning in the 1750s and 1760s that created a more homogeneous, smoother-looking page. Emphasized words were no longer set off typographically by being capitalized or italicized. This affected dozens of words in every issue. By mid-century, nouns were no longer to be found set in full capitals or italics. Use of italics for any word disappeared. Large capital letters beginning paragraphs were eliminated too.

The biggest physical change to the page of the *Gazette* was the reduction in the number of quotation marks. Quotations marks were originally used at the beginning of every line of a quoted paragraph before the 1750s. After the 1750s, quotation marks appeared only at the beginning and end of a paragraph, as is the case today. If this had been the only change made in the mid-eighteenth century, it would have reshaped the appearance of the page by itself. Long, vertical, irregularly aligned, wobbly lines of quotation marks on the left edges of paragraphs were gone by the 1750s. This was a major change in the shape of the printed page.

If a printer's job was to produce a page that was so complex and well designed by the use of rules for word recognition, then the printer as page stylist began to retreat from the design of meaning by the 1750s and 1760s, because meaning came from the proper use of rules, not the shape of words. The result made nouns more equal to verbs, adjectives, and all other parts of speech. The result made primary and quoted information more equal to each other and took away some meaning between the two kinds of knowledge, as designated by form.

After 1773, all nouns were printed the same way, without italics, regardless of their contexts' origin in Britain or the colonies. The larger issue in this development was the meaning of all words, including nouns, which appeared in the same type form and face. This change implied that all parts of speech and all ways of communicating meaning through print had equal value. Did a more uniform shape mean that nouns lost the special intrinsic naming value they were once thought to possess? The submergence of the distinctive marks of the noun signified that words did not stand by themselves with their meaning speaking through their form, any more than individuals could be recognized socially without all their possessions or markers. Thus, grammatical and visual context became essential in order to understand the meaning of any word. Michel Foucault observes that

> throughout the Classical age [sixteenth to eighteenth centuries], language was posited and reflected upon as . . . the spontaneous analysis of representation. . . . in the seventeenth and eighteenth centuries, the theory of the name had its place as near as possible to representation and thus gov-

erned, to a certain degree, the analysis of structures and character in living beings [making language a mirror image and a true description of re-
ality]. . . . all the words of a language were bearers of a more or less hidden, more or less derived, signification whose original raison d'être lay in an
initial designation. Every language, however complex, was situated in the
opening that had been created . . . by archaic cries. . . .

   Until the end of the eighteenth century, this . . . analysis has its place in
the search for the representative values of languages. . . . [Then,] through
the inflectional system, the dimension of the purely grammatical is appearing: . . . [and] consists . . . of formal elements, grouped into a system,
which impose upon the sounds, syllables, and roots an organization that
is not that of representation. . . . Languages are no longer contrasted in
accordance with what their words designate, but in accordance with the
means whereby words are linked together; from now on they will communicate, not via the intermediary of that anonymous and general thought
they exist to represent, but directly from one to the other, thanks to those
delicate instruments [grammars], . . . by which words are arranged in relation to each other.

   As long as language was defined as discourse, it could have no other
history than that of its representations: if ideas, things, knowledge, or feelings happened to change, then and only then did a given language undergo
modification, and in exactly the same proportion as the changes in question. But from now on there is an interior "mechanism" in languages which
determines . . . the bearer of identity and difference, [i.e.] the sign of ad-
jacency, the mark of kinship.

Foucault 1973, 233–36

The establishment of a set of grammatical and syntactical rules independent of humans and intrinsic to language was the most abstract
way in which authorship was eliminated. An author learned the rules
and used them more or less successfully. A writer could know them but
did not create them. The same was true of reading and readers. Perception and meaning lay in the individual's ability to recognize form, function, and meaning as they existed apart from him or her. But the meaning was not inherent in the form; it was taken from the context in which
the form occurred. Thus the reader had to learn and recognize what was
apart from himself, which appeared to be neutral.

   Much of the process of making grammar and syntax a seemingly independent system is illustrated by the way Harris made her discoveries.
She used printer's guides, mostly published in England, that contained
clear rules for virtually every decision a typesetter needed to make. She
listed most of these rules, evaluated whether or not they could be observed systematically by looking at structured samples of the *Gazette*,

and then charted occurrences. She produced graphs of the use of italicized nouns, capitalized nouns, running columns of quotation marks, and the long, or medial, form when the letter *s* fell within or at the beginning of a word. Thus, she produced graphs of how closely the *Gazette* followed the commonly used rules for printing. Her research was a remarkably comprehensive and precise effort that showed exactly the opposite of what had been predicted. The face of the *Gazette* had changed dramatically beginning about 1750. It was not stable.

There were four popular guides used by printers that focused on what was called grammar, which would mean design for us. In England, guides were published by Joseph Moxon in 1683, John Smith in 1755, and Caleb Stower in 1808. Cornelius Van Winkle produced one in the United States in 1818. Theresa Harris extracted twenty-two possible rules for observing the *Gazette* from all of these, but only about eight rules could actually be observed.

All of the printers' guides preferred shorter sentences, created by dropping semicolons. Moxon's *Mechanick Exercises on the Whole Art of Printing* (1978 [1683]) advocated beginning new sentences and paragraphs with a large capital letter and setting words to be emphasized in small capitals or italics. All proper nouns were to be italicized. The later guides rejected the use of italics in roman-type settings, however, and Smith's (1965 [1755]) rule was to set all proper nouns in capital letters of equal size. Smith began every line of a quoted paragraph with quotation marks, whereas Stower's (1965 [1808]) rules put them only at the beginning and end of the paragraph. These were the main rules that affected massive spatial alignments on a page. Harris also traced the change in use of commas, hyphens, apostrophes, and syllabic breaks.

The rule books helped us to isolate the changes on the printed pages by focusing on how type was set. But the point was not to study how far from or close to the rules the printer was. The point was to study typographic change. Thus, what was actually important to know was that setting words entirely in upper case dropped off significantly and had fallen out of use by the early 1770s. "Up until 1750, large quantities of the text were capitalized; capitalization was common for emphasis in every sentence," Harris notes; however, by 1795, "all words in a sentence [had become] more uniform or standardized, and . . . leave placement of emphasis to the individual [reader]" (Harris 1986, 15).

Use of italics diminished steadily over a long period. The drop began in 1755, and italics were all but eliminated by 1823. First, italics were not used in news from Europe, then were not used in local news, then

The
Maryland Gazette

Samuel Gz...

From TUESDAY December 3, to TUESDAY December 10, 1728. (Numb.

Look round the habitable World how few
Know their own Good ! or knowing it pursue !
How void of Reason are our Hopes and Fears !
What in the Conduct of our Life appears
So well defign'd, fo lucki'y begun,
But when we have our Wifh, we wifh undone ?

Dryden's Ju...

SIR,

IN my fecond Paper, I intimated my Defign of improving the FAIR-SEX, by giving fome finifhing Touches to Them who are already the moft beautiful Pieces in human Nature: I propofed to divert their Minds from ufelefs Trifles, and inftead thereof to ... their Breafts with valuable Knowledge; to point out thofe Imperfections which are the Blemifhes, as well as thofe Virtues which are the Imbellifhments of the Sex, fo as in the End, ... foft upon the Level with the Men in their boafted Superiority of Reafor.

How unmercifu! ... ... for many Ages has feclued the m ... and confined them chiefly to the divine Pleafures o—Learning, and confined them chiefly to the Bufinefs of the Needle ! How rarely are they taught or inured to think out of the Common Way, and beyond the legend of the Nurfery. They who under proper Directions might have ac ... the moft refined Knowledge, are fo ... by a filly Education, that generally fpeaking, they know little more than their Work, a fmall Share of Houfewifery; and a great deal of Goffiping.

IT would ill become the PLAIN-DEALER to compliment his Fair Pupils at the Expence of Truth, I therefore think it incumbent on Me to treat them with Sincerity; and hope to be excufed for mentioning the Defects in their Education, when I have offered them that in my Opinion, their Imperfections proceed rather from their miftaken Tutors, than from any Perverfenefs in their own Difpofition.

To rectify thefe Defects, I would earneftly advife them to Pay ... with Attention: From Books they may receive ... Improvements, as will make them lovely, when the Charms of their Faces lie buried in Wrinkles.

GOOD Writers have it in their Power to furnifh the tender Sex with Charms more lafting than thofe which they derive from Beauty, and which can fupply the Lofs of Youth and Gaiety with more valuable Qualities; but few Authors have taken fufficient Pains to point out proper Employments and Diverfions for the Fair Readers: The Pieces which they generally meet with, are too ferious too loofe! For their Perufal. I fhall therefore in the Courfe of thefe Papers, endeavour to entertain them in a more agreeable Manner; and introduce them to Reading, I fhall at my

leifure prefent them with a Set of Hiftories, collected from the Records of a powerful, invifible People, with whom I hold fome Correfpondence. My gentle Readers will undoubtedly be curious to know the Tranfactions of the FAIRIES, of whom they have heard fo many Tales from their Nurfes; but I muft take Notice in this Place, that I fhall never offer them a Fairy-Tale, which will not inftruct as well as amufe them. As the firft Specimen of this kind, I recommend the following Relation to my Fair Pupils.

THERE was a Country-Woman, who upon her whom I hold fome Correfpondence. ... defired her to come and affift Labour: The Good-Woman was delivered of a Da ... Mother; make your Choice: The Child a Mind) fhall be exquifitely Handfom, excell in V ... more than in Beauty, and be the Queen of a mighty p ... re, but withall, Unhappy: Or (if you had r she shall be an ordinary Country Creature like y ... but contented with her Condition. The Mother inn chofe Wit and Beauty for her Daughter, at the Hazard Misfortune.

As the Child grew, new Beauties open'd daily Face; till in a few Years, She furpaffed all the Rur ... that the oldeft People had ever feen. Her turn of gentle, polite and infinuating: She was of a read hension; and foon learnt every Thing fo as to Teachers. Every Holiday, She danced upo with a fuperiour Grace to any of her Co ... Voice was fweeter than any Shepher!'s Pip the Songs, which fhe uf ... to Sing ... So ... time Time fhe was not apprized when diverting her felf with her Play flowery Border of a Fountain, fhe Reflection of her Face: She ... Features and her Complexion f Company; and admired her from Day to Day to obtain a more fenfible of her Beauty the Predictions of the Fair Queen, and fpoil'd her ... D ... fel would neither Se Sheep: Her whole Amu ... drefs her Hair with the ...

FIGURE 30. *Maryland Gazette,* December 3–10, 1728. William Parks used a narrow range of type sizes, two columns, printer's flowers, and a few words in italics in 1728, giving the paper a carefully decorated, handcrafted look. Format courtesy of the Maryland State Archives.

THE   N°. 142.

MARYLAND GAZETTE,

Containing the freſheſt Advices, Foreign and Domeſtic.

WEDNESDAY, *January* 13, 1748.

From the South-Carolina GAZETTE, November 2, 1747.

Mr. *Timothy*,

A Maiden-Friend of mine in the Country, has engaged me to ſend you the incloſed Letter, and begs you'll not fail to give it a Place in your Gazette. It the Publication of it does not anſwer her End, ſhe hopes it will, at leaſt, be uſeful to ſome (to whom it may ſerve as a Hint), and that it may be an A-muſement to your Readers in general.

            S. S.

The following is the LETTER, &c.

YOU muſt know, Mr. Timothy, that with a tolerable Perſon, very good Fortune, and Lovers in Abundance, I have a particular Fancy to live and die a Maid. This Way of thinking, I proteſt, do s not ariſe from my not having it in my Power to have any Man; but from my not having ſeen any one Man, who had thoſe Accompliſhments which I think neceſſary for a Huſband. Perhaps you will imagine, that I dont know myſelf what ſort of a Man I would have; but Sir, to evince the contrary, I have ſent you a Deſcription of a Perſon, whom, notwithſtanding my preſent Humour, I would willingly marry, and bring to him 10000 l. for my Portion. When there are ſo many Fortune-Hunters, witty Sparks, pretty Fellows, and grave Widowers, about this Town, I dont not but I ſhall for firſt ſtrike ſome Scores with a flattering Hope thus they will eaſily carry me off; but to ſilence their Claims, thus follows the Deſcription of the only Man that I will have : You may juſtly entitle it

THE CHARACTER OF A MAID's HUSBAND.

HO' it is generally too fatal a Maxim among Women, to pleaſe their Eye if they torment their Heart, yet I am ſo far of that Opinion, that I muſt have ſuch a Perſon, whoſe Form, Shape, Air, and Mein, are intirely graceful and engaging. The Features of his Face muſt be regular and agreeable: His Eyes muſt be lively, ſparkling, and affecting; and over the whole Face there muſt appear a chearful Complexion, a healthful Air, and a chearful ſmile: His Stature muſt be of a riſing Height, eaſy and well proportion'd; a Gate free and genteel. His Behaviour ſerious, but natural : His Laugh, Speech, Action, and his whole Manner, muſt be juſt, without Affectation ; and free, without Levity.

BUT the Form of his Perſon is the leaſt of which I ſhall conſider as a Charm : His Genius and Knowlege muſt be extenſive, but not rambling into an Immenſity ; not ſkill'd in one Science, yet ignorant of all others ; not converſant in Books, yet knowing nothing of Mankind ; not a mere Scholar, nor a mere pretty Fellow ; but Learning, Freedom, and Gallantry, muſt ſo nicely be mingled together, that I might always find in him an improving Friend, a gay Companion, and an amuſing Gallant. In Converſation he muſt ſay nothing with Study, nor yet nothing as at Random ; the worſt he ſays muſt raiſe Attention, nor in the beſt muſt there appear any Labour for them.

HIS Soul muſt be generous without Prodigality, humane without Weakneſs, juſt without Severity, and fond without Folly ; to his Wife endearing, to his Children affectionate, to his Friends warm, and to all Mankind benevolent : Nature and Reaſon muſt join their Powers, and to the Openneſs of his Heart add Oeconomy ; making him careful without Avarice, and giving a Kind of Unconcernedneſs without Negligence : With Love he muſt have Reſpect, and by a continued Complaiſance always win upon the Inclinations ; as his firſt charm'd, he muſt ſtill endeavour to retain his Conqueſt ; and eternally look and ſpeak with

the ſame Deſires, the ſame Affection, tho' yet ſomewhat more Freedom.

IT is ſaid, that Experience proves the Soul attains a Kind of Blindneſs by loving, and Love never eſtabliſhes his Power without deſtroying of our Reaſon ; but the Man I chuſe muſt have Power to make his Sentiments become more paſſionate, as his Knowlege became more refin'd ; and the Paſſion, which in others is look'd on as a Mark of Folly, be in him the true Effects of Happineſs.

To all theſe Qualities I muſt add, that the Charm which is to be conſidered before all the reſt ſtill remains unſpoke of : He muſt have that which is very ſcarce in this libertine Age, Religion ; but tho' devout he muſt not be ſuperſtitious, tho' good not melancholy ; far from that Infirmity which makes Men uncharitable Bigots, averſe to that ſevere Temper which iaſen-ſibly diffuſes in the Heart of a Man a moroſe Contempt of the World, and a good Antipathy to the Pleaſures of it. He muſt not be ſo great a Lover of Society, as to mix with Aſſemblies of Fools, Knaves, and Blockheads, ; nor yet of Opinion that he ought to retire from human Society to ſeek God in the Horror of Solitude, but he muſt think the Almighty may be found amongſt Men, where his Goodneſs is moſt active, and his Providence moſt employed ; there his Religion muſt enlighten his Reaſon, perfect his Manners, regulate his own Conduct, both in the Cares of Salvation, and to the Duties of Life.

NOW, Sir, if any one Man will ſay, and then prove this Character to be his, my Fortune ſhall be his, as the only Man who deſerves it : But I believe I have made a Deſcription of a Man, as ſome Painters do of a Monſter, a Thing which is not in Nature ; which neither is, ever was, or ever will be : Therefore I fancy, Sir, I may as well make myſelf contented, not repine at dying a Maid (and I hope an old one), ſince I muſt not expect a Huſband to the Wiſhes of

         Your humble Servant,
         Reader, and Correſpondent,
         TAMAR SINGLE.

L O N D O N.

The P——M Bitt.

TO manage horſes P——M try'd
    His new invented Bitt ;
And not a little ſwell'd with Pride
    To ſee his Humour hit.

To manage Men our Artiſan
    Next took it in his Head ;
Conven'd one Night his flexile Clan,
    And to them thus he ſaid :

My Friends if you will lend a Hand,
    I'll riſe this E——d Old,
Mount, Sir, we're all at your Command,
    And will your Stirrep hold.

'Tis done—and ſo ſome necks he fits
    With halters and with axes,
The reſt the Freeborn reſt, he bits,
    And faddles with new Taxes.

O ENG-D! ENG-D! Country dear,
    What ROBIN long deviſ'd,
Hal in a Trice has brought to bear,
    Thou art at laſt Exciſ'd,

FIGURE 31. *Maryland Gazette*, January 13, 1748. This early version of Jonas Green's *Gazette* shows frequent use of italics, spaces separating advertisements, and very large capital letters, as well as paragraph headings indicating subject matter. Format courtesy of the Maryland State Archives.

were dropped from political speeches and personal letters. All of these changes affected proper nouns, which were always a large number of the words used at any place in the paper's pages.

Harris focused on individual printed words and on the use of quotation marks. But words were arranged in blocks in a page, and Simon Coleman and Matthew Johnson (1985) focused on the use of columns, lines separating them, horizontal lines separating parts of a column, like those separating stories in individual columns, and lines separating advertisements. They counted how segregated the space became (B. Little 1987, 245–48).

By 1750, two vertical columns had become three on every page of the paper; by the early nineteenth century, there were five vertical columns. Lines were used to separate sections of a column by 1750; to separate stories by 1805. But there were lines between advertisements by 1745; there had been none at all in 1734. William Parks's *Maryland Gazette,* which he printed between 1727 and 1734, was a two-column, two-page, large-print paper with the look of an early printed book.

The size of the individual items on a page, particularly the first two pages, also became uniform. Stephen Austin and Samuel Brainard (n.d.) found that the number of items on pages one and two, that is, news, editorials, advice, and letters, increased from a half dozen in 1728 to about twenty in 1770. The items top out at twenty per issue by the 1770s.

Advertisements increased steadily overall, except during the postrevolutionary depression, when "for sale" notices went way up. There was thus a grid of information on the page into which daily facts were fitted. This grid became more and more finely divided, with smaller and smaller boxes, more and more uniform compartments, marked out by obvious lines, and with clearer and clearer internal limits. The parts of the grid became quite predictable. Harris showed that words began to look more and more uniform, and Austin and Brainard showed that the boxes to hold the words did too.

At this point, it was easy enough to see that by the 1750s, the *Maryland Gazette* had become like Jim Deetz's dining table: lots of equal places, repeated regularly, over and over again, filled with separate items, and all for visual consumption. From the *Gazette's* tone, we know that the individual was the person addressed through its rhetoric and content. The monarch or the state was the object of the street plan. The great homeowner and his visitor were the objects of the tour of the falling garden. The individual desiring information for profit, self-improvement, and news held in common with the community was the object of the

119

[XXIII[d]. YEAR.] THE [N°. 1168.]

MARYLAND GAZETTE.

THURSDAY, JANUARY 28, 1768.

LETTERS *from a* FARMER *in* PENNSYLVANIA, *to the Inhabitants of the* Britiſh *Colonies.*

L E T T E R VI.

MY DEAR COUNTRYMEN,

IT may perhaps be objected againſt the Arguments that have been offered to the Public, concerning the legal Power of the Parliament, "that it has always exerciſed the Power of impoſing Duties, for the Purpoſe of raiſing a Revenue, on the Productions of theſe Colonies carried to *Great-Britain*; which may be called a Tax on them." To this Objection I anſwer, That this is no Violation of the Rights of the Colonies, it being implied in the relation between them and *Great-Britain*, that they ſhould not carry ſuch Commodities to other Nations, as ſhould enable them to interfere with the Mother Country. The Impoſition of Duties on theſe Commodities, when brought to her, is only a Conſequence of this her parental Right; and, if the Point is thoroughly examined, they will be found to be laid on the People of the Mother Country. Whatever theſe Duties are, they muſt proportionably raiſe the Price of the Goods, and conſequently the Duties muſt be paid by the Conſumers. In this Light they were conſidered by the Parliament, in the 25th *Charles* II. *ch.* 7, §. 2. which ſays, that the Productions of the Plantations were carried "from one to another, free from all Cuſtoms, while the Subjects of this your Kingdom of *England* have paid *great Cuſtoms and Impoſitions for what of them have been* SPENT HERE," &c.

Beſides, if *Great-Britain* exports theſe Commodities again, the Duties will injure her own Trade, ſo that ſhe cannot hurt us without plainly and immediately hurting herſelf; and this is our Check againſt her acting arbitrarily in this Reſpect.

It * may, perhaps, be further objected, "that it being granted that Statutes made for regulating Trade, are binding upon us, it will be difficult for any Perſons, but the Makers of the Laws, to determine, which of them are made for the regulating of Trade, and which for raiſing a Revenue; and that, from hence, may ariſe Confuſion."

To this I anſwer, that the Objection is of no Force in the preſent Caſe, or ſuch as reſemble it, becauſe the Act now in Queſtion, is formed *expreſsly* for the ſole Purpoſe of raiſing a Revenue.

However, ſuppoſing the Deſign of the Parliament had not been *expreſs'd*, the Objection ſeems to me of no Weight, with regard to the Influence, which thoſe who may make it, might expect it ought to have on the Conduct of theſe Colonies.

* If any one ſhould obſerve, that no Oppoſition has been made to the Legality of the 4th *Geo.* III. ch. 15, which is the *FIRST* Act of Parliament that ever impoſed Duties on the Importations in *America*, for the expreſt Purpoſe of raiſing a Revenue there, I anſwer, firſt, that though that Act expreſsly mentions the raiſing a Revenue in *America*, yet it ſeems that it had as much in View, "the improving and ſecuring the Trade between the ſame and *Great-Britain*," which Words are Part of its Title: And the Preamble ſays, "Whereas it is expedient that new Proviſions and Regulations ſhould be eſtabliſhed for improving the Revenue of this Kingdom, and for *extending* and *ſecuring* the *Navigation* and *Commerce between Great-Britain*, and your Majeſty's *Dominions* in *America*, which, by the Peace, have been ſo happily extended and enlarged, &c." Secondly, All the Duties, mentioned in that Act, are impoſed ſolely on the *Productions* and *Manufactures* of *foreign Countries*, and not a ſingle Duty laid on any Production or Manufacture of our Mother Country. Thirdly, The Authority of the Provincial Aſſemblies is not therein ſo plainly attacked, as by the laſt Act, which makes Proviſion for defraying the Charges of the Adminiſtration of Juſtice, and the Support of Civil Government. Fourthly, That it being *doubtful*, whether the Intention of the 4th *Geo.* III. ch. 15, was not as much to *regulate Trade*, as to *raiſe a Revenue*, the Minds of the People here were wholly engroſſed by the Terror of the *Stamp-Act*, then impending over them, about the Intention of which there could be *no Doubt*.

Theſe Reaſons ſo far diſtinguiſh 4th *Geo.* III. ch. 15, from the laſt Act, that it is not to be wondered at, that the firſt ſhould have been ſubmitted to, though the laſt ſhould excite the moſt univerſal and ſpirited Oppoſition. For *this* will be found on the ſtricteſt Examination to be, in the *Principle* on which it is founded, and in the *Conſequences* that muſt attend it, if poſſible, more deſtructive than the *Stamp-Act*. It is, to ſpeak plainly, a *Prodigy* in our Laws, not having one *Britiſh* Feature.

It is true, that Impoſitions *for raiſing a Revenue*, may be hereafter called *Regulations of Trade*, but Names will not change the Nature of Things. Indeed, we ought firmly to believe, what is an undoubted Truth, confirmed by the unhappy Experience of many States, heretofore free, that UNLESS THE MOST WATCHFUL ATTENTION BE EXERTED, A NEW SERVITUDE MAY BE SLIPPED UPON US UNDER THE SANCTION OF USUAL AND RESPECTABLE TERMS.

Thus the *Cæſars* ruined the *Roman* Liberty, under the Titles of the *Tribunitial* and *Dictatorial* Authorities,——old and venerable Dignities, known in the moſt flouriſhing Times of Freedom. In Imitation of the ſame Policy, *James* II. when he *meant* to eſtabliſh Popery, *talked* of Liberty of Conſcience, the moſt ſacred of all Liberties; and had thereby almoſt deceived the Diſſenters into Deſtruction.

All artful Rulers, who ſtrive to extend their Power beyond its juſt Limits, endeavour to give to their Attempts as much Semblance of Legality as poſſible. Thoſe who ſucceed them may venture to go a little further; for each new Encroachment will be ſtrengthened by a former *. "That which is now ſupported by Examples, growing old, will become an Example itſelf," and thus ſupport freſh Uſurpations.

A free People, therefore, can never be too quick in obſerving, nor too firm in oppoſing the Beginnings of Alteration, either in *Form* or *Reality*, reſpecting Inſtitutions formed for their Security. The firſt leads to the laſt: On the other Hand, nothing is more certain, than that the Forms of Liberty may be retained, when the Subſtance is gone. In Government, as well as in Religion, "the Letter killeth, but the Spirit giveth Life †."

I will beg Leave to enforce this Remark, by a few Inſtances: The Crown, by the Conſtitution, has the Prerogative of creating Peers; the Exiſtence of that Order, in due Number and Dignity, is eſſential to the Conſtitution; and, if the Crown did not exerciſe that Prerogative, the Peerage muſt have, long ſince, decreaſed ſo much, as to have loſt its proper Influence. Suppoſe a Prince, for ſome unjuſt Purpoſes, ſhould, from Time to Time, advance ſo many needy, profligate Wretches, to that Rank, that all the Independance of the Houſe of Lords ſhould be deſtroyed, there would then be a manifeſt Violation of the Conſtitution, *under the Appearance of legal Prerogative*.

The Houſe of Commons claims the Privilege of forming all Money Bills, and will not ſuffer either of the other Branches of the Legiſlature to add to, or alter them; contending, that their Power, ſimply extends to an Acceptance or Rejection of them. This Privilege appears to be juſt; but, under Pretence of this juſt Privilege, the Houſe of Commons has claimed a Licence of tacking to Money Bills, Clauſes relating to many Things of a totally different Kind, and have thus forced them, in a Manner, on the Crown and Lords. This ſeems to be an Abuſe of that Privilege, and it may be vaſtly more abuſed. Suppoſe a future Houſe, influenced by ſome diſplaced, diſcontented Demagogues, in a Time of Danger, ſhould tack to a Money Bill ſomething ſo injurious to the King and Peers, that they would not aſſent to it—and yet the Commons ſhould obſtinately inſiſt on it; the whole Kingdom would be expoſed to Ruin, *under the Appearance of maintaining a valuable Privilege*.

In theſe Caſes, it might be difficult for a while to determine, whether the King intended to exerciſe his Prerogative in a conſtitutional Manner, or not; or, whether the Commons inſiſted on their Demand factiouſly, or, for the Public Good: But ſurely the Conduct of the Crown, or of the Houſe, would in Time ſufficiently explain itſelf.

Ought not the PEOPLE therefore to watch? To obſerve Facts? To ſearch into Cauſes? To inveſtigate Deſigns? And, have they not a Right of JUDGING, from the Evidence before them, on no ſlighter Points than their *Liberty* and *Happineſs*? It would be leſs than trifling, wherever a *Britiſh* Government is eſtabliſhed, to make Uſe of any other Arguments to prove ſuch a Right. It is ſufficient to remind the Reader of the Day on which King WILLIAM III. landed at *Torbay* ‡.

I will now apply what has been ſaid to the preſent Queſtion. The *Nature* of any Impoſitions laid by Parliament on theſe Colonies, muſt determine the *Deſign* in laying them. It may not be eaſy in every Inſtance to diſcover that Deſign. Whenever it is doubtful, I think Submiſſion cannot be dangerous; nay, it muſt be right: For, in my Opinion, there is no Privilege theſe Colonies claim, which they ought, in Duty and Prudence, more earneſtly to maintain and defend, than the Authority of the *Britiſh* Parliament to regulate the Trade of all her Dominions. Without this Authority, the Benefits ſhe enjoys from our Commerce, muſt be loſt to her. The Bleſſings we enjoy from our Dependance upon her, muſt be loſt to us; her Strength muſt decay; her Glory vaniſh; and ſhe cannot ſuffer, without our partaking in her Misfortune.—*Let us therefore cheriſh her Intereſts as our own, and give her every Thing that it becomes* FREEMEN *to give, or to receive.*

* Tacitus.

† [illegible] iii. 6.

‡ [illegible] ber 5, 1688.

The *Nature* of any Impoſitions ſhe may lay upon us, may, in general be known, by conſidering how far they relate to the preſerving, in due Order, the Connexion between the ſeveral Parts of the *Britiſh* Empire. One Thing we may be aſſured of, which is this; whenever a Statute impoſes Duties on Commodities, to be paid only upon their Exportation from *Great-Britain*, to theſe Colonies, it is not a Regulation of Trade, but a Deſign to raiſe a Revenue upon us. Other Inſtances may happen, which it may not be neceſſary now to dwell on. I hope theſe Colonies will never, to their lateſt Exiſtence, want Underſtanding ſufficient to diſcover the Intentions of thoſe who rule over them, nor the Reſolution neceſſary for aſſerting their Intereſts. They will always have the ſame Rights that all free States have, of judging when their Privileges are invaded, and of uſing all prudent Meaſures for preſerving them.

"Quocirca vivite fortes
"Fortiaque adverſis opponite Pectora Rebus."

Wherefore keep up your Spirits, and gallantly oppoſe this adverſe Courſe of Affairs.——

A FARMER.

W A R S A W, *October* 7.

THE Day before Yeſterday the extraordinary Dyet was opened here, with the uſual Formalities. The King began with addreſſing the Aſſembly in a pathetic Speech, wherein he exhorted them to Concord. This was followed by another, ſpoken by the Biſhop of Cracovia. They have not proceeded to the Nomination of a Marſhal, but it is agreed that Prince Charles de Radzivil ſhall perform the Functions of that Dignity.

HAGUE, *Oct.* 13. The Prince Stadtholder having notified in Form, the Completion of his Marriage, with the Princeſs Wilhelmina of Pruſſia, to the different Colleges of the Government reſiding here; that agreeable Event was Yeſterday made known to the Town, by the firing of Cannon, diſplaying of Flags, and by other Demonſtrations of Joy; and Prince Lewis of Brunſwick gave an Entertainment upon the Occaſion, to a great Number of the principal Perſons of the Country. Their Serene and Royal Highneſſes the Prince and Princeſs of Orange were to leave Berlin Yeſterday; and, as they will reſt at Potzdam, Brunſwick, Loo, and Soeſdyck, in their Way home, they are not expected at the Houſe in the Wood before the 3d of November, when the Rejoicings here will begin again. The States of Frieſland have ſet the Example to the other Provinces, by voting an Annuity to the Princeſs of Orange; and, it is probable, that other Preſents will be made, by other Provinces, to ſhew their Satisfaction upon this Occaſion.

WARSAW, *Oct.* 14. The Aſpect of Public Affairs, in this Kingdom, becomes every Day more alarming. The Dyet ſat on the Day fixed, but proved extremely tumultuous. The Biſhop of Cracovia, the Biſhop of Kiovia, ſome other Prelates, and ſome of the Magnates, declared that they would never conſent to the Eſtabliſhment of a Commiſſion furniſhed with full Power to enter into Conference with the Ruſſian Ambaſſador, and at the ſame Time, ſpoke with more Vehemence than ever againſt the Pretenſions of the Diſſidents. Some of the Deputies replied to this, with great Warmth; and the Animoſity among them roſe to ſuch a Degree, that the Marſhal of the Dyet prorogued the Meeting to the 16th Inſtant.

The Day after the tumultuous Meeting abovementioned, the Biſhop of Cracovia, the Biſhop of Kiovia, Count Rzewuſki, the Waywode of Cracovia, and his Son, and ſome other Deputies, were carried off by ſome Detachments of the Ruſſian Troops, and have not ſince been heard of. We have likewiſe received Advice, that other Detachments of the ſame Troops have marched into the Eſtates of thoſe Noblemen, and live there at Diſcretion.

October 14. It is not yet known to what Place the Biſhops of Cracovia and Kiovia and the other Noblemen, who were carried off by the Ruſſian Troops, are carried. Very ſtrong Repreſentations are made to the Prince de Repnin, to get them ſet at Liberty.

MOSCOW, *Oct.* 5. The Miniſters of the Court have repeatedly declared to the Deputies of the Two general Confederacies of Poland and Lithuania, that the Empreſs, in taking Part in the Affairs of the Poliſh Nation, had only Two Objects in View; one of which is to re-eſtabliſh the Diſſidents in the Poſſeſſion of their Rights; the other, to maintain the antient Form of Government in the Kingdom.

Oct. 21. It is ſaid that the Biſhop of Cracow is carried through Lithuania into Ruſſia, along with the

FIGURE 32. *Maryland Gazette*, January 28, 1768. By mid-century, tiny roman typefaces had come to dominate. Frequent horizontal divisions created by spaces, use of capitalized words to indicate subject matter, and few printer's flowers and few quotation marks combined to produce a more mechanical, homogenous-looking page. Format courtesy of the Maryland State Archives.

newspaper. Everything, walking, seeing, hearing, and reading, occurred in the city. And in these ordinary ways, Annapolis made its subjects. But how did it make its citizens? The paper communicated to individuals. We knew, in the long run, that the Greens, who were always there as the actual printers, receded into a less authorial and more anonymous place. But how did individuals, who were citizens after 1776, see themselves as a unified entity through their newspaper? I guessed that the answer would be through a paper whose pages came to look more and more the same, less and less decorated or designed by a well-known talented, long-standing, middle-class printing family.

Little has frequently pointed out that the *Gazette's* type underwent very little change. The same four typefaces dominate its whole history. But I wondered about the implications of that statement. Looking at the face of the *Gazette,* I could see that a crude, fuzzy, very old-fashioned, two-column page had been so changed by the Greens that they produced a modern-looking newspaper well before the Revolution and continued to do so after it. To be sure, the same four typefaces dominated statistically, but the Greens nonetheless also completely changed the paper's appearance. How did they achieve this change?

The answer came from my students' examination of the printed pages of the *Gazette,* which showed increasingly more columns, fewer capital letters, fewer quotation marks, fewer words in italics, and a much tighter and more uniform grid of information. If typefaces stayed virtually the same, what did our catalogue of recovered type show? In 1997, after Little had catalogued 4,000 pieces, Matthew Moyer made a table that showed frequency of font face by stratigraphic level, which produced a chronology of font face use.

Moyer worked closely with Little and used the stratigraphy she had painstakingly established for the site. He also catalogued 2,000 more pieces of type using Little's system, producing a total sample of 6,000 pieces. He then arranged these on a table with stratigraphic data on the left and face sizes across the top (tables 6, 7, and 8). Face size is not just size but also has small stylistic variation. Sizes go from small to large, with Diamond being the smallest. From smallest to largest, the sizes are called Diamond, Pearl, Brevier, and Bourgeois, and some larger sizes are called Pica, Line English, and French Canon. The middle sizes were always the most commonly used faces and were called Bourgeois, Long Primer, Small Pica, and English. Statistically, from the beginning of the print shop's archaeological history to its end, 1745 to 1830, these middle sizes dominated the assemblages. But by the Revolution, there were three

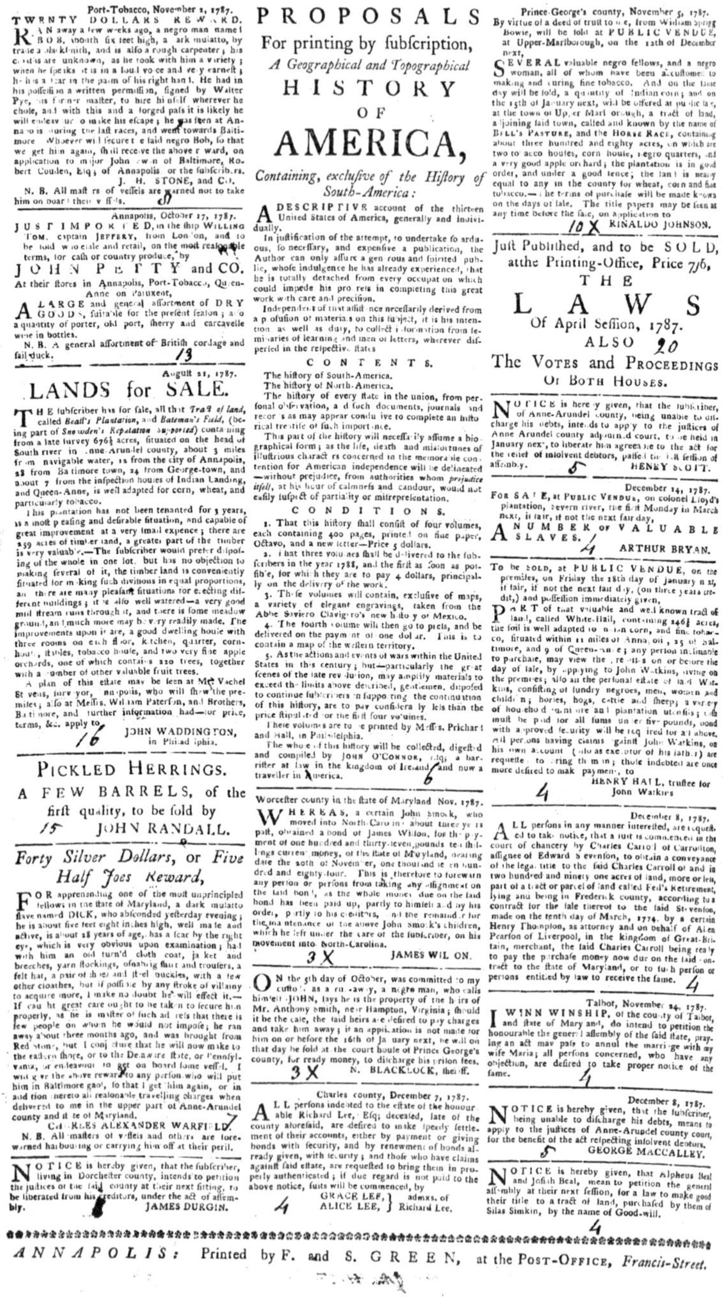

Port-Tobacco, November 2, 1787.

TWENTY DOLLARS REWARD.

RAN away a few weeks ago, a negro man named BOB, about ſix feet high, a dark mulatto, by trade a blackſmith, and is alſo a rough carpenter; his cloaths are unknown, as he took with him a variety; when he ſpeaks it is in a loud voice and very earneſt; he has a ſcar in the palm of his right hand. He had in his poſſeſſion a written permiſſion, ſigned by Walter Pye, his former maſter, to hire himſelf wherever he choſe, and with this and a forged paſs it is likely he will endeavour to make his eſcape; he was ſeen at Annapolis during the laſt races, and went towards Baltimore. Whoever will ſecure the ſaid negro Bob, ſo that we get him again, ſhall receive the above reward, on application to major John Swan of Baltimore, Robert Couden, Eſq; of Annapolis or the ſubſcribers.

J. H. STONE, and Co.

N. B. All maſters of veſſels are warned not to take him on board their veſſels. 8

Annapolis, October 17, 1787.

JUST IMPORTED, in the ſhip WILLING TOM, captain JEFFERY, from London, and to be ſold wholeſale and retail, on the moſt reaſonable terms, for caſh or country produce, by

JOHN PETTY and CO.

At their ſtores in Annapolis, Port-Tobacco, Queen-Anne on Patuxent,

A LARGE and general aſſortment of DRY GOODS, ſuitable for the preſent ſeaſon; alſo a quantity of porter, old port, ſherry and carcavelle wine in bottles.

N. B. A general aſſortment of Britiſh cordage and ſail duck. 13

Auguſt 21, 1787.

LANDS for SALE.

THE ſubſcriber has for ſale, all that *Tract of land*, called *Beall's Plantation*, and *Bateman's Field*, (being part of *Snowden's Reputation ſupported*) containing from a late ſurvey 676½ acres, ſituated on the head of South river in Anne-Arundel county, about 3 miles from navigable water, 12 from the city of Annapolis, 28 from Baltimore town, 24 from George-town, and about 7 from the inſpection houſes of Indian Landing, and Queen-Anne, is well adapted for corn, wheat, and particularly tobacco.

This plantation has not been tenanted for 3 years, is a moſt pleaſing and deſirable ſituation, and capable of great improvement at a very ſmall expence; there are 259 acres of timber land, a greater part of the timber is very valuable.—The ſubſcriber would prefer diſpoſing of the whole in one lot, but has no objection to making ſeveral of it, the timber land is conveniently ſituated for making ſuch diviſions in equal proportions, and there are many pleaſant ſituations for erecting different buildings; it is alſo well watered—a very good mill ſtream runs through it, and there is ſome meadow ground, and much more may be very readily made. The improvements upon it are, a good dwelling houſe with three rooms on each floor, kitchen, quarter, corn-houſe, ſtables, tobacco houſe, and two very fine apple orchards, one of which contains 220 trees, together with a number of other valuable fruit trees.

A plan of this eſtate may be ſeen at Mr. Vachel Stevens, ſurveyor, Annapolis, who will ſhew the premiſes; alſo at Meſſrs. William Paterſon, and Brothers, Baltimore, and further information had—for price, terms, &c. apply to

16 JOHN WADDINGTON, in Philadelphia.

PICKLED HERRINGS.

A FEW BARRELS, of the firſt quality, to be ſold by

15 JOHN RANDALL.

Forty Silver Dollars, or *Five Half Joes Reward*,

FOR apprehending one of the moſt unprincipled fellows in the ſtate of Maryland, a dark mulatto ſlave named DICK, who abſconded yeſterday evening; he is about five feet eight inches high, well made and active, is about 28 years of age, has a ſcar by the right eye, which is very obvious upon examination; had with him an old turn'd cloth coat, jacket and breeches, yarn ſtockings, oſnabrig ſhirt and trouſers, a felt hat, a pair of ſhoes and ſteel buckles, with a few other cloathes, but if poſſible by any ſtroke of villainy to acquire more, I make no doubt he will effect it.—If caught great care ought to be taken to ſecure him properly, as he is maſter of ſuch addreſs that there is few people on whom he would not impoſe; he ran away about three months ago, and was brought from Red-ſtone, but I conjecture that he will now make to the eaſtern ſhore, or to the Delaware ſtate, or Pennſylvania, or endeavour to get on board ſome veſſel. I will give the above reward to any perſon who will put him in Baltimore gaol, ſo that I get him again, or in addition thereto all reaſonable travelling charges when delivered to me in the upper part of Anne-Arundel county and ſtate of Maryland.

CHARLES ALEXANDER WARFIELD. 7

N. B. All maſters of veſſels and others are forewarned harbouring or carrying him off at their peril.

NOTICE is hereby given, that the ſubſcriber, living in Dorcheſter county, intends to petition the juſtices of the ſaid county at their next ſitting, to be liberated from his creditors, under the act of aſſembly.

JAMES DURGIN.

PROPOSALS

For printing by ſubſcription,

A Geographical and Topographical

HISTORY

OF

AMERICA,

Containing, excluſive of the Hiſtory of South-America:

A DESCRIPTIVE account of the thirteen United States of America, generally and individually.

In juſtification of the attempt, to undertake ſo arduous, ſo neceſſary, and expenſive a publication, the Author can only aſſure a generous and ſpirited public, whoſe indulgence he has already experienced, that he is totally detached from every occupation which could impede his progreſs in completing this great work with care and preciſion.

Independent of that aſſiſtance neceſſarily derived from a profuſion of materials on this ſubject, it is his intention as well as duty, to collect information from ſeminaries of learning and men of letters, wherever diſperſed in the reſpective ſtates.

CONTENTS.

The hiſtory of South-America.

The hiſtory of North-America.

The hiſtory of every ſtate in the union, from perſonal obſervation, and ſuch documents, journals and records as may appear conducive to complete an hiſtorical treatiſe of ſuch importance.

This part of the hiſtory will neceſſarily aſſume a biographical form; as the life, death and misfortunes of illuſtrious characters concerned in the memorable contention for American independence will be delineated—without prejudice, from authorities whom *prejudice itſelf*, at his hour of calmneſs and candour, would not eaſily ſuſpect of partiality or miſrepreſentation.

CONDITIONS.

1. That this hiſtory ſhall conſiſt of four volumes, each containing 400 pages, printed on fine paper, Octavo, and a new letter—Price 5 dollars.

2. That three volumes ſhall be delivered to the ſubſcribers in the year 1788, and the firſt as ſoon as poſſible, for which they are to pay 4 dollars, principally on the delivery of the work.

3. Theſe volumes will contain, excluſive of maps, a variety of elegant engravings, taken from the Abbe Saviero Clavigero's new hiſtory of Mexico.

4. The fourth volume will then go to preſs, and be delivered on the payment of one dollar. This is to contain a map of the weſtern territory.

5. As the actions and events of wars within the United States in this century; but—particularly the great ſcenes of the late revolution, may amplify materials to exceed the limits above deſcribed, gentlemen, diſpoſed to continue ſubſcribers in ſupporting the continuation of this hiſtory, are to pay conſiderably leſs than the price ſtipulated for the firſt four volumes.

Theſe volumes are to be printed by Meſſrs. Prichard and Hall, in Philadelphia.

The whole of this hiſtory will be collected, digeſted and compiled by JOHN O'CONNOR, Eſq; a barriſter at law in the kingdom of Ireland, and now a traveller in America. 6

Worceſter county in the ſtate of Maryland Nov. 1787.

WHEREAS, a certain John Smock, who moved into North-Carolina about three years paſt, obtained a bond of James Wilſon, for the payment of one hundred and thirty-ſeven pounds ten ſhillings current money, of the ſtate of Maryland, bearing date the 20th of November, one thouſand ſeven hundred and eighty-four. This is therefore to forewarn any perſon or perſons from taking any aſſignment on the ſaid bond, as the whole money due on the ſaid bond has been paid up, partly to himſelf and by his order, partly to his creditors, and the remainder for the maintenance of the above John Smock's children, which he left under the care of the ſubſcriber, on his movement into North-Carolina.

3 X JAMES WILSON.

ON the 5th day of October, was committed to my cuſtody, as a runaway, a negro man, who calls himſelf JOHN, ſays he is the property of the heirs of Mr. Anthony Smith, near Hampton, Virginia; ſhould it be the caſe, the ſaid heirs are deſired to pay charges and take him away; if an application is not made for him on or before the 16th of January next, he will on that day be ſold at the court houſe of Prince George's county, for ready money, to diſcharge his priſon fees.

3 X N. BLACKLOCK, ſheriff.

Charles county, December 7, 1787.

ALL perſons indebted to the eſtate of the honourable Richard Lee, Eſq; deceaſed, late of the county aforeſaid, are deſired to make ſpeedy ſettlement of their accounts, either by payment or giving bonds with ſecurity, and by renewment of bonds already given, with ſecurity; and thoſe who have claims againſt ſaid eſtate, are requeſted to bring them in properly authenticated; if due regard is not paid to the above notice, ſuits will be commenced, by

4 GRACE LEE, ALICE LEE, } admxs. of Richard Lee.

Prince-George's county, November 5, 1787.

By virtue of a deed of truſt to me, from William Sprigg Bowie, will be ſold at PUBLIC VENDUE, at Upper-Marlborough, on the 12th of December next,

SEVERAL valuable negro fellows, and a negro woman, all of whom have been accuſtomed to making and curing fine tobacco. And on the ſame day will be ſold, a quantity of Indian corn; and on the 15th of January next, will be offered at public ſale, at the town of Upper Marlborough, a tract of land, adjoining ſaid town, called and known by the name of BELL'S PASTURE, and the HORSE RACE, containing about three hundred and eighty acres, on which are two tobacco houſes, corn houſe, negro quarters, and a very good apple orchard; the plantation is in good order, and under a good fence; the land is nearly equal to any in the county for wheat, corn and fine tobacco.—The terms of purchaſe will be made known on the days of ſale. The title papers may be ſeen at any time before the ſale, on application to

10 X RINALDO JOHNSON.

Juſt Publiſhed, and to be SOLD, at the Printing-Office, Price 7/6,

THE

LAWS

Of April Seſſion, 1787.

ALSO 20

The VOTES and PROCEEDINGS

OF BOTH HOUSES.

NOTICE is hereby given, that the ſubſcriber, of Anne-Arundel county, being unable to diſcharge his debts, intends to apply to the juſtices of Anne Arundel county adjourned court, to be held in January next, to liberate him agreeable to the act for the relief of inſolvent debtors, paſſed the laſt ſeſſion of aſſembly.

5 HENRY SCOTT.

December 14, 1787.

FOR SALE, at PUBLIC VENDUE, on colonel Lloyd's plantation, Severn river, the firſt Monday in March next, if fair, if not the next fair day,

A NUMBER OF VALUABLE SLAVES.

4 ARTHUR BRYAN.

To be SOLD, at PUBLIC VENDUE, on the premiſes, on Friday the 18th day of January next, if fair, if not the next fair day, (on three years credit,) and poſſeſſion immediately given,

PART of that valuable and well known tract of land, called White-Hall, containing 246½ acres, the ſoil is well adapted to Indian corn, and fine tobacco, ſituated within 11 miles of Annapolis, 25 of Baltimore, and 9 of Queen-Anne; any perſon inclinable to purchaſe, may view the premiſes on or before the day of ſale, by applying to John Watkins, living on the premiſes; alſo all the perſonal eſtate of ſaid Watkins, conſiſting of ſundry negroes, men, women and children; horſes, hogs, cattle and ſheep; a variety of houſehold furniture and plantation utenſils; caſh muſt be paid for all ſums under five pounds, bond with approved ſecurity will be required for all above. All perſons having claims againſt John Watkins, on his own account (alſo as executor of his father) are requeſted to bring them in; thoſe indebted are once more deſired to make payment, to

4 HENRY HALL, truſtee for John Watkins

December 8, 1787.

ALL perſons in any manner intereſted, are requeſted to take notice, that a ſuit is commenced in the court of chancery by Charles Carroll of Carrollton, aſſignee of Edward Stevenſon, to obtain a conveyance of the legal title to the ſaid Charles Carroll of and in two hundred and ninety one acres of land, more or leſs, part of a tract or parcel of land called Fell's Retirement, lying and being in Frederick county, according to a contract for the ſale thereof to the ſaid Stevenſon, made on the tenth day of March, 1774, by a certain Henry Thompſon, as attorney and on behalf of Allen Pearſon of Liverpool, in the kingdom of Great-Britain, merchant, the ſaid Charles Carroll being ready to pay the purchaſe money now due on the ſaid contract to the ſtate of Maryland, or to ſuch perſon or perſons entitled by law to receive the ſame. 4

Talbot, November 24, 1787.

I WINN WINSHIP, of the county of Talbot, and ſtate of Maryland, do intend to petition the honourable the general aſſembly of the ſaid ſtate, praying an act may paſs to annul the marriage with my wife Maria; all perſons concerned, who have any objection, are deſired to take proper notice of the ſame. 4

December 8, 1787.

NOTICE is hereby given, that the ſubſcriber, being unable to diſcharge his debts, means to apply to the juſtices of Anne-Arundel county court, for the benefit of the act reſpecting inſolvent debtors.

5 GEORGE MACCALLEY.

NOTICE is hereby given, that Alpheus Beal and Joſiah Beal, mean to petition the general aſſembly at their next ſeſſion, for a law to make good their title to a tract of land, purchaſed by them of Silas Simkin, by the name of Good-will. 4

ANNAPOLIS: Printed by F. and S. GREEN, at the POST-OFFICE, *Francis-Street*.

FIGURE 33. *Maryland Gazette*, January 10, 1788. After the Revolution, a few very large sizes interspersed with several very small sizes, horizontal spaces, and a substantial amount of mid-sized roman type combined to produce a more modern look. Handwritten materials did not appear in print and indicate how many times an ad was to appear. This copy is from the Green's morgue. Format courtesy of the Maryland State Archives.

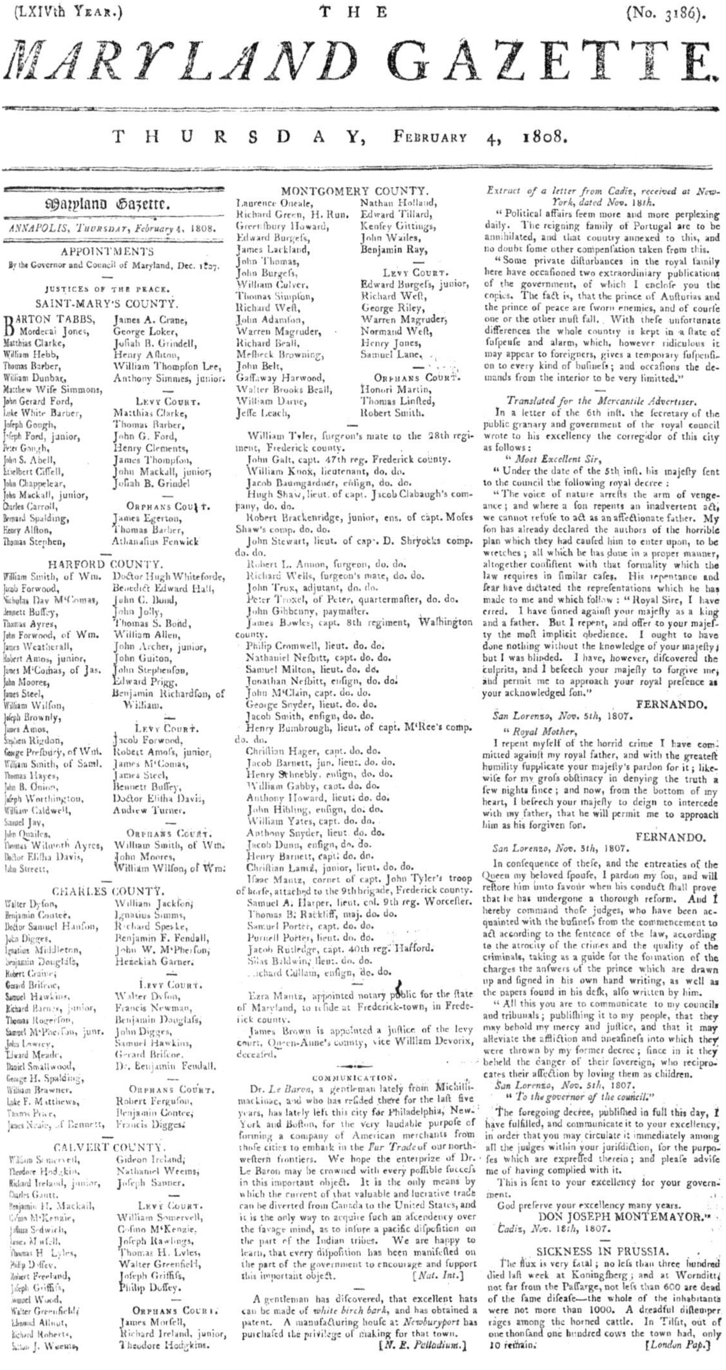

(LXIVth Year.) THE (No. 3186).

MARYLAND GAZETTE.

THURSDAY, February 4, 1808.

Maryland Gazette.

ANNAPOLIS, Thursday, February 4, 1808.

APPOINTMENTS

By the Governor and Council of Maryland, Dec. 1807.

JUSTICES OF THE PEACE.

SAINT-MARY'S COUNTY.

BARTON TABBS,
Mordecai Jones,
Matthias Clarke,
William Hebb,
Thomas Barber,
William Dunbar,
Matthew Wise Simmons,
John Gerard Ford,
Luke White Barber,
Joseph Gough,
Joseph Ford, junior,
Peter Gough,
John S. Abell,
Ethelbert Cissell,
John Chappelear,
John Mackall, junior,
Charles Carroll,
Bernard Spalding,
Henry Alston,
Thomas Stephen,
James A. Crane,
George Loker,
Josiah B. Grindell,
Henry Ashton,
William Thompson Lee,
Anthony Simmes, junior.

Levy Court.

Matthias Clarke,
Thomas Barber,
John G. Ford,
Henry Clements,
James Thompson,
John Mackall, junior,
Josiah B. Grindel

Orphans Court.

James Egerton,
Thomas Barber,
Athanasius Fenwick

HARFORD COUNTY.

William Smith, of Wm.
Jacob Forwood,
Nicholas Day M'Comas,
Bennett Bussey,
Thomas Ayres,
John Forwood, of Wm.
James Weatherall,
Robert Amos, junior,
James M'Comas, of Jas.
John Moores,
James Steel,
William Wilson,
Joseph Brownly,
James Amos,
Stephen Rigdon,
George Presbury, of Wm.
William Smith, of Saml.
Thomas Hayes,
John B. Onion,
Joseph Worthington,
William Caldwell,
Samuel Jay,
John Quailes,
Thomas Wilmoth Ayres,
Doctor Elisha Davis,
John Streett,
Doctor Hugh Whiteforde,
Benedict Edward Hall,
John C. Bond,
John Jolly,
Thomas S. Bond,
William Allen,
John Archer, junior,
John Guiton,
John Stephenson,
Edward Prigg,
Benjamin Richardson, of William.

Levy Court.

Jacob Forwood,
Robert Amoss, junior,
James M'Comas,
James Steel,
Bennett Bussey,
Doctor Elisha Davis,
Andrew Turner.

Orphans Court.

William Smith, of Wm.
John Moores,
William Wilson, of Wm.

CHARLES COUNTY.

Walter Dyson,
Benjamin Contee,
Doctor Samuel Hanson,
John Digges,
Ignatius Middleton,
Benjamin Douglass,
Robert Craine,
Gerard Briscoe,
Samuel Hawkins,
Richard Barnes, junior,
Thomas Rogerson,
Samuel M'Pherson, junr.
John Lowrey,
Edward Meade,
Daniel Smallwood,
George H. Spalding,
William Brawner,
Luke F. Matthews,
Thomas Price,
James Neale, of Bennett,
William Jackson,
Ignatius Simms,
Richard Speake,
Benjamin F. Fendall,
John W. M'Pherson,
Hezekiah Garner.

Levy Court.

Walter Dyson,
Francis Newman,
Benjamin Douglass,
John Digges,
Samuel Hawkins,
Gerard Briscoe,
Dr. Benjamin Fendall.

Orphans Court.

Robert Ferguson,
Benjamin Contee,
Francis Digges.

CALVERT COUNTY.

William Somervell,
Theodore Hodgkin,
Richard Ireland, junior,
Charles Gantt,
Benjamin H. Mackall,
Cosmo M'Kenzie,
Joshua Sedwich,
James Mansell,
Thomas H. Lyles,
Philip Dossey,
Robert Freeland,
Joseph Griffiss,
Samuel Wood,
Walter Greenfield,
Edmund Allnut,
Richard Roberts,
Sutton J. Weems,
Gideon Ireland,
Nathaniel Weems,
Joseph Sanner.

Levy Court.

William Somervell,
Cosmo M'Kenzie,
Joseph Rawlings,
Thomas H. Lyles,
Walter Greenfield,
Joseph Griffiss,
Philip Dossey.

Orphans Court.

James Morsell,
Richard Ireland, junior,
Theodore Hodgkins.

MONTGOMERY COUNTY.

Laurence Oneale,
Richard Green, H. Run.
Greenbury Howard,
Edward Burgess,
James Lackland,
John Thomas,
John Burgess,
William Culver,
Thomas Simpson,
Richard West,
John Adamson,
Warren Magruder,
Richard Beall,
Mesheck Browning,
John Belt,
Gaffaway Harwood,
Walter Brooks Beall,
William Darne,
Jesse Leach,
Nathan Holland,
Edward Tillard,
Kensey Gittings,
John Wailes,
Benjamin Ray,

Levy Court.

Edward Burgess, junior,
Richard West,
George Riley,
Warren Magruder,
Normand West,
Henry Jones,
Samuel Lane,

Orphans Court.

Honori Martin,
Thomas Linsted,
Robert Smith.

William Tyler, surgeon's mate to the 28th regiment, Frederick county.
John Galt, capt. 47th reg. Frederick county.
William Knox, lieutenant, do. do.
Jacob Baumgardner, ensign, do. do.
Hugh Shaw, lieut. of capt. Jacob Clabaugh's company, do. do.
Robert Brackenridge, junior, ens. of capt. Moses Shaw's comp. do. do.
John Stewart, lieut. of capt. D. Shryocks comp. do. do.
Robert L. Annon, surgeon, do. do.
Richard Wells, surgeon's mate, do. do.
John Trux, adjutant, do. do.
Peter Troxel, of Peter, quartermaster, do. do.
John Gibbenny, paymaster.
James Bowles, capt. 8th regiment, Washington county.
Philip Cromwell, lieut. do. do.
Nathaniel Nesbitt, capt. do. do.
Samuel Milton, lieut. do. do.
Jonathan Nesbitt, ensign, do. do.
John M'Clain, capt. do. do.
George Snyder, lieut. do. do.
Jacob Smith, ensign, do. do.
Henry Bumbrough, lieut. of capt. M'Ree's comp. do. do.
Christian Hager, capt. do. do.
Jacob Barnett, jun. lieut. do. do.
Henry Schnebly, ensign, do. do.
William Gabby, capt. do. do.
Anthony Howard, lieut. do. do.
John Hibling, ensign, do. do.
William Yates, capt. do. do.
Anthony Snyder, lieut. do. do.
Jacob Dunn, ensign, do. do.
Henry Barnett, capt. do. do.
Christian Lantz, junior, lieut. do. do.
Isaac Mantz, cornet of capt. John Tyler's troop of horse, attached to the 9th brigade, Frederick county.
Samuel A. Harper, lieut. col. 9th reg. Worcester.
Thomas B. Rackliff, maj. do. do.
Samuel Porter, capt. do. do.
Purnell Porter, lieut. do. do.
Jacob Rutledge, capt. 40th reg. Harford.
Silas Baldwin, lieut. do. do.
Richard Cullam, ensign, do. do.

Ezra Mantz, appointed notary public for the state of Maryland, to reside at Frederick-town, in Frederick county.

James Brown is appointed a justice of the levy court, Queen-Anne's county, vice William Devorix, deceased.

COMMUNICATION.

Dr. *Le Baron*, a gentleman lately from Michillimackinac, and who has resided there for the last five years, has lately left this city for Philadelphia, New-York and Boston, for the very laudable purpose of forming a company of American merchants from those cities to embark in the *Fur Trade* of our north-western frontiers. We hope the enterprize of Dr. Le Baron may be crowned with every possible success in this important object. It is the only means by which the current of that valuable and lucrative trade can be diverted from Canada to the United States, and it is the only way to acquire such an ascendency over the savage mind, as to insure a pacific disposition on the part of the Indian tribes. We are happy to learn, that every disposition has been manifested on the part of the government to encourage and support this important object. [*Nat. Int.*]

A gentleman has discovered, that excellent hats can be made of *white birch bark*, and has obtained a patent. A manufacturing house at *Newburyport* has purchased the privilege of making for that town. [*N. E. Palladium.*]

Extract of a letter from Cadiz, received at New-York, dated Nov. 18th.

"Political affairs seem more and more perplexing daily. The reigning family of Portugal are to be annihilated, and that country annexed to this, and no doubt some other compensation taken from this.

"Some private disturbances in the royal family here have occasioned two extraordiniary publications of the government, of which I enclose you the copies. The fact is, that the prince of Austurias and the prince of peace are sworn enemies, and of course one or the other must fall. With these unfortunate differences the whole country is kept in a state of suspense and alarm, which, however ridiculous it may appear to foreigners, gives a temporary suspension to every kind of business; and occasions the demands from the interior to be very limitted."

Translated for the Mercantile Advertiser.

In a letter of the 6th inst. the secretary of the public granary and government of the royal council wrote to his excellency the corregidor of this city as follows:

"*Most Excellent Sir,*

"Under the date of the 5th inst. his majesty sent to the council the following royal decree:

"The voice of nature arrests the arm of vengeance; and where a son repents an inadvertent act, we cannot refuse to act as an affectionate father. My son has already declared the authors of the horrible plan which they had caused him to enter upon, to be wretches; all which he has done in a proper manner, altogether consistent with that formality which the law requires in similar cases. His repentance and fear have dictated the representations which he has made to me and which follow: "Royal Sire, I have erred. I have sinned against your majesty as a king and a father. But I repent, and offer to your majesty the most implicit obedience. I ought to have done nothing without the knowledge of your majesty; but I was blinded. I have, however, discovered the culprits, and I beseech your majesty to forgive me, and permit me to approach your royal presence as your acknowledged son."

FERNANDO.

San Lorenzo, Nov. 5th, 1807.

"*Royal Mother,*

I repent myself of the horrid crime I have committed against my royal father, and with the greatest humility supplicate your majesty's pardon for it; likewise for my gross obstinacy in denying the truth a few nights since; and now, from the bottom of my heart, I beseech your majesty to deign to intercede with my father, that he will permit me to approach him as his forgiven son.

FERNANDO.

San Lorenzo, Nov. 5th, 1807.

In consequence of these, and the entreaties of the Queen my beloved spouse, I pardon my son, and will restore him unto favour when his conduct shall prove that he has undergone a thorough reform. And I hereby command those judges, who have been acquainted with the business from the commencement to act according to the sentence of the law, according to the atrocity of the crimes and the quality of the criminals, taking as a guide for the formation of the charges the answers of the prince which are drawn up and signed in his own hand writing, as well as the papers found in his desk, also written by him.

"All this you are to communicate to my councils and tribunals; publishing it to my people, that they may behold my mercy and justice, and that it may alleviate the affliction and uneasiness into which they were thrown by my former decree; since in it they beheld the danger of their sovereign, who reciprocates their affection by loving them as children.

San Lorenzo, Nov. 5th, 1807.

"*To the governor of the council.*"

The foregoing decree, published in full this day, I have fulfilled, and communicate it to your excellency, in order that you may circulate it immediately among all the judges within your jurisdiction, for the purposes which are expressed therein; and please advise me of having complied with it.

This is sent to your excellency for your government.

God preserve your excellency many years.

DON JOSEPH MONTEMAYOR."

Cadiz, Nov. 18th, 1807.

SICKNESS IN PRUSSIA.

The flux is very fatal; no less than three hundred died last week at Koningsberg; and at Worndittz, not far from the Passarge, not less than 600 are dead of the same disease—the whole of the inhabitants were not more than 1000. A dreadful distemper rages among the horned cattle. In Tilsit, out of one thousand one hundred cows the town had, only 10 remain. [*London Pap.*]

FIGURE 34. *Maryland Gazette,* February 4, 1808. By the early nineteenth century, there was much more variation in the size of roman type, but a more homogenous appearance to the paper. Very little italics, few quotation marks, few horizontal bars, and a general choice of smaller faces produced a more mechanical look. Format courtesy of the Maryland State Archives.

or four larger sizes that also began to be used that had not been used before: Great Primer, Double Pica, and 2 Line Great Primer. This came as a surprise. And then came the real surprise. Three very small sizes appeared for the first time just before the Revolution: Diamond, Pearl, and Brevier. These findings were the opposite of what I had predicted over a decade earlier. The number of typefaces, and therefore the number of sizes, actually increased. This is what helped to give the newspaper a more mechanical, much less hand-designed appearance. More variation, using both large sizes and small, was required to produce more homogeneity.

Little's observation about four faces dominating the paper is a correct generalization that is also true when the type is counted. Relatively small percentages showed the expansion of very large and very small typefaces. For the largest and smallest sizes, only 1, 2, and 3 percent of a sample size within a stratum were involved. But, even so, by the Revolution, the Greens were buying and using several sizes of type different from those they had bought earlier.

Matthew Moyer asked what percentage of the sizes in a stratigraphic context was made up of the main font sizes, Bourgeois and Long Primer. He wanted to know whether a small number of fonts was becoming a larger portion of the assemblage. He found the opposite: the standard sizes go from being two-thirds of a context early in the eighteenth century to about half by the early nineteenth century. This drop is "gradual and consistent." He sees this as a broadening of the different sizes used (Moyer 1997).

I concluded that it took more, not fewer, typefaces to produce a homogeneous-looking newspaper. Only the archaeology could show this. There was no way anyone could tell the percentages of increase of the various fonts themselves from the pages of the *Gazette*, because it was very hard or impossible to tell one font from another on the printed page. With counts of type pieces by point size, we could know the number of sizes available, by dates. And as a result, we found that some of the newly used type faces got smaller and some got bigger. There was a lot more variation in size. This was Matthew Moyer's counterintuitive discovery, and it is quite important, because it showed a great deal of change actually occurring.

To conclude, then, there was considerable change in the production requirements of the *Gazette* from about 1750 on. Around a stable core of four mid-range sizes, far more variation came into use. This variation was actually used to reduce the visual variation apparent on the printed page. The homogeneity that came to characterize the look of the page

TABLE 6. Percentages of the typefaces used in the *Maryland Gazette* from the early eighteenth to the late nineteenth century by stratigraphic context

Context and Date								Typeface								
	Diamond	Pearl	Brevier	Bourgeois	Long Primer	Small Pica	Pica	English	Great Primer	Paragon	Double Pica	2 Line Pica	2 Line English	2 Line Great Primer	2 Line Double Pica	French Canon
Early eighteenth century (n = 12)				42	25	8		25								
Mid eighteenth century (n = 36)				33	36	19		6	3		3					
Late eighteenth century (n = 23)			9	26	35	13		14	4							
Late eighteenth century (n = 59)			2	10	27	19		31	3		7			2		
Late eighteenth–early nineteenth centuries (n = 236)	1		9	33	23	17		13	2		2		1			
Late eighteenth–early nineteenth centuries (n = 553)	1	1	8	31	23	19	1	12	4		1	1	1	1	1	1
Mid-late nineteenth century (n = 72)			6	25	29	15		18	3	1					3	

SOURCE: Data assembled by Matthew Moyer

TABLE 7. Percentages of spaces used by typeface in the *Maryland Gazette* from the early eighteenth to the late nineteenth century by stratigraphic context

Context and Date	Diamond	Pearl	Brevier	Bourgeois	Long Primer	Small Pica	Pica	English	Great Primer	Paragon	Double Pica	2 Line Pica	2 Line English	2 Line Great Primer	2 Line Double Pica	French Canon
Early eighteenth century (n = 4)				50	25			25								
Middle eighteenth century (n = 39)				33	13	8		38	3		5					
Late eighteenth century (n = 27)	4			26	33	22		15								
Late eighteenth century (n = 33)			3	21	27	12		27	6				3			
Late eighteenth-early nineteenth centuries (n = 230)			5	30	30	12		19	3				1			
Late eighteenth-early nineteenth centuries (n = 452)			7	28	29	15	1	14	4		1			2		1
Mid- late nineteenth centuries (n = 73)			3	18	34	21		16	4		3			1		

SOURCE: Data assembled by Matthew Moyer.

TABLE 8. Percentages of the typefaces and spaces used in the early eighteenth- to late nineteenth-century *Maryland Gazette* based on the total number of pieces found

Context and Date	Diamond	Pearl	Brevier	Bourgeois	Long Primer	Small Pica	Pica	English	Great Primer	Paragon	Double Pica	2 Line Pica	2 Line English	2 Line Great Primer	2 Line Double Pica	French Canon
Early eighteenth century (*n* = 16)				44	25	6		25								
Middle eighteenth century (*n* = 75)				33	24	13		23	3		4					
Late eighteenth century (*n* = 50)	1		4	26	34	18		14	2							
Late eighteenth century (*n* = 92)			2	14	28	16		29	4		4		1	1		
Late eighteenth-early nineteenth centuries (*n* = 466)	1		7	32	27	15		16	2		1		1			
Late eighteenth-early nineteenth centuries (*n* = 1,005)	1	1	8	30	26	17	1	13	4		1	1	1	1	1	1
Mid-late nineteenth centuries (*n* = 145)			4	21	32	18		17	3	1	1		1	1	1	1

SOURCE: Data assembled by Matthew Moyer.

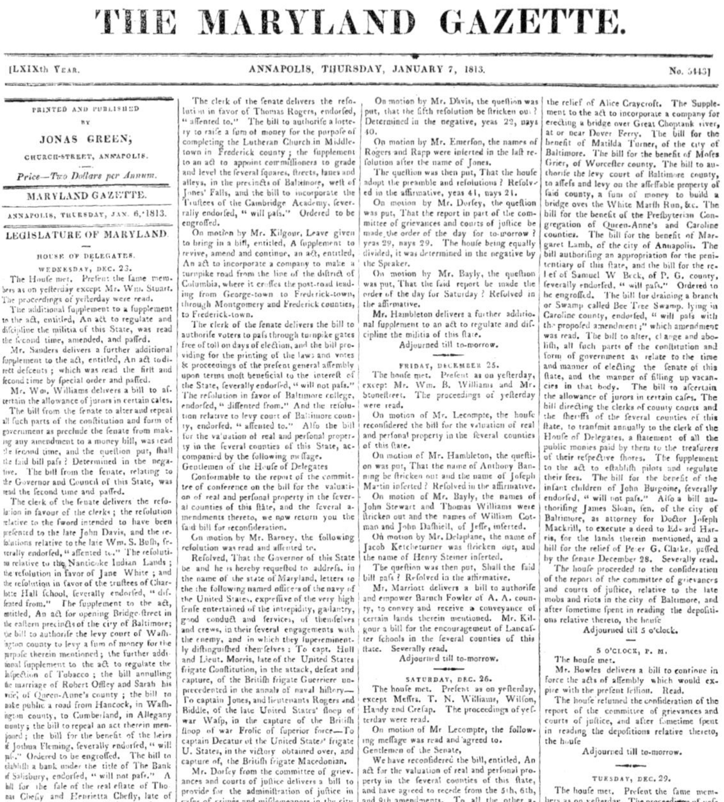

THE MARYLAND GAZETTE.

[LXIXth Year. ANNAPOLIS, THURSDAY, JANUARY 7, 1813. No. 5443]

PRINTED AND PUBLISHED BY JONAS GREEN, CHURCH-STREET, ANNAPOLIS. *Price—Two Dollars per Annum.*

MARYLAND GAZETTE.

ANNAPOLIS, THURSDAY, JAN. 6, 1813.

LEGISLATURE OF MARYLAND.

HOUSE OF DELEGATES.

WEDNESDAY, DEC. 23.

The House met. Present the same members as on yesterday except Mr. Wm. Stuart. The proceedings of yesterday were read.

The additional supplement to a supplement to the act, entitled, An act to regulate and discipline the militia of this State, was read the second time, amended, and passed.

Mr. Sanders delivers a further additional supplement to the act, entitled, An act to direct defects; which was read the first and second time by special order and passed.

Mr. Wm. Williams delivers a bill to ascertain the allowance of jurors in certain cases.

The bill from the senate to alter and repeal all such parts of the constitution and form of government as preclude the senate from making any amendment to a money bill, was read the second time, and the question put, shall the said bill pass? Determined in the negative. The bill from the senate, relating to the Governor and Council of this State, was read the second time and passed.

The clerk of the senate delivers the resolution in favour of the clerks; the resolution relative to the sword intended to have been presented to the late John Davis, and the resolutions relative to the late Wm. S. Bush, severally endorsed, "assented to." The resolution relative to the Nanticoke Indian Lands; the resolution in favor of Jane White; and the resolution in favor of the trustees of Charlotte Hall school, severally endorsed, "dissented from." The supplement to the act, entitled, An act for opening Bridge-street in the eastern precincts of the city of Baltimore; the bill to authorise the levy court of Washington county to levy a sum of money for the purpose therein mentioned; the further additional supplement to the act to regulate the inspection of Tobacco; the bill annulling the marriage of Robert Offley and Sarah his wife, of Queen-Anne's county; the bill to make public a road from Hancock, in Washington county, to Cumberland, in Allegany county; the bill to repeal an act therein mentioned; the bill for the benefit of the heirs of Joshua Fleming, severally endorsed, "will pass." Ordered to be engrossed. The bill to establish a bank under the title of The Bank of Salisbury, endorsed, "will not pass." A bill for the sale of the real estate of Thomas Chesly and Henrietta Chesly, late of Calvert county, deceased, passed by the senate Dec. 23d. The further additional supplement to the act to provide for the organization and regulation of the courts of common law in this state, and for the administration of justice therein, endorsed, "will pass with the proposed amendments;" which amendments were read. Also the bill to alter the time of holding Baltimore county court, accompanied by the following message.

Gentlemen of the House of Delegates

We return to your house the bill to alter the time of holding Baltimore county court, and hope, on reconsideration, you will agree to pass the same. By changing the time of sitting of said court to the day proposed by the bill aforesaid, the convenience of Baltimore county will in our opinion be greatly promoted. Read.

Adjourned till to-morrow.

THURSDAY, DEC. 24.

The house met. Present as on yesterday. The proceedings of yesterday were read.

The House proceeded to the second reading of the bill authorising an appropriation for the Penitentiary of this State; and, on motion by Mr. Stansbury, the question was put, That the blank in said bill be filled up with eleven thousand seven hundred and sixty seven dollars and forty-seven cents? Determined in the negative—Yeas 10, Nays 48.

On motion by Mr. L. Duvall, the question was then put, That the said blank be filled with six thousand dollars? Determined in the negative.

On motion by Mr. Barney, the question was then put, that the blank be filled up with five thousand five hundred dollars? Determined in the negative.

On motion by Mr. Dorsey, the question was put, That the said blank be filled up with [illegible] thousand dollars? Resolved in the affirmative—yeas 35, nays 25.

The question was then put, Shall the said bill pass? Resolved in the affirmative.

The clerk of the senate delivers the resolution in favor of Thomas Rogers, endorsed, "assented to." The bill to authorise a lottery to raise a sum of money for the purpose of completing the Lutheran Church in Middle-town in Frederick county; the supplement to an act to appoint commissioners to grade and level the several squares, streets, lanes and alleys, in the precincts of Baltimore, west of Jones' Falls, and the bill to incorporate the Trustees of the Cambridge Academy, severally endorsed, "will pass." Ordered to be engrossed.

On motion by Mr. Kilgour, Leave given to bring in a bill, entitled, A supplement to revive, amend and continue, an act, entitled, An act to incorporate a company to make a turnpike road from the line of the district of Columbia, where it crosses the post-road leading from George-town to Frederick-town, through Montgomery and Frederick counties, to Frederick-town.

The clerk of the senate delivers the bill to authorise voters to pass through turnpike gates free of toll on days of election, and the bill providing for the printing of the laws and votes & proceedings of the present general assembly upon terms most beneficial to the interest of the State, severally endorsed, "will not pass." The resolution in favor of Baltimore college, endorsed, "dissented from." And the resolution relative to levy court of Baltimore county, endorsed, "assented to." Also the bill for the valuation of real and personal property in the several counties of this State, accompanied by the following message.

Gentlemen of the House of Delegates

Conformable to the report of the committee of conference on the bill for the valuation of real and personal property in the several counties of this state, and the several amendments thereto, we now return you the said bill for reconsideration.

On motion by Mr. Barney, the following resolution was read and assented to.

Resolved, That the Governor of this State be and he is hereby requested to address, in the name of the state of Maryland, letters to the the following named officers of the navy of the United States, expressive of the very high sense entertained of the intrepidity, gallantry, good conduct and services, of themselves and crews, in their several engagements with the enemy, and in which they supereminently distinguished themselves: To capt. Hull and Lieut. Morris, late of the United States frigate Constitution, in the attack, defeat and capture, of the British frigate Guerriere unprecedented in the annals of naval history.—To captain Jones, and lieutenants Rogers and Biddle, of the late United States' sloop of war Wasp, in the capture of the British sloop of war Frolic of superior force.—To captain Decatur of the United States' frigate U. States, in the victory obtained over, and capture of, the British frigate Macedonian.

Mr. Dorsey from the committee of grievances and courts of justice delivers a bill to provide for the administration of justice in cases of crimes and misdemeanors in the city and county of Baltimore, which was read.

Adjourn untill 5 o'clock

5 o'clock, P. M.

The House met.

On motion by Mr. Wright, the following message was read, assented to, and sent to the senate.

Gentlemen of the Senate,

We return you the bill, entitled, An act for the relief of the heirs of John Chaires, under an expectation that on a reconsideration thereof, which we solicit, you will give it your concurrence.

On motion by Mr. Barney, Ordered, That the depositions taken before the committee of grievances and courts of justice, relative to the mob or riot that took place in the city of Baltimore, and the conduct of the civil officers of that place, be printed for the use of the members.

The clerk of the senate delivers the resolution in favour of the debtors to the state, endorsed, "assented to with the proposed amendment;" which amendment was read and assented to. The bill for the benefit and relief of William Harrison, of Jas. of Talbot county, endorsed, "will not pass." The supplement to the act to lay out a road from Wm. Sinclair's plantation to Vaughan's mine run and gun-powder mills, and from thence to the owl branch; and the bill to correct a mistake in the record therein mentioned, severally endorsed, "will pass." Ordered to be engrossed. And the additional supplement to the act to regulate and discipline the militia of this state, endorsed, "will pass with the proposed amendments," which amendments were read

The house proceeded to the consideration of the preamble and resolutions relative to the war, and on motion by mr. Lewis Duvall, the question was put, That the words "and New Jersey" be inserted after the words Rhode-Island in the fifth resolution? Determined in the negative, yeas 25, nays 46.

On motion by Mr. Davis, the question was put, that the fifth resolution be stricken out? Determined in the negative, yeas 22, nays 40.

On motion by Mr. Emerson, the names of Rogers and Rapp were inserted in the last resolution after the name of Jones.

The question was then put, That the house adopt the preamble and resolutions? Resolved in the affirmative, yeas 41, nays 21.

On motion by Mr. Dorsey, the question was put, That the report in part of the committee of grievances and courts of justice be made the order of the day for to-morrow? yeas 29, nays 29. The house being equally divided, it was determined in the negative by the Speaker.

On motion by Mr. Bayly, the question was put, That the said report be made the order of the day for Saturday? Resolved in the affirmative.

Mr. Hambleton delivers a further additional supplement to an act to regulate and discipline the militia of this state.

Adjourned till to-morrow.

FRIDAY, DECEMBER 25.

The house met. Present as on yesterday, except Mr. Wm. B. Williams and Mr. Stonestreet. The proceedings of yesterday were read.

On motion of Mr. Lecompte, the house reconsidered the bill for the valuation of real and personal property in the several counties of this state.

On motion of Mr. Hambleton, the question was put, That the name of Anthony Banning be stricken out and the name of Joseph Martin inserted? Resolved in the affirmative.

On motion of Mr. Bayly, the names of John Stewart and Thomas Williams were stricken out and the names of William Cotman and John Dashiell, of Jesse, inserted.

On motion by Mr. Delaplane, the name of Jacob Ketcheturner was stricken out, and the name of Henry Steiner inserted.

The question was then put, Shall the said bill pass? Resolved in the affirmative.

Mr. Marriott delivers a bill to authorise and empower Baruch Fowler of A. A. county, to convey and receive a conveyance of certain lands therein mentioned. Mr. Kilgour a bill for the encouragement of Lancaster schools in the several counties of this state. Severally read.

Adjourned till to-morrow.

SATURDAY, DEC. 26.

The house met. Present as on yesterday, except Messrs. T. N. Williams, Wilson, Handy and Cresap. The proceedings of yesterday were read.

On motion of Mr Lecompte, the following message was read and agreed to.

Gentlemen of the Senate,

We have reconsidered the bill, entitled, An act for the valuation of real and personal property in the several counties of this state, and have agreed to recede from the 5th, 6th, and 9th amendments. To all the other amendments we have adhered. We have also added three other amendments. We hope that the bill, as now amended, will receive your concurrence.

On motion of Mr. Bowles, the following resolution was read.

Resolved, That the executive be requested to have printed, on the most reasonable terms, all the testimony taken before the committee of grievances and courts of justice relative to the late mobs and riots in the city of Baltimore, and cause one copy to be forwarded to each member of the general assembly; and they are hereby authorised to draw an order on the treasurer of the western shore for the amount of the expense of said printing.

Adjourned till Monday.

MONDAY, DECEMBER 28.

The house met. Present the same members as on Saturday, except Messrs. Banning, Frey, Potter and M'Donald. The proceedings of Saturday were read.

The clerk of the senate delivers the resolutions in favour of the Rev. Joseph Wyatt, and James Hood, of John, severally endorsed, "assented to." The bill to incorporate a company for the purpose of building a bridge over the river Susquehanna at or near Rock run. The bill to lay out and open the a road in Baltimore county. The bill, entitled, A supplement to revive, amend, and continue an act, entitled, An act to incorporate a company to make a turnpike road from the line of the District of Columbia where it crosses the post road leading from George-town, to Frederick-town through Montgomery and Frederick counties, to Frederick-town. The bill for the support of William M. Charey, of A. A. county. The bill to repeal an act to change the name of George-town Cross roads, in Kent county. The bill to encourage the education of youth in Worcester county. The bill to establish and confirm the Falls turnpike road from the city of Baltimore to Richard Caton's Lime Kiln. The bill for the relief of Alice Craycroft. The Supplement to the act to incorporate a company for erecting a bridge over Great Choptank river, at or near Dover Ferry. The bill for the benefit of Matilda Turner, of the city of Baltimore. The bill for the benefit of Moses Grier, of Worcester county. The bill to authorise the levy court of Baltimore county, to assess and levy on the assessable property of said county, a sum of money to build a bridge over the White Marsh Run, &c. The bill for the benefit of the Presbyterian Congregation of Queen-Anne's and Caroline counties. The bill for the benefit of Margaret Lamb, of the city of Annapolis. The bill authorising an appropriation for the penitentiary of this state, and the bill for the relief of Samuel W Beck, of P. G. county, severally endorsed, "will pass." Ordered to be engrossed. The bill for draining a branch or Swamp called Bee Tree Swamp, lying in Caroline county, endorsed, "will pass with the proposed amendment;" which amendment was read. The bill to alter, change and abolish, all such parts of the constitution and form of government as relate to the time and manner of electing the senate of this state, and the manner of filling up vacancies in that body. The bill to ascertain the allowance of jurors in certain cases. The bill directing the clerks of county courts and the sheriffs of the several counties of this state, to transmit annually to the clerk of the House of Delegates, a statement of all the public monies paid by them to the treasurers of their respective shores. The supplement to the act to establish pilots and regulate their fees. The bill for the benefit of the infant children of John Burgoine, severally endorsed, "will not pass." Also a bill authorising James Sloan, sen. of the city of Baltimore, as attorney for Doctor Joseph Mackrill, to execute a deed to Edward Harris, for the lands therein mentioned, and a bill for the relief of Peter G. Clarke, passed by the senate December 28. Severally read.

The house proceeded to the consideration of the report of the committee of grievances and courts of justice, relative to the late mobs and riots in the city of Baltimore, and after sometime spent in reading the depositions relative thereto, the house

Adjourned till 5 o'clock.

5 O'CLOCK, P. M.

The house met.

Mr. Bowles delivers a bill to continue in force the acts of assembly which would expire with the present session. Read.

The house resumed the consideration of the report of the committee of grievances and courts of justice, and after sometime spent in reading the depositions relative thereto, the house

Adjourned till to-morrow.

TUESDAY, DEC. 29.

The house met. Present the same members as on yesterday. The proceedings of yesterday were read.

The clerk of the senate delivers the resolution in favour of the Examiner General, endorsed, "assented to." The resolution relative to an order of the court of appeals for the Eastern Shore, endorsed, "dissented from." The bill for the relief of James Patton, of Talbot county, endorsed, "will not pass."—And the bill to lay out and open a road in Anne-Arundel county; the bill annulling the marriage of Vincent P. Taylor, and Elizabeth his wife; the bill for the relief of Andrew Porter Evans, a purchaser of confiscated property; the bill respecting certain land certificates in Washington county. The bill to stop a public road in Prince-George's county; the bill for the relief of George Michael Conradt of Frederick county; the supplement to an act passed at November session seventeen hundred and ninety-six, entitled, An act respecting the roads in Somerset and Worcester counties; the supplement to an act authorising the levy court of Prince-George's county to open a road in said county; the bill for the relief of Elizabeth Peters of Prince-George's county; the bill to make public a road in Queen-Anne's county, and the bill to sell part of the real estate of Nicholas Carroll late of the city of Annapolis deceased, severally endorsed, "will pass." Ordered to be engrossed. Also the supplement to an act to extend M'Elderry-street in the eastern precincts of Baltimore; the bill to make public an old road leading from South River Church to intersect the Annapolis road to West River, and the bill for the relief of Debby Ann M'Coy an infant, of A. A. county, severally endorsed, "will pass." Ordered to be engrossed. The bill for the benefit of James, Mary, Lucretia and John Stevens Gouty of Caroline county, and the bill for the relief of Charles Thompson of Dorchester county, severally endorsed, "will pass with the proposed amendments;" which amendments were read, assented to, and the bills ordered to be engrossed. Also

FIGURE 35. *Maryland Gazette,* January 7, 1813. Four columns, vertical spaces, a great deal of tiny print, no flowers, and no decoration, plus a clear rational order of information produced a modern-looking newspaper. Overall, greater variety of type sizes but fewer visual boundaries like quotation marks, capitalized letters, and horizontal bars were used to print a paper with an ever more mechanical, modern, and less hand-crafted appearance. Format courtesy of the Maryland State Archives.

was not produced by uniformity of type but rather through the use of much greater diversity in its size.

This discovery could be contested because the numbers from which it was derived were fairly small and more than the *Gazette* was printed at the shop. In the later strata of the print shop, where the newly used smaller and larger font sizes appeared, each new size represents only between 1 and 3 percent of all pieces of type from that layer. But I never bought the idea that they represented minor variation. If they were found, they were used. Because one piece from a font represents anywhere from hundreds to 10,000 pieces from the same font, I argue that if one piece was present, the font was used, and at the time of the stratum in which it was found. But for what and how often?

How could Moyer's findings be used to query the *Gazette* itself? The answers came, once again, from undergraduates who did the research. Angela Arias, Anna Hill, and Laura Figueroa (2002) collaborated in 2002 to study the pages of the *Gazette* using leads from Matthew Moyer. Figueroa took Moyer's main discovery and turned it into questions. Did type get smaller? If it did, where did it get smaller? Where did the type get larger? And exactly what and how did you measure in order to answer these questions? She queried the *Gazette;* she did not turn to it to confirm Moyer's work. Instead, she problematized his findings.

Figueroa used a ruler that measured height of letters, called a point ruler, because type size is measured in a unit called points (Arias, Hill, and Figueroa 2002). She sampled (1) the body of the *Gazette* separately from (2) the masthead, and measured (3) the signature separately from (4) advertisements. These were the four major divisions of the paper.

She found that the size of capital letters used to print nouns went down by two point sizes between 1755 and 1770 and remained small. Her samples extended from 1745 to 1785. There was a lot of variation in the size used for nouns from 1760 to 1775, but there was an overall increase in the use of smaller sizes, which became a permanent drop by 1776. This meant that the print size of all nouns got smaller, which was a very big change.

There were also some new, larger sizes of type. But where? Moyer could not tell from the archaeological collection of type. Figueroa found out. The type used in the masthead was made a great deal larger. By 1755, the size of the masthead was increased by six point sizes. Except for a brief drop in 1780, it stayed large. The signature size stayed about the same, becoming slightly smaller just before 1760. But the basic size for the body of the newspaper went down by 1755, varied during the 1760s, and then went down further and remained small. The bulk of the news-paper was the body, which got much smaller in point size. Advertisements helped pay for the newspaper and showed increasing variation in the sizes of the fonts used. Overall, from 1750 to 1785, ads were composed us-ing a larger variety of sizes. This, of course, required more font sizes.

To summarize, the body of the paper became smaller and thus more visually homogeneous; the masthead became bigger and more prominent visually; and the advertisements started to contain a lot of sizes. All this required more font sizes. We had not known this. Moyer discovered the general trend to more variation; Figueroa discovered what the variation was used to produce.

The main argument I have been interested in developing is that the *Gazette* did not stay the same throughout its history but was systemat-ically redesigned just before and around the time of the American Rev-olution. There was a lot of variation in size of type, which developed around a core of medium-sized type that was used consistently. The news-paper was thus redesigned using variation around a stable core.

We already know that the vast majority of printed words looked dif-ferent by the 1760s. Thus we have already seen significant visual changes. Now we also know where the size of these words was shrunk by using significantly smaller sizes of type.

The purpose of the argument about orderly subdivisions in the news-paper was to extend Deetz's argument by saying that the pages of the *Gazette* were like the top of a mid eighteenth-century dinner table. Struc-turally, they were the same. Deetz links material changes to explaining how a person became defined as an individual. Little and I argue that the individual was the core of the analysis, because in a colonial setting, he or she was the subject of the early modern state. On the other hand, Deetz argues that there was a conceptual change in everyone's perceptions in the eighteenth century and that it was a way of thinking.

Deetz ignores the Revolution in his analysis. Come the republic, or early nation-state, the subject was the citizen, who subjected him- or her-self to the republic, not to the monarch. This was done through the same self-disciplines, or technologies of the self, as before. One of these disci-plines was reading, which became more common before and during the Revolution, and certainly became prominent in the nineteenth century in the new United States.

But reading was not just a conscious, rational process. Benedict An-derson, also building on Foucault, points out that people saw themselves as having a lot in common when they actually read the same material.

They did not even have to see each other reading for this to happen. They did not actually have to do the reading: citizenship's common bonds could be imagined through the simple availability of a newspaper (Anderson 1991, 62–65). The result of having the same sorts of information available—tides, phases of the moon, ship arrivals, merchants' new inventories, advice on how to dress and on how to play music, news from London—all produced an imagined sense of community among a growing and increasingly diverse group of people who actually had little in common. Once these same people were no longer British and did not express loyalty to the British king and army, they had even less in common, of course. They not only had to become American, they had to make themselves into American citizens.

Eliminating the author, that is, the owner of the paper, from its appearance was part of this process. Eliminating the author also occurred when people assumed that language had its own natural processes, separate from a user's intentions. Just when the newspaper became a more homogeneous document, the Greens also signed it in such a way that its actual composition by members of the family became less and less obvious and they became more and more anonymous.

The Greens' submergence into anonymity was charted by Anna Hill (Arias, Hill, and Figueroa 2002). From 1745 on, when Jonas Green began to print the *Maryland Gazette*, his name appeared clearly. After he died in 1767 and Anne Catherine Green became the printer, there were more design elements like flowers and bars and a new section devoted to poetry. She also introduced the phrase "letters to the printer," whose oblique reference to herself is indicative of a process that removed her appearance from what she was actually doing.

In 1775, the Greens' son Frederick began to print the paper. "We," meaning the Greens, was replaced by third person designations, which acted to make the author appear omniscient and the audience worldwide. By 1779, the printer's signature, which always appeared at the end of the paper, was reduced from four lines to two, used only the Greens' surname and initials, and the address. All this was reduced to one line by 1782. By then, use of graphics, which were printer's flowers and bars—really anything decorative like large initial letters—was gone. Only advertisements remained eye-catchingly distinctive, and they subsequently became more so.

If the printer's signature could be defined as name, title, pronouns referring to the Greens, size of print for these, and number of lines used to sign the paper, then all decreased in size, length, and style. The Greens became "they" and thus anonymous. This was one way the reader could see himself or herself represented in the paper and imagine that his or her opinion was expressed in its pages.

Little and I derived our initial hypothesis about the *Gazette*'s organization from Deetz. But I derived my hunch about why the pages of the *Gazette* took on a mechanical, mass-produced, or homogeneous look, and why signatures were less emphasized, from Jacques Derrida (1986). The key was the signature. Derrida concentrates on actual signatures, making no distinction between those that were handwritten and those that were printed. Although Derrida does not add this, in the eighteenth century, handwriting and signatures were marks of character, and integrity. Benjamin Franklin says as much (Rothstein 1997, B1). Signatures showed personality, integrity, and honesty. There was a tie between a person's signature and the whole man or woman. I argue that Jonas Green, Anne Catherine Green, and the family created a signature for themselves with the look of the *Maryland Gazette,* not just with the lines at the end of the paper that had their names and address on it. The look was the quality of design: lines, columns, close adherence to printer's rules, decorations, and the quality and variety of what was published. The design of the paper was the signature, and at the end of each issue, it contained a more literal one.

The literature on American colonial printing tells us that Jonas Green was famous for the way he produced the *Maryland Gazette.* The fame did not spring from the contents, but from the printing. At first, I thought this meant the quality of the page design and production, and, of course, it did. But my students' and colleagues' figures show that the design became more homogeneous, regular, and anonymous from at least 1750. Jonas Green and his family tended to disappear as authors, people with opinions, or with reputations. I began to wonder whether the Greens' fame as a printing family was derived from producing so regular-looking a newspaper that they as editors actually disappeared from public view exemplifying the rise of popular opinion.

Derrida (1986) explains the process of submerging the identity of the author beneath the veneer of anonymity, while preserving authorship and opinion in fact. He uses the story that Jefferson's feelings were hurt, and he was offended, when his draft of the Declaration of Independence was discussed by those about to sign it, who requested changes. The Declaration was to be a committee document, something Jefferson had not foreseen. According to Derrida, Franklin had to explain to Jefferson that, not only did it have to be that way, but the authorship of the document would have to be anonymous, because the effect would be stronger if all fifty-five delegates signed unanimously. For the Declaration to belong to all, it could not be obvious that it had been written by one man.

Derrida explains that in the half-generation between the many signatures on the Declaration of Independence representing popular opinion and the writing of the United States Constitution, the major change that reduced authorship to anonymity had been completed. The Constitution had no signatures at all. No one signed it, nor did anyone have to. It was a common document because of the voting process and was even further removed from authorship than was the Declaration.

Franklin thus understood that authorship had to be submerged in order to facilitate the appearance of commonly held opinion (Rothstein 1997, B1; Thornton 1997), and Derrida points out that the new idea of citizenship required this process and accelerated it. The difference between Franklin in the eighteenth century and Derrida in the 1980s is important. Franklin believed in the vote, citizenship, and popular government. Derrida, no doubt, did too, but also realized that while people believed in deriving power from individual rights exercised through voting, the power of the wealthy and that of any elite did not come from that source. It came from citizens believing that their own opinions mattered, despite the "irreconcilable inconsistencies, controversy, and propaganda" that they read and saw around them (B. Little 1988, 286; 1992, 88). But, as Foucault had pointed out earlier, it was also a result of the processes of seeing written language as having grammatical laws and not being seen as direct representations of speech.

The idea of popular opinion was that citizens—who did not know one another and frequently shared little or nothing except citizenship—could share opinions. For Derrida and Anderson, this is an illusion or a fantasy, but it was the basis for creating linked citizenship and thus the imaginary community that was the basis for a new nation.

Jefferson had to submerge his authorship of the Declaration of Independence for the common good. Jonas, Anne Catherine, Frederick, Jonas (son of Anne Catherine and Jonas), and Samuel Green did something similar with regard to the *Maryland Gazette,* probably in part consciously, between 1760 and about 1810. The analysis of printer's type and grammatical rules for newspaper design shows this. Submerging individual authorship, while appearing to place power in the hands of citizens, created the origin of the state's authority in popular opinion and simultaneously the opportunity to have such opinion in a newspaper appear as belonging to all. Derrida demonstrates that the process of creating authorless authority had been established by the ratification of the Constitution in 1789, a document without signatures, but with votes behind its acceptance.

Going well beyond Derrida and Franklin, and with the help of Foucault's (1973, 344–86; 1979, 195–292) ideas on citizenship, Anderson specifies that ordinary people who did not know one another, but who were newly linked by being legally equal citizens, saw one another reading the same documents, including newspapers. Newspapers contained local items, international items, advice on behavior, and reports on tides, temperatures, merchandise, and slaves to be sold or captured, and they thus created a community among readers and listeners that cut across different languages, measurement systems, money, and political values. Such reading of common material, using common grammar, allowed people to imagine unity when there was in fact a hierarchy.

The uniformity of the printed page and the reduction of the public role of the printer as author thus had a role in convincing readers that they not only shared the news but were linked to many others by reading it. Citizens could believe that they knew they were like others because they saw themselves and their opinions in the pages of newspapers and saw others reading identical pages. Thus, the printed page helped to create citizens. And our excavated printer's type has shown how the page was designed and manufactured to promote the reader seeing himself or herself on the page and not the Greens.

Benjamin Franklin, who was so persuasive to Jefferson, according to Derrida's story about dropping his singular authorship, also partially misunderstood other elements of a signature. Franklin lamented both the deterioration of penmanship and the disappearance of the signature from public writing. Without good penmanship and a signature, he reasoned, one could not tell responsible from disreputable opinions. Because a signature was an authenticating symbol and could be used to hold an author responsible, at least in theory, its disappearance from public discourse meant the absence of a social guarantee. Franklin did not see that the social guarantee would grow from people's capacity to watch one another and themselves in gardens, streets, buildings, and in the social settings where they could publicly practice the rules of behavior, called "advices," that the Greens regularly dispensed through the *Gazette*.

By 1765, Franklin's advice to Jefferson in 1776 had thus already been taken by Jonas Green, Franklin's former apprentice (Thomas 1975, 126). The Declaration looks to us like an enormous experiment, and even more so the Constitution. And they were. But authorless public opinion did not commence with the Founding Fathers. It had been rehearsed earlier. This occurred at a time when colonial American society was focused on the definition of the individual as the basic unit of society (Isaac 1982, 264–69, 273–95) and saw that an individual's attention was appropriately focused on the center of the state: the monarch. Baroque theory in urban design, garden design, theater, music, and all forms of etiquette was centered on the monarch, the top of the hierarchy. The individual was to look to that center, whether in State Circle, Church Circle, or one of the eleven baroque gardens in the city of Annapolis and the hundreds scattered all about beyond it, and willingly place himself in that hierarchy.

To be sure, such an individual had possessions, including things learned, a personality to be shaped, as well perhaps as land and slaves. But the state attempted to capture that individual's attention for itself, thus commanding an individual to be a subject. The state, or monarch, did this by putting itself or himself directly in the line of vision and hearing. This was the era of the liberty-loving individual, but one who was also commanded to be loyal to a hierarchical state. Deetz's individual possessed a plate, knife, fork, spoon, mug, serving portion, bedroom (or at least a bed), privacy, a personal history that was permanent in his or her obituary and epitaph, and many deliberately learned characteristics, including reading, proper speaking, and time telling. But the focus of this entity was the state, at least as far as the monarchical authority was concerned. The state, for its own success and accumulation of power, called on individuals to be its subjects.

The liberty required to own property and to be a subject was also mixed with acknowledging that the state watched. One performed one's knowledge and used one's possessions for the state. This is how baroque theory worked, at least in a colonial city like Annapolis, but obviously also in baroque Rome, Versailles, and London. The state watched as it commanded. The state authored everything and in turn was authored by the deity, so the argument went. Not so in the new republic. There was no author except nature and the citizen and groups of citizens who expressed themselves through popular opinion. Such opinions were a new source of national power.

The imaginary became a real source of power because the citizen watched both himself and his or her fellow citizens. This kind of eternal vigilance was expressed through the advice given by the *Gazette* on behavior and politics. Everybody could see it and respond. The watchfulness had no author, however, and appeared to have no beginning either. Once unsigned, the rules of behavior had no history. They appeared to be a function of nature, the way grammar and syntax had their own internal rules. And when the rules were shared through reading, they became popular opinion. Thus, the newspaper linked citizens, who were to be the basis of the new state's power, with the concept of the individual as autonomous. The newspaper fostered the creation of a new community, whose members saw themselves as free, while watching one another and themselves.

Once rules were placed in nature, or as Foucault shows, within what appeared to be the natural structure of language, which was within the domain thought to be beyond human motivation, or control, they tended not so much to be invisible as to be beyond human action to challenge or control. This is a hallmark of ideology according to Althusser (1971, 158–62; 168–69). Accompanying this process was the one that saw the elimination of the marks, or signatures, of those who wrote an opinion, or the source of any written piece's actual origins. The motivation and context disappeared and seemed to become internal to the words, and as we have seen, to how they were actually made to look.

Althusser points out that ideology and ideological propositions like individualism presented themselves as though they had no history, that is, no origin in a context that would explain their economic, political, or psychological function. This was a way for an ideological proposition to appear to have been always with us, or inevitable. This raises the place of history and use of precedent.

Rational presentations of both North America's paleontology and native prehistory formed part of the process. Charles Willson Peale of Annapolis began North American natural history and Native American history with his early museum in Philadelphia (Richardson, Hindle, and Miller 1983, 22–105). His correspondent Thomas Jefferson, often cited as our first rational archaeologist (Fagan 1995, 29), encouraged both the collecting of material and its exhibition by Peale. Origins were to be traced and proper histories written that could be relied on because of the assembled evidence. Every once in a while in the *Maryland Gazette,* one saw reports of attempts by the king or the Royal Academy to promote scientific work (April 22–29, 1729), such as the invention of a much needed chronometer; accounts of earthquakes (July 4, 1750) or great storms; and accounts of failures by the British government to protect American colonial interests (March 20, 1755; May 30, 1765). There was plenty of history, precedent, and chronological citation in the *Gazette* by the 1750s. It tended to displace reports of the use of magic to explain events (December 3–10 and 17–24, 1728; July 12–19, 1734; July 4, 1750; January 2–7 and 11, 1753). The invocation of history and precedent is like the assumption that written language has its own internal, natural rules. Language may be written by an individual, but its meaning is far more general than its author. So too with history. Events may be caused by individuals, but their explanation can be found in larger, naturalistic trajectories, which may be beyond human control but not beyond human observation or understanding. This reasoning was, of course, the origin of geology, paleontology, and archaeology in both Europe and the new United States. The purpose was to explain how the present came to be and, possibly, how the future could be understood.

While we think of these as sciences because of their dependence on amassed and assessed evidence, the stories they were used to produce were eventually taken to be true. But nobody wrote a history of individualism or of public opinion. These were either so new or so self-evident—as Jefferson himself said—that they could not have a context of class from which they appeared. This is at least what Althusser would likely say.

Because the whole process of creating a history or a set of precedents for action is a part of granting natural right, divine justification, or inevitability, it is as ideological as creating a disembodied public opinion. It is not only a social construct, but is also just as partial to those in charge. Did anyone see through this arbitrary and ideological procedure? Who did not believe what they were being told? Illustrations of answers to these questions can be seen in quotations from the mid eighteenth-century parody of politics in Annapolis in the *History of the Ancient and Honorable Tuesday Club.*

The purpose of the club, now well known in scholarly circles, was to criticize local government through humor, which was actually satire and parody and thus above governmental sanction. Proprietary government for the colonies was attacked through criticism of the governor and his appointees, but this was done obliquely, in the actual body of the club's monthly activity. The club not only elected a president, Charles Cole, as a stand-in for the proprietor, and possibly the king, but also satirized what his role was and ought to be (Breslaw 1975, 295–97):

'Tis Cole, 'tis Cole demands our annual praise
For Cole I Sing, For Cole I wear these bays,
Long live and prosper Cole the great.
May he the favorite of fate

FIGURE 36. Charles Willson Peale supervising the excavation of a mammoth skeleton in Newburg, New York. Peale reassembled the mammoth's bones in his museum in Independence Hall, Philadelphia, in order to show the public the historical depth associated with the new republic. Photograph by Howard Erenfeld.

Still on his Club benignly Shine,
    From that exalted place
    May his most gracious face
On our long standing members Shed a radiance divine.

Breslaw 1988, 468

Cole was a substitute subject for the theme of unearned wealth. His clothing was said to be that of a dandy, and his table was always lavish. These deliberately provocative displays by Cole, explicitly against club rules, became a play on the proprietor and the king, whose patronage outweighed his ability to govern (Breslaw 1975, 132). Dr. Alexander Hamilton noted in April 1748 that "the President himself may be said to be the Solar Center . . . that kindly planet the Moon, who reflects the light She receives from the former, less constant and vigorous than the Sun himself indeed, but milder and more benign. The rest of our officers, according to their talents, may be accounted the Smaller planets and our Commoners are Second rate Stars or Sattelites, that move round the greater or more Splendid orbs" (Breslaw 1988, 71).

This should be read as parody. Cole did not govern the club as its president; that was done through self-imposed rules that served as a play on the colonial Maryland Legislature. Cole is made to appear oblivious to this parody of the state in the Tuesday Club's *Records* and *History*, with his interest taken up instead by ceremonial prerogative and lavish protocol.

Cole's role as a parody of the governor was mediated through several objects symbolic of the contemporary political situation. Club member and historian Dr. Alexander Hamilton created a scalloped-edge canopy for the president's chair, which is portrayed in all the pictures that include Cole. The chair is raised above all others and is intended as a throne. Hamilton made plans for a "grand Tiara or Cap of State" to grace Cole's head (Breslaw 1988, 189, 274). Several versions of this metaphorical crown of England were ultimately inspired by Hamilton's plan, and in February 1750/51, a "Great Ceremony of the Capation" was held, at which Cole was crowned and it was proclaimed: "By the permission the longstanding members of this here ancient and honorable Club constitute and declare your Lordship a head of heads . . . Chief cap and Cap'd head of all the caps and Cap'd heads . . . of his majestie's dominions in America" (ibid., 275). This led to club antics over the proper formalities that members should observe towards this "Cap of State" (ibid., 235).

Analogous to contemporary political debate regarding royal authority, the club eventually began to argue over the role of the presidency— "whether he ruled by 'divine right' or was established by 'civil institution'" (Breslaw 1975, 301)—which almost led to a civil war among the members and reproduced the revolt against the proprietary government by the lower house of the Maryland General Assembly (ibid., 302). During the debates on this issue, the role of the presidential props such as the chair and canopy were also called into question. In December 1751, Cole left in great wrath over the attempted constraints on his power, and a member suggested burning the canopy and chair. Others asked whether the canopy, box, and record book should be sold, although nothing came of either proposal.

This relationship of Tuesday Club activities to the contemporary political scene had been demonstrated earlier (Micklus 1983; Breslaw 1975), but I and my former students Janice Bailey Goldschmidt and Elizabeth Kryder-Reid argued that its political humor was a "veil" for commentary on the political milieu that ultimately allowed members' expressions of resistance to be seen as socially legitimate (see Bourdieu 1977, 164, 169). The club's "gelastic rule" wrapped the tone and topic of its activities in socially acceptable humor, that is, parody, and allowed its explicit ambitions to remain unacknowledged (Bailey-Goldschmidt, Kryder-Reid, and Leone n.d., 30–32). This mockery, recorded by Dr. Alexander Hamilton, is important, because it shows how deeply buried disgust with nonrepresentative government had become by the 1750s and how violence was avoided by proprietary authority.

Even so, the issue here is the purpose of making a history or a set of precedents for action. The Tuesday Club needed to justify its own existence, and so Hamilton wrote a history of it showing that he understood that he could influence—that is, make—popular opinion, and that the result was a fabrication. He thus saw through the origins of popular opinion and attempted to use one of ideology's mechanisms, a rational history, to expose the mechanism's workings.

I learned from *In Small Things Forgotten* that individuals can possess a history that is permanently recorded, even if only in a few words on a gravestone. An epitaph is a record of a person's achieved merit, a kind of earthly social possession. This is self-composed, although we tend to forget that unless we also connect such a composition to autobiography and the beginning of the celebration of the self in the Renaissance. Even if we forget our college lessons in these practices, they were well known to Dr. Hamilton.

Hamilton is important here, indeed, is a kind of hero in my application of Althusser, because he understood ideology, at least one of its apparatuses, and came to a similar conclusion as Althusser, which is the same one I have come to over the long run: even if you can see ideology, you probably cannot escape it. Here is Hamilton on history and its tie to individualism, and what to do when you see ideology and its impact:

> While I am penning these prologomena, to this most excellent history, my genius and parts, are not a little furbished up, sharpened and exalted, by the delightful prospect, of procuring to myself thereby Immortal fame, and a lasting character. . . . I shall share the same rank of honor with Herodotus . . . Xenophon, Plutarch, Caesar, Tacitus . . . and Livy. . . . These great . . . advantages, I shall Enjoy, as being Historiographer, to the most Honorable Mr. President [C]ole [Club president] some degree I hope, above those celebrated authors, who have penned the Histories of "Tom Thumb," "Jack and the Giants" . . . and a hundred degrees above our modern french Romance compilers . . . to whom only the Tobacconists and spice shops . . . have been of late years so Infinitely Indebted, who, had they not been supplied from these vast piles of waste paper, would have been at a sad loss to wrap up their grocery and haberdashery.
>
> Hamilton 1990, 21–22

Hamilton raises his own mock history to the purpose of popular history and ranks it with the classics. Here is his parody of the standard historical discourse:

> From this position, which certainly no man in his senses will deny, may be clearly prov'd, the Dignity, grandeur, worth and excellency of that Club, of which I now Compile the History, since it can be made evident, by authentic Records, that it is ancient as Time itself.
>
> Wealth, a royal or noble birth, offices of honor, titles and dignities, in all polite Societies have a Certain fixed value, and may be called excellencies of the first Class; Honesty, Truth, Candor, Charity, Humanity, Piety, and other such Scholastic terms, which your Vendors of Ethics call moral virtues, are of a fluctuating nature, having sometimes a modicum of worth, at other times no worth at all Annexed to them, according as they tally or Correspond with the prevailing modes of the times in which they make their appearance, these are of the Second Class, their intrinsic worth being very hard to be ascertained by our polite modern Connoiseurs.
>
> But still at all time and in all Circumstances, Antiquity Carries with it a certain value, and takes place of everything else, being an Inestimable prize, for which Historians in all ages have eagerly contended, each aleging and maintaining that his own Nation has the Justest claim to it. . . .
>
> It has been the misfortune of most Historians, while they grope, fumble and blunder in the dark, among the Rubbish of Antiquity, and vainly try to tack together fragments, and broken hints of history, to produce a Chimera, or monstrous birth, which seems to every Judicious Reader, altogether Inconsistent in itself, ridiculous, and Indeed Incredible, hence we have, what are called the fabulous accounts. . . .
>
> That I may evade splitting upon this dangerous rock, I shall lay aside all disquisitions and Dissertations, concerning ancient times . . . and [instead] . . . shall trace in direct line, our ancient and honorable Tuesday Club of Annapolis, from a Celebrated Club, called the . . . Club of Laneric, in the ancient kingdom of Scotland, which was in its highest Glory, about two centuries before . . . Oliver Cromwell.
>
> Hamilton 1990, 25, 44, 45

Hamilton was preparing a mock history that he knew no one was going to believe. It was a parody of contemporary chronicles that he knew justified the circles in power. Hamilton knew what to do with these self-justifying histories too:

> If Histories of Nations and kingdoms then, are only capable to Instruct . . . with useful Remarks and observations, I hope the same may be allowed the Histories of Clubs. . . . [Otherwise] my Readers, if any there be, may Gather some Instructions from them, if so, my reward is Sufficient, but if none will be at the pains to read these historical Collections, which may be the case for aught I know, I am satisfied, and . . . they may . . .

apply these labored papers, to wipe a part which decency forbids me to name.

Hamilton 1990, 18

The hundreds of pages that compose Hamilton's *History* are filled with short essays on society, history, luxury, and music. They have a reflexive quality and comment on official as well as daily life, especially that of the upper middle and upper classes. The commentary seems especially modern, intellectually accessible, and always sustains a critique of the world around him; it laughs at the capacity to give stability through reference to the past. His message about history was that it was composed for use now, not for enlightenment about some distant time or the future. And that one needs to know this or face the fact

> that some other Historical Stuff is [like] . . . the tender leaves of vegetables [which give] . . . that most grievous distemper called the piles, by means of the Corrosive down that often abounds upon the leaves of said vegetables, which like so much low Itch, would vellicate [twitch] in a dreadful manner . . . the Rectum, where it terminates in the anus; and here I shall terminate this Chapter, lest I vellicate [or pluck] the ears of my reader by talking too much in my own praise.
>
> Hamilton 1990, 22

When you finish reading *The Maryland Gazette,* you realize that whoever read and followed the shape of its writing and the guidance of its content was likely to become more and more an individual because it, and they were within the ideology of individualism even while they witnessed the inequities of a hierarchical society. The idea of a hierarchy based in nature was coming apart by the 1750s. The middle-class Tuesday Club members showed this when they resisted the technologies of writing, speaking, and historical citation, which were the technologies of possessive individualism, an ideology placed in nature. When we read Dr. Alexander Hamilton's parody of hierarchy and history, we can see that the the British had a tool for controlling subordinated groups in the ideology of individualism, but the control was becoming partial. Personal liberty and freedom within the idea of a natural hierarchy, at least in Annapolis, failed beyond the 1760s.

When the ideology of possessive individualism was linked to the technology of panoptic citizenship in the Declaration of Independence and the Bill of Rights, the contradiction between a promised equality in law and an actual hierarchy of wealth and power became much more difficult for many whites and some blacks to see. In fact, the Tuesday Club member Jonas Green, who used his public protest against the 1765 Stamp Act to help direct anti-British protests, ultimately enhanced the ideology of individualism when it became embedded in the technology of panoptic citizenship. He propagated the ideology of possessive individualism when it was transformed from a naturalizing ideology to a masking ideology even though he had glimpsed in the 1750s that the devices used to support the ideology were a lie.

When we examine printed and written material from eighteenth-century Annapolis, we see that there were occasional glimpses through ideology. The rarity of the glimpses leads me to conlude that Althusser's hypothesis is largely correct. But because some people do see clearly once in a while, like the African Americans who gardened for their own freedom and Dr. Alexander Hamilton's social parodies, there is hope for challenge and reform.

CHAPTER 5

Time and Work Discipline

James Deetz wanted to know how New Englanders thought in the eighteenth century and whether or not the way they thought changed in the course of it (1977, 133–36). He argued that thinking organized the rest of life by using a few central habitual patterns, and that if we knew them, those patterns would be the organizing thoughts that could be found reflected throughout the built world of New Englanders.

The Georgian pattern began in Boston and spread into the countryside. It featured people seeing themselves—and memorializing themselves at the end of their lives—as unique individuals. Life, full of individuals, was lived in a materially different way after about 1750. People had portraits done of themselves, just as they had one or two of their main accomplishments inscribed on their gravestones. This individuality was expressed, and probably also was taught and reinforced at the table. There was a set of places, but also spaces between them, marking each as separate. This separateness is essential to my understanding of the conceptual strength of Deetz's analysis (1977, 46–61).

This change in eating habits originated in England but was preceded by changes in France and Italy. Because of the ebb and flow of intensity of contact with England, the New England colonies followed, more or less closely, what was done in England. The colonies copied depending on the level of integration with England, Deetz argued.

Because the heart of what was changing was an idea out of the Italian Renaissance, which was the person defined as an individual, Deetz made the powerful argument that the concept of the person that he was studying could be expressed as a unique history, which could be seen in his or her epitaph. New England Puritanism went from a future in death controlled by predestination to a permanent history of one's earthly accomplishments. Puritanism's most dour and controversial idea was of life's course being seen and chosen by a God whose sacrifice and love were a cocoon of comfort and judgment. This unworkable, if revolutionary, idea changed in the hands of the Renaissance idea of the individual's freedom of action and personal responsibility into New England's Calvinistic crisis. With the introduction of the Renaissance idea of the individual, a cold utopia gave way to a transatlantic market world.

Around an individual was a space, like the one made by a place setting centered on an equal, individual chair. That space was a social division marked by a face, a personality, cultivated or learned habits, a history of accomplishments, often called an (auto)biography, a wardrobe, and some warts, that is, flaws overcome yet displayed for others to see as examples of self-corrected behavior. Deetz did not choose to develop these ideas fully, but he did see that individuals led lives in divisions of activities that took place in divided spaces in and around houses that accommodated and facilitated them.

Material culture forces an emphasis on things and their dimensions, and then on the activity made possible by the things, an activity learned through making, using, and keeping things. Such activities are Deetz's habits of mind, Michel Foucault's technologies of the self, and the daily array of ways fellow and sister citizens of the new American republic measured one another, and themselves, in the self-inspection station I argue that Annapolis was. Material culture comprised the instruments of power people used on one another and on themselves. These instruments were important because they were used to teach time, work habits, orderliness, and many other behaviors. No armies were required for punctuality when people told time. My colleague Paul Shackel (1993) has shown in convincing detail that dining habits formed one of the ways in which functioning individuals were manufactured. The individual was made by learning rules and by watching to see whether or not they were being observed. The most powerful watcher, according to baroque theorists, was the monarch, or the state (Bacon 1968, 112–47). Republican theorists thought that citizens were the best enforcers, but some of them later came to doubt the willingness or the ability of the poor and propertyless to engage in this process of becoming individuals, because the poor knew they would be victims of the idea and certainly not its beneficiaries. There was some disagreement as to whether black slaves were excluded because of their accidental, but nonetheless permanent, social condition or because they were inherently inferior. Even if free, they could never be individuals, according to this second justification for slavery.

Because Deetz connected the arrangement of dishes on the dining table to a major social change that had its most abstract expression in the mind, I was interested in asking three questions about his results so that I could study them in Annapolis. What caused the idea of the individual to move throughout New England? How was the idea tied to making money, that is, to European capitalism? Third, could the process be seen in Annapolis? If so, how did it get expressed in an aggressively commercial city?

I changed the idea of individualism to possessive individualism in order to address these questions. The possessive individual is supposed to own himself or herself. The concept of possessive individualism sees an individual as composed of a virtually limitless array of skills, abilities, and traits, which can be learned and perfected and are meant to be displayed. The acquisition of skills defines an individual as constantly changing and never finished. Because skills are separate from one another, like being a good father or the skillful user of a machine, an individual has many compartments. These are separate, and a full complement is never actually achieved. This accumulation and separation creates people who see themselves as incomplete, because they can never see themselves, or be seen by others, as finished. I argue that this social product is a function of capitalism and historically of the production process of early industrialization, where people constantly had to remake themselves.

My original analysis of the archaeology of Annapolis was as a study of Deetz's ideas. This was what led me to develop his concept of the individual and work it out on broken dishes. In my analyses of gardens, urban landscapes, and the organization of the newspaper, I needed the concept to define to whom the garden's and city's views were addressed. The individual, as I have reworked Deetz, was their subject. He or she visited, saw, was lectured to, and was taught and learned. The individual built, copied, and exemplified the laws of nature. The individual was the social unit Jonas Green, Anne Catherine Green, and their sons addressed when they designed the *Maryland Gazette*. The reader as actor was the subject of the *Gazette*. It was designed for eyes, which could belong to readers and users in different ways.

Deetz and I differ substantially on one point. In my opinion, these individuals were not really individual in the sense of having real privacy or rights. Individualism was a mask disguising the social reality of wealth and power held by a few, who could be so placed because others believed in their own special abilities and rights. Believing in such social aspirations at an individual level could be achieved by people thinking they could learn the many laws of nature by observing them. This was the ideology associated with the development of classes of wealth in Annapolis. Maybe individualism was a frame of mind, as Deetz suggests, but I argue that it was also a material expression of ideology, visible in the city's landscapes, printed pages, and dining tables. Individualism was not uniqueness at all; it was the material production of interchangeable people who thought they were unique and believed that they had the personal freedom and liberty to develop to the best of their abilities. This hid the reality of a city's occupants whose wealth was very fluid and increasingly amassed by very few people.

Exemplifying this material culture, there was a trend in Annapolis toward multiplying tableware shapes, indicating an increasingly "modern" or disciplined way of eating (see table 9). Although the evidence for this varied at different archaeological sites, more types of tableware were increasingly used overall (Kristopher Beadenkopf, personal communication, May 1, 2003). The increasing complexity of the dining table—the number of types of tableware, the corresponding number of courses, and how the meal was structured by rules of etiquette—marks the trend toward possessive individualism.

Individualism consisted of learned skills, or habits of mind created by the little technologies of seeing, reading, listening, and eating properly. These possessions could never be completely assembled and yet were always being assessed. I originally derived this idea from Richard Handler (1988; Handler and Saxton 1988), an anthropologist at the University of Virginia, who took the idea of possessive individualism from the philosopher C. B. Macpherson (1962) and developed it as an explanation for the popular infatuation with history, particularly the undisciplined kind evident at American outdoor history museum settings.

Macpherson went far enough to see that if one were considered an individual, one owned one's self, including one's past. Macpherson did not see this as a creation, however. Handler understood that a person as an individual not only had to have a past but could hope to refresh it with a sense of precedent by being in the presence of origin points or original practices, which could happen outdoors in places like Colonial Williamsburg or like the settings Historic Annapolis was creating with the William Paca House and Garden.

Handler (1986), explicitly or implicitly with reference to Foucault's

TABLE 9. Variety of tableware shapes from nine archaeological sites in Annapolis, 1700–1900

Functional variation $(V/W) \times F^a$

	Hyde/Thompson	Victualling	Jonas Green[b]	Maynard-Burgess	Carroll	Gotts' Court	Bellis Court	22 West Street[b]	Bordley-Randall[b]
1700–1750	1 (3/3(1))	—	—	—	—	4 (14/19(5))	—	8	138
1750–1800	11 (32/21(7))	4 (4/4(4))	4	—	—	3 (12/5(4))	—	14	296
1800–1850	8 (9/6(5))	8 (14/11(6))	3	—	4 (11/10(4))	—	6 (46/36(5))	37	238
1850–1900	13 (34/21(8))	—	—	3 (8/6(2))	2 (2/2(2))	11 (71/27(4))	7 (13/10(5))	30	43
1900+	—	—	—	—	—	14 (48/32(9))	—	25	357

SOURCES: Data from Hyde-Thompson, Victualling, Jonas Green, and Maynard-Burgess sites from Shackel 1993 and Leone 1999: 195–216. Data from Gotts' Court, Bellis Court, 22 West Street, and Bordley-Randall sites from Beadenkopf et al. 2002.

NOTE: Hyde/Thompson was home to a physician. Victualling Warehouse was home to a laborer. Jonas Green was home to the middle-class printing family. Maynard-Burgess was owned by free African American workers. Carroll was rented. Gotts' Court and Bellis Court were early twentieth-century row houses, called alley dwellings, rented to African American laborers. 22 West Street was a wealthy home, but by 1800, it had become a boarding house. The Bordley-Randall House was owned by successive elite families.

[a] V = Total vessels present in a minimal vessel count. F = Number of different vessel forms present. W = Number of wares plus primary decorative techniques.

[b] Raw counts not available.

work on the disciplines or technologies of the self, taught me the idea that the self-possessing person was in possession of pieces of skills or items that were never complete and thus never integrated. Handler, however, not a Marxist, left this assembly unconnected to industrial production and failed to see that it was a production line, but for people, and that it came from a far earlier era. He did see that the end was not whole, like a car, but was rather a process that never stopped.

If one saw the idea of the individual as Deetz did, it was frozen in art history as the creation of the Renaissance and the expression of a cognitive pattern he described. If one saw, not the individual, but individualism and its insides, which was the constant acquisition of more and more in the process of making oneself, then the less idealistic and more material aspect of the idea was evident. Obviously, an individual was going to love personal freedom and liberty. That allowed maximum room for what he or she was supposed to own, get, possess, accumulate, learn, assemble, achieve, and display. But these possessions were all compartmentalized and could never be adequately assembled into coherence. It was this potential for incompleteness that laid the basis for constant remaking.

Seeing New England's pattern of material culture as the result of ideology was the major difference between my work and Deetz's. This difference allowed me to attempt an explanation of why, as the towns in the landscape were integrated into a market and the transatlantic economy, the Georgian pattern moved from Boston, the center of commerce, to the countryside. Because I was analyzing a small city, in which we had conducted several dozen excavations, as opposed to an entire region, I focused on neighborhoods and individual houses, and the resulting study allowed me to make sense of the ceramics of the city as a whole.

Our study of Annapolis ceramics was conducted in two phases. In the early 1990s, we took the collections from five sites and compared them and published the results. All of our excavations since 1982, when Archaeology in Annapolis began work in the city, have been conducted using natural stratigraphy, so everything was chronologically ordered. We used only minimum vessel counts. Initially, we took an array of five sites, dating from 1750 to 1820, and then four more a decade later, for a total of nine sites.

Our study of Annapolis ceramics covered the period from 1700 to 1900 and spanned wealth groups from renters without much money to two upper-middle-class homes occupied by their owners to one very wealthy household. All nine collections of ceramics were important because, through probate inventories, we knew who had lived in each house

FIGURE 37. Creamware dishes, teacups, and filigreed ceramic basket. Later
eighteenth-century etiquette was expressed through the rules that accompanied
the use of these modular, mass-produced forms. Creamware was inexpensive
and commonly available soon after it was invented. Today, its delicacy is mis-
represented as rarity. Photograph by Howard Erenfeld.

and thus what kind of financial environment was responsible for the
dishes bought, used, and discarded. I am not so interested in the idea
that money was needed to buy dishes of varying quality. While the prices
of dishes varied, they were so universally available that the presence or
absence of sets reflects a cultural preference, in the long run, not wealth.
While money was required, the sets, which is what I am most concerned
with, could have consisted of expensive or inexpensive dishes. My position, based on Deetz, is that the use of a set was the marker of how a
person was defined, and therefore whether or not a household moved
into or out of the code of the market economy.

Beginning with Paul Shackel, later adjusted by Christopher Nagle
(Leone 1999) and then by Kristopher Beadenkopf (Beadenkopf et al.
2002), we used measure(s) of variations in form and decoration to describe how well matched the dishes on dining tables in Annapolis were,
by stratigraphic period. I report our findings on form and decoration
through 1900 in tables 9 and 10. Decoration decreases because sets of
tableware—an indicator of being within the market—were being bought
and used. Resistance to the market is shown by larger amounts of dishes

that do not look alike. The results show that the degree of decorative variation was low in sites that were occupied by wealthier families and higher for those assemblages from households of lower incomes, as in the case of the boarding house at 22 West Street. Gotts Court was occupied by fairly wealthy families between 1700 and 1800, but by the turn of the century, the area had become the home of African American laborers. Bellis Court was also home to African American laborers, who were not matching their wares according to the Victorian style that others were employing (Beadenkopf, personal communication, May 1, 2003).

We sorted vessels by tableware, tea ware, dishes for cooking and storing, and items like chamber pots. I only report tableware at this point, which were dishes used for eating meals. The number of vessels was sorted by form and decoration, which means external embellishments. These attributes are indicative of function at a meal and style, which indicates whether or not a dish belonged to a set. The formulas that measured these collections were constructed so that high results (relative within each index) meant lots of variation in form or decoration. For instance, if the result from the formula that measures form (see table 9) was 30 or above, this meant that there were many different shapes of vessels appearing on the table. Conversely, if the result was 1–5, there was less variation in form on the table: the dining table was dominated by plates or bowls. If the result of the formula for decoration (see table 10) was low, say less than 10, then there was a low degree of decorative variation present. An index in the teens and higher indicated a lot of decoration and stylistic variety in the assemblage, or parts of several sets.

Through use of these two indices, we were able to determine whether a particular dining table was homogeneous or heterogeneous according to two different ways of looking at ceramics and how they define sets of dishes. If the results were 4 (form) and 5 (decoration), this meant a fairly homogeneous tabletop in terms of form, and only a little variation in style. The table setting had few forms belonging to several sets. Results that looked like 11 (form) and 3 (decoration) meant that the table was more homogeneous in terms of style but with many shapes. There was a more matched and more complex dinner setting. This might also indicate that several matched sets were owned.

The overall results show a general trend. Earlier, households that had more money adopted sets; a little later, poorer households did so too. Renters tended to be poorer and used more varied dishes. Black Annapolitans used a different pattern for a different cuisine and showed a much more varied table in terms of style. African American assemblages

TABLE 10. Variety of tableware decoration from four archaeological sites in Annapolis, 1700–1900

Decorative variation ([(V/W)/F] × D^a)

	Hyde/Thompson	Victualling	Jonas Green^b	Maynard-Burgess	Carroll	Gotts' Court	Bellis Court	22 West Street^b	Bordley-Randall^b
1700–1750	Not calculated					5 [(14/7)/5 × 12]	—	12	28
1750–1800						3 [(12/8)/4 × 7]	—	14	2
1800–1850						—	18 [(46/12)/5 × 24]	170	1
1850–1900						22 [(71/12)/4 × 15]	—	24	not calculated
1900+						23 [(48/6)/9 × 26]	10 [(13/2)/5 × 8]	152	1

SOURCE: Beadenkopf et al. 2002.
^{a} Total vessels present in minimum vessel count, divided by (W) number ware types. F = Number of different forms present. D = Number of primary decorative techniques.
^{b} Raw counts not available.

also had low numbers for forms, which may indicate a cuisine featuring stews, often argued to have been brought as a tradition from Africa, served in bowls. Adherence to this tradition fluctuated throughout the mid-to-late nineteenth century as African Americans moved in and out of the market economy.

The first result was a pattern we would all recognize and something Deetz would have noticed in New England by 1750. This pattern occurred early in Annapolis houses as seen through archaeology. There was a fully developed use of individual place settings at three of our sites between 1700 and 1750. The same pattern continued between 1750 and 1850. So the pattern appeared early and sooner or later was used almost everywhere in the city.

Several things became clear as we proceeded. Deetz's pattern of dish use to mark a person as an individual was found in Annapolis before 1750, which was possibly a little earlier than in New England. Second, the pattern was used throughout the whole nineteenth century. There was no alternative way to eat by 1800. The pattern was everywhere we measured. Because the level of use of sets varied and sometimes declined, I suspect the indices may show that a family removed itself from the market, as well as from the personal disciplines I argue fostered success in it. We also know ethnographically that some people of African descent did so in the nineteenth and twentieth centuries by fishing and non-market-driven farming. It certainly could have been the choice of others, and with these indices, we have had the chance to look (Mullins 1999, 127–54; Warner 1998, 236–86).

People who were defined as individuals were trained to two virtues. They saw themselves as responsible for their own training as a part of personal growth. Second, this training adjusted people to the needs of a market economy. Eating with manners, expectations, utensils, at specific times, with all the associated details, was the equivalent of learning parallel sets of rules about work. These included punctuality, cleanliness, polite speech, learning to be watched, and watching others. Much of this argument was developed much earlier by Norbert Elias, who argues that manners, and thus civilized behavior, arose in the context of fifteenth–sixteenth-century court society and then took on bourgeois form in the next two centuries (Elias 1978–82; see also Mennell 1989).

The person who lived this way lived within an ideology that allowed people to perceive great personal freedom instead of a world of laborers, renters, and interest-rate payers. Therefore, I think that individualism was an ideology, and we can find its adoption by finding matched dishes as its index. This pattern was found first among the wealthy, but its use by the not-so-wealthy began almost as soon. I argue that many families in the middle and lower income groups adopted such patterns as they entered the market as laborers and renters because they thought they were individuals and not because they were copying the stylish.

The value of my adaptation of Deetz's argument is that when the not-so-wealthy saw themselves as individuals and therefore as having personal freedom, liberty, the capacity to develop opportunities, and the ability to grow, the ideology masked the material truth of unequal wages and high rents. The latter two were always out of control, and in Annapolis in the eighteenth century, this applied to more and more people. Yet these were the very people who were becoming individuals in their own eyes. This certainly was the case by the time the middle and lower classes became American revolutionaries. If they had not seen themselves as individuals, they would not have fought for the rhetoric of American independence.

The processes involved in seeing people as individuals who were naturally free included placing such definitions in nature by saying they were part of natural law and thus true. The rights, the personality, and the capacity to accumulate things and knowledge were all resident in nature. Recall that this was described by Macpherson (1962) as possessive individualism. Because eighteenth-century conceptions of nature had long been established as including rules, laws, and principles, there was a well-known focus on these. The sciences and descriptive disciplines were directed to discovering these laws throughout the known universe, in the heavens, in water, geology, climate, geography, acoustics, and in the properties and abilities of humans. Society was also a natural entity, having already been seen as greater than and different from the individuals or groups of people who made it up.

Furthermore, society, as a natural form, had its own laws, which were often commented on by social theorists and philosophers, including Hobbes and Locke, who wrote about possessive individualism. The universe, the processes of the earth, and the societies people formed were all seen as natural forms with laws that were to be known through observation and experiment. Depending on the philosophy of the day, once the laws of nature were known, they could be used and improved upon or observed and adopted in order to be in harmony with an orderly universe. From my point of view, this was an ideological process.

The laws of nature could be used to build planned landscapes and, once built, such locales could be environments for observing and perfecting nature experimentally. Eventually, in the later eighteenth century and well into the nineteenth, this led to early American horticulture and scientific efforts at farming. But I tend to see these activities as aimed at arguing that power ought to be held by those who could observe, mimic, and explain natural laws. This was so because society was a natural hierarchy, with those who understood it best entitled to be in a position to make its laws available to others.

My colleagues Paul Shackel and Paul Mullins have worked out the context of ceramic use in Annapolis and period households in the eighteenth and nineteenth centuries so that the numerical patterns available archaeologically could be compared to written patterns. Following leads from Deetz, and using material from Annapolis and Anne Arundel County inventories, Shackel and I looked at items like dining tables, sets of forks, knives, cups and saucers, and napkins, and other things used to make uniform etiquette routine.

Shackel found that households adopted sets of dining items as early as 1720, including some headed by people who were not wealthy at all. He found that sometimes the wealthy led the way in adopting items and sometimes the not-so-wealthy did. Shackel and I agreed that the ups and downs signal two trends. There was nothing inevitable about the adoption of modernizing etiquettes, otherwise it would not have taken over 150 years (1720–1880) for it to have occurred in such a small city. Adoption is tied to something else. Second, we think ceramic use is an index of involvement in wage-labor and making oneself a member of the market. It is not a matter of copying novel styles so that a family could pretend to be like people whom they were, indeed, not like economically.

People did not emulate the rich because the rich set the trends and styles. People, rich, middling, and poor, entered the transatlantic market in hundreds of different ways, and as they worked for wages, made profits, bought and sold labor, they realized they had possessions, could have more, including rights and liberties, and became individuals as a function of movement into or out of the market. This is what guides the adoption of modernizing etiquettes, better called routines.

Dr. Alexander Hamilton provides the best description of what old-fashioned eating habits looked like, showing what sets of utensils, used with their rules, replaced:

> [The house] was kept by a little old man whom I found at vittles with his wife and family upon a homely dish of fish without any kind of sauce. They desired me to eat, but I told them I had no stomack. They had no cloth upon the table, and their mess was in a dirty, deep wooden dish which they evacuated with their hands, cramming down skin and all. They used nei-

ther knife, fork, spoon, plate, or napkin because, I suppose, they had none
to use. I look upon this as a picture of that primitive simplicity practiced
by our forefathers long before the mechanic arts had supplied them with
instruments for the luxury and elegance of life.

Hamilton 1948 (1744), 8, quoted in Shackel 1993, 77, 80

By 1746, good taste, manners, and a well-appointed table were linked
with many other forms of order, like music and geometry, and were made
the basis of happiness by being placed in nature:

A man who models his Taste a right, with relation to natural Objects, such
as Painting, Music, Architecture, or Geometry, will never attempt to bring
Truth to his own Humor, but leave these just where he found them, he will
accommodate his Taste and Fancy to their Standard; and if he does the
same in the moral System he will in reality become a great and a wise Man;
as he is on the other Side, a refined and polite Gentle-man; By the first Taste,
he understands how to lay his Garden, Model his house, fancy his Es-
quipage, appoint his table, and improve a leisure Hour; by the other he
learns the just value of these Amusements, and of what Importance they
are to a Man's Happiness, Freedom, and self Enjoyment, A Taste so truly
modeled would discover that the right Mind, and generous Affection, have
more Beauty and Charm, than all the Symetries of Life besides.

Maryland Gazette, August 26, 1746, quoted
in Shackel 1993, 71

Shackel relates dining habits to personal hygiene, which included both
brushing one's teeth and using a close stool, a toilet bowl beneath a chair.
He made these extensions because they were connected in the period literature and through their use in Annapolis to being up to date, with natural abilities, and good social graces:

By the 1790s advertisements for toothbrushes, tooth powder, and tooth-
picks became prominent in the *Maryland Gazette*. It is worth noting that
a 1793 advertisement regarding tooth-care products was in the middle of
a one-column advertisement for a "Hair Dresser and Perfumer." Included
in this ad were hair powders, soaps, oils, razors, and so forth, signifying
that tooth care was important to those who could afford these other luxury items. By selling and advertising these items, merchants helped to create and reinforce individuality and a socially segmented society.

Shackel 1993, 73

the teeth serve for mastication, for the distinct articulation of sounds, and
for ornament. The foulness of the teeth by some people is little regarded;
but with the fair sex, with the polite and elegant part of the world, it is
looked on as a certain mark of filthiness and sloth; not only because it
disfigures one of the greatest ornaments of the countenance, but also be-

cause the smell imparted to the breath by dirty rotten teeth, is generally disagreeable to the patients themselves, and sometimes extremely offensive to the olfactory nerves in close conversation. . . . And above all the art of pleasing in conver[sati]on and social life, are matters of the highest co[ncer]n to individuals: but in this no one can excel, whose loss of teeth, or rotten livid stumps, and fallen lips and hollow cheeks, destroy articulation, and the happy expression of the countenance.

Maryland Gazette, August 15, 1776, quoted in
Shackel 1993, 73

Skills like manners, musical ability, geometry, and pleasant looks and dress were all combined in mid eighteenth-century Annapolis. They could be acquired, gradually, by purchase, practice, and watching. They were all argued to be natural. While it is important to see that these skills appeared early in the eighteenth century in the city, they took a century and more to characterize the whole population.

Shackel and I extended Deetz's argument about eating habits to the use of time telling, sound or music making, and measurement of space. While I included scientific instruments and timepieces in the analysis of landscapes to show how the ideology of individualism was placed in nature, now I would like to show how the use of the technologies of precision and self-mastery made a modern individual. My argument is that the use of such items, whether for eating, personal hygiene, seeing, or any other purpose produced a habit that reproduced ideology within the user.

I want to move from sets of dishes to items that scholars still tend to see as luxury goods used in leisure moments by the wealthy. They all measured sound, time, or space and trained the human ear, voice, hand, and eye. They are Foucault's technologies of the self, as well as E. P. Thompson's (1967, 1974) instruments for learning and keeping the disciplines of time and work. I see them as just like dishes and associated table manners.

In order to make a case that such items were the technologies of ideology, Marlys Pearson searched the pages of the *Maryland Gazette* for the formulas, or rules of etiquette, for using them. Aside from the minutes and history of the Tuesday Club, the *Gazette* is the best contextual source for understanding Annapolis, because of the tie to daily life in all its varied aspects.

Because I am presenting an idea of what a person looked like who had taken on the ability to make himself, here is an example of what such a man ought to be according to the time:

Dr. Charles Carroll, who had been about 40 years resident of this town . . . followed the practice of physic with good success; but laying that aside, he applied himself to more extensive schemes of trade and merchandise, by which he amassed a very considerable fortune. He was educated in the mother country, in the principles of the Church of Rome but long since renounced the errors of that church and became a loyal subject and a true Protestant; and in the year 1737 was chosen to represent the people in the lower house of the Assembly . . . he spared no pains to be serviceable to the country and his constituents. . . . He was a gentleman of good sense.

Maryland Gazette, October 2, 1755

By the mid 1750s, rationality, in the sense of using articulated rules that could be learned, was being held up as a model. Individuals now possessed discrete traits that were observable and could be acquired.

E. P. Thompson (1967, 96–97) quotes Josiah Wedgewood on the energy of children and how productive it would be if properly harnessed. Thompson is incorrect, I think, as was Wedgewood, about how to use the seemingly unfocused energies of children. But two generations earlier, people in Annapolis were offered the rules for raising children within a rational system that would produce individuals like Dr. Charles Carroll. While this idea did not cite dining habits, it explicitly included punctuality, regulation of emotions, rationality, writing, numeracy, geography, and use of proportions. All of these skills were learned through the use of the instruments I have just cited. These were no different from Deetz's New England dishes arranged as place settings and rules for how to use them:

The government of children, with respect to manners, cannot be distinct from education, otherwise than a part from [the] whole. By manners the author means that part of education by which moral principles are inculcated and habits of virtue begun, and by education he means that part of it only which is confined to . . . natural knowledge.

The parent is earnestly interested for the present peace and welfare of the child to maintain his authority, and be punctually obeyed from the first moment a command is understood; by this means he will be able to regulate passions, to quiet discontent, and to be in every respect the substitute of reason to the infant til its own is sufficiently informed, corrected or invigorated.

After listing and commenting on several attitudes to be used on and with children,

The author observes that nothing is more talked of than consulting the genius [nature or personality] of a child, nor anything less practiced. . . . The absurdity of setting every boy to write verses . . . whatever be the inclination, capacity, fortune or intended profession of the scholar, has been sufficiently exposed. In general, if those lads who are intended for trade and business were, instead of dead languages, to learn English, writing, arithmetic, the rudiments of geography and drawing, they would obtain an acquisition which . . . would be perpetually useful.

Maryland Gazette, January 3, 1765

By the time this "Essay on the Government of Children" was finished, the reasoning looked modern, even if the writing style was not. We see in the last paragraph the skills to be learned in order to be useful. Emerging here was the idea that humans had variable talents and capacities and that these were what should be shaped. Two results became possible with this idea. One was that a person could be rationally trained for trades and businesses. These were seen as rule-governed professions and they produced wage-workers. Second, the whole educational process was neither inevitable nor derived from a natural hierarchy. That it did sustain a hierarchy is clear, but what people thought and said they were doing was discovering the genius—one's personal inclination—not producing a working class. Both trends were actually occurring: a working class was being produced through these educational ideas, but one whose members thought they were individuals.

Items by which one learned the technologies that made people into individuals were widely available early. To show these methods, William Parks advertised in 1730:

Bibles and Common Prayer Books of several sizes, some with the old and others with the new version of the psalms . . . testaments, psalters, spelling books, primers, hornbooks; book of devotions, . . . grammars and construing books; large and small copy books, with copies ready wrote in several curious hands for youth to learn to write by . . . minute books, overtures and songs with notes printed to them on copperplates . . . history books, arithmetic books and many other useful books.

Maryland Gazette, October 13–20, 1730

Here are divisions into religion, spelling, reading, writing, praying, designing or drawing, copying, dancing, playing music, singing, and learning history and arithmetic. This was modern, rational behavior. It was segmented, filled with rules to be copied, learned, and reproduced.

Furthermore, the practice of scientific, or experimental, observation for practical aims involved a wide range of human behaviors. Nevertheless, involved in all this observing, fixing, and discovering rules was the production of segmented, pragmatic, and routinized people.

A chronometer that kept Greenwich mean time at sea and that, with a nautical almanac, could successfully locate east-west position, or longitude, was not successfully invented until the 1760s, but over thirty years earlier, John Smith, a Maryland experimenter, no doubt motivated by the prize of £20,000 offered in Britain for such an invention, sought to come up with a device, incorporating a clock and other mechanisms, to be used at sea for this purpose. He reported this attempt to understand nature for useful purposes:

> Many have been the attempts . . . of finding the longitude at sea: so that to attempt such a discovery is now looked upon as madness and folly . . .
> I . . . have not only attempted to search thereof, but do assume to the possibility of attaining the same . . . I (by God's assistance) will discover it to any such as are capable of understanding the same. . . .
> I shall conclude . . . that what I have attained, I acknowledge God to be the giver of, (and not man) and therefore unto God I return my thanks. . . .
> Cecil County, May 22, 1729, John Smith.
>
> *Maryland Gazette*, May 20–27, 1729

The experiments in farming and livestock raising carried on by Chesapeake men and women throughout the second half of the eighteenth century are comparable. Smith's chronometer was like the work, often reported as experiments on their plantations, by founding fathers like Washington and Jefferson. Much of this work involved improving agriculture, but it also included machinery. In order to do any of this, people had to be willing to train themselves in measurement and then to make measured observations.

An advertisement in 1730 suggests how an individual could train him- or herself in the disciplines of daily life:

> Lately published . . . [and] lately imported by William Parks from London, The Dealers Pocket Companion. Containing tables for the Ready knowing the amount , or value of any commodity, either bought or sold, by the pound, ell, yard, ounce, or any other thing, under what denomination so ever, from a farthing to twenty shillings . . .
> The Virginia and Maryland Almanac. Showing the time of sun-rising and setting, length of days, new and full moon, eclipses, fixed and moveable feasts, stars rising and setting, weather, days of the several courts, etc. For the year of our Lord Christ, 1731 . . . Price 6 d. or 4 s. per dozen.
>
> *Maryland Gazette*, October 13–20, 1730

The first guide enabled quick calculation of commodities, plus their exchange value. The point is not only that there were a half dozen com-

mon currencies, including tobacco, but also that speed was tied to exactness in a way that made exchange a function of time. Money could
be made and spent better if things, including money itself, were speed-
ily interchangeable.

The second guide described how to use the major heavenly bodies as
interchangeable predictors of the calendar, including the civil courts. Thus
the use of the law, the calendar, and astronomical bodies was made to
appear meshed, and as they became enmeshed in the same measures, they
gave a sense of predictability to people's daily lives.

How was one learn to use these guides, almanacs, instruments, and
etiquettes? The answer was through lessons, daily practice, often recorded
in a daybook, and through classes that demonstrated experiments. Advertisements like the following one in Annapolis in 1749 for a course of
experiments on the subject of electricity were common enough and also
appeared in eighteenth-century Britain. Two elements are apparent here.
One is the ready availability to the public of disciplinary precision, and
the other is that the knowledge was promoted as easy to assimilate:

> Notice is hereby given to the curious, . . . A course of experiments on the
> newly discovered electrical fire; containing . . . a number of new ones lately
> made in Philadelphia; by which several of the principal properties of this
> wonderful fire are demonstrated; viz.
>   That it is an element, intimately united with all other matter. . . .
>   That although it will fire inflammable bodies, itself has no sensible heat.
>   That it doth not, like common matter, take up any perceptible time in
> passing through great portions of space. . . .
>   That it will live in water. . . .
>   To be shown, an artificial spider, animated by electrical fire, acting like
> a live one, and endeavoring to catch a fly. . . .
>   Various representations of lightning, the cause and effects of which will
> be explained by a more probable hypothesis than has hither to appeared;
> and some useful instructions given how to avoid the danger of it. . . .
>   Eight musical bells rung by an electrical phial. . . .
>   A battery of eleven guns discharged by fire issuing out of a man's
> forefinger. . . .
>   The price . . . a single person five shillings.
>   Any gentleman proposing a new experiment may have it tried at a va-
> cant time; and the reasons, as far as hitherto known, of every operation,
> will be given at leisure to curious inquirers, by . . . The Operator.
>
> *Maryland Gazette,* May 24, 1749

Electricity was the topic here for personal observation, individual experiment, and questioning, all in a framework of entertainment. Such
public demonstrations presented the developing possessive individual

with an environment in which he or she could come to know nature simply, directly, and convincingly. There were also practical advantages, such as learning to avoid the dangers of lightning, and these probably added to the popular success of the demonstrations. There is no inference in this ad that these experiments will make the observer either more efficient or more socially adept. But in order to find these demonstrations acceptable, one already had to have internalized the whole idea of personal growth through absorbing natural, precise knowledge achieved on an experimental basis.

If electrical experiments were not available except through public demonstrations, many others could be performed at home whenever their practical value permitted. Advertised as useful to anyone in the city or countryside who had to deal with land, the *Farmer's Companion* of 1760 promised

> Directions on how to set off any one or everyone, of the points of the compass, or any of the degrees, even in a strange place, without any instrument of any kind, so easily apprehended, that a man of the least ingenuity, with a small share of learning, may be directed in a few minutes how to set off one or two courses, so true as to correct the compass.
>
> II. How to tell the true distance to or from any one or several object or objects; and the true distance they are from one another, without any instrument.
>
> III. How to make a circle or circumference divide itself into points or degrees. . . .
>
> IV. How to make a square to run land without any compass.
>
> V. A sure and certain method for setting clocks and watches, without any regard to the time of year, or latitude of the place. . . . By Abraham Milton, Inspector, at Chestertown [Maryland]
>
> *Maryland Gazette,* April 10, 1760

This pocket guide was based on assuming a grid that preexisted over land and water using the heavenly bodies and their predictability as the nodes. With it, the whole surface of the earth was conceived of as divisible and subdivisible into an infinite series of lines, joining one another in predictable ways. The *Farmer's Companion* thus created the same sense of precision and interchangeability that electrical experiments did for matter and that a ready reckoner like the *Dealers Pocket Companion* did for money and commodities. This ad and others proclaimed the infinite divisibility of the physical and cultural worlds by rational means, a process that could be learned and mastered by the individual, they suggested.

Medicine had not been fully professionalized in the 1760s, and training in it was remarkably public. In the following advertisement, we can see its divisions, and that its basis in profit-making had not yet been hidden by guild-like professionalization.

> A course of anatomical lectures will be exhibited this winter in Philadelphia, for the improvement of young gentlemen, now studying physic and surgery in America.
>
> The course will consist of about sixty lectures, in which the situation, figure and structure of the human body will be demonstrated, . . . their respective uses explained, and their diseases, with . . . method of cure . . . ; all the necessary operations in surgery will be performed . . . and the whole conclude with a few plain directions in the practice of midwifery. . . .
>
> Each person that attends only the lectures, to pay six pistoles. Those who intend also to learn the arts of dissecting and injecting, to pay ten pistoles.
>
> *Maryland Gazette*, October 6, 1763

Public and semi-public lectures and demonstrations like these were regularly advertised and commonly held in American cities. They continued into the nineteenth century and were based on a mixture of public education, entertainment, reason, and direct experience. Reason and experience were themselves dependent upon seeing the world in rationalized units. Such units took space and chronology, or time, as major dimensions and subdivided much of the observable world into what were taken to be natural, preexisting units, like the individual himself.

The discipline to be produced by using rules embedded in learning, experience, and careful, free choice appeared quite early in the *Gazette*. An entry from 1756 illustrates how learning and knowledge were to be acquired and used. The point here is not the external means of imposing discipline, which were easy enough to see, but rather the process of imposing self-discipline. There could never be enough force to make external discipline work; but there was always enough force for it to work as soon as, and as long as, discipline was a matter of self-directed effort at self-fulfillment:

> It is no shame not to know that which one has not had the opportunity of learning; but it is scandalous to possess knowledge and remain ignorant . . . and by your own heedful observation, you may the sooner make a good improvement of your time; and you would do well to get yourself provided with some of the best books, describing the modern way of military discipline, for books are great assistance to those who every day compare their reading and practice. . . .
>
> A good commander will use his soldiers, just as a good father uses his children; and he who governs otherwise, through covetousness, negligence, pride, or ill-nature, shall never get any great honor himself. . . . It is in dis-

pensing rewards and punishments, which keeps the world in good order. They never had their business well done, who through an excess of goodness reward mean services too highly, or punish great miscarriages lightly. Therefore as you must take care of the back and the belly, the pay and provisions of your soldiers, so you ought to be very severe in your discipline; the two former will gain you the love of your men, the latter their fear, and all mixed together, produce complete obedience.

Maryland Gazette, December 2, 1756

On the face of it, the subject here is leading soldiers and what an officer can learn and how. But the nature of a discipline, its roots and effect, and ultimately its impact on family life are clear in the metaphor of a father and his children. The place of books in the systematic comparison of practice, advice, and shared knowledge shows how rational categories are routinized, and embedded in experience, rather than in nature or the divine.

What was printed in the pages of the *Gazette* that both appeared authorless and shaped people as individuals, using disciplines people thought would make them more productive? In other words, how were people instructed so that they internalized the ideology of individualism and the hierarchy that went along with it?

The rules for how to be a female in the eighteenth century are the clearest expression we have from Annapolis of the mix of rationality and hierarchy, particularly for creating its lower end. We now call this sexism. The following quotation exemplifies how women were to be placed in an inferior position in a natural-appearing hierarchy:

I intimated my design of improving the fair sex by giving some finishing touches to them who are already the most beautiful pieces in human nature: I propose to divert their minds from useless trifles, and instead thereof [fill] their breasts with valuable knowledge . . . to consort upon the level with the men in their . . . reason.

How unmerciful is that custom which for many ages has secluded the most admirable creatures on earth from the divine pleasure of learning. . . . How rarely are they taught or inured to think out of the common way, and beyond the [?] legend of the nursery. . . .

To rectify these defects, I would earnestly advise them to read . . . from books that they may receive such improvements as will make them lovely. . . . Good writers have it in their power to furnish the tender sex with charms more lasting than those which they derive from beauty. . . . I shall . . . endeavor to entertain them . . . and entice them into reading . . . with a set of histories collected from the records of a powerful invisible people . . . fairies.

. . . a country woman . . . was delivered of a daughter . . . the fairy [gave] the mother . . . your choice: the child . . . shall be exquisitely handsome, excel in wit more than in beauty, and be queen of a mighty empire, but withall [be] unhappy: or . . . shall be an ordinary ugly country creature like yourself but contented with her condition. The mother immediately chose wit and beauty for her daughter, at the hazard of misfortune.

Maryland Gazette, December 10, 1728

The writer goes on to tell how the daughter was chosen by a king to be his queen, the king died, the queen ruled, but had a mother-in-law called Invidessa, who was "jealous of her daughter-in-law." The mother-in-law was about to murder the daughter-in-law when the fairy asked, "[A]re you willing to renounce that beauty, quit the title of a queen, return to your village . . . contented to live an ugly, poor, unknown creature at her village where she tended sheep [?]" She accepted and "thought of herself as happy with her little flock" (ibid.).

In 1749, women were still meant to be mute, a condition brought about through an explicitly enforced and internalized self-discipline:

A cordial for the ladies . . . Miss Molly . . . was fair and young, had wealth and charms,—but then she had a tongue! . . . with snarling meals, and each a separate bed,

> To an old uncle of, she would complain,
> Beg his advice, and scarce from tears refrain,
> Old Wisewood smoked the matter as it was,
> "Cheer up (cried he) and I'll remove the cause,
> A wondrous spring within my garden grows,
> Of sovereign virtue [?] to compose . . .
> Strange are the effects, the qualities divine,
> Tis water called, but worth its weight in wine . . .
> Three spoonfuls take, hold in your mouth, then mum:
> Smile and look pleased when he [husband] shall rage and scold,
> Still in your mouth the healing cordial hold,
> One month this sympathetic medicine tried,
> He'll grow a lover, you a happy bride. . . .
> The water's water:—be thy self thy friend,
> Such beauty would the coldest husband warm,
> But your provoking tongue undoes the charm:
> Be silent and complying, you'll soon find
> Sir John [the husband] . . . will be kind."

Maryland Gazette, November 8, 1749

In a man, similar disciplines produced a more elevated result:

Mr. Thomas Ringgold, late of Chestertown, merchant and one of the Delegates of Kent County. He discharged the trust reposed in him by the people in their appointment of him to serve in that elevated department with fidelity, and yet did not acquire more esteem, respect and honor from his public than private conduct. His extreme sensibility disposed him to beneficence, while prudence, smiling on his unwearied diligence, crowned his labors with a great fortune, which confirmed him a real friend to the poor. Nor was his liberality confined here alone; many of his relatives largely participated in his wealth, and public contributions flourished on the fruits of his industry. But it would be needless to enumerate . . . his virtues.

Maryland Gazette, April 9, 1772

These were the virtues of self-disciplined people who saw themselves as and made themselves into individuals, as well as members of their class. This whole book is about making sense out of artifacts from Annapolis so that historical Annapolis will itself make more sense. Broken pieces of dishes are important to archaeologists because they are used, universally, to date the deposits they are found in. They make sense to other people because we all eat from them. We also know from childhood and child rearing that table manners are wrapped around the items on the table top and all are combined to civilize people so that individuals are predictable and, in turn, recognize the efforts of others to reciprocate.

The case with African Americans is rather different, and in the long run, rather more revolutionary. Many of my former students have studied with African Americans in Annapolis, whose archaeology dates from 1790 to the present, as is apparent from our excavations. The material on ceramics and dining I cite here comes from Paul Mullins's analysis (1999) of the archaeology of the Maynard-Burgess House in the city. Mark Warner (1998) also analyzed material from this same property, and I borrow from his material as well.

The archaeological material available from Mullins and Warner dates from the second half of the nineteenth century and continues well into the twentieth. The ceramics I have used in this discussion of discipline begin in the eighteenth century, continue well into the nineteenth, and end around 1900. There is some overlap with Mullins and Warner's (1993a) materials from the Maynard-Burgess House.

Mullins and Warner mount an argument that is crucial to placing ceramics in the context of daily domestic use. For urban African Americans, especially those who were free, which was a large percentage of those in nineteenth-century Annapolis, the problem was how to be free and subordinate simultaneously. Although American racism and slavery were far more severe than American class distinctions, the problem I have been addressing throughout this book is the making and reproduction of a class of workers who thought that they were free but who were in fact willing wage workers.

Mullins and Warner described the racism of Annapolis throughout the nineteenth and twentieth centuries and the efforts of people like John and Maria Maynard and their family to be middle-class in the face of white society's conflicted desires to keep them at the racial bottom and have them be customers simultaneously.

Mullins (1999, 127–54) found that the ceramics used by the middle-class Maynard and Burgess families represented a mixed dining table. Dishes were neither matched nor of the same age. Our oral histories of African Americans in Annapolis found that middle-class families sought, bought, kept, and used sets that came out on special occasions, such as when the minister came to eat with them. Such Victorian ware has very little archaeological presence. Two patterns of ceramic use are evident. The sets used for formal dining events were Georgian, as described by Deetz for the eighteenth century, and Victorian, which was an elaborated version of Georgian etiquette that still featured individual place settings and matched dishes. The dishes predominating in the kitchen for daily use were not so regular, and Mark Warner (1998) has shown that food was from a different tradition, featuring stews, more pork, more fish, and a connection to African cuisine. We do not know from Annapolis how slaves used ceramics, so from that point of view, I cannot say whether they saw two traditions operating at once among themselves.

Both Mullins and Warner draw heavily on black intellectuals to describe the world free African Americans lived in, which we obtained access to through archaeology. Using the literature on consumption, Mullins describes a world of things that could be purchased, often fairly cheaply and that were as available to whites as to blacks. There was therefore the kind of equity and even access that looked democratic. But the world of goods was also racialized, as with Aunt Jemima images, which were a stereotype of ugliness and domestic subservience. Commercially produced goods offered equal access to Victorian and middle-class—often called genteel—taste. But many of these goods told the white and black worlds of the inferiority of blacks. And for this reason, as well as to avoid spending cash on status items, some black intellectuals urged their listeners not to shop in an attempt to gain acceptance in a world that would not welcome them for long, if at all.

Mullins shows that a certain amount of freedom was obtained through the use of consumer goods. Even if dishes did not provide freedom, access to mass-produced goods just like them made domestic life easier. But is this to be seen as the action of the ideology of possessive individualism? The answer to this question has to be balanced and careful:

Double consciousness was described by Du Bois (1969, 16–17) as a "second-sight in this American world—a world which yields him no true self-consciousness, but only lets him see himself through the revelation of the other world." The underside of this heightened "second-sight" vision was that it was formulated through the veil of race, which "only lets him see himself through the revelation of the other world"—a racialized White world that stifled African-American self-consciousness. For Du Bois, this yielded a struggle in which African Americans constantly negotiated the contradictions of "two-ness, an American, a Negro; two souls, two thoughts, two unreconciled strivings; two warring ideals in one dark body whose dogged strength alone keeps it from being torn asunder."

When this idea appeared in *The Souls of Black Folk* in 1903, it was an astounding notion that envisioned an African-American subjectivity that could be African as well as American. Du Bois believed struggle would produce an African-American subjectivity that comprehended its Africanness and unique historical experience, as well as its American identity. He confronted the fundamental contradiction of all public space when he observed that African America:

> Would not Africanize America, for America has too much to teach the world and Africa. He would not bleach his Negro soul in a flood of white Americanism, for he knows that Negro blood has a message for the world. He simply wishes to make it possible for a man to be both a Negro and an American, without being cursed and spit upon by his fellows, without having the doors of Opportunity closed roughly in his face. (Du Bois 1969, 4)
>
> Mullins 1999, 186

Certainly, by the period after the Civil War, the education, architectural ideas, and domestic crockery of African Americans like the Maynards and Burgesses in Annapolis gave them some of the appearances of the white middle-class. Both the archaeology and the literature used by Mullins and Warner show this, but they also show that these African Americans were and wanted to be different. They desired the traits, rights, and accomplishments that went with being liberty-loving citizens, but this does not mean that they wanted to be white. Racism in any case made that impossible, as they well knew. The impossibility confronted them every day and was articulated by their own leaders, which was the very opposite of the way that William Faris's leaders spoke to him and his fellow middle-class white citizens.

Earl Conrad (1947, 231) suggested that a struggle much like that Du Bois described was still being waged in all public space:

> The resistance in the Negro is one which utilizes all the weaknesses in the economy, politics, philosophy, and religion of the dominant group. On the one hand, it drives the Negro to integrate himself as fully as possible into the broad national fabric, and on the other hand compels him to create a

world of his own in his ghettos and in the areas of the South where he is massed. He builds his own economy, while battling to penetrate the white man's economy. He fights for the realization as a national or mass group of his own, yet concurrently seeks to join the nation's mainstream. I find that both these processes are historical and inevitable, and not contradictory, inevitable to a greatly outnumbered group which must seek all methods of advance.

quoted in Mullins 1999, 187

Mullins observes:

Conrad soberly understood that the African-American struggle was a tactical negotiation that preyed on racism's interstices. Within racism's ideological fissures African America fashioned a material, social, and cultural foothold that was both within and apart from American society. Racialization never utterly vanquished African-American aspiration or cultural integrity, but it always compelled African Americans to warily survey the ambiguous distinction between empowering incorporation and escalated subordination.

Mullins 1999, 187

After reading Paul Mullins and Mark Warner on consumption, it is possible to see that black Annapolitans did accept the ideology of individualism and endeavor to live it out, to reproduce themselves within it. It is also clear that some of their national leaders said that the ideology was a disguise for exploitation and worse. We could probably find American social reformers like Joseph Smith and Ann Lee who either said the same thing or acted as though they consciously knew the same thing. (Faris might have heard Mother Ann Lee, and anyone in Annapolis in the Federal Era could have read about the Prophet Joseph Smith.) They had just as much reason to, but I think the power of the ideology acting on them may have deafened them.

My material on ceramics covered the mid eighteenth century to the late nineteenth. My commentary on African American ceramic use cannot begin before the mid nineteenth century, and some of the quoted material falls within our own lifetimes. I believe I can do this safely, regardless of chronology, because ideology in capitalism operates by continually shifting and changing its subjects, but not its objective: cheap labor and new markets. The concept of the free individual is ever new and has a deeply embedded luster that appears to its receivers to transcend class. But it does not actually transcend class; it is embedded in the protection of class. Such embeddedness creates the contradiction that the most despised can come to see themselves as free and equal. And those who see themselves as individuals may recognize ideology's effect on others outside their class and, sometimes, can see the conflict produced in such movement. They can sometimes see their own ideological position. Within such a contradiction lies a dawning consciousness of the falseness of the dominant ideology (Abercombie et al. 1980; Miller 1972; Patterson 1985; McGuire 1992b, 140–43). Archaeology provides the history of the passage of the technologies of ideology down through classes. Through archaeology, we can see ideology questioned, as well as the consequences of these moments of consciousness.

CHAPTER 6

From Althusser
and Lukács to Habermas

Archaeology in Public in Annapolis

Did the action of the technologies of the self and the ideology they fostered penetrate below the members of the class that benefited most from them? Yes, to a great degree, but with consciousness of the results visible to the middle class and those lower down the economic and political order. This was a visibility we can notice through the satire of the Tuesday Club and its members' outright criticism of class. But the ideology of individualism worked. It was used even if it was inverted and parodied. And ideology avoided violence for the most part.

When I designed Archaeology in Annapolis, I did not have analyses of ideology such as I have described here available to me. But even so, the beginning of this project in 1981 was like this moment decades later. The question was then and is now how to use archaeological knowledge to promote awareness of conditions and change. Even in the early 1980s, there was enough historical knowledge to create an environment in which to be explicit about the existence of ideology and some of its content so as to promote change.

Through the 1980s and early 1990s, I adopted and adapted the Marxist strategy of explaining the origins of ideology to those whose condition was continued by it as elaborated by Georg Lukács (1971, 83–160). Archaeology in Public in Annapolis was an effort to show how the built and made worlds, as these were available through archaeology, acted to reveal how the givens of daily life worked, and particularly their origins, when they came into being.

Archaeology in Public (Potter 1994) was part of the commitment the
Historic Annapolis Foundation made to its own constituents when it
founded and sponsored Archaeology in Annapolis. My idea was to replace the make-believe you-are-there versions of teaching about the past
that I had found at many places in the United States and, in particular,
had written up at Colonial Williamsburg and at Maryland's Historic
Saint Mary's City. In those places, I had found a pattern of presenting
a view of important past life to visitors as though they had immediate
access to it, as though the past weren't dead, but somehow still alive in
the interpreter's play (Leone 1981a, 1981b). I found two problems with
the way Williamsburg and St. Mary's City presented the past to visitors, which became one of my points in creating Archaeology in Public in Annapolis. One was the assumption that living history was history alive for you to see, experience, and understand now. And the other
was their inability to deal with the idea that the information presented
about the past was the information that the museum took for granted as
the most important it could teach. The idea that a presentation of the
past could be a function of the present was missing in these places. Missing along with this possibility was an interest in who might have been
left out of the story and that the structure of the story itself, including
its politics and economics, might be embedded in the message taught
to visitors.

This set of problems, known to historians as presentism, to Freud as
projection, and to Marx as ideology motivated me as I struggled to understand how Americans made a past for themselves to live by, be inspired by, and unify themselves at the time when the United States was
becoming the world's greatest power. If presentations of the past did have
a structure that was used to choose elements of the past so that they made
sense, then how could I use these assumptions, whether learned from
Freud or Marx?

In answering this question, I turned to Lukács, as suggested to me by
JoAnn Magdoff (personal communication) and Steve Barnett (Barnett and
Silverman 1979, 41–81). I had originally been introduced to Louis Althusser by anthropologists at Princeton through students of my colleague
Steve Barnett. Janet Dolgin and JoAnn Magdoff also pointed me to Althusser, and I saw in his modern Marxist thought a complement to the
ecologically oriented prehistoric archaeology I was already familiar with.
Materialist social thought was already current in prehistoric archaeology
but was nowhere present in the scholarship on modern material culture
that was beginning. The Princeton anthropologists created this transition

for me and then, with the suggestions of Lukács, helped make a tie to public uses and presentations of historical knowledge.

The issue for me was how to put Marx to work in public and, without knowing it, I put an elderly idea to work. If exposing ideology was our task, and if Althusser provided scholarly ways of doing it through empirical work, then Lukács argued that a historian's job was to trace how an ideology came to be. Give ideology a history.

I tried to join together the ideas of Althusser and Lukács. Althusser pointed out that ideology appeared not to have a history. It did not give itself beginnings or ends, or the appearance of being connected to historical circumstances. Ideologies gave themselves the aura of being timeless and eternal, or of deriving from God or being natural forms. The appearance of not having a history or of being tied to specific historical circumstances could be addressed and corrected by historians, and here I read archaeologists, who could explore the origins and reasons for specific ideologies. Lukács provided me with a way of doing so. Althusser was not able to do this because he defined ideology as virtually impossible to behold for very long.

I tried to create awareness of ideology through a public program in Annapolis based on archaeology (Potter 1994; Leone and Potter 1996; Leone n.d.). The central element of it was a site open to the public, free, with students giving tours of methods, and then of a message that showed the archaeological origins of some element of ideology.

I worked with a theater producer, Philip Arnoult, to train undergraduate students and some graduate students to give 12–15 minute tours of ongoing archaeological sites that were open to the public. We did this from 1982 to about 1993. On one site, we used the archaeology of a series of houses built from 1680 to the 1880s to show how the divisions of home and yard reflected the divisions of daily and personal life into ever more discrete functions, separating domestic and work life, and then work and leisure time. We commented that these were divisions within the notion of people as individuals, and that there had been a time before our lives were so subdivided and when we were not so isolated from the parts of our own lives (Leone, Potter, and Shackel 1987). Thus, our sense of our lives as compartments and of ourselves as isolated was relatively new, arbitrary, and mutable.

Our final message was devoted to asking people to think about their notion of leisure and vacation time, which was the time they were spending with us right now, and that these were new concepts, were arbitrary definitions of a person, and were part of how we now defined individuals. We pointed out that archaeologists interpret the past for the present, in the present. "We don't dig up the past, we think up the past," was our parting idea. We finished by explaining that there is always a message like ours in interpretations of the past and that one can find it by asking questions at other historic sites, because "if you don't, the past will be done to you." People were urged to take charge of what they were taught.

The connection of most use here is to landscapes, since I have spent time trying to explain how the technology embedded in them operated to define people as individuals operating in a naturally preexisting hierarchy, and then in the revolutionary era, as individuals operating in the context of a watchful citizenship.

We gave two tours of landscapes that were being excavated in Annapolis. In the later 1980s, we excavated in the eighteenth-century landscape rebuilt by Charles Carroll of Carrollton (Palus and Kryder-Reid 2002). In the early 1990s, we excavated all around the Maryland State House on State Circle (Read et al. 1990). Both sites were opened to the public, the first with a structured tour and a booklet, the second with a brief explanation and a pamphlet. All this was presented by my students or graduate students.

The surface subject matter of the tours and explanations was the function of perspective in such eighteenth-century landscapes. We showed how the land had been shaped to create illusions to fool the eye about closeness and distance. Then we explained how that placed the builder in charge of using and explaining the operation of natural law, thus placing him closer to the top of the natural hierarchy of leadership. Landscapes built this way, which were common and relatively simple to design, were not best interpreted as for food, farmed by slaves, or the result of money or leisure. They were devices for controlling access to power. They depended on people seeing themselves as individuals with the freedom to understand the laws of nature, to model themselves on natural processes, and to improve their lives by acquiring such knowledge by observing and learning from nature. This was how individualism was learned by a person. The solid geometry of these places and of the city as a whole could operate successfully because it operated on people who saw themselves as capable of responding individually and personally to being instructed in natural law.

I chose landscapes and ideology as the subject of the public program. The point was to explain the operation of ideology and to show its origins. The aim of our archaeology was to demystify the way the landscape of the city had been explained and to collect enough accurate ar-

chaeological information to make a scientifically responsible alternative
explanation possible. I called this a critical approach, because it was to
illuminate the current operation of ideology, in this case the ability of
the city's landscape to create illusions and to make those in charge of
them appear to be more worthy of their social positions.

One of the easiest ways for us to focus on individualism was through
exhibits on ceramics and on toothbrushes. We mounted a public exhibit
of matched sets of dishes from the eighteenth and nineteenth centuries.
This was put together with originality and effort by Christine Hoepfner
in 1987 in a small, free museum at the Annapolis waterfront (Hoepfner
and Potter 1987). We explained the use of individual place settings and
their role in creating a sense among people of their equality and separateness. We tried to show the shift from use of common eating equipment in the late seventeenth century to the use of elaborate, matched en-
sembles by the mid-nineteenth century. The exhibit was popular and was
taken as our way of showing what we had recovered archaeologically.
But it was not seen by visitors as any kind of new awareness of how modern individuals were conceived.

Toothbrushes were more successful. These were presented as an archaeological collection and were organized by Paul Shackel (1993, 5–6, 42–
50). We mounted this small exhibit of two or three dozen toothbrush
handles in the Historic Annapolis tour headquarters in the Old Treasury
Building next to the Maryland State House on State Circle. To bring the
exhibit into the nineteenth century, we borrowed toothbrushes from Elizabeth Comer's excavations in downtown Baltimore. We wanted to show
strong connections to the Baltimore Center for Urban Archaeology.

We did not have brochures for either exhibit, as I recall, so we were
limited to labels with brief explanations in the cases. The point of the
exhibit on toothbrushes was to show the advent of the idea of personal
hygiene, cleanliness, and a sweet-smelling body. These were maintained
by people who assumed personal responsibility for themselves and who
were ready for mutual inspection of their keeping the rules for good conduct. These were the implements of well-disciplined individuals. The exhibit was frequently visited but caused neither public debate nor dispute.

Not so with our film *Annapolis: Reflections from the Age of Reason*
(Leone n.d.), which was meant to be a visitor's introduction to archaeology in the city. The purpose of the site tours, a guidebook, exhibits,
and this film was to put on public display all our conclusions drawn
from landscapes, ceramics, and items of personal discipline (Potter 1994:
190; Potter and Leone 1986). We attempted to show the ideology of

possessive individualism and its role in the eighteenth century in maintaining society with a great disparity of wealth in it, and how it was
kept peaceful.

Our audiovisual production was designed as an introduction to questions to be asked. Next came a visit to an excavation, followed by a guidebook. The slide show was produced in the mid 1980s by Gary Aten of
Telesis, Inc., in Baltimore. We used a then up-to-date technology and
mounted twelve slide projectors holding over 700 slides of Annapolis,
all synchronized by a computer, so that twelve images were projected at
once on a large, very long screen, and in sequences, which could be set
up to show motion. The analogue today would be streaming video, but
without any modular potential except reduction to videotape, which we
eventually did, courtesy of Elizabeth Comer. Because the production was
almost half an hour long and had so many slides, all taken by a very
good photographer, Howard Erenfeld, the whole supporting analysis of
data could be played out. The audiovisual presentation linked all the data
on the ideology of possessive individualism that I have outlined.

In the presentation, I argued through the narrator that the technologies that link landscapes, architecture, scientific and musical instruments,
and place settings imposed the self-disciplines that sustained the hierarchy in which the liberty-loving individual produced himself as a willing
worker. The material culture constituted the implements of the ideology.

The presentation failed to excite and to create alliances among groups
who could work for change probably because we were speaking to members of the middle class, who were largely uninterested in serious social
change. The presentation was not politically timid but was ineffective
because these instruments of ideology had changed so much since the
eighteenth and early nineteenth centuries that they were not immediately
important to our listeners and viewers. The latter may not have wanted
a more egalitarian society, but people could also see no connection between the material culture of an earlier time and their own.

The third and last part of our public program was a guidebook called
Archaeological Annapolis, which took people around the city on foot
and in pictures and showed how the city's historic structure had been
remade into its present. The photographs, which were of important spots
in the city, showed what the city had looked like before it was homogenized into what it is today. The point was to provide a way for visitors
to see that the appearance of the past is a modern creation, not an eternal and fortunate survival, and that visitors can ask how and why this
occurred, as well as what and who were not provided with this presti-

gious look. It was a modern version of Dr. Alexander Hamilton's parody of the purpose of history.

By 1990, two things about Archaeology in Annapolis struck me. We had given tours to over 50,000 visitors, many of whom provided feedback through questionnaires. Part of this first success was the popular and official support we experienced. People who visited liked what they saw, how they were treated, and what they heard. Mayors and members of the city council expressed support.

Second, little or no critical awareness of the action of the material culture of ideology had been created either in visitors or in Annapolitans themselves. The public program had made little or no difference in the consciousness of Annapolitans, so far as I could tell. The sole exceptions were some in the local scholarly and preservation community who objected to the facts they had heard and to our conclusions. At first and in the long run, these behind-the-scenes objections meant less to me than the rather more surprising reaction of warm public support for an interpretive program aimed at adults that was free and frequent. I could not figure out why something that was focused on exposing the ideology of inequality and domination would be popular. It was, but I concluded that it had changed little or nothing about life in the city.

Between 1988 and 1990, I came to the conclusion that the way I was doing a critical archaeology was ineffective. I know in retrospect that the messages were muted in our pamphlets, although not in our many tours. Although the guidebook was a success, it was easily misinterpreted. Instead of concluding that the past had been invented for political purposes, some concluded that interpretations changed as increasing information and new knowledge allowed them to be improved. Scholarship on Annapolis was ever better, not just different. The audiovisual presentation was too long to sit through for many people, much, much too provocative for virtually all professional preservationists and local historians, and it could not be mounted in public for more than about six months.

I concluded that my effort at using critical theory had failed both because I was timid in my attempt at using it in public and because I had either misunderstood the theory or the theory available to me was inadequate. I therefore changed my use of critical theory. Some of the reasons for doing so were suggested by archaeologists opposed to a Marxist interpretation, either in general or in Althusser's version as used by me (Hodder 1986, 63–65, 166–67; Beaudry, Cook, and Mrozowski 1991, 150–91; McGuire 1992b, 140–42). These doubted the validity of the hypothesis that ideology was so powerful that it blinded people to exploitation. Ian Hodder, Mary Beaudry, Lauren Cook, and Stephen Mrzow-ski do not think class and exploitation are effectively explored using the dominant ideology thesis. Randall McGuire argues that the exploited see and understand their condition but are so subjected to violence they can do little about it.

Our public presentations were from the top down, or from the archaeologist out. I created them without understanding what the public, or community members, or the preservation community wanted to hear. The interpretation was what I as an archaeologist thought people needed to hear, based on what I believed was fully defensible in light of the remains. In this sense, I thought Annapolis was more like a classroom than the mature and varied community of equals it is. This was both my mistake and one embedded in Lukács's thinking. It is not embedded in Althusser's work, because, at least reading between the lines, he does not hold out hope for the ability of democracies to reform themselves. Illumination through teaching does not pierce ideology. But I could not agree to be so pessimistic, even though his definitions of ideology hold so much potential.

My motivation in creating and running Archaeology in Public in Annapolis was to connect past and present using archaeology to explain some useful link. I hoped that a presentation of landscapes, ceramics, print, and scientific and other instruments would show people the beginnings of the notion of individualism that we use today. The public program did not achieve the goal I had hoped for.

These analyses of the technologies of ideology contribute to explaining the origins of American patriotism and of the independent American state, as well as to resolving puzzles about the Annapolitan landscape. Because these are lively questions whose answers are still clouded by illusions of freedom, liberty, and inclusion, the archaeology offers important antidotes to popular, received wisdom. The issue is not the value of a Marxist analysis but rather how to teach the analysis.

I did not want to give up either a public program based on interpreting archaeology or an effort to use Althusser's take on ideology to make sense of the material culture of an administrative center like Annapolis (Leone 1995). After all, the city was not a serious port, a market center, or a manufacturing hub. It was a small, powerful capital that I was sure was about manufacturing and using the apparatuses of power. Ideology was the way into exploring that. I turned to Jürgen Habermas at the suggestion of one of my graduate students, Priscilla Saulsgiver, as a new way of dealing with the effects of capitalism. Habermas was not concerned with Althusser's definition of ideology but with the enhancement of the operation of democratic processes to moderate the effects of modernity, and capitalism in particular (Habermas 1984).

What caught my attention was Habermas's notion of the "lifeworld" (Habermas 1984–87, 1: 386–91; 2: 391–97), which as I interpret it means the articulated, lived-out response of the exploited to the dominant culture's intrusions. Lifeworlds, which are cultures, exist within and also apart from capitalism. Beginning about 1990, I began to use this idea as a way to work with African Americans in Annapolis on archaeology that was of interest to them and to the public, white and black.

Habermas continued the effort of members of the Frankfurt School who created modern Marxist critical theory to understand and challenge capitalism. For him, the issue was how to change capitalism's effects without using the violence that was employed by Bolsheviks, Communists, Nazis, and Fascists.

Among the ways to bolster the democratic societies and processes that Habermas wanted to foster was one that seemed to me to come right out of anthropology. He argued that there would be people who had not yet been fully incorporated into capitalism's quest for markets, resources, or colonies. Lifeworlds could either be outside capitalism's orbit or could characterize people within a capitalist society. These might be groups within capitalist societies that had dealt with some of capitalism's effects and had moderated some, eliminated some, and resisted others. This was a fertile idea and allowed me to see a process I had never noticed before. There were living or past groups, or some leaders of some groups, who plainly saw what was to them most destructive in the trade, missionary activity, land acquisition, natural resource depletion, importation of unhealthy food, plantations, slavery, disease, and a hundred other by-products of Western contact. After all, the Pueblos resisted, the Navajos resisted, the Inuit resisted, modern Iran rebelled completely, and so on. So, who in Annapolis had resisted, fought back, or built a shell for survival? Who did so with a critique that could serve others as a model in mainline society for thinking and doing similarly? For Habermas, a lifeworld could show alternatives, possibilities, and strategies, and these could be based on critiques of capitalism drawn from their experience with it and, particularly, with keeping its worst aspects at bay.

I came to understand that African American culture in Annapolis might fit Habermas's concept of lifeworlds. But this was only a gradual realization and is not complete even now. It is also based on my own particular reading of Habermas. This realization in any case allowed me to add a vital dialectic to critical theory. If the job of the historical scholar was to explore the origins of modern conditions and to give ideology a history, then the job of a scholar using Habermas was to engage in a dialogue about how to work with people on the edges of capitalism for their purposes and for those he thought were his. In Annapolis, this created a dialogue between individuals connected to various institutions supporting African American interests and those of us in Archaeology in Annapolis. It linked past and present through archaeology, and I hoped it would be about class as well as race relations.

I began this dialogue before I understood fully that critical theory expressed through our public program did not produce adequate change, except popular support for archaeology. I began the dialogue because of what I had seen in South Africa while teaching in the Department of Archaeology at the University of Cape Town in 1988. Many South Africans held that historical archaeology had great potential in South Africa because it could be organized to comment on European intrusion into native South Africa in a way that no other field could find the evidence to do. I was able to visit several townships in South Africa, near Cape Town, Johannesburg, and Pretoria. My wife and I went with Africans and people of Indian descent, all themselves segregated by residential rules under apartheid. Conditions in the townships were never good compared to where we were living in Cape Town. One day we were being driven through a township outside Cape Town that our friends wanted us to see. Conditions were miserable in the streets, with no paving, puddles and mud everywhere, and with shanties the only housing, yet with white laundry hung from clotheslines like some heroic effort to remain clear of all this degradation, speaking of hope and determination above the concentration camp conditions. The police enforced control from tubelike armored vehicles called "Hippos," about twenty feet long, with gun ports at regular intervals, stationed on the muddy streets between the houses throughout these segregated neighborhoods. Then I knew that I could make no difference there, but maybe I could in Annapolis. That drive was the pivotal moment. It was one among many township visits, but the one that told me what apartheid had created and done.

Earlier on in my stay in Cape Town, I met Omar Bradshaw, who had helped guide me through "clearance" to teach in South Africa despite the United Nations ban on academic visits. We were talking soon after I got there, and he had opinions about archaeology, which he called a site of struggle in South Africa. I had never heard the term, let alone its usage. He saw archaeology as central to South Africa's identity. He saw the practice and substance of archaeology in South Africa as part of national consciousness and as central to his country's free future. I had one of the single most exhilarating moments in all my time as a professional archaeologist. At no time in my experience in the United States as an archaeologist had anyone seen or presented archaeology this way. My family had thought it was a low-paying job of luxurious irrelevance. American archaeologists were either bothered with their field's scientific irrelevance or accepted that condition as inevitable. Here was a vision I longed for and had already tried to use through critical theory and a public program in Annapolis.

Behind the hopes in South Africa for historical archaeology was the possibility that archaeology could produce an alternative history to that composed for the nation by Europeans and white South Africans. The commonly taught and dominant version of the past had disfranchised Africans and was ever present in the monuments, restored historic buildings, history museums, famous plantation farm houses, the great fort in Cape Town, and the very look, that is, the plan, of the cities. It was all European. Africa was almost nowhere.

An African history and a past for peoples whose ancestors had been brought there as slaves and servants from India, Indonesia, and other places in the Dutch South Asian trading empire was what was longed for (Schrire 1988, 1995). This amounted to a whole alternative story, and one that included a commentary on the Europeans who had created the current state of affairs. So although I was not fully aware of all the elements of this way of writing a critical alternative history while I was in South Africa, the elements were there, and they came together later in Annapolis for me. The key early piece in Annapolis was to be a close collaboration with people who understood archaeology, and who were not afraid of it or of archaeologists. These were people who knew they could use it for cultural and political purposes and who were immediately ready to make an alliance based on knowing what archaeology could do. Our earlier ineffectiveness in Annapolis had raised the question of how to deal with resistance to capitalism's actions to impoverish, mask its actions, and counteract efforts at challenge and change. African America offered an alternative for archaeological action. Because we subsequently went to a group and not a collection of upper-class artifacts, we bridged past and present far more effectively. Because we worked with people who were interested in using historical things to institute change, we had allies for the first time. Preservationists were already in power and had no need to see how they got into that position. Even though they were our patrons and sponsors, they were not allies; they saw us as handmaids and themselves as owners.

Work with African Americans always came with their clear vision of conditions in the present, although not always with clarity about how to interpret what we found through archaeology. For me this became a viable alternative to my use of Lukács and of a top-down critical theory. A dialogue among archaeologically competent equals who saw the need to improve social conditions now became possible. This was an advance for critical theory.

Ultimately, Habermas, the theorists I began using, and I all seek to understand modernity and correct its pathologies as they are expressed through racism and class antagonisms (Hermann 1999).This accords with the social purpose of archaeology since the time of its founding as a science. Archaeology's purpose has been to discover the ways the world has come to be as it is. For example, originally, archaeology was closely associated with demonstrating the so-called long chronology of human existence, as opposed to the short chronology proposed by a narrow reading of the Bible, and it also provided evidence for the origin of humans from evolutionary processes that linked us to other primates. This was explicitly designed to undermine a church-supported hierarchy and European history that privileged peoples tied to Rome and Greece. I have tried to show that archaeology can also write a history of personhood like possessive individualism and in so doing can produce an alternative to a social pathology, that is, blindness to poverty and powerlessness, within the way modernism works.

Jürgen Habermas outlines two ways in which those who have been denied human rights can ameliorate modernism by using history. The oppressed can describe their condition against the official cant of our society, thus providing from their lifeworld a contrast with what the dominant say. Second, they can describe what they have done historically to change their condition: How they have resisted, found alternatives, used hidden times, secret practices, and exempted moments to make a life outside the official system.

Although Habermas does not suggest it, we learn from Homi Bhabha that everyone contains some element of the other; we are all hybrid (Bhabha 2002 [1994], 64–65, 123–38, 236–56). Thus, when the other writes a history, it is a history of the dominant part of society and of the system. A hybrid history can be a reflection on both the repressed and on who did the repressing. We shall see all this in the next two chapters, which are on African America. We can also choose to see that every one of these efforts at a narrative discourse about power and identity is a way to preserve rational representative government through the creation of consciousness. I have come to see that only the enslaved, formerly enslaved, or those who were free but extremely close to racism saw or see through ideology. In Annapolis, the poorest whites may have seen through it too, but I have little archaeological or documentary evidence for that.

CHAPTER 7

African America

My students and I at Cape Town worked hard, but I left realizing full well that they would eventually have to make the difference there, not me. The only difference I could make would be in Annapolis. When I returned there, I went to the Banneker-Douglass Museum to meet the director and the associate director, Barbara Jackson. I told them I wanted to work on archaeology with them. The director laughed at me. But Jackson said: "We want to know if we have archaeology; we want to hear about freedom—we're tired of hearing about slavery." And, "Tell us what is left from Africa." I had never been given a bigger gift as an archaeologist than at that moment. I know this more now than I did then, but I knew it then too. She articulated the problems that I have worked on ever since in Annapolis, which include the role of archaeology itself.

DO WE HAVE ARCHAEOLOGY?

The puzzle for scholars, African Americans, and other members of oppressed cultures, or lifeworlds, is what happens to their members within capitalism. What does resistance to exploitation and its powerful ideology embodied in personal liberty and freedom look like? Sticking with Louis Althusser meant using the concept of ideology to understand how a large, creative group that was homogeneous when viewed from outside, but really internally diverse, handled the threats of living alongside capitalism. How could we learn; what would we learn; how had African Americans in Annapolis made many lives for themselves?

If Jürgen Habermas wanted alternative forms of resistance, how could archaeologists preserve the heterogeneity of the black experience in the city? If Habermas wanted an antidote to capitalism, how could we avoid essentializing and naturalizing people who wanted to be and were members of the middle class. If Althusser wanted no one outside ideology, how could I both want to find African traditions of kin-based communities intact after two centuries and also accurately describe archaeological remains that were able to sustain several levels of complex interpretation, including one that showed that Africa survived and another that showed membership in the middle class?

Where would I find the ideology of possessive individualism? If this ideology were breached by African Americans, what would that look like and who would it include? And then, who would care enough about these discoveries to use them to reflect back on the dominant culture of Annapolis today? How could such knowledge contribute to making critical theory work for people in the city?

Wanting to know whether there is archaeology for your group was asking whether knowledge of the past mattered and whether or not your people could use it for their own purposes. Would it make your people look right? Would your people belong more to mainstream society and be more acceptable? In other words, would it reverse racist treatment? That is what I think Barbara Jackson's questions meant. But there was also concern about the use of archaeology as a process. Would using it appear so neutral that its ability to create chronologies, origins, and successive elites just continue current efforts to maintain inferiority and then domination, while also deepening these relationships by absorbing people of African descent into the results of archaeology and into the middle-class sciences, some of whose results they had been able to avoid so far?

Shortly after these questions were asked, my field school began to dig in the parking lot immediately adjacent to Jackson's Banneker-Douglass Museum, where a new county courthouse was eventually to be built. The museum is in a Victorian church, once home of an African Methodist Episcopal congregation, whose parishioners had lived in houses surrounding it. Some of the houses had been taken down in the 1950s and 1960s and others in the 1970s for the parking lot that now covered their old neighborhood and surrounded the surviving church. We dug our units in the lot, discovered the old backyards and cellars, and found lost slate pencils, buttons, and thousands of other items from the nineteenth and early twentieth centuries that had belonged to the owners and renters who lived there.

Because Barbara Jackson told us who had lived in the houses, their names, address by address, we automatically answered her first question. Yes, there was archaeology by and of African Americans, and we knew what it looked like, in great detail (Mullins and Warner 1993b). There was material that was directly connected to people who had lived there. From systematic analysis, we discovered the patterns of purchase and use of the bottles, tin cans, buttons, pins, plates, bowls, and animal and fish bones. These produced different patterns of purchase, cooking, and discard. The patterns all answered the question of whether or not an archaeology of black life existed. The archaeology turned out to be there, as we found in 1992 and beyond, and it was both immediately recognizable and different in important ways from that of sites that had been occupied by people of European descent.

An analysis of tins cans showed that residents preferred national brand-names, because weight, quality, and price were guaranteed. The local grocer could circumvent such guarantees where he sold loose produce. Bottles were discarded quickly according to a match between their manufacturing dates and the associated stratigraphy. This meant that few containers were reused for canning and preserving fresh goods. Food could evidently be bought fresh and probably inexpensively. Fish scales, a sign of fresh fish caught locally and cleaned at home, disappeared after 1880. Fresh fish were bought from black vendors after this date. These were the patterns that attempted independence. They were also explained through oral histories (Jopling 1991, 1992) obtained from former residents of the courthouse block by Hannah Jopling at Barbara Jackson's request.

Jopling is the first cultural anthropologist to work with Archaeology in Annapolis. While she was learning archaeology, she introduced oral history and, later, life histories into Annapolis by recording and teaching others to record the stories that African Americans tell, told, and wanted others to hear, which were regarded as one of the essential ways of documenting, cementing, sharing, and celebrating their experiences, lessons, and testimonies. Jopling's first oral histories, when recorded, were crucial to Warner's and Mullins's work. Her own later work has been mainly with African American women's oral histories in a traditionally African American area near places we have excavated.

Because censuses, as well as people's memories, told us that the foundations and backyards we dug in had belonged to people of African descent, the archaeological discoveries were unambiguous. African Americans visiting the Banneker-Douglass Museum saw archaeology in their neighborhood, and it was theirs. Supported by both the museum and a grant from the Maryland Humanities Council, we dug on Sunday afternoons and opened our excavations to people from all the black congregations in town, after having been invited to speak to several of the congregations directly. People from those churches came to visit. Many African Americans from the city came during the annual Kunta Kinte Festival devoted to celebrating African American culture. Many, many more read about our work and discoveries. When we exhibited our findings in the Banneker-Douglass Museum a short time later, hundreds of African American youngsters came (Leone et al. 1995). When we moved the exhibit to the headquarters of the Historic Annapolis Foundation, thousands of schoolchildren came. There was no doubt that there was an African American historical archaeology.

The content of local archaeology from backyards, basements, privies, and wells was perfectly ordinary: bones, buttons, bottles, glass, broken dishes, pins, cans, and everything you would expect. Because we conducted oral history interviews with some of the block's former residents, we knew that a woman had done laundry in a yard where an unusual number of buttons was recovered, including some with U.S. Naval Academy insignia on them. We also knew that discarded uniforms were often given to Naval Academy workers who lived in this neighborhood. Slates and pencils were from turn-of-the-century schools. Some chicken bones came from chickens raised in backyards. Some ham bones were from the Naval Academy, where many African Americans worked. Bric-a-brac and fine china sets were sometimes gifts from employers, but much more often were bought new from street vendors to be used on special occasions. Very little was said to be hand-me-down; much was from hard work and "makin' do." Thus, former residents remembered what the recovered remains meant, which provided the look of daily life among working-class and property-owning people of African descent. And after that came the results of archaeology that showed little fine china and frequently mismatched and hand-me-down dishes (Paul R. Mullins, written communication, 2004).

During the history of these houses, the neighborhood changed. By the time of its destruction for urban renewal—courthouse expansion and a parking lot—the houses were either all or almost all owned and occupied by African Americans. But it had been a mixed neighborhood earlier, with people of African and European descent living there in the later nineteenth and early twentieth centuries. It became mostly black in the twentieth century. Bellis Court, behind the African Methodist Episcopal Church, was built for poor black renters.

TELL US ABOUT FREEDOM

Our first excavations and our first oral histories were along Franklin Street, an African American neighborhood in which people owned their own homes from the 1830s to the 1970s. The neighborhood included Wylie Bates's store and William Bishop's properties in the later nineteenth and early twentieth centuries. Both men owned real estate in Annapolis, became wealthy, and left impressive legacies. Bishop was one of the wealthiest men, black or white, in Annapolis. Bates was influenced by Booker T. Washington's idea "that hard manual labor would compel white America to grant African Americans political rights" (Mullins, written communication, 2004), and in his autobiography (Bates 1928) he describes his efforts to circumvent the racism of his time. The segregated high school for African Americans was named for him. Although we excavated houses once owned by Bishop and wanted to include Bates's store, which had been disturbed by later building, the archaeology did not include them specifically. The archaeology was, however, about Annapolis middle-class black families whose material culture showed them to be trying to be both in and outside the middle class. Racism pushed them to the margins, but American ideology drew them in.

Wylie Bates's critique no doubt speaks for many members of the black middle class:

> The North tried to saddle the responsibility for Slavery upon the South. Slavery was an American Institution, and America is responsible for the past and present treatment of the Negro, and must account to God for her sins both of omission and commission. Americans to a great extent are still unwilling to recognize the Negro as a *bona fide* citizen, a member of the body politic, a loyal patriot. Five hundred thousand foreigners came to America during the last year, and it is easier for that half-million to get remunerative employment than for the same number of Negroes, who would lay down their lives for the Flag of this Country; and would also experience great difficulty in receiving fair and just treatment.

> Bates 1928, 18

Wylie Bates had a clear view of reality, but he wanted to be middle-class and succeeded. His autobiography shows him to be fully within the ideology of possessive individualism. Yet his people were excluded and exploited. The combination occurring so clearly here shows the conflict between a steeply hierarchical society that used racism and segregation to keep workers as poor as possible and an ideology that fooled the two-thirds of society that employed the other third, which combined clear knowledge of its condition with a hope for inclusion that would prove very damaging to a hierarchy of unequal wealth.

Most of the archaeology along Franklin Street was about free people, because most of the neighborhood's houses dated to after 1865. But once we touched free blacks before Emancipation and then the survival of African traditions in Annapolis, both excitement and controversy were there all at once. Our discoveries produced different reactions, depending on race.

When we started to excavate the Maynard-Burgess House, attitudes to us started to change. This house had come onto the real estate market in the mid 1980s and been sold to a woman who soon found that it was too eaten by termites and deteriorated to restore. She then sold it to Port of Annapolis, a for-profit preservation group that was interested in it because of its location and historic fabric. The land was once owned by Charles Carroll of Carrollton, and the house had a Federal Era look about it and was part of a block of similar houses opposite the Annapolis City Hall on a historic street.

The Historic Annapolis Foundation got Archaeology in Annapolis involved. We dug a great deal there over three seasons, and ultimately both Paul Mullins (Mullins 1999a; Mullins and Warner 1993) and Mark Warner (1998) wrote dissertations based on their work at the house, which we proved to be far more special than was at first suspected.

Whose house had this been? Had they been black or white? Someone connected to Charles Carroll of Carrollton, who was white, rich and famous, but Catholic? Or John Maynard and Willard Burgess, who were black? John Maynard was born free in the early nineteenth century, bought his wife out of slavery and step-daughter later, and then, in 1847, built or bought, moved, and reassembled in changed fashion, this house for his family. It was always lived in by the Maynards from then on until it was sold early in the twentieth century to one of the Maynard's boarders, a relative and member of the Burgess family, whose descendants lived there uninterruptedly until the 1980s. So potentially this was a site where only African Americans had lived.

Preservationists, local historians, and architectural historians focused on the fact that some parts of the house dated from before 1847, must have been built somewhere else, and had perhaps been bought, disassembled, and reconstructed in their present form and location by John Maynard. Thus, part of the house had presumably originally had a white owner. The archaeology showed that nothing on the site dated from before 1847. There was nothing that could be tied to Charles Carroll or anyone else before then. The land had been unoccupied, and there was neither trash nor yard scatter. Nothing existed to show a tie to an architecturally earlier house. Indeed, for the Maynard house to be older than 1847, it had to have been built somewhere else and moved piecemeal to its current location, and architectural historians argue this to be the case.

The Maynard-Burgess House produced a rich archaeology that showed, when analyzed by Mullins and Warner (1993a), how its black owners developed different strategies over time to preserve their economic independence, fishing the Bay, using black street vendors as opposed to white grocers, and patronizing national, regulated brands, while keeping up a conventional Victorian exterior and an interior of their own choosing, following W. E. B. Du Bois and other black intellectuals. Mullins points out that some of the behavior behind the archaeological remains like changes in the consumption of fish occurred because of anti-black stereotyping. He argues that many blacks—at least the Maynards—stopped consuming fish because of the anti-black racial caricatures associated with fishing (Mullins 1999: 110, 118). "If anything, racism drove Blacks away from fish consumption and toward marketplace consumption, so the ideological caricature of Blackness and fishing served market interests. Vendors did provide a halfway point; i.e. Black consumers could have fish but avoid the caricatures associated with fishing" (Mullins, written communication, 2004). This was how they negotiated the town's racism and preserved their own integrity. All these patterns are fully described by Paul Mullins and Mark Warner.

To this day, Annapolis has not decided how independent blacks can be or have been, which is to say, how much it wants to see and hear from them about their mutual lives and conditions. The Maynard-Burgess House became more and more derelict, even as it passed from private, to nonprofit, to city ownership. It has been stabilized by an intrusive internal wood skeleton that both keeps it from collapsing and prevents anyone from seeing its insides. It is a very long way from housing a demonstration to anyone in or out of Annapolis of the many lives that free people of color made for themselves there from 1847 to 1980. But by excavating it and analyzing the material from the courthouse neighborhood and two turn-of-the-century tenements built largely for people of African descent, the archaeology of Annapolis unlocked black communities living in freedom, escaping racism, and making independent lives, with integrity and consciousness of their condition.

Although Barbara Jackson Nash told us that there were differences in wealth and standing within the Annapolis black community, and other black intellectuals and leaders told us to see communities and not one large group, Mullins's archaeological results provided nuanced results. He argues that the most striking distinctions were really in social space—church memberships, family lineage, skin color, education, home ownership—and less in portable material culture. The Maynard probate and Maynard's earliest deposits contain stylish things, but the similarities with poorer African Americans are more striking than the differences. This suggests that archaeology can provide an important comment on difference along the color line because it demonstrates similarities in material culture while also showing radically distinct social and cultural worlds (Mullins, personal communication, 2004). The archaeology of the Maynard-Burgess House and our associated research did show such distinctions, which led to a better understanding of black Annapolis. They had archaeology, and it commented on capitalism, democracy, and the ideologies of both.

WHAT IS LEFT FROM AFRICA?

I want to turn to what was left from Africa. I had no expectation that this question could be answered when Barbara Jackson asked it around 1990. I knew that there was a scholarly search for Africanisms like house forms, food ways, and some musical styles that preserved African traditions. But I thought that a place like Annapolis was so middle-class, had been so completely the home of government bureaucrats for so long, so utterly the home of people who thought they were descendents of eighteenth-century European traditions that it could not be a place to find Africa alive.

The search for Africa is well established in archaeology, folklore, American history and literature, and American studies. The comprehensive *Archaeology of the African Diaspora in the Americas* by Theresa Singleton and Mark Bograd (1995) offers hundreds of citations and a clear overview. The demographic, ethnic, and cultural composition of the Chesapeake area in particular, and of the U.S. East Coast and Caribbean in general are described by Lorena Walsh (1997), Michael Gomez (1998), Michael Mullin (1976, 1999), and Robert Ferris Thompson (1983, 1991,

1993). Detailed analyses of African origins and traditions come from Margaret Washington Creel (1988), Gwendolyn Midlo Hall (1971, 1992), and Charles Joyner (1984, 1999). My own effort here is a local contribution to their larger, older and more comprehensive effort.

Africa survived in Annapolis and flourishes. It is hard to get hold of what you do not know, and archaeologists are no better at this than any other scientists. But within archaeology there is a tradition of recording almost everything that is excavated. If you dig it up, you write it down, count it, identify it, say what it is made of, and save it. You certainly do not throw it away, even if you have no idea of what it is or was.

So, one afternoon in 1991 at the Charles Carroll House in Annapolis (Logan et al. 1992), Dr. Robert Worden, who had taken the lead in preserving the historic structure and its grounds, and who was excavating with us as a volunteer on a project he had funded in his capacity as head of the museum house, showed me what he had just found that day. He knew the material was important; so did I. He had kept it separate from the rest because he had found all the pieces together about eighteen inches below the modern dirt floor in a ground-floor room of the house that was called the East Wing.

He showed me an as yet unwashed group of fourteen rock crystals, at least half a dozen white bone discs about one and a half inches in diameter, a black pebble that was very smooth, two coins with dates, one 1790, one 1810, the bottom of a pottery bowl with a blue asterisk on it, and some common pins. There was an ensuing debate about those items, which continues to this day. On one side, the stuff was trash; nothing. The room, whose function we did not know then, had produced large amounts of small bones, pins, and other archaeological finds from the upper few inches, which told us that it had been some kind of work or disposal space. The material could be waste from a workroom associated with the house's main kitchen, which was immediately adjacent. But what Robert Worden was showing me was not scatter. It had all been concentrated and packed together and found as a unit, he said. He knew it belonged together. And because none of it looked broken up into small fragments, even though everything was mostly pieces, it did not appear to be discard. The pieces were also bigger than much of the material coming from the rest of the room.

The material "was concentrated in very loose soil underneath a layer of hard-packed soil or clay—like the clay was a covering for what came next. The excavation area was very small—between floor joists and against a wall. To me it seemed like a chamber now filled with loose dirt—

FIGURE 38. The Charles Carroll House in Annapolis, where the first cache of spirit materials was discovered. This house was begun in 1699 and was extended and enlarged through the 1770s. Its current shape and height were imposed by Charles Carroll of Carrollton. Archaeology in Annapolis excavated the ground floor of the house, the ruins of its extension, and through-out the large garden laid out by Charles Carroll when he enlarged the house. Courtesy of the Anacostia Museum and Center for African American History and Culture, Smithsonian Institution. Photograph by Steven M. Cummings.

unlike the rest of the hard-packed area adjoining, and above and below. The cache was also near a door (to the outside) [on the] northeast [corner]" (Robert Worden, personal note, November 2004.)

One opinion was that the material was household discard. A pebble was a rock. The pierced discs were button backs; the crystals had perhaps occurred there naturally. In other words, the first inclination among some early viewers was to identify things based on their own experience. Because the material Robert Worden found had no obvious meaning in anyone's experience, it was regarded as bits and pieces of virtually no importance, which should perhaps simply be counted and then discarded, like brick fragments or oyster shells. Worden himself had no intention of treating it this way, and he carefully recorded and photographed it.

I had two thoughts, one automatic and one based on an old experience of my own. Because we archaeologists do not discard anything, except bricks and oyster shells, and then only after counting or weighing them, there was never any chance that we were going to throw this material away.

FIGURE 39. The room in the Charles Carroll House where the main cache of spirit materials was found. Substantial archaeological deposits from the eighteenth and nineteenth centuries were recovered here. The cache was discovered in the northeast corner. Courtesy of the Anacostia Museum and Center for African American History and Culture, Smithsonian Institution. Photograph by Steven M. Cummings.

That was the first antidote to discarding these materials actually or intellectually. The second antidote came from my own field school training in Arizona in 1964. I dug in a prehistoric pueblo ruin at Grasshopper, Arizona, the site of the University of Arizona's field school under the direction of Raymond Thompson. At the bottom of the twelfth- or thirteenth-century room where I was digging, on its floor or just below it, was a set of crystals, and, as I remember, a pebble or two. These were identified at the time as a magician's cache or bundle. They were said to have belonged to a practitioner. This did not mean that what I was looking at in Annapolis was something similar, but it seemed familiar.

Shortly after this find, and for reasons I no longer remember, I encouraged a campus newspaper reporter who was the local stringer for the *New York Times* to write up the material. He did, and it was published in the Sunday *Times* ("Scientists Find Slaves Kept African Culture," September 15, 1991), beginning a process that still continues. Monday, the next day, Dr. Frederick Lamp, a former student of Robert Ferris Thompson's, and curator of West African Art at the Baltimore Museum

of Art, called me up and said we had discovered a spirit bundle whose
origins were in West Africa and that must have been made by an African
or African American. A little while later, Professor John Vlach of George
Washington University called and said there was a whole American tradition of African beliefs that had been transferred here from West Africa
and was well known.

Lamp explained that the crystals we had discovered at the Charles Carroll House were used to contain spirits (personal communication). White
buttons with their four holes, were a cosmogram, often referred to as an
X, Vlach explained (see Vlach 1978, 1987, 1991, 1993). White clay, or
ash, or the opacity of a crystal looked like the water through which spirits of dead relatives traveled home, back to the sea from which we and
they ultimately came. The cosmogram was sometimes represented as an
X, but more fully as an X within a circle or lozenge. The arms of the X
are encircled to show both motion and completeness. It is a combination of a horizon line that divides the living world from the world of the
dead and a vertical line that is the axis between the living and the dead,
who live in the world of spirits below. The cosmogram is the circle of
life, seen as a life cycle from birth to midlife to death, and to life in the
spirit or underworld (Ferguson 1992).

The cache or bundle that we had discovered had probably been put
in the ground by a ritual specialist, Lamp said. It would have been used
to manage the spirits in the house or to protect the inhabitants from spirits. This was a practice from the BaKongo tradition, brought directly from
West Africa. Although we did not know it fully at the time, we had found
materials from the larger diasporic world of which these African spirit
practices were a part.

I knew I was a beginner in this field, but I felt that the archaeological
and folkloristic search for items and practices deriving from Africa was
weak. I knew the search was important to people of African descent, because Barbara Jackson and John Vlach had said so, and I knew there
was a literature in anthropology on the issue. Beyond this discussion, I
was interested in why African practices and religious traditions had survived, in what contexts, and for what larger reasons.

My students and colleagues' work at the Charles Carroll House helped
expand on the opening to West Africa provided by a public discussion
of the crystals in two other ways. On the other side of the wall from the
room where Robert Worden had discovered the cache was the main
kitchen of the great house. Under the kitchen hearth was a single enormous crystal weighing several pounds. The large kitchen and the origi-

FIGURE 40. Artifacts in the main cache of spirit materials in the Charles Carroll House. The cache contains at least a dozen rock crystals (not shown in this photograph), two dated coins, many white pierced discs, buttons, and a black pebble. The cache was capped by a pearlware bowl fragment with a blue asterisk in its bottom. Courtesy of the Anacostia Museum and Center for African American History and Culture, Smithsonian Institution. Photograph by Steven M. Cummings.

nal room were connected by another smaller room, and under one of its thresholds was a set of three crystals. We now had a pattern that was neither random nor trash.

We were more firmly establishing an African presence in the Charles Carroll House. These basement rooms, which had had no particular identity before, were now seen to have been the rooms of Charles Carroll's cook, whom he wrote about. Archaeology now showed that she had protected her environment with these ritual bundles, and she may have worshipped through them as well. Thus, while the Jesuits were upstairs saying Mass, she was in an African safe zone beneath. At least that was our hypothesis.

"Poor old Grace died suddenly last Friday morning between the hours of 10 & 11: her death was instant and without groan . . . she had been sick, but that morning she eat [sic] a hearty breakfast & told her mistress she hoped now the warm weather was coming on, she should get well. I saw her about 5 o'clock in the old kitchen that morning poor old creature. I hope she is happy" (Worden 2004, April 3, 1773). Grace's death as recorded by Charles Carroll of Carrollton, may have preceded the placement of caches but not the domestic uses of the rooms.

The Carroll households, including that in Annapolis, saw frequent floggings, whippings, and sometimes the chaining of slaves in an iron collar. There are many, many references to these, their frequency and apparent necessity. In the correspondence between Charles Carroll of Annapolis and his son Charles Carroll of Carrollton, it is clear that such violence was an accepted and routine part of daily life for them and their many slaves (Carroll and Carroll 2001, Appendix III, 1585) on their thousands of acres (ibid., 646, 655; Worden 2004, September 28, 29, 30, and October 6, 1774.) This violence provides some of the context for the use of spirit caches. Two notations by Charles Carroll of Carrollton from the Annapolis house serve to illustrate it:

October 19, 1772,

I lost a pair of thread stockings when last with you, pray enquier for them, Nanny is not the only thief in your house, I think to give Molly and Henny a severe whipping when I go down if my stockings are not found.

Carroll and Carroll 2001, 646

November 23, 1772,

Little Nan has been whipt about Mrs. Moreton's shifts, she confessed she stole them and said she gave them to Moll, search Moll's box etc., privately, but it is probably she has sold them. I am determined to see Moll and Henny well whipped when I go down.

Carroll and Carroll 2001, 655

A short time later, I was asked by the Historic Annapolis Foundation to run an excavation just across the street from the Carroll House, at Slayton House, a building newly donated to the Foundation (see Jones 2000). Slayton House is a late eighteenth-century row house built just before the Revolution. It has five stories, and its basement workrooms, including its kitchen, are accessible from the street by a separate stair and lower passage well below street level. Work yards were at the rear of the house, and the kitchen can be entered directly from these. The basement kitchen is large, with a huge fireplace, like the others in eighteenth-century Annapolis great houses, and a separate laundry room that also had a fireplace. There are also a lower foyer, which receives a descending stair and the shaft of a dumbwaiter, and some smaller, newer rooms for storage and an early twentieth-century electric and gas kitchen.

FIGURE 41. Slayton House, street façade, 1920s. A
separate entrance to the basement workrooms led from
the street and was immediately below the elaborate
front door.

By the time we excavated in these spaces, we knew that such places
were the domain of African Americans who worked there and of the possibility of finding spirit bundles in certain locations beneath the floor,
which in this case was made of cement-covered bricks. By the time we
began work at Slayton House, we had already begun to understand that
caches of the kind we first found at the Carroll House constituted efforts
to control the passage of potentially harmful, or helpful, spirits, who used
chimneys, doors, pipes, stairs, and northeast corners to gain entrance to
people whom they were to harm or protect (Jones 1999; Leone and Fry
1999). Spirits use drain pipes, gates, arbors, doors, chimneys and there-

fore hearths and fireplace openings to come and go. Caches to control this movement are properly called hands, mojos, bundles, or tobys. They trap and contain the spirits and direct their powerful action to or at someone. Spirits can cure, protect, foretell, control, or harm. At this point, I did not understand much about these traditions derived from Africa, and I did not yet know much about the religions from which they came or into which they changed. I was even confused about whether there was a religion or a scattering of magical practices.

My former student Lynn Jones, who ran our archaeological laboratories, also ran the excavations over two years (Jones 2000). We discovered seven caches in these workrooms (table 11). A large cache with a porcelain doll's head, arms, and legs, a ring, pins, and buttons were found under the kitchen hearth. Pins with a pierced Chinese coin were found in the northeast corner near a doorpost in a twentieth-century storeroom. A painted bottle filled with solidified black material was buried in a niche in the northeast corner of the new kitchen under the floor. A pile of white plaster with a broken sherd from a crock showing a dolphin swimming in waves was found in the old kitchen's northeast corner mixed with a white powdery material. Pins and glass fragments were found under the threshold of the door connecting the kitchen to the stair hall. And pins and buttons were found at the base of the staircase. Because some of the caches had been disturbed by rodents and by trenches for drains and pipes, we could not be sure that all the objects we found were part of a cache. But with years of retrospection and learning, I am confident that this was a carefully marked space protected by spirit bundles. The cook and others were probably protecting themselves, but such protection has an active component to it and might have aimed the spirits at the owners, which might have had an effect if the whites who owned the house had been raised by people of African descent who explained the ways of spirits to them as children. This was a much later insight provided by Gladys-Marie Fry.

Our finds at Slayton House received substantial, unsolicited publicity. Because our finds at the Carroll House had become better known, the circle of people seeking to contact us got larger. Professor Fry, a folklorist in the University of Maryland's English Department and an expert on African American material culture (Fry 2001 [1975], 1990), told me of her long-standing hope of exploring the sorts of things we were discovering in archaeology through written materials about them. Fry explained two things to me when we first met. One caused substantial relief and the other a transformation in how I thought about my group's discoveries.

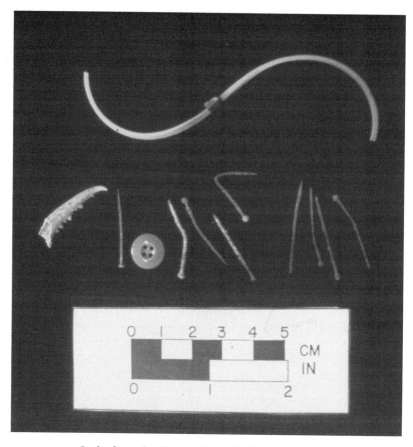

FIGURE 42. Cache from the Slayton House kitchen. There are nine common pins, a crab claw, a button, and a bead with a modern thread through it.

For the first time since I had begun to learn about crystals, caches, or West African religious traditions, I learned that large amounts of similar material had been discovered throughout the American South in houses and workplaces associated with slaves (Brown and Cooper 1990; Galke 1992, 2000; Jones 1999; LaRoche 1994; LaRoche and Blakey, 1997; Logan et al. 1992; Orser 1988a, 1986b, 1994; Patten 1992; Wilkie 1997, 2000). I knew, as most historical archaeologists did, of Leland Ferguson's (1992) colonoware pots and spoons with Xs on them. But Fry had heard of a whole pattern of archaeological discoveries from Virginia to Texas that involved caches or bundles from chimneys, hearths, and beneath floors and doors. Suddenly, I did not have to worry about my

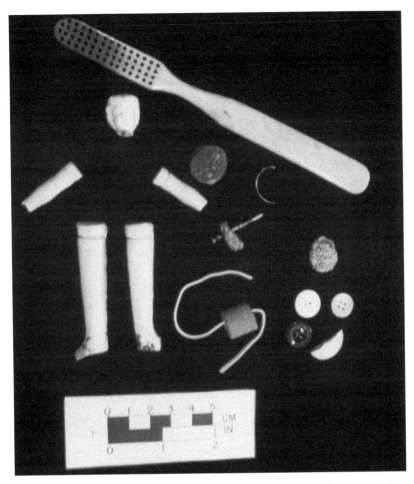

FIGURE 43. Cache from the hearth, Slayton House kitchen. These materials come from beneath the hearth and were recovered close together and intact. Doll fragments, rings, and discs are common in these caches. The kitchen contained at least two other caches.

own narrow frame of reference. Instead of making a unique discovery that some local professionals dismissed as trash, our discovery was one example of a pattern that Fry saw emerging from the archaeology done in the South since the 1970s.

The second part of my conversation with Fry was about the records of slave life that came from the stories recorded by and with former slaves

TABLE 11. Caches of artifacts from the Slayton House
in Annapolis tied to African spirit traditions

Artifacts	Unit where found	Location of unit	Date of artifacts
Porcelain doll parts, peanut shell with pin, brass button, white shell buttons, a gold ring	Unit 8, level B, throughout	In front of hearth in old kitchen	ca. 1870
6 white glass buttons, 2 white shell buttons, a straight pin	Unit 7, level E, throughout	Northeast corner of old kitchen	after 1845
Whiteware soup plate sherds, ironstone wash basin, stoneware butter crock, a white button, a gray shell button	Unit 7, feature 27a	Along east wall of old kitchen (northeast corner)	after 1845
A bone button, a white glass button, a metal button, whiteware soup plate sherds, ironstone wash basin sherds	Unit 7, feature 28a	Along east wall of old kitchen (northeast corner)	after 1845
A black bead, a gray glass button, 9 straight pins, a fragment of crab claw	Unit 12, level B	Northeast corner of present-day kitchen	after 1828
Tumbler base, bottle base, lamp chimney glass, lamp globe glass (white with pink painted decoration)	Unit 12, feature 42b (inside wall in corner)	Northeast corner of present-day kitchen	after 1870
Chinese coin, brass bell, 3 straight pins	Unit 18, level A	Storage room under the stairs	after 1870

SOURCES: Jones 2000, 59–60, table 1.

in the 1930s as part of the Works Progress Administration (WPA) Federal Writers' Project (FWP), which produced the so-called slave narratives, better known now as slave autobiographies (Hyatt 1970–78 [1935]; Rawick 1972, 1977, 1979; and see http://memory.loc.gov/ammem/snhtml/ snabout.html [accessed October 23, 2004]).

There are 11,000 pages of typescripts of narrative answers to standardized questions given by people in the 1930s who led their early lives in slavery before Emancipation in 1865. There was a protocol of over

FIGURE 44. Cache from the kitchen, Slayton House. A set of white buttons, each with four holes representing the cosmogram, distinguish this cache. Courtesy of the Anacostia Museum and Center for African American History and Culture, Smithsonian Institution. Photograph by Steven M. Cummings.

350 questions that were asked, mostly by white interviewers, of anyone who had grown up in slavery. Many hundreds of people were interviewed, from Delaware to Indiana, and from Texas to Florida. Some of the richest narratives come from the deep South. These narratives, published under the title *The American Slave: A Composite Autobiography* (Rawick 1972, 1977, 1979), are readily available in research libraries.

Some of the questions are about religion, and Gladys Fry planned a survey of them for us to find statements about the materials we were excavating. She opened my eyes to a written source that might help understand and explain the bundles. This process opened up the possibility of a better, more comprehensive understanding of the practices associated with the bundles and their meaning. But beyond this was the possibility of seeing the world of late American slavery from the vantage point of those who had lived in it and survived it. What did slaves think about their world, and how did they create it and understand their circumstances? The tension in a democracy whose economic base is capitalism is between external power and power from instruments of self-discipline. Capitalism inevitably creates opportunities, both to be achieved and already taken. Because it produces both great wealth and the power to protect it, and is defended as producing opportunities in the future for others, it is a system that mixes armed might, like that required to keep slaves, with self-discipline exercised through aspirations.

Neither capitalism nor democracy was extended very far after the Revolution. Capitalism, to be sure, did not look like the coherent system we know it to be now, nor had it been fully described analytically by the later eighteenth century. It was still possible to escape. And it certainly was possible to mount temporarily successful critiques of it, as was done throughout the early industrializing world by religious and secular utopianists. A parallel constraint on social life was that at first democracy was restricted to property-owning men in the new United States. Democracy was not to be extended to those without property, to women, to slaves, or to free people of color. Not only were all those outside the boundaries of the alliance of those who won the Revolution, but so was the optimism that the alliance generated. What then were slaves to do?

Slaves were property, but they were people in everybody's eyes, even if there was a debate among some whites about what kind of humans they were. Certainly, in their own eyes, they were not slaves. They never ceased resisting. Individually, there was subservience, but collectively this was less and less the case. This was especially true after the Haitian Revolution of 1793. And free people of African descent were constantly under threat of having their freedom removed, trumped by racism and by having no voting rights at all. What did these people have to say about the republic to which they belonged? Did they accept the self-improvement and self-monitoring vehicles of their masters and surrounding whites? Or, did they see the lie in its tale of opportunity and find something different? This is one question.

I have used Althusser (1971) so far as a basis for my analysis, and my final question about escape comes from the critiques of Althusser's ideas on ideology (e.g., Abercrombie, Hill, and Turner 1980). Individualism and its ally citizenship, Althusser would argue, are masks hiding a sharp hierarchy of wealth and power. Can anyone of a class of people see through the mask so that underlying relationships are visible? In Annapolis, the underlying relationship throughout the eighteenth century was that fewer and fewer people possessed more and more of the city's total wealth, and more and more of their neighbors possessed less and less of it. This inequality, I argue, was possible without violence largely because of the effectiveness of the ideology of individualism, with explicit personal freedom and individual liberty, and finally citizenship. This

ideology appeared so true to so many that it was not regarded as de-
batable. Did an ideology that included personal freedom and opportunity persuade those kept outside the promises of liberty before and after
the Revolution, particularly slaves and free people of African descent?
And how would an archaeologist know? Through the collaboration suggested by Fry, we discovered much of what we had hoped for about
African traditions in Annapolis and how people of African descent handled their place in Annapolis society.

Part of the surprising mix of events along my way came from the dates
of our archaeological discoveries. The earliest, 1790–1810, were dated
by pierced coins in the Charles Carroll House cache. The cache material
from Slayton House was as recent as 1920, however, so it had been made
or used, not by slaves, but by free workers in the twentieth century. When
we published these findings in newspapers, I was invited to speak to a
radio talk show in New York City with a predominantly African American audience. Six women called in, and five of them identified relatives
who used the practices described in the narratives and materials related
to what I described from Annapolis. Five of the six were happy to have
archaeology comment on traditions they knew. The sixth thought a white
guy could not be knowledgeable enough to comment on black culture.
When I finished listening, I knew that some aspect of the materials from
Annapolis was still alive now. I also knew I had to work at my relation
to African American culture.

One day, I got a call from Catherine Yronwode, who lives in northern California and runs a business on the Internet supplying authentic
and pure materials for making mojos or hands, material that we were
calling caches or bundles (Yronwode 2002). Yronwode sells most of the
well-known components for mojos, tobys, or hands from a website of
over 600 pages (www.luckymojo.com). She had read the FWP narratives
and then collected for sale the materials for hands mentioned there. She
began to advertise and sell them to a large customer base that was mostly
in the U.S. South, about 80 percent of whom are African American. But
she also had a customer near my own office at the University of Maryland, College Park. We talked for thirty minutes, and I realized that our
Annapolis discoveries were important to people far beyond archaeology
and African American folklore.

Yronwode obtained authentic St. John the Conqueror root, black dog
hair, bluing, red flannel, and a dozen other key, standard ingredients for
making hands. She had a knowing clientele who came to her with a clear
understanding of what each wanted. Furthermore, she had read some of

the 1930s narrative sources and used those as definitions of authenticity and purity. She did not sell substitutes or corrupted material. She sent me a box of about two dozen of these items. My conversation with Ms. Yronwode showed me that the tradition was alive, large, and in my own backyard, which is to say, on the edge of Annapolis. Now there was no gap between 1920 at Slayton House and today. The tradition was alive and was called Hoodoo, or conjure, conjuration, or root work. It is probably best to refer to it here as African spirit tradition. It had been in America since the eighteenth century, and had its origins in West and West Central Africa, so it was both African and American. It is part of what is left of Africa in America.

My students and I were guided by Herskovits (1958 [1941]) to the debate over whether or not anything is left of Africa in America, which dates from about 1900 and includes discussions of African dance, music, food, dress styles, and religion. But the more recent question of what happened to African traditions in the New World also seemed important (see Gundaker 1998a, 1998b; Price 1990; Price and Price 1999; Thompson 1983, 1991; Theophus Smith 1994). There is little or no evidence for West African religious traditions in seventeenth-century Anglo-America through historical archaeology, certainly in Annapolis. Even though there were African indentured servants, for example, from the Caribbean, and some slaves late in the 1600s, African spirit traditions or their early forms are not visible archaeologically. They are not apparent until early in the eighteenth century as far as I know.

There is thus a century in North America with people of African descent but without evidence of their religious traditions. So when African spirit traditions appear archaeologically in the early eighteenth century, they are African, but are probably also American, and they may be the beginning of an amalgam of several African traditions, such as the BaKongo, Fan, Ifa, and Yoruba traditions. I and others thus tend to see them as coming from a combination of sources and as a creation in America of African origin. But there is another, more traditional position that argues that spirit use is what is left of religious traditions torn from their origins and practiced secretly, largely bereft of specialists and their original web of meaning. It is thus a remnant, but is purely African, not part Native American religion, Christianity, or English witchcraft. It is not creole.

This debate was the context for our excavations at the James Brice House, where initially we did not expect to find much related to African Americans, but where we certainly would not have missed it. The Brice House was built late in the eighteenth century and is one of the largest and best preserved of the great Annapolis houses. It is a five-part Georgian house with the west wing devoted to an office and stable or warehouse and the opposite east wing containing a kitchen and laundry. Our job was to excavate within and around the west wing and inside the east wing and its connection to the main block of the house. In the 1980s, during renovation and restoration of the house, then newly bought and owned by the not-for-profit arm of the bricklayer's union, called the International Masonry Institute, the attic of the main house was substantially altered. This was supposed to have been where the family's slaves had lived. Whether they lived there or not, the various owners did have slaves, and the current owners were also interested in that aspect of the house's past. We found that past in a number of different places in the house. At the base of one of the house's lightning rods, which was near a downspout, we found a dense, compact cache of oyster shells, a crystal decanter top, and a broken up tortoise shell; there was also a pierced coin with the bundle. Both the downspout and lightning rod provided an obvious connection with the flash of the spirits and a pathway for them, probably marked by the whiteness of the oyster shells. The likely meaning of the artifacts as a hand was clear, and we did not doubt that this find was African American. The discovery was made and immediately recognized by Colin Beaven.

The major scholar of West African religious traditions in the United States is Robert Ferris Thompson of Yale. His best-known books on the topic, *Flash of the Spirit* (1983) and *Face of the Gods* (1993), use the known connection between the ways spirits express themselves and ways to contain and direct them. Spirits are associated with beams of light and things that flash like mirrors, crystals, decanter tops, pie plates, and, more recently, hubcaps. These embody spirits. They capture and control them and then direct them. This is called a metonym. The thing controlling spirits is not what it appears to be; it is actually something entirely different. It doesn't stand for something else; it is something else, so a crystal or mirror actually held the spirit.

The Brice House excavations were conceptualized by James Harmon (Harmon and Neuwirth 2000), who began our work in the west wing and moved us to the east wing after the first excavation was well along. Two of our archaeologists, Colin Beaven and Matthew Cochran, were already very familiar with the work we had done on spirit traditions, and Cochran had independently discovered Yronwode's website. These men dug in the east wing along with a prehistorian who insisted that the archaeology of African spirit use was intellectually unconvincing, because there was no way to distinguish its remains from scatter or trash. Because a number of other local archaeologists continued to hold this opinion, they constituted a useful foil to our work.

The east wing of the Brice House (Harmon and Neuwirth 2000) became a treasure trove of African spirit usage over the year, from the beginning of our work there until Jessica Neuwirth and Matthew Cochran figured out fully what was really there (Neuwirth and Cochran 1999; Cochran 1999). During the excavations, several members of our team knew virtually immediately that we had discovered several caches. The first two seemed independent of each other. On the north side of the room that we knew as the laundry, a room we believed to have been thoroughly disturbed by gutting and installation of central heating early in the twentieth century, asbestos removal, the tearing up of two or three layers of twentieth-century wooden flooring, and general careless treatment, we began to find significant collections below the floor. Cochran and Beaven right away saw interesting things that were as yet new to them.

The deposits were dry and included beads, peach pits, pins, a medicine bottle with a stopper in place and a seed inside it, buttons—including one with what looked like a handmade letter M impressed on its top, three pieces of red cloth, and many more things, forming a circular deposit about eight feet wide and two to three inches deep, ending at a bricked-up doorway that had led to a hallway and then to the kitchen. The old doorway was in the center of the wall, on the centerline between the hearths at either end of the long axis of the whole wing itself. My students thought this collection was a cache but had never heard of one so big, so flat, so oriented, so rich, and so stratified. Why was it more or less oval, why had it been used over about forty-five years, as dated by its ceramic contents and through its internal stratification, why did it have between 500 and 1,000 items in it, why was it so oddly placed in the room? Its being in front of a doorway made sense, but not much else.

The modern door that connected the laundry to the modern hall and then to the north room and former main kitchen was only a few feet from the original door, now bricked up. Another and far more recognizable collection of materials was discovered near the new door, but on the other side of the threshold—the hallway side of the now closed-up door. Two iron rings, each about an inch and a half in diameter were in the deposit, along with buttons and pins. Because rings are so well known from archaeological deposits of spirit use, and in part too, because the materials were close together—not spread out—and in front of the older doorway, we thought right away that we had a spirit deposit. We were elated,

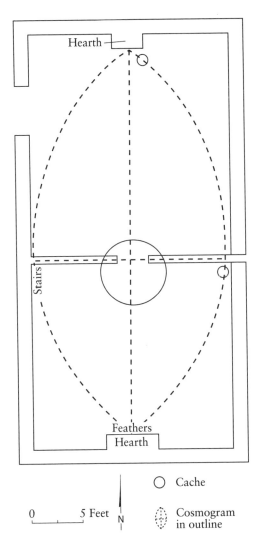

Hearth

Stairs

Feathers
Hearth

FIGURE 45. Brice House cosmogram. This diagram schematically shows the deposits, consisting of about a thousand items, buried below the floors of the kitchen and laundry of the Brice House. The deposits date from the 1880s to the 1920s. Drawing prepared by Bill Nelson based on original by Jessica Neuwirth and Matthew Cochran.

0   5 Feet   N

○   Cache

⋰⋱   Cosmogram in outline

except that no amount of our logic placated the prehistorian. It was meaningless to him.

The prehistorian supervisor was excavating what was left of the very large hearth for the original kitchen fireplace. I knew this was a very important locale for African traditions. Even when he turned up porcelain doll fragments under the hearth, he refused to believe he had found anything significant, refused to record associated materials, and left me exasperated. I wanted more and more context, but I was grateful that the hearth had yielded enough to guarantee our understanding of its role in managing spirits in the house. More and more, I knew, this had been an African environment; on the one hand, we should have expected it, on the other, we were delightfully surprised to find it.

Next, on the inside of an exterior door, we found a pierced coin. The door was in the center of the outside wall of the east wing, directly opposite a staircase to the second floor and on the short axis of the building. Next, at the southern fireplace, which had been heavily reconstructed, but near some of its hearth area that remained undisturbed, we found a clump of feathers, meaningless to us at the time, but recorded. The staircase to the upper floor, where slaves or free servants might have lived, had originally ascended from near the big oval deposit in the laundry. This stair had been moved so that it now centered on the hall between the kitchen and laundry. Furthermore, pipes insulated with asbestos had been installed at the location of the earlier staircase. The entire surrounding floor area had been disturbed, and we never excavated it. If I had the dig to do over again, I would try to excavate there, as well as at the base of the newer, twentieth-century stair.

About six months after our excavation was finished, and long before our report was complete, Jessica Neuwirth and Matthew Cochran (1999) called me up with an amazing discovery made from their much deeper reading of materials connected to African spirit traditions. They believed that rather than there being a series of unconnected caches in the workrooms, the entire space was laid out as a cosmogram. In the middle of the two rooms was the cosmogram's center, located at the crossing of the east wing's long and short axes, as marked by the openings through the two chimneys at either end and the outside door and the staircase at either end of the short axis. The floor, plus the flues, the outside door and the stair opposite, composed a large, three-dimensional environment both illustrating and enabling a life's safe journey.

A cosmogram is not representational, like most uses of a cross. It facilitates. A cosmogram made up of bundles, mojos, or hands, controlled the passage of spirits who came and went. Spirits pass up and down chimneys, in and out of doors, up and down stairs, and caches control their intent and action.

The cosmogram's center is its key element, because it is the crossing point of the lines that connect the land of the living and the spirits in the world of the dead, as well as the beginning and end of life's path. The first is the vertical axis; the second is horizontal. Not only do these crossed axes represent life and its relationship to death, but they help control the

FIGURE 46. Black mirror and black and white beads, Brice House cosmogram. Mirrors, like crystals, can capture and direct spirits. Courtesy of the Anacostia Museum and Center for African American History and Culture, Smithsonian Institution. Photograph by Steven M. Cummings.

relationship as well. The crossed axes are often seen as an X. Once we knew we had a cosmogram, we realized that the whole space was protected by a coherent set of moves that showed us we had made a mistake in seeing individual bundles as the largest unit of this tradition's operation. Upon reflection, we also began to understand that at least the kitchen in Slayton House (Jones 2000) was probably just as completely marked, and that we had only seen individual bundles, not a whole cosmogram. This may have been true of the Charles Carroll House finds as well. Because our own internal debate had centered on whether or not we actually had bundles, we completely missed the bigger picture. That mistake did not happen again.

The debate within my own team was an unpleasant one. Unless you could be sure something was a cache, it was best to be scientifically conservative and conclude nothing. Some argued that this should be our way of operating to avoid more criticism from the local archaeologists, who always proclaimed these discoveries to be trash and not discoveries at all. Why add fuel to the fire of criticism, after all? The political side effect of this position was our silence, with little or no understanding of how this denied historical access to the black community.

My response to this position was to suggest that all such caches be

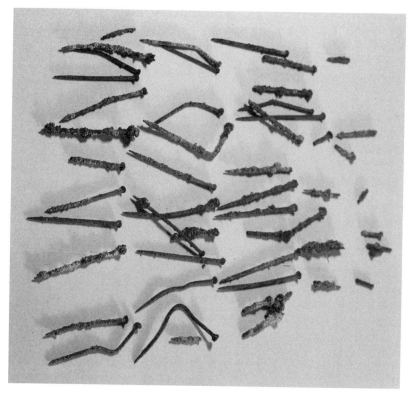

FIGURE 47. Pins from the Brice House cosmogram, one of the few ever discovered with datable layers. The large number of pins may represent either replenishing of the cosmogram's power or its constant use. Courtesy of the Anacostia Museum and Center for African American History and Culture, Smithsonian Institution. Photograph by Steven M. Cummings.

studied comparatively so as to note the common elements. I figured that once an archaeological signature for a cache was found by such a comparative study, the debate would be ended. This was a somewhat primitive technique, but the more we discovered such materials archaeologically, the easier such a technique would be, and the more it would be needed and appreciated. No dice from my crew at first.

The idea of comparison was behind Gladys Fry's suggestion that she had long wanted to survey the Cultural Resource Management literature on slave houses, quarters, and other living spaces. To quiet the doubts voiced by my own staff, I followed Fry's suggestion and we created a research design. Cultural Resource Management archaeological projects, normally mandated by some level of law, require an excavation and a site report that is descriptive. Such reports normally contain no coherent analysis and follow various formats. In other words, they are hard to follow if you are not an archaeologist, and Fry readily admitted that she could not find her way through them to get coherent results. I knew she was right.

She and I hired Jane Cox to begin a survey of such reports, and Cox obtained remarkable results. We began with CRM reports on slave environments in Virginia. She found that the major collection of archaeological reports was in a state library in Richmond, with some in Williamsburg. As she visited, counted, called around, explored, and convinced people of what she needed, Jane Cox found there were about thirty-four sites in eastern Virginia that had been excavated and were connected with slaves. These were quarters, field houses, tenant farms, slave pens where people were held while awaiting sale, places where free people had lived, and places in plantation houses assigned to slaves or freed people of African descent.

Of the thirty-four such sites, only seventeen were useful to our survey. There were no written reports on many of the thirty-four sites, and others had no evidence of bundles or caches. Cox counted each item in each cache at the seventeen sites by location, like the northeast corner, hearth, chimney base, door threshold, or doorpost. She made a table of the results, which we subsequently published in the *Journal of American Folklore* (Leone and Fry 1999). Cox's survey produced both more and less than I expected. It covered a little more than the eastern half of the state. The survey showed that very much more had been done in Virginia for and on African Americans through archaeology than is true in Maryland even up to the moment of this writing. This is true despite Virginia's noted past in sustaining slavery and segregation, while Maryland was home to a very large number of free black people from well before Emancipation.

The survey showed that caches were found in only three locations: (1) northeast corners, (2) hearths, or chimney bases, and (3) thresholds or bottoms of staircases or steps. They were composed of a combination of things, often pins, buttons, coins, glass bits, rings, bone pieces, and stones. No one thing or set of things was always there. There was no set of things that was a common denominator. But when a deposit was found, the original archaeologist noted it, because all the items were found very close together, often dug into the ground, in one of the three

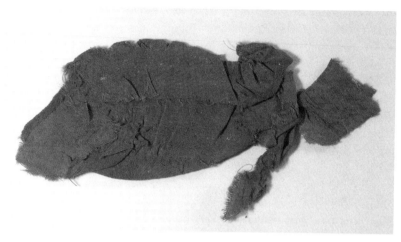

FIGURE 48. Red flannel from the Brice House cosmogram, a powerful element in the spirit practices derived from West Africa. The Brice House deposit was dry and provides a rare surviving example of the use of this cloth. Three swatches of it were recovered, along with a separate mass of threaded material and a root mass. Courtesy of the Anacostia Museum and Center for African American History and Culture, Smithsonian Institution. Photograph by Steven M. Cummings.

locations. As a result of Cox's work and our team's subsequent analysis, our finds in Annapolis had a comparative context and became indisputably associated with African American use of spirit traditions in both slavery and freedom.

There was no material associated with these practices in the seventeenth century in Virginia. The earliest date in Virginia is 1702; the earliest in Annapolis is 1790. The latest date in Virginia is 1880; the latest archaeological date in Annapolis is 1920. These dates are important, because the chronology of West African traditions cannot be established through the FWP composite slave autobiographies (Rawick 1972, 1977, 1979). From those narratives, one can tell that spirit use was a part of people's lives and beliefs and had African origins. But archaeology gave it a beginning, an end, and a spatial context.

At first, I thought that African spirit use was associated with slavery, then after the Slayton and Brice Houses, I realized that it had continued, so that it must be associated with living in a racist context. Was the absence of seventeenth-century evidence because there was little permanent slavery in Virginia in the seventeenth century or because there were comparatively few slaves? If African spirit traditions were a "slave religion" as Albert Raboteau (1978) said, then it would not be found where slav-ery did not exist or was a marginal part of society. But there were Africans and there must have been African beliefs. I would rather leave this issue unresolved with a search that expects African traditions to have been alive in the seventeenth century but yet to be uncovered through ar-chaeology. I have come to suspect that while African spirit traditions may have been fostered in slavery and racism, they were not created within them. While there is a strong component of fear in conjure, there is in other religions as well, and it is not the dominant theme. Thus, I do not think the West African traditions should be associated with slavery as a matrix that explains them. I think they should be understood in the con-texts of diasporic religions like Santeria, Condomble, Voodoo, and Palo Mayombe that appeared among Africans exposed to Christianity, and Native America, in the New World. Sorting out a combination may be fruitless, but acknowledging the combination as creative is essential to seeing how the religions work in the New World circumstance of slavery and racism.

I have read and been influenced more by Rabateau (1978) and Theo-phus Smith (1994) than by Michael Gomez (1998). My own former stu-dents Lynn Jones (1995, 1999) and Christopher Fennel (2000, 2003) have been oriented more to Robert Ferris Thompson than to individual ethno-graphic areas of Africa or the different influences of Muslim and non-Muslim peoples. As a result, our interpretations tend to stress Congo and BaKongo-speaking traditions, while attempting to recognize the ethnic variety among these, as well as the hierarchical order of the Congo king-dom itself, which emerged in the centuries just before the initiation of the European slave trade.

I recognize that neither a search for the specific African religious tra-ditions nor an attempt to assess the actual ethnographic variety within them has been accomplished by the work I report here. This is the case even though such a search has been initiated by scholars on whom I rely, like Theophus Smith (1994), Grey Gundaker (1993, 1998a, 1998b), and Christopher Fennel (2000, 2003). My effort has been an intermediate step, to produce a correlation of the archaeology of spirit traditions with the FWP slave autobiographies.

All around the periphery of my archaeological work was the possibil-ity that reading the FWP autobiographies would produce a reconstruc-tion of what the caches meant. Citations from them regarding religion, charms, spells, magic, and curing were frequent in the scholarly litera-ture, but as isolated, evocative quotations. Fry and I did not want to be impressionistic, because that work had already been done; we wanted to be comprehensive and, therefore, comparative.

Timothy Ruppel, a colleague of Fry's, who also knew the FWP composite autobiographies very well, began to work with us, teaching me a great deal. Following guidelines laid out by Fry, Ruppel read all the composite autobiographies, recording every single mention of an item found in our archaeological caches for magical purposes. He took the list of Jane Cox's research of everything discovered in archaeological caches in Virginia, went through the composite autobiographies searching for a mention of these items, and found the contexts of their use.

Table 12 lists the thirty-six items found in secure archaeological provenients in the eastern half of Virginia that come from known African and African American contexts. While these have been published before by our research team, it is important to see the material here, because it helps constitute our case for knowing the material pattern. The number of occurrences by object is particularly significant, because it indicates frequency.

Table 13 extends the list to items mentioned in the FWP composite autobiographies, which is where most details of perishable items necessarily come from. To achieve this list, Ruppel did not read only for items by themselves but also for mentions of charms, hands, or tobys. There were 239 such occurrences in the narratives, and they are the base for extending the thirty-six items in table 12 to the seventy-four or so items listed in table 13. This is the universe of things that an archaeologist can expect to find when looking for the remains of West and Central West African traditions. The list could be expanded through spreading the survey into other archaeological areas in the South, although not likely by much.

The point of our surveys was to establish both the universe of materials used for spirit purposes and their meaning, which is essential in order to create an understanding of how West African religions functioned in Annapolis and elsewhere in North America. Table 13 shows only the list of items mentioned in the slave narratives and what each was intended to do. It is quickly clear that the majority of items were worn, not buried. According to the FWP autobiographies, however, twenty-two items— beads, bones, bricks, brooms, buttons, claws, coins, corn shucks, feathers, graveyard dirt, matches, nails, needles, pins, red pepper pods, rings, roots, salt, saltpeter, shoes, sticks, and yellow dust—were to be buried or used outside, and so some of them might be expected to be found archaeologically. (Note that these items are distinct from and in addition to those in

TABLE 12. Artifacts in caches from
archaeological sites in Virginia tied to
African spirit traditions, 1702–1920

Items	Frequency
Beads	87
Bottles	13
Bones	93
Broach	1
Buckles	30
Buttons	285
Cameo	1
Ceramics	10
Chisel	1
Circular frame	1
Coins	19
Comb	2
Crystals	47
Discs	48
Gaming pieces	4
Glass	11
Hinge	1
Hook	2
Horse bit	1
Horseshoe	3
Jewelry	5
Keys	2
Knife blade	2
Nails	49
Necklace	1
Needles	3
Pendant	2
Pins	625
Rings	4
Sinker	1
Spring	1
Stones	8
Strainers	1
Watch fob	2
Wire	149
Wood	1

SOURCE: Leone and Fry 1999. Compiled by C. Jane Cox.

TABLE 13. Textual references in the Federal Writers' Project composite autobiographies listing purposes and placement of artifacts tied to African spirit traditions

Charm (with key ingredients)	Function	Location worn or placed
Bag (toby)	prevent whipping	unspecified
dimes	protect from conjure	over heart
red ants	ease teething	around neck
asafetida (herb)	prevent smallpox, prevent chills, protect from conjure, ease teething	around neck
devil's snuff	make friendly	under steps
lodestone	protect from conjure	around neck
powder	protect from conjure	around neck
salt	prevent palpitations	over heart
sand	avoid whipping	carry
sulfur	protect from conjure	around knee or in shoe
wood ash	fix court case	carry
Ball (silver)	protect from conjure	unspecified
Band (red flannel)	gain strength, prevent rheumatism	wrist, arm, or leg
Beads	prevent sickness	around neck
Belt (snakeskin)	not given	wear; place unspecified
Bone (black cat)	avoid whipping	pocket
	bring luck with law	carry
	make disappear	unspecified
	avoid detection	carry
bones	not given	unspecified
brick (powdered)	protect from conjure	steps
broom	protect from witch	before door
buckeye	bring luck	carry
	prevent sickness	in pocket or around neck
Button	bring luck	carry
charm string	bring luck	neck
white	bring luck/ease teething	neck
pearl	ease teething	neck
shiny	prevent sickness	wear
Calf dropping	escape patrol	feet
Claw (buzzard)	ease teething	neck

TABLE 13 *continued*

Charm (with key ingredients)	Function	Location worn or placed
Coin	protect from conjure	ankle, neck
	prevent rheumatism	ankle
	bring luck	carry
	prevent sickness	ankle
Coin (brass)	avoid indigestion	neck
Coin (dime)	not given	on string of beads
	protect from conjure, swallow with tea	shoe, ankle
	prevent cramps	neck
Coin (penny)	prevent sickness	ankle
	protect from conjure	floor by door
	avoid indigestion	neck
Coin (pierced dime)	prevent rheumatism	unspecified
Corn shuck	protect from conjure	shoe
Crab	make invincible	hold in mouth
Feathers (bird)	protect from conjure	shoe
Flaxseed	protect from witch	around bed
Fork	protect from witch	by bed
Frog (dried)	ease teething	neck
Graveyard dirt	escape patrol	feet
Hand	control mistress	unspecified
Hand (red flannel)	protect from witch	under armpit
	bring luck	pocket
	protect from conjure	neck
Horseshoe	protect from spirits	over door
	avoid whipping	over door
	bring luck	over front door
	protect from spirits	over door
Jawbone (hog)	ease teething	unspecified
Lead disc (with holes)	prevent palpitations	around neck
Matches	prevent headache, protect from conjure	hair
Mole foot	ease teething	neck
Nails (5 new)	avoid whipping	in ground
Needles (2)	protect from conjure	crossed in hat
Newspaper (with red pepper)	protect from conjure	shoe

TABLE 13 *continued*

Charm (with key ingredients)	Function	Location worn or placed
Nutmeg	prevent rheumatism	neck
	ease toothache	neck
	prevent headache	neck
	ease teething	neck
Peace plant	protect from conjure	pocket or shoe
Pins (in pincushion)	protect from witch	side of bed
Rabbit foot	bring luck	carry
	protect from witch	wear
	avoid detection	carry
	avoid whipping	neck
Raccoon foot	protect from witches	wear
	bring luck	carry
Rattan	avoid whipping	wave in face
Rattlesnake rattles	ease teething	neck
Red pepper pod	protect from conjure	over door
Ring (black)	bring luck	hand
Ring (brass)	prevent croup	finger
	prevent heart pains	left hand
	prevent rheumatism	finger
Root	avoid whipping	chew and spit
Anjillico	prevent sickness	neck
Devil's shoe string	bring luck	unspecified
	get money or job	chew
Drink	protect from conjure	drink
Five-fingered grass	protect from conjure	over bed
John the Conqueror	protect from conjure	pocket
	bring luck	carry in pocket
Rattle snake master	bring luck	unspecified
Devil's shoestring	obtain favors	chew
	release from jail	spit in cell
	avoid whipping	tie around waist
Salt	avoid ill will	footprint of guests
Saltpeter	protect from conjure	shoe
Shoe	protect from conjure	over door
old	protect from spirits	over door
Sifter (flour)	protect from witch	by bed
silver	remove conjure	wear
pieces	protect from conjure	boil and drink

TABLE 13 *continued*

Charm (with key ingredients)	Function	Location worn or placed
Snakeskin	protect from conjure	wear
Stick	avoid pursuit	crossroads
	avoid whipping	under master's door
	avoid mistreatment	under master's door
String	protect from witch	on image
		in hair
	prevent sickness	neck
	prevent cramps	wrist and ankle
		wrist
	ease teething	neck
Teeth (alligator)	ease teething	unspecified
Turpentine	escape patrol	feet
Urine	protect from conjure	back steps
Urine and salt	protect from conjure	around door
Yellow dust	avoid mistreatment	sprinkle

SOURCES: Rawick 1972, 1977, 1979; Leone, Fry, and Ruppel 2001, 150n.
NOTE: These items together with those in table 12 compose a complete list of material used in the African spirit tradition from our sources.

Table 11, which were actually found archaeologically.) A further twenty four items—bottles, broaches, buckles, cameos, ceramics, chisels, circular frames, combs, crystals, gaming pieces, glass, hinges, hooks, horsebits, jewelry, keys, knife blades, necklaces, pendants, sinkers, springs, stones, watchfobs, and wire—that were found through archaeology in Virginia, as shown in Table 12, are not mentioned in the slave narratives, and we thus have only an approximation of what they might mean.

Some very important patterns are thus now clear for the first time. The first is that the FWP composite autobiographies are not a complete guide to explaining the archaeology of the spirit traditions. Only fourteen of the items found archaeologically are mentioned in the narratives. To be sure, the most commonly used are mentioned, usually multiple times. However, only twenty-two of the sixty items mentioned as being associated with spirits were put in the ground. The rest were worn or carried. This means that putting items apart from a person and not wearing them was a much less frequent practice. It does not mean that such a way of dealing with spirits was less significant or less powerful; it was just less frequent. We also saw with these lists that establishing an archaeological signature for the spirit tradition was going to be difficult, because buttons, coins, pins, beads, and rings were frequently worn or carried, as well as buried, and thus could be associated with different purposes. So, while we might find an archaeological cluster, it would not be easy to establish its meaning or purpose.

To summarize the newly discovered pattern: thirty-six items are visible through Virginia archaeology for African spirit traditions. This list includes most of the items found in similar deposits in Annapolis, but not all, for example, peach pits from Brice House. The archaeological list should be expected to be expandable, because spirits shape shift in their expressions and cannot be pinned down completely by way of this kind of archaeological categorization (Grey Gundaker, personal communication, October 25, 2003).

The composite autobiographies mention sixty items, some more than once, that are involved in spirit use. These sixty items include thirty-eight not so far found archaeologically. Tables 12 and 13, taken together, show all the items from both archaeology and the narratives, but the latter do not mention twenty-four items that were found archaeologically. Thus, almost a third of all the archaeological items found were never mentioned by former slaves in their FWP autobiographies.

Finally, as shown above, forty-six items were meant to be buried or used outside in the yard, where some of them might be found archaeologically. Twenty-four of these were actually found in Virginia, and twenty-two of them are mentioned in the composite autobiographies. This is over half of all the seventy-four items used to manage spirits. The rest of the items were worn, usually singly for protection or curing. The items buried or used outside involved fixing, that is, turning spirits used against a person away, or directing spirits onto others. While this is so, it is also clear that rings, pins, and coins, for example, could be carried as well as buried and thus their meaning depends on use, not just on location. This, too, indicates shape shifting in the spirit tradition. A form like a ring does not mean only one thing, but its meaning comes partially from its location and context.

The composite autobiographies are quite clear on the purposes of items worn or carried as charms. Fry, Ruppel, and I could see two patterns. One was the full inventory of seventy-four items involved in spirit traditions, which was a basic discovery in itself. The second pattern was the effect of using them. Use was to prevent disease, to cure it, or bring luck by controlling the future of events in about two-thirds of all recorded cases. The diseases were limited to rheumatism, headache, the pain of teething, smallpox, chills, indigestion, and protecting from conjure itself. Table 13 shows the variations.

After we discovered the purposes of the items listed in table 13, we also found a substantial discrepancy between our archaeological discoveries regarding spirit traditions and the FWP composite autobiographies' description of what was used and where the items were placed. The archaeology showed us bundles of items buried permanently or added to over a long period, say for the forty or so years of use at Brice House. The bulk of the data from the autobiographies refer to single items worn for a purpose and relatively briefly.

Then we had a breakthrough that began to explain the discrepancy between those items found through archaeology and where the same items were to be placed as listed in the FWP autobiographies. I looked at the combination of location and purpose and realized that buried bundles were used for fixing. Fixing is often called conjure, refers to harming someone, and is a part of Hoodoo. Hands, mojos, tobys, root work, fixing, conjure, and malign conjure can all mean the same thing. Hands, mojos, tobys, bags, bundles are the actual material used. Conjure, fixing, and malign conjure are the processes of harming, killing, making crazy, crippling, or otherwise causing some kind of physical injury—often extremely serious—to some intended victim. This side of spirit use required a cache.

In the FWP autobiographies, when fixing was to be done, the bag was usually put under the steps where the intended victim was going to walk. That was the most common location in the thirty-five times bags are specifically mentioned in the composite autobiographies. In the fireplace, in the ground, in running water, and near the bed of the victim are also specified as effective locations. The bag had to be near the person to be harmed for it to work.

Suddenly, I realized that I was quite wrong. Our work in Annapolis was not just about protection and health; it was also not just about building a cosmogram for symbolic purposes and celebrating African antecedents. It was also about using spirits to keep dangerous, burdensome people away and in their place. It was not passive; it was aggressively about wishes to kill, drive crazy, and cause sickness and harm. Bad conjure is dangerous to engage in.

Our discovery is that within a hierarchically organized household there was symbolic violence. There was rebellion and resistance. The Annapolis households where we find fixing were not tranquil places as we saw with the Charles Carroll household, where we should see just African superstitions and African survivals. There was violence and not social harmony. This conclusion, suggested by Ruppel, comes from our analyses and should be taken as a hypothesis and explored. Its virtue comes from allowing a view of Annapolis as a torn society made up of two cultures, not as a hierarchical one living in subdued peace. It calls for seeing a clear consciousness of conditions of the part of people of African descent.

Who was it aimed at? The kind of conjure that is fixing was normally done away from home according to the narratives. It was done on others, rarely to people in one's home. In the Virginia cabins, which were marked by buried caches and bundles and in the Annapolis kitchens and surrounding workrooms, who could the object be? One item in the Brice House cache was a button with resin on top and with pieces of mother of pearl pressed into it to form what seemed like an M. Matt Cochran pointed out that the Martins had owned the house at the time of the cache's use. Might fixing have been aimed at owners, overseers, employers, masters, mistresses, and those who caused the working conditions in which people of African descent found themselves?

In the composite autobiographies, it is clear that fixing was done to people who were likely to believe in it, especially people of African descent. Some scholars are reluctant to believe that it was directed against whites (Raboteau 1978), but the question arises from our work. When we see fixing in the narratives, it was usually done away from home. Yet the archaeology shows fixing done at one's workplace at home. We do not know why yet. We know from the autobiographies that it was sometimes directed at family members. But because it was the most dangerous part of spirit practice, we have a puzzle about the relation between the owners/employers and those doing the fixing.

This newly discovered question posed a problem because it brought fixing into the house, where the FWP composite autobiographies do not mention it. For people who know, use, and care for spirits, especially in their yards, there is a daily practice known as sweeping. A sweeper begins at the door and sweeps carefully to the gate, guiding and pushing out spirits who are not wanted. The gate is one of two dividing lines. The safest zone, with the most domesticated spirits, is in the house. The yard also has spirits under control, but is a zone for further domestication of those who are out of control, or wild. The zone of greatest danger is beyond the gate. New spirits can be discovered all the time in the woods or wilderness. They can be brought closer and closer to home in

FIGURE 49. Button with inlaid bits of mother of pearl from the Brice House cosmogram. The inlays in this created piece may form an M, perhaps standing for the surname of the family that owned the house at the time the cosmo-gram was laid down. Courtesy of the Anacostia Museum and Center for African American History and Culture, Smithsonian Institution. Photograph by Steven M. Cummings.

a deliberate process of control. But the safest spirits are those in the house. This is the paradigm in some Caribbean islands, not necessarily in Annapolis, but I cite it here for a purpose.

Fixing occurred in the wild, outside the gate, in the composite autobiographies, so that a spirit could be brought under control. According to the autobiographies, that is where bundles, which were like those found archaeologically, were supposed to be placed. The autobiographies rarely discuss the elaborate array of protections or conjure items we found in houses in Annapolis or throughout Virginia. Who, then, were they used against?

It should be kept in mind that the composite autobiographies, gathered in the 1930s, were obtained from people who had been children or at best teenagers in the slavery era almost sixty years before. They may thus not have been fully informed about what was going on. It might not be safe to tell a child that one was putting a hex on the master. Children under a certain age might also not be initiated into all the details of religious practice.

I think there are three hunches to hold in mind that come from this juxtaposition of two quite different, equally valid sources. When I realized, quite gradually, that there were cosmograms made of bundles in Annapolis houses, I began to see that, because they were maintained for decades, possibly over whole lifetimes, the environment their makers created was one akin to worship—in this tradition, it is called centering—and were not just momentary acts for protection, no matter how potent. A cosmogram served to placate, domesticate, and direct spirits for the long term, possibly even to teach. Second, in a world of spirits that moved and were powerful, and where competing and neighboring social forces directed them, a well-marked space or yard offered long-term protection or was a safety zone. Third, since the bags mentioned in the FWP autobiographies that best describe those we found archaeologically had a single, general purpose, which was to cause harm, the role of masters and employers needs to be specifically examined for antagonisms, more than that of family members of the user of the cache.

As a result of systematically comparing the whole range of archaeological material found within the autobiographies' formulas, we saw a clear division between items used for curing, prevention, and foretelling the future, on the one hand, and warding off danger and provoking vengeance, on the other. There is little archaeology for the first, but it is extensive for the second. The very close, domestic placement of items used for fixing raises a provocative question about at whom such fixing was aimed. Even with this new question, we still have an archaeological signature we did not have before. But what does the signature mean within African American culture?

We have African households in the middle of historic Annapolis with practices so different, so secret, so effectively coherent in their own terms, that we have found a whole part of Annapolis society outside the Georgian city.

What did African spirit traditions accomplish? I think there are two answers. The first is how caches work. They work by containing three elements, and this is the signature. At first, I made the mistake of supposing that there could be common denominator items, like pins or buttons, or graveyard dirt, that were somehow interchangeable and had to be in any bundle. This was incorrect when we compared the lists of archaeological bundle contents to the lists from the FWP autobiographies of spirit use. Theophus Smith led me to see that a bundle always had a purpose, like curing, protecting, or driving a specific person away. It was always aimed at a person, for a specific reason, and was placed in a specific location. As a result, there were three items, or a set of elements, in a hand. There was something to identify the person, like hair or a small possession. There was something allied to a wish, a bent pin or nail to cure rheumatism or a crab claw for tenaciousness or strength. Third, there was something to contain the spirit, like a crystal, a piece of red cloth, a mirror fragment, graveyard dirt, or white powder. When the object of the bundle or hand passed near it, the spirit caused the desired result. These were the three elements as represented by things in a cache.

This appears simple enough, but it does not explain the bundles in the workrooms of the big Annapolis houses or in some of the slave cabins and tenant homes of Virginians of African descent. There, something much longer-term and akin to centering, or teaching, or continual maintenance was likely.

The second answer is that Africa's spirit traditions have their origins in societies organized by kinship, where face-to-face knowledge was essential to social control (William Stuart, personal communication). Under these circumstances, magic was worked by some on others and was based on close, direct knowledge of one another and universally shared beliefs. Ancestors were important because everyone shared them and they were in direct relationship to the hierarchy among the living, because they had once been the living. Because of virtually universal beliefs, spirits reflected the organization of society and managed ties among the living, whose needs and sore spots were known. On these bases, spirits could be used in transplanted African communities in the New World and form part of how Santeria, Condemble, Voodoo, and North American variants work. These beliefs helped to achieve order.

This leads to asking whether spirit use is an African remnant. Or is it part of a new religion? African religions did not have to explain and create ways to deal with racism, permanent inferior statuses, or long-term racial hatred. African religion in America did.

One major explanation advanced for how people of African descent dealt with hatred is that they did so by using aspects of Christianity and making it their own; they created a combination of African religious beliefs and Christianity. From the standpoint of archaeology, there is no evidence of anything from Christianity in the bundles from anywhere they have been excavated. The FWP autobiographies tell of no use of Christian ideas or definitions when wearing charms or fixing enemies or witches. But, the FWP autobiographies very often show that people who used or believed in spirits were devout Christians. The composite autobiographies show a bifurcated world, where there was neither a connection nor a contradiction between going to church and wearing a pierced dime around your ankle at the same time.

Theophus Smith (1994) argues for a profound connection, however, even though there is only partial evidence for it. And here is the link to Habermas's lifeworlds, or cultures, outside capitalism that may provide insight into what exploitation produces. The insight comes through seeing how different something familiar can be when it is in another's hands, thus showing the artificial and arbitrary way the dominant society has arranged its relations between peoples.

Smith starts with black churches in the United States and asks why Moses, Jesus, and the saints of the Gospels are held in such high but equal regard in them. Indirectly, he asks why black churches are different from other churches. For him, this is a positive distinction. His answer comes from the heart of West African religion. Humans can make spirits do things (Smith 1994, 39–45). By using and understanding the means for controlling elements of the supernatural, as happens in African spirit traditions in North America through the use of charms and bundles, people can advance their causes through managing spirits to act. Moses, Jesus, and the saints caused God to act. God acted when Moses asked it; when Jesus asked, God obeyed; the saints got action, which is why they were saints. These heroic Christian figures caused God to do things. And this is what people achieved through caches and bundles within their use of African practices. The same is true (Smith 1994, 48–49n27) in the other diasporic religions like Santeria, Condomble, Voodoo, and Palo Mayombe.

Within Calvinistic Protestantism, there is the central understanding that the life and sacrifice of Jesus is the core of redemption. Unity with God is God's choice. One listens to the preached word in order to exemplify choices already determined. Within the Orthodox and the Roman traditions of Christianity, the sacraments are ways to grace and may lead to God's intercessions. In all of these, God's ways are mysterious, his actions remote, unforeseeable, yet ever-present. But there is no sense of commanding God to act. Imploring and waiting are different from direct commands with expectable results.

On this basis, Theophus Smith shows that managing spirits is an African tradition in North America. Afro-Christianity is a combination of Christian text and West African ideas of direct action taken by believing people who get God to act. And the models, beyond Jesus, are Moses, the prophets, and the early Christian saints. It follows that using spirits, which anyone can see from the FWP autobiographies is largely devoid of explicit theology or a large practitioner class, is a set of practices for specific purposes, for example, charms against rheumatic pain and aids for teething babies. But when all the information from the composite autobiographies is added together, devout Christians can worship as all Christians do and also obtain specific aid for specific causes by using charms and bags as their African forebears had done. Thus, modern African spirit traditions and black Christianity are not within the zone of the highly rationalized, ritualized, and hierarchical Christianity that characterized eighteenth- and much of nineteenth-century Annapolis. They were largely closed to whites by mutual agreement and practice.

What happened in African American Annapolis between 1790 and 1920 that can shed light on work, racism, slavery, individualism, and American citizenship? Were Africans and African Americans made part of the work environment through the same means of individualism as an ideology that appeared to have worked relatively well for the middle classes? Beyond this question, were the processes of capitalism, including the constantly shifting exploitation in the service of profits, visible to people of African descent? And if so, what did they do that we can use to educate ourselves? Where did their beliefs fit into their lives to describe and improve their existence? Did the spirit traditions form an alternative set of actions and understanding for African Americans that were separate from those of their masters and employers? Did these religions save by being very different and removing believers from the world? Or did they save by being violent, symbolically or otherwise? What were their believers up against? The answer to that comes next and last.

The archaeology showed what bundles and hands were composed of, and our systematic survey of the FWP autobiographies expanded the array of items and identified their range of use so that we could present a catalogue of this spirit tradition. The full meanings of the practices that involved the objects are available. The following materials were collected by Timothy Ruppel under the direction of Gladys Fry. I have been reporting our work using the composite autobiographies, as edited by George Rawick. The following very clear description of practices comes from Harry Hyatt's famous collection, *Hoodoo–Conjuration–Witchcraft–Rootwork: Beliefs Accepted by Many Negroes and White Persons, These Being Orally Recorded among Blacks and Whites* (1970–78 [1935]). This large set of interviews was made during the 1930s by an Episcopal priest and contains lengthy clarifications of how the spirit tradition worked. I have chosen a few quotations from a large number that either show the detailed context of intentions or the materials used that can be expected from archaeological work. I have not sought out materials only from Maryland for these illustrations. Indeed, there is not enough from Maryland to do that. I have used the most convincing material regardless of the state of origin. While we do not actually know how coherent the use of spirits was, it is normally treated as a fairly coherent creole tradition by the time it was recorded.

> Ah wus troubled an' worried ovah life. Dat fo' fo'ks [four forks] of de road means where mens will perceive where he wus goin'. It's a fact dere's turn in de road, isn't dere—dere's a real turn. Yo' kin go dis way an' yo' kin go dat way. Well now, de fo'ks de road means de turn of life.
>
> Yo' go out to the fo' fo'ks of de road an' there, there's where yo' kin git the real spirit—now, listen to me—of Jesus or de devil. If yo' are a man that's pullin' an' strivin' fo' the right, the Holy Spirit will give you whut end of de road tuh take. Then, if yo' wanta come tuh be a evildoer of evil things an' learn how tuh put evil things ovah, yo' kin learn it right there in de corner of that road. Satan will meet chew right dere wit great power an' great strength, an' take an' tell yo' jes' whut route tuh take an' jes' whut uh do fo' that individual.
>
> Now, heah whut chew do. If yo' wanta git a real message from Satan in de fo' corners of de road, dere's a certain bath whut yo' should use. Yo' take a tea-spoonful of red peppah—listen good—a teaspoonfulla blue-stone, a teaspoon of soda an' a teaspoon of alum. An' then yo' have a tea-spoon of very common table salt. Put those seven [five] ingredients into chamber lye [sixth ingredient]—one quart—put those seven ingredients into one quart [of water, seventh ingredient]. Then yo' po' all of that into yore bath. Then yo' begin tuh bath yo'self. Now, if yo' want Jesus tuh cleanse youre soul from all uncleanness, say, "Ah'll dry this of de Jordan Rivah."
>
> . . . Now regardless to yore bad luck or regardless of whatevah comin' agin yo', . . . or whatevah yo' gotta [do], if yo' will only give yo'self up an' apply that bath to yo', an' turn yore face to de east an' repeat de Lord's Prayer three times, an' then when yo' are through wit that, go to de fo'ks of de road, say, "Now, Lord, show me jes' whut end of de road tuh take." An' de one that yore mind follows, that's the one yo'll be successful in. That's de way that ah got this spiritual gift that ah've got.
>
> . . . Then you go out to the forks of de road an' come quiet with de whole mind an' sit there fo' bout ten or fifteen minutes. An' then whate-vah yo' wanta do, right or wrong, that spirit will meet chew there.
>
> Hyatt, 2: 1116

This general view shows that use of the spirit tradition was involved with life's problems including one's overall sense of purpose. It also shows the overlay of Christianity on the African use of spirits. Such an amalgam justifies people like Theophus Smith, who saw a novel religion coming from the mixture of African spirits, who were immediate and could be made to act, and Christian spiritual beings. The red pepper, blue stone (probably bluing), (baking) soda, alum, and salt probably involve the invocation of red, blue, and white. Red was the color of communication, blue prevented unwanted spirits from entering, and white was the way to enter the world of the spirits of the dead.

This use of pins, a doll, four corners, crossing, and evil spirits comes from Maryland. These items were found in many of the archaeological caches.

I remember one time when I wus in Philadelphia. There wus a lady, her husband left her, she wanted to bring him back. So she got ready an' she went to this *doctor.* So she ast 'er, she said, "Could joo get my husband back?"

She told 'er, "Yes."

She said, "Whut way could joo get 'im back?"

So she said, "I'll tell you wha' choo do." She said, "You get a black cloth, you make it up like you do a baby, an' you stick out one pin an' one needle in it—new needle an' new pin."

An' she [the wife later] taken the needle an' she stuck it up one place, here [she demonstrates]. (In the head.)

I guess it must have been the eyes she makin'—an' [she half-pantomimes]. (The pin.)

Another place. [Many persons acted out everything they did.] (For the other eye.)

She put it [the doll] right up over the doah [still demonstrating].

So that it was held there by the needle and pin stuck through the eyes and into the plaster.) [Final result of my commenting.]

I was in the house. I seen that mahself.

An' she [the *doctor*] said, "Ev'ry time you come to this house [the wife's own]," she said that—"an' I'll pin it up here over the doar—an' ev'ry time you come in," [she] said, "before you speak to anybody," she said, "you cuss at it, an' that'll bring 'im back again an' make 'im stay with you."

So, after that, another time, I seen her *dress* [prepare magically] a letter, this lady [the wife]. She *dressed* that letter she took an' went down there [the page] jes' like that with her fingernails—you know, went down jes' like that. Den she had somepin, ever now an' then she dip her fingernails into this mess—it was jes' like perfume. She'd dip her fingernails into it, she'd make a straight line, she'd go straight on down [the page] for to make him start writin'.

So they went on at dat an' went on at dat [using various devices to bring the man back].

So the next two weeks—I think it wus, yes—the moon wus shinin'. You

see, this wus dark nights when this happened. So the next two weeks there
would be a moon shinin' at night. So after that [in the light of the moon],
she said to dis lady, she said, "When you come again," she said, "you bring
me a piece of money, but let it be silver—a ten-cent piece, but don't bring
it in two nickels."

So when this woman [the wife] came [home] again she ast me to go with
'er, an' I went back with 'er. An' it wus some way out in de country, see.
We taken de trolley [or streetcar] because we went a long ways. You know
I'd heard tell of these things an' I wanted to see 'em. So when I went with
'er, she taken this money—she tied it up. It wus tied up in four corners—
it was a handkerchief. She made it [the four corners of the handkerchief]
in a cross like—like a baby. An' after she got way out de country, she taken
an' threw it to the end of this road. The road was crossed up. She threw
it to the end of the road [down the left prong which was crooked]. She
threw it over her right shoulder an' said somepin three times.

So I said to the lady, I said, "Whut did you do that for?"

She said, "We got to pay off the evil spirits whut we git our work to
act, so they'll do whut we want to do, see."

So I imagine that's whut dey did that for. That's all I know about that.
But anyhow I went with 'er.

So after that, why she [the *doctor*] said to this woman, she says, "When
this baby falls down off of the doah," she says, "in seven days after that,
if not seven days then the ninth day," she says, "he'll come home."

I didn't go back with 'er though after dat baby fell, but I went with 'er
for to pay off, you know, dat concern to the ends of that road. I went with
'er den.

So after that I ast the lady, I said, "Did your husband came?"

She said, "Yes, he come back all right."

I said, "Well, how he's treatin' you?"

She said, "Fine, better than he did before."

Hyatt, 1: 54–55

This use shows the actions taken through the use of pins, black cloth,
the door through which spirits enter, a powerful liquid, a shiny ten-cent
piece, and a handkerchief, with clear reference to spirits who were invoked to work specifically for a person.

Cosmograms were not symbols like flags or crosses. They were active
and causal and drawing one or renewing one was to be engaged with
spirits. Here is a brilliant example of how use of a cosmogram worked.

Well, yo' run along den, after yo' do dis, yo' see. Well, yo' take an' set
down, jis' lak yo' settin'. Set down an' fix yo' out a little—yo' take jis' lak
yo' take a sort of a little clay doll or somepin in de shape of a person. It's
de form of a person, yo' see. Yo' take dat doll an' make it outa rags. Jis'
as well say yo' make yo' a rag doll, yo' understand. Yo' see, take an' make
de two eyes an' evah'thing an' bear [bury] it in de front of yore' do'. But

chew let dis be purtty late at nighttime, yo' see. But chew take befo' yo'
do dis now—yo' take an' draw yo' a circle. Yo' see, take an' draw yo' a
circle on a clar [clear] sheet of paper, yo' see. Write it with ink pen, yo'
see. Yo' don't have tuh put de stars around dere 'cause yo' ain't gotta burn
no candles now, yo' see. Jis' draw dis circle an' inside of dis circle yo' put
dat cross inside dat circle, which like yo' put it on de ground, but chew
put it inside de circle yo' see. [He demonstrates and I comment for my own
benefit.] (Like quartering a pie.)

Dat's right. But it inside dat circle. Yo' put dat little rag doll on top of
dat. Well, understand, yo' write *O. L. Young* an' *L. L. Young,* yo' see, an'
yo' put chure name under de bottom of dat, right up under de bottom of
his name, yo' understand. Well, yo' explain yore condition to them—to
him, yo' see. Tell him jis' whut chew wants to do, an' whut chew wanta
be successful in, yo' see, an' jis' why dat yo' controllin' de other ones. An'
explain things to him jis' lak yo' talkin' to a person ord'nary [ordinary
person]. Den yo' take an' bear dat man, dat little rag doll on top of dat—
jis' bear it an' smooth it, smooth de ground right smooth yo' see.

(Where do you bury it?)

Right in front of yore business, yo' see, but let dat be—whenevah yo'
doin' dis work, buryin' de rag doll in de circle, let dat be at nighttime, yo'
understand, real late at night. But it mus'n't be befo' twelve a'clock—[yo'
mustn't] take an' bury it anytime befo' twelve, yo' know.

Hyatt, 2: 1186

This example is particularly helpful because it shows the generic wish
to be successful to be behind the cosmogram's use. An actively composed
cosmogram can be done at any time. As the next description tells, the
cosmogram is an action that achieves its purpose while a person com-
poses it. The bag not only contained the desired person's track, but was
buried for permanent effect under the corner of the house.

Dey say yo' could take an' git chew Adam-an'-Eve root an' *High John de
Conkah,* see. An' git chew some *Hearts Cologne,* dis [just a] little—called
Hearts Colgne—an' take an' put dis heah root on dis. An' evah time yo'
git ready tuh go out wit—git close tuh 'ah [her] enough, in conversation somewhere, an' let 'ah [her] git de scent of dat. An' if she come anywhere about chew, pick up 'ah tracks see, an' put dem 'em in a bag yo'
undahstan'.

Take an' put 'em in de sack yo' see an' take an' bury 'em undah de cor-
nah of yore house, an' dat will keep 'ah love. Dat will make hah come dere
all de time. Jes' stay right roun' yo'.

Hyatt, 4: 2818

Many spirit items were found in water, although it is the action of
composing a hand, with its implements of a new shiny spoon, a rusty

nail, dirt from a track, and a rock, that leaves some remains that are visible archaeologically. This quotation shows the ritual that accompanies the making of a cosmogram in a footprint and then using the kalunga line, the horizontal line between this world and the world of spirits, to get the spirits to be available. The latter move is to have the named individual to be dealt with by them.

> Yo' take a person dat yo' dislike an' yo' wan' 'em away from yo'. Yo' meet 'im. He's comin' dat way an' yo's comin' dis way. Take a bran'-new piece of papah, a piece like dat [he changes this for cloth later]. Take a bran'-new teaspoon. When ah say bran'-new, ah mean one dat was nevah used fo' any purpose. An' yo' put it—take a piece of cloth, white cloth dat yo' have nevah used fo' any othah purpose. Take dat wit yo'. An' prepare tuh meet yore man, whomsoevah it is. An' meet 'im dere, an' git a smile if yo' kin. Pass 'im an' pass 'im a certain distant [distance]. But gauge yoreself so as tuh not allow 'im tuh git away too far. An' yo' take de track up wit dat teaspoon. Begin right at de toe, don' cha know an' pull it directly back tuh de heel. An' git de spoonful an' put it intuh dis cloth, an' wrap it up so it won't—yo' know, it will be out of de way. An' yo' take a rust nail an' yo' cross de track directly in de centah, an' den cross it ag[in from de heel tuh de toe—away from yo', directly. An' throw de nail ovah yore left shouldah. Den yo' keep de stuff dat yo' got in de cloth, take dat an' take de spoon an' throw dat ovah yuh right shouldah. Take dat cloth right on, roll it up tight, tie it away from yuh, don' cha know. Take a piece of rock an' put in it, in de othah part of it, an' yuh care [carry] it an' yuh throw it ovah uyh lef' shouldah, right ovahbo'd intuh runnin' watah. Or if de tide is goin' down, on de tide, when yuh throw it ovah. An' yuh mention de person's name. Dey goes right on out like dat [with the tide]. As it go ovahbo'd, dey die. An' if it's comin' up, yuh know what yuh call a spring tide, huh, when it's comin' up, why dey'll git almos' crazy until de tide turns. An' as soon as de tide turns ag'in, dey gone.
>
> Hyatt, 4: 2879–80

Discs, dimes, Chinese coins, buttons, and spoon bowls could be used to create spirit movement on behalf of the practitioners. Embodied in this quotation is the idea that anyone could employ spirits; there is very little mention of professional root doctors compared to ordinary folks who were adepts. Dimes were the most common form of discs, and, like buttons, could easily be remade into the movement of life that invoked spirit action. It is like a constant centering (Grey Gundacre, personal communication).

> Yes sir, ah've heard dat yo' take an' steal a dime—a sliver dime—an' carry it to de . . . (You steal this dime?) Yes sir, steal it from someone. (And then you cross it. How do you cross it?) Right cross de piece. Take a pocketknife

or sompin an' cross a cross mark cross de face [on the dime]. An' carry it
to de cemetery an' bury it, an' she'll follow yo' ev'ywhere yo' want her tuh.
(Whom would you steal this dime from?)
Anyone. It be best tuh steal it from her, providing if she got one.
(Oh, I see. To make her love you?)
Yes sir.

Hyatt, 5: 4423

Because dimes like other coins were widely used, the following array
is essential to see. Both shape and shine could be important. The seven
formulas below serve to show the multiple uses such coins could be put
to. However, what this array actually shows is that the spirits doing the
curing, protecting, and diagnosing are subject to the action desired, and
this is what determines the definition of what the colors and treatment
of the dimes actually mean. In other words, the dime has meaning imposed, given the need or use sought.

13007. Dey tell me dey take a piece of silver money an' put it in a red
sack—flannel—an' put a piece of garlic to it an' tote it on yo'. That be fo'
good luck. . . .

13008. Nine silver dimes, file them, wear in *NATION SACK* [brand
name of bag worn by women] with lodestone for protection and trade. . . .

13009. Jes' lak if yo' didn't know whether yo' wus *poisoned* or not, but
a piece of silver is de best. If yo' think yo' were *poisoned* an' don't know
enough fo' shore, if yo' put a piece of silver in yore mouth an' hold it in
dere, in de length of time it will turn black if dey is any *poison* in yo'. . . .

13010. A dime under the tongue turns black if you are *hurt*. . . .

13011. "Hold it in your mouth . . . if you is always *hurt* like dat, dat
dime will turn black." . . .

13012. "Take a silver dime, if you think somebody is trying to *hurt*
you. Put it in your mouth right under your tongue and you can drink and
eat all you want. That dime takes [absorbs] everything." [This must be a
unique experience, to keep a silver dime under your tongue while eating
and drinking!] . . .

13013. "You take a silver dime and put it in your mouth under your
tongue, and take a thimbleful of sulphur, swallow it, and keep this dime
under there about one or two hours and take it out. If it's black, it's bad
[you are hoodooed]; if it's not black [the sickness] it's nashural." . . .

13014. Well, if yo' git poisoned, yo' kin take a dime an' tie it round
yore laig, roun' yore neck, an' if yo' poisoned, dat dime will turn green an'
it'll cure it.

Hyatt, 5: 4426

These quotes establish a whole other world apart from European medicine and social control. It is another lifeworld or culture and it does not

matter whether it was creole or wholly African. It does matter that it was coherent and so integrated into the lives of people of African descent that it extricated them from some aspects of capitalism's actions.

There are no possessive individualism, no measurement, no self-improvement, virtually no property, and no rights in the world of people using African spirit traditions. The archaeology and citations from the FWP autobiographies show a culture apart from the rest of Annapolis and English North America. The sources show it to have been coherent; that is, another culture. It provided a complete, separate identity and tied people from Africa to one another. Thus, to use Habermas's term, it was a separate lifeworld.

Can we learn from it? Certainly. The purpose of seeing the survival and florescence of African religion is not to borrow what it was but to see where and what an alternative looked like. The alternative showed that the ideology in the rest of Annapolis was not as inevitable, natural, God-given, or superior as it said it was and hoped it would become. Now that we can see that the people at the bottom created an option for them-selves, can we know why? Can we know what they saw that made them stay different?

CHAPTER 8

What Do We Know?

What does African American culture in Annapolis, from between 1790 and 1920, teach us about our own conditions? How does it shed light on work, slavery, racism, equality, and the level to which African Americans were within or lived beyond the ideology of individualism? The picture so far shows that middle-class people like Jonas Green and William Faris, white men with slaves, lived within and duplicated the ideology and its technologies. They may have seen through the ideology, but they also did not find a way to avoid it. How did people of African descent, slaves, and free men and women behave, given the ideology alive in the city? Were the processes of capitalism like low wages, poor working and living conditions, treating people like sources of profit, and the constantly shifting means of exploitation, like encouraging members of economic groups to despise each other through racism and ethnic hatred, visible despite the ideology of individual freedom? What did they say and what did they do? If we can know the answers to these questions, then can we use them to educate ourselves?

We can see how deeply the ideology penetrated, and the conflict it produced, in the figure of Wylie Bates, a prominent African American Annapolitan, born a slave in North Carolina in 1859, who founded and ran a grocery store in a mixed neighborhood in Annapolis from the late nineteenth through the early twentieth centuries. There were dozens of businesses in the city owned by African Americans, although they often flourished only briefly, for lack of either an adequate clientele or capital. Such entrepreneurs saw themselves and were seen by people like W. E. B. Du Bois and Booker T. Washington as models for other African Americans, and they were held up to the white world as having succeeded in business by using principles supported by the white community.

Bates both internalized the ideology of individualism and propagated it. His privately published autobiography, *Researches, Sayings, and Life of Wylie Bates* (1928), constitutes a remarkable investment in seeing himself as an individual, and the mere fact that he wrote it shows that he felt himself to be in sufficient possession of his own experience to be able to categorize it as a life of accomplishment and pass it on as a lesson. "The Negro must learn the secret of the application of wealth; he acquires it, but he does not know how to apply it to advantage," he asserted. "The Negro is a spendthrift; he is reckless and also a hypocrite. He tries to make people believe what he is not, by the imitation of the shadow and not the real substance" (Bates 1928, 14, quoted in Mullins 1999, 102). Because Bates made the largest contribution to buy the land for the black high school in Annapolis, it was named after him.

Bates was not unique in his success in Annapolis or in his advice to his fellows, but he typifies the effort to make the idea of individual labor and self-discipline, which he expressed as frugality, work for him and for others. At one level, he saw himself as an equal, or a potential equal, if he worked hard enough. He was within ideology as he wrote and was more like Booker T. Washington than W. E. B. Du Bois.

Bates saw the truth of racism clearly enough. He felt that he was an equal despite it and that he would be a full individual if the law allowed it. However, I agree with Paul Mullins, who criticizes Bates's absorption into ideology by juxtaposing his ideas with those of his contemporary, A. Philip Randolph, who wrote: "Workingmen and women of my race don't allow Republican and Democratic leaders to deceive you. They are paid by Rockefeller, Morgan, Armour, Carnegie, owners of Southern railroads, coal mines, turpentine stills, cotton-plantations, etc., who makes [sic] millions out of your labor. Don't be deceived by the small increase in wages which you are receiving; the capitalists are taking it back by increasing the cost of food, fuel, clothing and rent" (Randolph 1919, 12, quoted in Mullins 1999, 102).

Two realities lived simultaneously within the black community in Annapolis (although blacks in Annapolis were also stratified and cannot comfortably be called one community). These two realties are those seen and clearly called the two souls and double vision of American blacks.

Du Bois said these two realities, which he called the two strivings, American and Negro, or African, sought to be included in the American ideology of personal freedom and liberty and yet outside the state-sponsored exploitation that accompanied it. Certainly, Wylie Bates and possibly even Booker T. Washington did not see that these two realities were not warring ideals at all. They were, in fact, one and the same, if we accept Althusser's argument, based on Marx. The promise of and quest for freedom masked the inescapable reality of capitalism's base and essence. Althusser was right in thinking that the middle class was absorbed in ideology, but he was wrong in supposing that its members could not see this. They did see, even though they were absorbed.

Africa and the sense of unity and community it was used to foster survived, however, and still does, in several ways. This survival may be the way around ideology that Habermas theorizes in arguing that those most harshly affected by capitalism can develop a critique of it and, sometimes, tactics that may moderate it. A. Philip Randolph had a critique and, in interracial unionization of railroad workers, a corrective action using a powerful political means within mainstream American society. Habermas's concept of other lifeworlds may be an alternative to Althusser's suspicion that we cannot escape ideology, let alone reform the economic system it masks. Habermas theorizes an escape from the dilemma caused by Althusser's view in two ways. In the first place, he sees some lifeworlds offering a critique of capitalism, and, secondly, he sees some as offering ways of living so as to avoid its worst impact. Both may mean that ideology is permanently breached.

The issue for me in this book is to link the archaeology of the world of things and of people of African descent in Annapolis and other areas in North America to a world outside capitalism. There are two reasons to do this, according to the theories I am using. One is to have a clear vision or critique of capitalism, including its history. The other is to have a view of how to build a world different from it. The FWP composite autobiographies, which expose capitalism's repellent consequences, provide the first. A religion like spirit use that embodies beliefs and practices quite different from those of Christianity, yet linked to it, provides the second. A separate religion forms a commentary on the central tenets of Christianity and yet can be used to question its origins and function. This in turn provides a balance from outside ideology to those of us within it. Certainly, the details of how to use conjuration and root work do that. This was a world that was outside that of whites but was also within a particular variant of Christianity, one with an active view of spirits who went beyond the activities usually imputed to the Holy Ghost and that saw the devil as capable of being imminently and personally engaged by and in an individual's life.

This world of spirits was for immediate and effective personal use. Thus, spirit use existed outside mainstream Christianity but occasionally within a creole variant of it as practiced by some people of African descent. For some, spirits may have been used without any reference to or amalgamation with any part of Christianity, but whether within or outside of Christianity, spirit usage was a very different world and provoked quite different behavior.

Albert Raboteau (1978) argues that religion acted as an escape from and partial antidote to slavery and racism. This accords with the logic of social scientific treatments of religion and begins to compose an explanation for why people can be so closely tied to their spiritual lives while living in harsh circumstances.

> Religious suffering is at one and the same time the expression of real suffering and a protest against real suffering. Religion is the sigh of the oppressed creature, the heart of a heartless world and the soul of soulless conditions. It is the opium of the people.
>
> The abolition of religion as the illusory happiness of the people is the demand for their real happiness. To call on them to give up their illusions about their condition is to call on them to give up a condition that requires illusions. The criticism of religion is therefore in embryo the criticism of that vale of tears of which religion is the halo.
>
> Marx 1970 (1843–44)

Religious practices ease, explain , and moderate by creating closely bound communities of people who determine to help each other. But against what?

Answering this requires an understanding of the world people of African descent inhabited in the United States. Throughout the FWP composite autobiographies there are many powerful descriptions of the treatment of slaves: burning, brandings, whippings in innumerable forms, torture, selling members of families, hunting, and in general enough shocking material to disturb anyone. Many of the descriptions are of specific events and do not extend explicitly beyond the circumstances an interviewee lived through or saw, usually firsthand.

Dempsey Jordan, who had been born a slave in New Orleans in 1836, was interviewed by the Federal Writers' Project in Texas. He had seen and participated in his master's slave auctions, and his account is formal enough to constitute a global critique:

I'se seen him [the master] when he had most a hundred at a time but he would trade on them all the time. He woke us every morning about 5 o'clock so'es we could tend to his stock and open his saloon in time to have everything cleaned by the time people began to stir good. He worked us till 9 or 10 o'clock every night except Saturday nights and he stayed open till 12 o'clock, then he would turn us a loose to prowl around until Monday morning again then the same old job again. Yes we had jail there in town for the bad and wild slaves that was captured in their home country. I seen master have some of them kind of slaves and he would keep them chained all the time he had them. At night he would put them in jail and lock them up so they could not get away. I'se seen him ship lots of slaves because they would not do what he told them to do

Some of them he traded for came direct from Africa and he would have to tame them. He had to whip them to get them under control. He had to handle them every way. He had one I'se remember, he first put chain on and locked him up at night, but that slave was stubborn and he tried every way to handle that slave. Finally he put a chain around that negro's neck and fastened it to a rafter in the jail so that negro would have to stand up every night and in the morning before let him loose, would hit that negro 25 licks with a raw hide. He finally made a pretty good negro out of him while he owned him. Then maser sold that negro for a pretty good price for he was a healthy, stout negro. After his new Maser got him you know that negro killed his Maser and tried to run off, but his Mistress was too much for him. She got on her horse and overtaken that negro and shot him twice with one of these old cap and ball guns. She thought she had killed him, but she didn't. He lay around out there in the woods several days and some Spanish people nursed him back to health. One morning he came back to Maser and said he wanted to stay with him. Maser went to the negroes Mistress and bought him back for about one-half price and kept him nearly a year. He never did give Maser anymore trouble but he finally sold him to another man and I never did see or hear of that negro again. I expect they finally had to kill him because he was a real mean negro, didn't care for nothing or nobody.

Yes, I have seen and helped dress lots of slaves for sale. When Maser would get a buyer he had us wash and clean up the negroes so when we got that done we would grease their face, hands and feet so they would look real good or fat just like you would want a good fat yearling to look when you wanted to sell him. Maser said they would bring the best price then when he would sell a slave. When they would be sold and separated from their people you never heard such bawling and hollering that would take place. But Maser made good money buying and selling slaves as long as he lived, course Mistress quit that when he died. Maser would set a regular day for his slave trading and people came from everywhere on that day to bid on the slaves cause they knew he always had a big bunch on hand to pick from.

No sir, Maser or the white folks did not teach us to read or write, Maser did not have much to do with church life although he gave money to the

work of the church, he never did go out much. Mistress was a religious
woman, and I had to drive her to church when she wanted to go or wherever she went. She taught me to always tell the truth regardless of how it
hurt me. We had a place fixed there at the white folks church when we
wanted to go to church.

                                        Rawick 1972–79, supp. ser., 1, 6: 2158–60

Contrast Jordan's description of the marketing of slaves with A. Philip
Randolph's analysis of how employers treated railroad workers. In principle, which is the extraction of profit from human labor, there is no difference. Both men saw it for what it was.

A. Philip Randolph proposed a solution. So did Dempsey Jordan. His
too is a critique and an alternative:

When we were freed there was not a negro in all the south that could read
and write his name. We was most like a herd of mules, did not know anything at all in the way of making a living here in this country, but we gradually started to building schools and sending our children to school and
they began to learn how to read and write and learn the ways of this country. Some of the negroes began to learn different kinds of trades to where
we have some pretty well educated negroes and some that can hold good
paying jobs. If I had my way we would deport all of our negro race and
send them back to there home country or cut them a state off to its self,
cause we are now educating all these negroes and sending them to hell
fast as we can. The more you educate one of them the bigger rascal he
becomes and gets further away from God and the less he will tell the truth.
Of course I think as long as we are going to let the negro live here and
have to pay taxes and be a soldier for his country in time of war, he ought
to be allowed more voting privileges here in Texas, as the negro he does
not have rights here in Texas. We do not have the right to vote if we don't
pay our taxes. We have got to pay pole taxes and only use it once. I can't
see how the party that stays in power here in Texas are elected because
the negroes all vote the other way. Some day we will change all that because they tell me that the negro race is increasing faster than the white
people, then we will be in the way that we can get something done for
the poor negro. They are in a terrible fix here in this county because the
white people can work them and gib them what they want to give and
the negro he can't say anything, he has to take what they will give him
and keep his mouth shut. I does believe that is the reason these her youngsters are so sorry. They get to where they won't tell the truth and steal all
the time. They say if you get after them about their stealing, Uncle we will
not go to Heaven if we don't steal from the white people. Son I think that
is a terrible condition for any race of people to get in regardless of their
race or color.

What have I done since the War between the states? I done just what I
could get to do, farm mostly, but I'se worked some for wages—mostly farm

wages, although I worked one year for a railroad company helping them build a railroad from New Orleans, Louisiana.

Rawick 1972–79, supp. ser., 1, 6: 2164–65

Jordan proposed return to Africa, voting privileges, other rights, and education.

When I began work in Annapolis in 1981, one of the founders of Historic Annapolis Incorporated told my wife that there had been no slave market or auction in Annapolis. Certainly, from my long experience now in the city and having taught since 1976 at the University of Maryland, there is neither memory nor recognition of the conditions of slavery either in Maryland in general or in Annapolis in particular. The only presence found now in Annapolis is the dawning recognition of slavery through the story of Kunte Kinte provided by Alex Haley, including the new memorial at the city's dock.

It is not clear to me how the heritage of slavery has been so altered. Nor is it clear to me why the vivid description of Maryland slavery provided by the FWP composite autobiographies (Rawick 1972–79, 16, 8 (Maryland): 1–78) is virtually unread and unused in Maryland historical circles and public celebrations of its past.

I use the FWP composite autobiographies here because they provide good descriptions of local conditions, including conditions in Annapolis. There is a description of a conjurer, as well as of the motivating consciousness of slaves and former slaves. The citations vivify conditions in Maryland in a way that archaeology never can. Archaeology's job is to provide undeniable patterns for those who forget, doubt, deny, get lost, and become rootless. The composite autobiographies for Maryland also show that slavery probably did not belong in Maryland and certainly could not continue there. It was an institution that ripped white Maryland apart. But the composite autobiographies also show that while people of African descent forgave it, people of European descent never lost their hurt and the guilt that they had tolerated, used, and legalized the violence and hierarchy that slavery produced. Slavery's heritage in Maryland is not only not over, it is incompletely integrated into its public memory.

The composite autobiographies sometimes describe general living conditions, but usually they are specific. The one below is abstract enough to provide a general picture without raising doubts about its accuracy. The material conditions described here occur time and time again in these autobiographies. All this material is from Maryland. Dennis Simms, a

former slave, was interviewed in 1937 at his home in Baltimore and described his life on the Contee plantation in Prince Georges' County, abut-
ting Anne Arundel County, whose seat is Annapolis:

> We would work from sunrise to sunset every day except Sundays and on
> New Year's Day. Christmas made little difference at Contee, except that
> we were given extra rations of food then. We had to toe the mark or be
> flogged with a rawhide whip, and almost every day there was from two
> to ten thrashings given on the plantations to disobedient Negro slaves.
>
> When we behaved we were not whipped, but the overseer kept a pretty
> close eye on us. We all hated what they called the 'nine ninety-nine', usu-
> ally a flogging until [the victim] fell over unconscious or begged for mercy.
> We stuck pretty close to the cabins after dark, for if we were caught roam-
> ing about we would be unmercifully whipped. If a slave was caught beyond
> the limits of the plantation where he was employed, without the company
> of a white person or without written permit of his master, any person who
> apprehended him was permitted to give him 20 lashes across the bare back.
>
> If a slave went on another plantation without a written permit from his
> master, on lawful business, the owner of the plantation would usually give
> the offender 10 lashes. We were never allowed to congregate after work,
> never went to church, and could not read or write for we were kept in ig-
> norance. We were very unhappy.
>
> Sometimes Negro slave runaways who were apprehended by the pa-
> trollers, who kept a constant watch for escaped slaves, besides being
> flogged, would be branded with a hot iron on the cheek with the letter
> "R."
>
> We lived in rudely constructed log houses, one story in height, with huge
> stone chimneys, and slept on beds of straw. Slaves were pretty tired after
> their long days' work in the field. Sometimes we would, unbeknown to
> our master, assemble in a cabin and sing songs and spirituals.
>
> Rawick 1972–79, 16, 8: 60–61

The creation of the degradation essential to the physical and psychological
sense of inferiority needed to make slavery work is described by "Parson" Resin Williams, who was interviewed in 1937 in Baltimore. He had
been born free on a large plantation in Prince Georges' County, next to
Anne Arundel County. Williams was completely familiar with slave life
and describes the slave market in Baltimore:

> Williams, though himself not a slave by virtue of the fact that his grand-
> mother was an Indian, was considered a good judge of healthy slaves, those
> who would prove profitable to their owners, so he often accompanied slave
> purchasers to the Baltimore slave markets.
>
> He told of having been taken by a certain slave master to the Baltimore
> wharf, boarded a boat and after the slave dealer and the captain negoti-
> ated a deal, he, Williams, not realizing that he was being used as a decoy,

led a group of some thirty or forty blacks, men, women and children, through a dark and dirty tunnel for a distance of several blocks to a slave market pen, where they were placed on the auction block.

He was told to sort of pacify the black women who set up a wail when they were separated from their husbands and children. It was a pitiful sight to see them, half naked, some whipped into submission, put into slave pens surmounted by iron bars. A good healthy negro man from 19 to 35 would bring from $200 to $800. Women would bring about half the price of the men. Often when the women parted with their children and loved ones, they would never see them again.

Such conditions as existed in the Baltimore slave markets, which are considered the most important in the country, and the subsequent ill treatment of the unfortunates, hastened the war between the states.

Rawick 1972–79, 16, 8: 76–77

From Camp Parole, now a suburb of Annapolis, Page Harris an ex-slave, described the ways used to keep slaves on the land and in submission in this area of study. These were general techniques, widely used throughout the South, and created the conditions of terror frequently referred to in the FWP composite autobiographies:.

I have a vague recollection of the Stafford's family, not enough to describe. They lived on a large farm situated in Charles County, a part bounding on the Potomac River and a cove that extends into the farm property. Much of the farm property was marshy and was suitable for the purpose of Mr. Stafford's living—raising and training blood hounds. I have been told by my mother and father on many occasions that there were as many as a hundred dogs on the farm at times. Mr. Stafford had about 50 slaves on his farm. He had an original method in training young blood hounds, he would make one of the slaves traverse a course, at the end, the slave would climb a tree. The younger dogs, led by an old dog, sometimes by several older dogs, would trail the slave until they reached the tree, then they would bark until taken away by the men who had charge of the dogs.

Mr. Stafford's dogs were often sought to apprehend runaway slaves. He would charge according to the value and worth of the slave captured. His dogs were often taken to Virginia, sometimes to North Carolina, besides being used in Maryland. I have been told that when a slave was captured, besides the reward paid in money, that each dog was supposed to bite the slave to make him anxious to hunt human beings.

Rawick 1972–79, 16, 8: 23

The violence needed and used to maintain slavery was perpetually present, something largely unacknowledged in the world of historic preservation and history museums.

In Annapolis, life in and after slavery was described by Page Harris who understood some of the practices of conjure and made clear some of the contexts of its use. This is the material for the Maynard-Burgess house as a museum. He lived in Annapolis starting in 1866.

> There was a slaveholder in Charles County who had a very valuable slave, an expert carpenter and bricklayer, whose services were much sought after by the people in Southern Maryland. This slave could elude the best blood hounds in the State. It was always said that slaves, when they ran away, would try to go through a graveyard and if he or she could get dirt from the grave of some one that had been recently buried, sprinkle it behind them, the dogs could not follow the fleeing slave, and would howl and return home.
>
> Old Pete the mechanic was working on farm near La Plata, he decided to run away as he had done on several previous occasions. He was known by some as the herb doctor and healer. He would not be punished on any condition nor would he work unless he was paid something. It was said that he would save money and give it to people who wanted to run away. He was charged with aiding a girl to flee. He was to be whipped by the sheriff of Charles County for aiding the girl to run away. He heard of it, left the night before he was to be whipped, he went to the swamp in the cove or about 5 miles from where his master lived. He eluded the dogs for several weeks, escaped, got to Boston and no one to this day has any idea how he did it; but he did.
>
> In the year of 1866 my father returned to Maryland bringing with him mother and my brothers and sister. He selected Annapolis for his future home, where he secured work as a waiter at the Naval Academy, he continued there for more than 20 years. In the meantime after 1866 or 1868, when schools were opened for colored people, I went to a school that was established for colored children and taught by a white teacher until I was about 17 years old, then I too worked at the Naval Academy waiting on the midshipmen. In those days you could make extra money, sometimes making more than your wages. About 1896 or '97 I purchased a farm near Camp Parole containing 120 acres, upon which I have lived since, raising a variety of vegetables for which Anne Arundel county is noted. I have been a member of Asbury Methodist Episcopal Church, Annapolis, for more than 40 years. All of my children, 5 in number, have grown to be men and women, one living home with me, one in New York, two in Baltimore, and one working in Washington, D.C.
>
> Rawick 1972–79, 16, 8: 24–25

It is clear from the Maryland FWP composite autobiographies that some African Americans had served as Union soldiers in the Civil War. It is also clear that there was a level of deep ambivalence within Maryland society that led to an understanding of the conflicting social principles at work within a democratically rationalized society, but one rooted in good part in a complete lack of freedom for a major portion of the population.

Finally, from the Maryland FWP composite autobiographies comes an analysis of feelings in Anne Arundel County about slavery and the conflicting circumstances in which everyone there lived. It is these conditions that produced the critique of Maryland society that we see in the maintenance of African spirit traditions, Wylie Bates's autobiography, Gladys Fry's streaming video, and Maisha Washington's teaching archaeology as a method for historical discovery to Annapolis youngsters of African descent (http://anacostia.si.edu/academy/academy.htm [accessed October 24, 2004]).

James Wiggins described black and white life in a 1937 interview:

> I was born in Anne Arundel County, on a farm near West River about 1850 or 1851, I do not know which. I do not know my father or mother. Peter Brooks, one of the oldest colored men in the county, told me that my father's name was Wiggins. He said that he was one of the Revell's slaves. He acquired my father at an auction sale held in Baltimore at a high price from a trader who had an office on Pratt Street about 1845. He was given a wife by Mr. Revell and as a result of this union I was born. My father was a carpenter by trade, he was hired out to different farmers by Mr. Revell to repair and build barns, fences and houses. I have been told that my father could read and write. Once he was charged with writing passes for some slaves in the county, as a result of this he was given 15 lashes by the sheriff of the county, immediately afterwards he ran away, went to Philadelphia, where he died while working to save money to purchase mother's freedom, through a white Baptist minister in Baltimore.
>
> I was called "Gingerbread" by the Revells. They reared me until I reached the age of about nine or ten years old. My duty was to put logs on the fireplace in the Revell's house and work around the house. I remember well when I was taken to Annapolis, how I used to dance in the stores for men and women, they would give me pennies and three cent pieces, all of which was given by me to the Revells. They bought me shoes and clothes with the money collected.
>
> Mr. Revell died in 1861 or '62. The sheriff and men came from Annapolis, sold the slaves, stock and other chattels. I was purchased by a Mr. Mayland, who kept a store in Annapolis. I was sold by him to a slave trader to be shipped to Georgia, I was brought to Baltimore, and was jailed in a small house on Paca near Lombard. The trader was buying other slaves to make a load. I escaped through the aid of a German shoemaker, who sold shoes to owners for slaves.
>
> The German had a covered wagon, I was put in the wagon covered by boxes, taken to a house on South Sharp Street and there kept until a Mr. George Stone took me to Frederick City where I stayed until 1863, when Mr. Stone, a member of the Lutheran Church, had me christened giving me the name of James Wiggins. This is how I got the name of Wiggins, af-

ter my father, instead of Gingerbread, through the investigation and the information given by Mr. Brooks.

You know the Revells are well known in Anne Arundel County, consisting of a large family, each family a large property owner. I can't say how many acres were owned by Jim Revell, he was a general farmer having a few slaves, you see I was a small boy. I can't answer all the questions you want.

There were a great many people in Anne Arundel who did not believe in slavery and many free colored people. These conditions caused conflicts between the free colored who many times were charged with aiding the slaves and the whites who were not favorably impressed with slavery and the others who believed in slavery. As a result, the patrollers were numerous. I remember of seeing Jim Revell coming home very much battered and beaten up as a result of an encounter with a number of free people and white people and those who were members of the patrollers.

Rawick 1972–79, 16, 8: 66–67

Slaves, former slaves, and African Americans in general saw clearly through the ideology of individualism. These descriptions pierce it and do so permanently. Having pierced it, my conclusion is that they show that Althusser is incorrect in describing ideology as invisible. Many people, like Wylie Bates, who used conventional ideology anyway and tried to master the workings of capitalism despite what ideology did, were not blind to it. Althusser is correct, however, when he calls ideology almost inescapable for members of the middle class. People saw through the ideology of possessive individualism but did nothing about it, or could do nothing. They lived their lives behind this mask anyway.

Mark Warner (2001) quotes the following declaration from a Washington-based newspaper intended for African Americans:

A NEGRO TO DIE

Some negro in Maryland must hang. That is a settled question. The unwritten law of Maryland is that if a white person is killed and the murderer cannot be found some negro must hang for it. In this country if there is no law on the statute books to fit a colored man's case the law is supplied.

Washington Bee, June 6, 1896

In 1922, over 1,000 members of the Ku Klux Klan paraded past the Maynards' house on Duke of Gloucester Street in Annapolis. They would have also gone right past the St Mary's Catholic Colored School, then maintained by the Redemptorist Order just a block from the Maynard-Burgess house:

Members of the Ku Klux Klan came into the wide open Saturday night. Marching behind a huge emblazoned cross, symbol of the organization, the illumination being by acetylene gas, and clad in the full regalia of the order of white robes and hoods, except that the face-capes of the hoods were thrown back, to comply with legal requirements, about 1,000 Klansmen—from various parts of the state . . . participated in a spectacular parade through the principal streets of Annapolis. . . . The visiting K.K.'s were the guests of those of Annapolis and Anne Arundel County, of whom there are reported to be in the neighborhood of 1,000, and the street parade had its finale in an oyster roast and feast at Horn Point. . . . Hundreds of residents of the city, who had never before seen a parade of the secret organization, gathered along the principal streets covered by the line of the march—Gloucester, West and Main.

Evening Capital, October 30, 1922

Watching from within the Catholic Church, its schools, and convent, the priests record:

Ku Klux Clan visited Annapolis–Eastport Saturday evening and caused quite a sensation. Baltimore lodge numbered about 500—about 9 1/2 arrived in 100 auto cars and caroused in Eastport until midnight. May they return to better judgment. Amen.

Redemptorist House Chronicle for St. Mary's, November 1, 1922, Redemptorist Archives, Brooklyn, N.Y.

Mark Warner and Paul Mullins want the Maynard-Burgess House, which they excavated, to illustrate the role of race in nineteenth- and twentieth-century Annapolis. The house is to be restored and turned into a museum. What will it show? Historic houses in the city illustrate patriotism, taste, wealth, and little that ties them to people's lives today. Mullins thinks that the house, if opened as a museum, could show the attempt to achieve the middle-class American dream despite racism. Blacks did it amid Klan marches, lynchings, and constantly shifting economic conditions. They did it despite the failure of Reconstruction. This is a window into an alternative to the worst of capitalism's tactics. Its details need to be on exhibit for everyone to learn from. The black middle-class dream is an effort to live within capitalism but to purge it of anti-black racism. The Maynard-Burgess House could help serve to illustrate the lifeworlds of those who saw capitalism as it was, including Wylie Bates and the narrators of the FWP autobiographies.

HOW TO TEACH

How powerful is archaeology to challenge capitalism? This question is a version of the one that asks about the importance of the role of the past in society's identity. Because society is made up of people and individuals who possess a history, there is little debate about whether or not a sense of the past is significant. We do not always know how important it is, but no one doubts that some sense of the past is central to life, individually and collectively. This book is about what to say and how to teach people about the past in order to explain the operation of their lives within the United States today. It is not only about substance but about means as well.

But the question for me and others (e.g., Matthews 2005; n.d.) is how one presents an alternative and less ideologically bound picture of the past. Using Lukács's ideas as the basis for a model of education did not work. And Habermas does not come with any model. Although static exhibits in Annapolis have been largely foreclosed to a project like ours through dislike and fear of embarrassment by the museum community, many other media have been open to us, and we have used them.

Newspapers and local television with both black and white audiences have been regularly approached with stories on archaeology. This includes Black Entertainment Television. All of the most popular introductory archaeology textbooks in the United States for college-level courses include sections on Archaeology in Annapolis, increasingly dealing with our joint work on African American discoveries. Streaming video reaches a middle-class audience, white and black, but requires a powerful enough computer, which many people do not have access to. The Smithsonian's Anacostia Museum is devoted to African American culture and uses streaming video in its Online Academy to reach beyond the museum with consistent information on African American scholarship (http://anacostia.si.edu/academy/academy.htm [accessed October 24, 2004]). Each clip or cameo presentation is five to ten minutes long and appears "live." Gladys-Marie Fry explains African symbols sewn into the designs of quilts. I explain BaKongo traditions revealed through Archaeology in Annapolis and our comparative work along the Atlantic Coast. Maisha Washington, formerly curator at the Banneker-Douglass Museum, located in the AME Church building whose neighborhood Barbara Jackson Nash invited us to explore through archaeology and oral history in the late 1980s, explains how archaeology works to young African Americans in Annapolis. Since the summer of 2001, she has taught Annapolis youngsters from public housing projects through programs at the museum. Her focus has been on African American cuisine and foodways and on archaeology as a way of understanding, learning about, and conducting research on and for African Americans.

There are two parts to Maisha Washington's archaeological lessons, one methodological, the other substantive. Following the Society for American Archaeology's guidelines for conducting model excavations by using large sandboxes filled with unmixed layers of sand, peat moss, and potting soil, into which artifacts have been placed, she has teams of two to three youngsters place a grid of stakes and string over the box and use a line level and ruler to measure depth. The teams take notes, bag artifacts by provenience, and cross-mend finds in the laboratory. The youngsters dig with mason's trowels, recover everything strati-graphically, and measure all finds in three dimensions. They do not screen or photograph, but they perform most of the regular functions of a normal excavation.

During the summers of 2003 and 2004, Washington's three-week summer program, which met for archaeology three days a week, for three hours each time, took place in our laboratory adjacent to the William Paca Garden. There were twenty-four young people, aged six to twelve; most were girls. They also visited our field school excavation for a tour of the excavations given by our students and were taught about perspective in the Paca Garden.

Archaeology in Annapolis supplied some of the equipment, like the sandboxes. We did not provide the ideas. If we provided anything, it was a long-term, Annapolis-wide appreciation of archaeology, including among African Americans with whom we have worked as partners since 1988.

Maisha Washington's archaeology curriculum involves African origins for much of African American culture. She focuses on food, cooking, and items familiar to the children. She makes it clear to her students that archaeology is theirs to learn and use. She couples learning the method with exploring Annapolis and other areas of African American culture.

She discusses Egypt, which she explains is known through the work of archaeology. Egypt is African, and not just some free-standing ancient civilization divorced from the rest of Africa, as most European and American archaeologists usually put it. Much of African culture, she explains, comes from Egypt and so does some of European civilization. This is the thesis of Martin Bernal's *Black Athena: The Afroasiatic Roots of Classical Civilization* (1987; but see also Lefkowitz and Rogers 1996 for a critique of this position).

African religions have some of their expressions in this country as well, she explains. Africa provides the basis for some of Christianity. It is a commonly held scholarly hypothesis that black American churches have been influenced by African traditions, in a form known as Afro-Christianity. But the idea expressed by Washington is that African notions of queens, mother figures, and other spiritual powers were expressed through Christianity. They are the original forms, possibly even for Christianity itself, not just its manifestations in diasporic communities in the New World. Like Robert Ferris Thompson, she sees many American cultural origins as African and as improperly called European. This claims Africa as the origin of the West. It is the subordinate's alternative and has the possibility of taking the inevitability of truth away from the West's position.

At this point, engagement with African America provides two ways of commenting on the actions of capitalism's masking ideologies, both through archaeology. One is through a reading of the FWP composite autobiographies and itself has two parts. There, for any English-language reader to see, is the effort to make money by disciplining and selling human beings. The intense struggle of slaves, masters, and other implicated bystanders to move in and out of personal and social responsibility for the violence and even genocidal wickedness of nineteenth-century American slavery is vivid. Virtually everyone involved in slavery's mandatory violence saw through its covering lies. No one was at peace within American slavery, and no one could remain at peace after reading these penetrating indictments of our profit-making system. The FWP composite autobiographies demonstrate, not only that many people breached the ideology of individualism by revealing its extreme side, but that the ideology itself was used, while slavery existed, by people of African descent who internalized the ideology's sense of rights, possessions, and full personhood and made it indict the system and demand better of it. Regardless of what form it took, the contemporary ideology of slavery was thus unconvincing to people of both African and to many of European descent.

The FWP composite autobiographies also speak to us today in the archaeology of plantations, quarters, conjure, and independent living in tenancy and in towns. Archaeology is thus our current window into an understandable critique and our opportunity to consciously describe our society's masks, with the attendant hope of change. We can choose to use the FWP autobiographies to see a different culture, but one within our own, which has a religion like African spirit traditions. Regardless of what it is called—doctoring, fixing, or root work—it is a living diasporic religion like Santeria, Candomble, or Shango. Its practitioners were frequently Christians or used the deeply felt invocation of the names of Jesus, Moses, the saints of the Gospels, and Satan. These spirits moved

God in this world and in the other world. In moving God for immediate purposes, they show an alternative world to prayer and the formal origins of Christianity as provided by the Latin and Greek churches. They are magical, immediate, and compose an unfamiliar mix of traditions that is capable of showing us the same jumble of parts and pieces that goes into Western Christianity, despite its veneer of Italian marble and Protestant whitewash. The magic of African spirits and its difference from Christianity reveals the magic left within mainstream Christianity. This is not transubstantiation but the newly invented idea that life begins at conception and is never to be ended on the gallows, in the electric chair, or by lethal injection.

The third and final engagement with archaeology and critical theory comes in our tools being in the hands of those with a clear view of capitalism's ideologies. Maisha Washington's teaching of the methods and techniques of archaeology to African American children in Annapolis in our laboratory in the William Paca Garden makes archaeology their own. This idea does not come from Habermas, but from Homi Bhabha (1994). Bhabha is important (Matthews and Palus, n.d.; Palus, n.d.) here because he urges the writing of a postcolonial narrative that exposes the way the colonial narrative itself is written:

> For colonial and postcolonial texts do not merely tell the modern history of "unequal development" or evoke memories of underdevelopment. I have tried to suggest that they provide modernity with a modular movement of enunciation: the locus and locution of cultures caught in the transitional and disjunctive temporalities of modernity. What is in modernity more than modernity is the disjunctive "postcolonial" time and space that makes its presence felt at the level of enunciation [writing, telling]. [We are a hybrid society and] must be reconceived liminally as the dynastic-in-the democratic, race-[as] differences . . . and splitting the teleology of class-consciousness: it is through these iterative interrogations and historical initiations that the cultural location of modernity shifts to the postcolonial site.
>
> Bhabha 1994, 251

This unnecessarily difficult language means that when those who have been colonized or enslaved write of their pasts, they write of a society that was both free and enslaving, or a hierarchical society that was also democratic. In other words, it is one thing to read the FWP composite autobiographies and to discover the existence and breadth of African-derived spirit usage, but it is another to use an understanding of archaeology, not to redo modernist histories of society, but to illuminate the artificial basis for creating differences like race and gender and influence those who are conscious of their position in the system of profit-making.

The correctness or otherwise of Maisha Washington's Afrocentric archaeology can be tested in due course. But the idea behind its use in Annapolis and my invoking it here is to cite it as the extension of democratizing processes. In this context, archaeology extends democracy and protects freedom. It does so not because an Afrocentric archaeology is correct or incorrect. That will be known in time. It is a protection for democracy because it is in the hands of those with a keen view of our society, its history, and the ideology we live with, and it will enunciate its own many critiques and histories.

Homi Bhabha speaks of the colonized person being "less than one and double" (1994). It is easy to understand that less than one means less than whole and less than a member of the majority, who is in control. The colonized are made to seem and be inferior in the beholder's eyes and in their own.

The idea that the colonized do something creative with their inferior membership in the dominant culture is the location of culture for Bhabha, by which he means where a new culture, or cultural creation, can be found. This place is also likely to be the location of Habermas's alternative lifeworlds. Bhabha observes that the colonized—for our purposes, slaves or free people at the economic bottom—know the dominant society so intimately that they transform it into a farce or parody by copying it.

The colonized want to belong and are constantly rejected. As a result, they create African America. One element of the creation is a perfect but utterly different style of English, dress, cuisine, and religion. The creation is a complete copy but utterly original. It is so original that the original's very seriousness is called into question and can be laughed at.

Based one of the West's most arcane but popular sciences, archaeology, Maisha Washington contends not only that the West's oldest civilization, ancient Egypt, was African but that the notion of a mother with a divine child entered our tradition from Africa too. She thus asserts that archaeology can show that Western civilization's origins, including some of Christianity's symbols, are African. As Bhabha says, she takes the dominant culture, copies it, and produces a version that is both itself and brand-new. It is a double. But because the cause of the production is so obviously colonial circumstances, it is a parody of the original. This is not very different from what Dr. Alexander Hamilton did in *The History of the Ancient and Honorable Tuesday Club* both to tease the Crown's agents and to free himself from them by declaring himself and his peers to be their equals. American freedom was and is made through this process, which breaches the dominant ideology by using ridicule and the master's tools.

SUMMARY OF THE PROBLEM

The problem is who is the individual who acts. If we are all within ideology, then what is the vehicle for breaching possessive individualism and how can consciousness of its operation be gained and maintained? I want to return to C. B. Macpherson (1962) and his analysis of the idea, before concluding with my impression of the state of the ideology of individualism. Macpherson does not extract the idea of the individual from archaeology the way Deetz does. He analyzes it from its origins in political theory in Hobbes and Locke. Althusser expands on Marx's insight that the idea was a function of the ruling class, not a freestanding element of reality.

For Macpherson, the idea is a fundamental link in modern political theory, because he sees it as the basis for liberal democratic government. By "liberal," he means a government of rights and laws. By "democratic," he means that elected officials can be held responsible for guaranteeing those rights and enforcing these laws. Even though it is hard to read between Macpherson's lines, it is relatively clear that he thinks Hobbes, Locke, and their interpreters, himself included, responded with adjustments to the theory of individualism as the world of political practice changed. Political practice meant the way daily life was led. This in turn meant that possessive individualism might not be a free-standing ideal good but had a meaning that shifted and changed with circumstances. But you have to read between Macpherson's lines and inconsistencies to perceive this.

Macpherson takes possessive individualism from reading Hobbes, in whose theory the individual possesses himself, his capacities, property, rights, and his labor. He alone can alienate these, which means sell them on the market. The fundamental obligation of the state is to protect these possessions by recognizing them. This mutuality is the social contract and existed because the property owners elected their representatives as the government. Thus, the property owners were the government and there was synchrony between the elements of civil society. Macpherson writes as though such a relationship might have actually existed in the seventeenth century.

How was the relationship made to appear as though it did exist? As one reads both the archaeology of Annapolis as a colonial capital and its surviving ideas, for example, in the *Maryland Gazette,* the belief and conviction that individuals possessed personal liberty as a right appeared by the middle of the eighteenth century. If my interpretation of the archaeology and material culture of Annapolis is correct, and if James Deetz's is correct for New England, many people in the colonies saw themselves defined this way by 1700. Possessing rights, including personal liberty, goes with individualism, and thus individual liberty also appeared here by 1700.

Macpherson does not use the notion of ideology in his analysis, because he believes the theory of possessive individualism is true in and of itself. But he does understand that Hobbes and Locke produced a theory that was either an ethnographic description of the workings of part of their society or widely shared as a public belief. Macpherson's analysis is sufficiently tied to living reality to allow him to observe that by the middle of the nineteenth century, industrialism had made many members of society unable to see the social contract as involving them, even though they saw themselves as individuals. Such alienation produced and continues to produce a crisis of legitimacy in governance. Macpherson argues that the idea of possessive individualism has not lost its power, and that there is no alternative to replace it as a way of defining the basis for membership in the state. Therefore his debate is over how to define it in a sufficiently universal way that all individuals belong equally to society. In other words, how to fix the basis of government?

Macpherson clearly missed the American Revolution, at least historically, if not in principle. He did not ask what actually happened in society when those who had lived their lives on the basis of possessive individualism ceased to believe that the state guaranteed its part of the social contract. In Maryland, Virginia, and, in general, in the rest of the American colonies, a majority of the propertied groups failed to believe that the state represented or protected their liberty and other possessions. Instead, those who were to become American revolutionaries built their idea of possessive freedoms into a new Declaration of Independence, a war, a new Constitution, and a new government for those with property. And they alone could vote. Because the contract was with one another, the job of each was to look after each. This was sometimes called eternal vigilance, but I am calling it panoptic citizenship.

Macpherson (1962, 272) struggled with what happened when the franchise was extended to those without property, both endangering those who owned it with the will of those who did not, and revealing to the propertyless that they had natural rights no different from those who had long held them. Ultimately, he never solved the problem as a political philosopher.

Althusser too was a kind of political theorist. He did not imagine that the poor would see rights due them because they believed in personal liberty. He did not see that those with debt, or who were faced with foreclosure, or who were overworked, had little capital, or no insurance would ridicule the state or leave it. He did not see that they would rebel. He did predict that the middle class would remain within ideology; he did predict that they would not be revolutionaries and would be conservative. He did predict that they would remain blind, and although he was incorrect about that, he was right about their being conservative, even though we have found that they could see.

Both Habermas and, to a lesser extent, Macpherson make the propertyless worker with the vote the agent of change for society. Those theorists, using data I report from Annapolis and about it, make the poorest and most despised the agents of change, while Althusser does not. Habermas and Macpherson include slaves and former slaves because of their clarity of vision, their insistence on community over individualism, and their exercise of rights.

Some slaves, African Americans, and, for example, members of the Tuesday Club of the 1750s saw that possessive individualism would get them nowhere. The idea was not a lie for the Tuesday Club members, but because of the Revolution, it led only to deeper captivity in ideology. This is true of Wylie Bates in 1900 too. He tried to make possessive individualism work but blamed social circumstances—read the state—for its failure.

Here is where Macpherson is incorrect and Althusser is correct. It is the very idea, the ideology that we can own ourselves, that is a lie. Maybe the rich and powerful own their lives, although one wonders. More likely they do not. Members of the top and middle classes fool themselves, and they may be the most active victims, only to be given vision, sometimes accompanied by violence, by the poorest. And that vision is of the supremacy of profit, not self or freedom.

Habermas takes the possibility of a vision of the system as seen by its victims and as stated in the victimizer's terms and shines an accurate description at the dominant class, in the hope that a clear view of exploitation will lead to society's modification. I use the critique of capitalism in the FWP composite autobiographies to illustrate that possibility of a clear view of exploitation in our society. And I use the information on African spirit practices to illustrate what another culture, inside of and produced in part by capitalism, looks like, so that we can see alternate possibilities. Homi Bhabha and other postcolonial writers argue that a reconstruction of historical reality that contains critiques, through alternatives like parody, is more effective than Habermas's techniques. Alternative narratives would show that we are a hierarchy and a democracy at the same time, a society from Africa as well as Europe, and one that is pagan as well as Christian. We are not pure at all, we just think we are. All these authors struggle against the pessimism of Althusser. All struggle as well with what vehicles to use to teach the truths of a democratic society. All this is reflected and enacted in Annapolis.

Archaeological Sites Excavated in Annapolis

Amelia G. Chisholm

Site number	Site name	Site reports	Collection location*
18AP01	Paca House and Garden	Archaeological Investigations of the Paca House Garden (Powell 1966)	Historic Annapolis Foundation (HAF)
		Paca Garden Archaeological Testing 18AP01, 186 Prince George Street (Galke 1990) Summary of Archaeological Excavation Data from the Wm. Paca House (Peterson 1981) The Paca House (South 1967) The Archaeological Situation at the William Paca Garden (Spring House and Presumed Pavilion House) (Orr 1975a)	Maryland Archaeological Conservation Laboratory (MAC Lab)
18AP02	Hammond Harwood House	Archaeological Excavations at the Hammond-Harwood House (Dent 1985)	Hammond-Harwood Association
18AP03	Tobacco Prise	No report	HAF, Maryland Historical Trust (MHT)
18AP04	Weems Creek IV	Field Notes on Maryland Archaeology (H. T. Wright 1970)	H. T. Wright
		An Archaeology Sequence in the Middle Chesapeake Region (H. T. Wright 1973)	

Site number	Site name	Site reports	Collection location*
18AP05	Skorpas	Field Notes on Maryland Archaeology (H. T. Wright 1970) An Archaeology Sequence in the Middle Chesapeake Region (H. T. Wright 1973)	
18AP06	Shady Lake	Field Notes on Maryland Archaeology (H. T. Wright 1970) An Archaeology Sequence in the Middle Chesapeake Region (H. T. Wright, 1973)	
18AP07	Cady Cove	Field Notes on Maryland Archaeology (H. T. Wright 1970) An Archaeology Sequence in the Middle Chesapeake Region (H. T. Wright 1973)	
18AP08	College Creek	Field Notes on Maryland Archaeology (H. T. Wright 1970) An Archaeology Sequence in the Middle Chesapeake Region (H. T. Wright 1973)	H. T. Wright
18AP09	Taylor Avenue	Field Notes on Maryland Archaeology (H. T. Wright 1970) An Archaeology Sequence in the Middle Chesapeake Region (H. T. Wright 1973)	H. T. Wright
18AP10	19 South Gate Ave.	Field Notes on Maryland Archaeology (H. T. Wright 1970) An Archaeology Sequence in the Middle Chesapeake Region (H. T. Wright 1973)	
18AP11	Greens Farm	Field Notes on Maryland Archaeology (H. T. Wright 1970) An Archaeology Sequence in the Middle Chesapeake Region (H. T. Wright 1973)	Smithsonian
18AP12	Back Cove	Field Notes on Maryland Archaeology (H. T. Wright 1970)	Maryland Historical Society

Site number	Site name	Site reports	Collection location*
		An Archaeology Sequence in the Middle Chesapeake Region (H. T. Wright 1973)	
18AP13	Artisans House /43 Pinkney St.	Archaeological Investigations of 43 Pinkney Street (Kenyon 1972)	HAF, MHT
		Excavations at 43 Pinkney Street (1974–1975) (Liggett 1976)	
18AP14	Victualling Warehouse	A Preliminary Site Report for the Victualling Warehouse (Crosby 1984)	HAF
		Archaeological Excavations at 18AP14: The Victualling Warehouse Site, 77 Main Street, 1982–1984 (Pearson 1991)	
18AP15	Church Site	A Cultural Resource Survey of the College Creek Area (Williams, Ernstein, and Shackel 1987)	Robert Ogle Collection
18AP16	Depot Cemetery		Smithsonian
18AP17	Mann's Tavern	Report on 4 Possible Archaeological Sites in Annapolis (H. T. Wright 1963)	Smithsonian
18AP18	Upton Scott House	Scott House. Archaeological Feasibility Study (Cosans 1972)	HAF
18AP19	Meadow Point		
18AP20	Arundel Estates		
18AP21	99 Main Street	Preliminary Field Report on the Archaeological Excavations of the 99 Main Street Site (Orr 1975b)	HAF
		Phase II Archaeological Excavations at 99 Main Street 18AP21 (Sign of the Whale) (Cuddy 2005)	
18AP22	State House Lawn		HAF, Maryland State House

Site number	Site name	Site reports	Collection location*
18AP23	Reynolds Tavern	Archaeological Investigations at Reynolds Tavern, 4 ChurchCircle (Orr and Orr 1978) Interim Report on Reynolds Tavern Excavation (Dent and Ford 1983)	HAF, MAC Lab
18AP24	Saunders	No report	
18AP25	Glassworks	No report	HAF
18AP26	Dr. James Murray House	No report	
18AP27	Heise House (City Gates)	No report	
18AP28	Calvert House	Preliminary Analysis of Features from Period 1 Associated with Posthole Building(s) at the Calvert Site (Yentsch 1986) Summary of Excavations at the Calvert Site (Yentsch 1987) Preliminary Analysis of Vertebrate Remains from the Calvert Site in Annapolis, Maryland and a Comparison with Vertebrate Remains from Sites in South Carolina, Georgia, and Jamaica (Reitz 1987) Calvert Site, Seed Remains (N. F. Miller 1988)	HAF
18AP29	Jonas Green House	A Summary of Archaeological Excavations from 1983–1986 at the Green Family Printshop, 18AP29 (Cox and Buckler 1995)	HAF
18AP30	Shiplap House		HAF
18AP31	Hyde House	Report on 4 Possible Archaeological Sites in Annapolis (H. T. Wright 1963)	
18AP32	Ireland House Midden	Report on 4 Possible Archaeological Sites in Annapolis (H. T. Wright 1963)	

Site number	Site name	Site reports	Collection location*
18AP33	Shaw's Shop	Report on 4 Possible Archaeological Sites in Annapolis (H. T. Wright 1963)	
18AP34	Patrick Creagh House	Archaeological Testing at the Patrick Creagh House, AP 34 (Yentsch 1985)	HAF
18AP35	Quinn Site / 20 West Street	No report	HAF
18AP36	Dorsey House / Battery	No report	HAF
18AP37	Retallick-Brewer House	Archaeological Excavations at the Retallick-Brewer House (Sonderman 1988) Archaeological Excavations at the Retallick-Brewer House Site (Bodor 1992)	HAF
18AP38	Brice House	The James Brice House (Ridout 1978) Archaeological Testing at the Brice House, a National Historic Landmark (Basilik, Brown, and Epperson 1984) Excavations at 178 Prince George's Street, the Back of the Brice House, 18AP38 (Williams 1988) Archaeological Investigations at the James Brice House (18AP38) A National Historic Landmark Site 42 East Street (Harmon and Neuwirth 2000)	HAF
18AP39	Newman Street	Preliminary Report: Archaeological Site Excavations at the Newman Street Site (Hopkins 1985)	HAF
18AP40	Ridout House and Garden	A Map of the Ridout Garden (Hopkins 1984)	HAF
18AP41	25–27 West Street	No report	HAF
18AP42	State House Inn	Preliminary Report on Excavations at the State House Inn (Hopkins 1986b)	HAF

Site number	Site name	Site reports	Collection location*
18AP43	St. Anne's Church	Excavations at the State House Inn Site, 18AP42, 15 State Circle, (Shackel, Hopkins, and Williams 1988) Minimum Vessel Analysis State House Inn AP42 (Yentsch, Bescherer, and Patrick 1989) Archaeological Excavations at the Carroll Family Tomb in St. Anne's Church Yard (Dent, Ford, and Hughes 1984) Church Circle, Annapolis, 1986 Monitoring of Public Works Excavation (Hopkins 1986a) Excavations at St. Anne's Churchyard, 18AP43, Church Circle (Shackel and Galke 1988) Monitoring and Excavation in St. Anne's Churchyard, 18AP43 (Jones 2001)	HAF
18AP44	193 Main Street	Archaeological Testing at the 193 Main Street Site, 18AP44 (Shackel 1986) Bottle Glass Analysis, 193 Main Street Feature 12 (Privy) (Beavan 1988) Archaeological Excavations at 18AP44: 193 Main Street, 1985–1987 (O'Reilly 1994a)	HAF
18AP45	St. Mary's / Carroll House	Faunal Remains from Feature 82 (18AP45) (Warner 1992) 1991 Archaeological Excavations at the Charles Carroll House (Logan et al. 1991) Report on Archaeological Investigation Conducted at the St. Mary's Site (18AP45), 107 Duke of Gloucester Street (Palus and Kryder-Reid 2002)	HAF
18AP46	College Creek	A Cultural Resource Survey of the College Creek Area (Williams, Ernstein, and Shackel 1987)	HAF
18AP47	Sands House	Archaeological Excavations at the Sands House (18AP47) (O'Reilly 1994b)	HAF

Site number	Site name	Site reports	Collection location*
18AP48	Governor's Mansion	No report	Governor's Mansion, Annapolis
18AP49	Feldmeyer-Gassaway House	Limited Excavations at the Gassaway-Feldmeyer House 18AP49, 194 Prince George Street (Ernstein 1990b)	HAF
18AP50	Bordley-Randall House	Preliminary Report on Bordley-Randall Site (Yentsch 1988) Emergency Excavations at the Bordley-Randall House 18AP50, 9 Randall Court (Stabler 1990) "It is quietly chaotic. It confuses time": Final Report of Excavations at the Bordley-Randall Site (Matthews 1996)	HAF
18AP51	22–26 West Street	Continuity and Change on an Urban Houselot: Archaeological Excavations at the 22 West Street Back Lot, 8AP51 (Ernstein 1994)	HAF
18AP52	Gott's Court	Test Excavations at Gott's Court, 18AP52 (Warner 1992) Phase II/III Archaeological Investigations of the Gott's Court Parking Facility (R. Christopher Goodwin & Associates 1993)	HAF
18AP53	John Brice II House	Archaeological Testing at the John Brice II (Jennings-Brice) House 18AP53, 195 Prince George Street (Ernstein 1990a)	HAF
18AP54	Annapolis Federal Savings Bank	Archaeological Excavations around State Circle (Read et al. 1990)	HAF
18AP55	10 Francis Street	Archaeological Excavations around State Circle (Read et al. 1990) Archaeological Testing at 10 Francis Street (Galke and Jones 1993)	HAF
18AP56	Edwards	Archaeological Excavations around State Circle (Read et al. 1990)	HAF

Site number	Site name	Site reports	Collection location*
18AP57	Shaw House	Archaeological Excavations around State Circle (Read et al. 1990)	HAF
18AP58	Queen Anne House	Archaeological Excavations around State Circle (Read et al. 1990)	HAF
18AP59	Johnson Site	Archaeological Excavations around State Circle (Read et al. 1990)	HAF
18AP60	Nicholson's Lot	Archaeological Excavations around State Circle (Read et al. 1990)	HAF
18AP61	Public Well	Archaeological Excavations around State Circle (Read et al. 1990)	HAF
18AP62	YMCA	Archaeological Excavations around State Circle (Read et al. 1990)	HAF
18AP63	Courthouse Block	Ground Penetrating Radar Testing of the Franklin Street Site (Warner 1990) Phase I/II Archaeological Investigations on the Courthouse Site (18AP63), an Historic African-American Neighborhood (Warner and Mullins 1993) Three Centuries in Annapolis: Excavations at the Court House (Aiello and Seidel 1994) Three Hundred Years in Annapolis: Phase III Archaeological Investigations of the Anne Arundel County Courthouse Site, 18AP63 (Aiello and Seidel 1995) Phase I/II Report for the Banneker-Douglass Museum Expansion: The Courthouse Site (18AP63), 86–90 Franklin Street, 2000 (Larsen 2001) Phase III Archaeological Investigations for the Banneker-Douglass Museum Expansion: The Courthouse Site (18AP63). 86–90 Franklin Street (Larsen 2002)	HAF

Site number	Site name	Site reports	Collection location*
18AP64	Maynard-Burgess House	Glass Analysis Made Difficult: Preliminary Analysis of a Bottle Glass Sample from 163 Duke of Gloucester Street (Greengrass 1991) Final Archaeological Investigations at the Maynard-Burgess House, 18AP64, a 1850–1980 African American Household in Annapolis (Mullins and Warner 1993a)	HAF
18AP65	172 Green Street	No report	HAF, 172 Green Street, Annapolis
18AP66	Wygant Landing	No report	
18AP67	Ellipse-USNA	Cultural Resource Survey at the United States Naval Academy (Bodor et al. 1993) Catalog of Historic Maps for Cultural Resource Management, United States Naval Academy (Cox et al. 1994)	United States Naval Academy (USNA)
18AP68	Porter Road-USNA	Cultural Resource Survey at the United States Naval Academy (Bodor et al. 1993) Catalog of Historic Maps for Cultural Resource Management, United States Naval Academy (Cox et al. 1994)	USNA
18AP69	Hells Point-USNA	Cultural Resource Survey at the United States Naval Academy (Bodor et al. 1993) Catalog of Historic Maps for Cultural Resource Management, United States Naval Academy (Cox et al. 1994) Archaeological Survey of the United States Naval Academy Shoreline (Aiello and Seidel 1996)	USNA
18AP70	Chase-Lloyd House		

Site number	Site name	Site reports	Collection location*
18AP71	Culvert Site	No report	
18AP72	Bottle Site	No report	
18AP73	Bladen Bridge Site	No report	
18AP74	Slayton House	An Architectural Investigation of the Slayton House at Ridout Row (Graham et al. 1998) Archaeological Investigations at Slayton House, 18AP74 (Jones 2000)	HAF
18AP75	209 Main Street	Cultural Resources Management Investigations for the Main Street Reconstruction Project (Fehr 1997)	
18AP76	141–143 Main Street	No report	
18AP77	"Site 3"	Phase I Cultural Resources Identification Survey: U.S. Naval Academy Golf Course, U.S. Naval Academy North Severn (Beauregard and Davis 1995)	MAC Lab
18AP78	"Site 4"	Phase I Cultural Resources Identification Survey: U.S. Naval Academy Golf Course, U.S. Naval Academy North Severn (Beauregard and Davis 1995)	MAC Lab
18AP79	"Site 7"	Phase I Cultural Resources Identification Survey: U.S. Naval Academy Golf Course, U.S. Naval Academy North Severn (Beauregard and Davis 1995)	MAC Lab
18AP80	MD 450– Gateway Circle	Phase I Archaeological and Architectural Investigations and Phase II Evaluation of Site 18AP80, Related to the MD 450–Gateway Circle Project (Sheehan 1998)	MAC Lab
18AP81	USNA Mess Hall / Seamanship Bldg.	Historic Preservation Plan: United States Naval Academy (Campbell et al. 1997)	MAC Lab

Site number	Site name	Site reports	Collection location*
		Phase I Archaeological Investigations, Phase II Evaluation, and Phase III Mitigation Studies Related to the Replacement of the HTW Piping, United States Naval Academy (Sheehan and Williams 1998)	
18AP82	Buchanan Road-USNA	Historic Preservation Plan: United States Naval Academy (Campbell 1997) Phase I Archaeological Investigations, Phase II Evaluation, and Phase III Mitigation Studies Related to the Replacement of the HTW Piping, United States Naval Academy (Sheehan and Williams 1998)	MAC Lab
18AP83	Chilled Waterline Upgrade-USNA	Intensive Level Reconnaissance at the United States Naval Academy: The Main Campus, NSWC Annapolis Housing, USNA North Severn, and the Naval Academy Dairy Farm (Seidel 1996) Historic Preservation Plan: United States Naval Academy (Campbell 1997) Phase I-III Archaeological Investigations for the Chilled Water Line Upgrade (P-165), Including Site 18AP83, U.S. Naval Academy, (Sheehan 1999)	MAC Lab
18AP84	Dunn Site	Phase II Archaeological Site Examination of the Dunn Site (18AP84), 44 West Street (Beisaw 2000)	
18AP85	Martin Street Parking Lot	No report	HAF
18AP86			
18AP87	Park Place #1	Phase I Archaeology Survey of the Proposed Park Place Development (Ward 2000)	

Site number	Site name	Site reports	Collection location*
		Phase IB/II Archaeological Investigation of Selected Portions of the Proposed Park Place Development (Ward and McCarthy 2001)	
18AP88	Park Place #2	Phase I Archaeology Survey of the Proposed Park Place Development (Ward 2000) Phase IB/II Archaeological Investigation of Selected Portions of the Proposed Park Place Development (Ward and McCarthy 2001)	
18AP89	Park Place #3	Phase I Archaeology Survey of the Proposed Park Place Development (Ward 2000) Phase IB/II Archaeological Investigation of Selected Portions of the Proposed Park Place Development (Ward and McCarthy 2001)	
18AP90	111/113 Chester Avenue	No report	
18AP91	24 Fleet Street	No report	
18AP92	112 College Avenue	No report	
18AP93	119 Chester Avenue	Preliminary Report on Archaeological Investigations in the Eastport Neighborhood of the City of Annapolis: 119 Chester Avenue (18AP93) and 110 Chesapeake Avenue (18AP94) (Palus 2003) Final Report on Archaeological Investigations in the Eastport Neighborhood of Annapolis: 2001–2004 (Palus 2005)	HAF
18AP94	110 Chesapeake Avenue	Preliminary Report on Archaeological Investigations in the Eastport Neighborhood of the City of Annapolis: 119 Chester Avenue (18AP93) and 110 Chesapeake Avenue (18AP94) (Palus 2003)	HAF

Site number	Site name	Site reports	Collection location*
		Final Report on Archaeological Investigations in the Eastport Neighborhood of Annapolis: 2001–2004 (Palus 2005)	
18AP95	Lincoln Park	No report	
18AP96	Railroad Repair Shop	No report	
18AP97	10 Cornhill Street	Digging for the Chalmers Mint (Mumford)	HAF
18AP98	Fleet Street Park	No report	
18AP99	Ogle Hall	No report	
18AP100	102 Chesapeake Avenue	Final Report on Archaeological Investigations in the Eastport Neighborhood of Annapolis (Palus 2005)	HAF
18AP101	201 Chesapeake Avenue	Final Report on Archaeological Investigations in the Eastport Neighborhood of Annapolis: 2001–2004 (Palus 2005)	HAF
18AP102	512 Second Street	Final Report on Archaeological Investigations in the Eastport Neighborhood of Annapolis: 2001–2004 (Palus 2005)	HAF
18AP103	127 Chester Avenue	Final Report on Archaeological Investigations in the Eastport Neighborhood on Annapolis: 2001–2004 (Palus 2005)	HAF
18AP104	207 Duke of Gloucester St.	No report	HAF
	520 Third Street	Final Report on Archaeological Investigations in the Eastport Neighborhood of Annapolis: 2001–2004 (Palus 2005)	HAF
	108 Eastern Avenue	Final Report on Archaeological Investigations in the Eastport Neighborhood of Annapolis: 2001–2004 (Palus 2005)	HAF

* The artifacts from these collections that are stored by the Historic Annapolis Foundation can be used for future research, through two steps. The first is to go through the site report, especially referencing the artifact catalogue that is in the appendix of the report, to determine which artifacts are to be seen. The researcher should take note of the provenience data and bag numbers. After this step, the researcher needs to consult the Archaeology in Annapolis Finders Guide for Collection (Chisholm 2004) to determine the specific box that each particular item is stored in. Once this process is finished, the artifacts can be easily located and removed for research.

Works Cited

Abercrombie, Nicholas, Stephen Hill, and Brian S. Turner. 1980. *The Dominant Ideology Thesis*. Boston: G. Allen & Unwin.

Adams, William Hampton. 1980. Waverly Plantation: Ethnoarchaeology of a Tenant Farming Community. Report prepared by Resource Analysts, Inc. Atlanta: Heritage Conservation and Recreation Service.

————. 1987. *Historical Archaeology of Plantations at Kings Bay, Camden County, Georgia*. Reports of Investigations No. 5. Gainsville: Department of Anthropology, University of Florida.

Adams, William Hampton, and Sarah J. Boling. 1989. Status and Ceramics for Planters and Slaves on Three Georgia Coastal Plantations. *Historical Archaeology* 23.1: 69–96.

Aiello, Elizabeth A., and John Seidel. 1994. Three Centuries in Annapolis: Archaeological Excavations at the Courthouse Block, Annapolis, Maryland. Report prepared by Archaeology in Annapolis. On file: University of Maryland, Archaeology in Annapolis Laboratory, College Park.

————. 1995. Three Hundred Years in Annapolis: Phase III Archaeological Excavations of the Anne Arundel County Courthouse Site (18AP63), Annapolis, Maryland. Report prepared by Archaeology in Annapolis. On file: University of Maryland, Archaeology in Annapolis Laboratory, College Park.

————. 1996. Archaeological Survey of the United States Naval Academy Shoreline. Report prepared by Archaeology in Annapolis, submitted to the Chesapeake Division Naval Facilities Engineering Command, United States Naval Academy. On file: University of Maryland, Archaeology in Annapolis Laboratory, College Park.

Akerson, Louise E. 1989. *The Albermarle Row House Excavation: An Archival Investigation of 44–50 Albermarle, Street, Baltimore, Maryland, Part 1*. Baltimore Center for Urban Archaeology Research Series Report No. 5.

——. 1990. *Baltimore's Material Culture, 1780–1904 — An Archaeological Perspective*. Baltimore Center for Urban Archaeology Technical Series No. 4.

——. 1993 *Fragments of City Life: Preserving Baltimore's Archaeological Heritage — Archaeology Trail Guide*. Baltimore: City Life Museums.

Althusser, Louis. 1971 [1969]. Ideology and Ideological State Apparatuses. In *Lenin and Philosophy, and Other Essays,* trans. Ben Brewster, 127–86. New York: Monthly Review Press.

Anderson, Benedict. [1983] 1991. *Imagined Communities: Reflections on the Origin and Spread of Nationalism.* Rev. ed. New York: Verso.

Arias, Angela, Anna Hill, and Laura Figueroa. 2002. Printer's Type: A Reflection of the Penetration of the Georgian Worldview in Annapolis, Maryland during the Eighteenth Century. Paper produced for the Department of Anthropology, University of Maryland. On file: University of Maryland, Archaeology in Annapolis Laboratory, College Park.

Armstrong, Douglas V. 1990. *The Old Village and the Great House: An Archaeological and Historical Examination of Drax Hall Plantation, St. Ann's Bay, Jamaica.* Urbana: University of Illinois Press.

Austin, Stephen, and Samuel T. Brainerd. N.d. A Preliminary Analysis of the Content of the *Maryland Gazette.* Paper produced for the Department of Anthropology, University of Maryland. On file: University of Maryland, Archaeology in Annapolis Laboratory, College Park.

Bacon, Edmund N. 1968. *Design of Cities.* New York: Viking Press.

Bailey-Goldschmidt, Janice, Elizabeth Kryder-Reid, and Mark P. Leone. N.d. Symbolic Violence and Contending Elites: The Tuesday Club in Eighteenth Century Annapolis. Unpublished manuscript. On file: University of Maryland, Archaeology in Annapolis Laboratory, College Park.

Barnett, Steve, and Martin G. Silverman. 1979. Separations in Capitalist Societies: Persons, Things, Units and Relations. In *Ideology and Everyday Life,* ed. Steve Barnett and Martin G. Silverman, 39–81. Ann Arbor: University of Michigan Press.

Bartlett, Lu. 1977. John Shaw, Cabinetmaker of Annapolis. *Antiques,* January–February, 362–77.

Basilik, Kenneth J., Ann R. Brown, and Terrence W. Epperson. 1984. Archaeological Testing at the Brice House, a National Historic Landmark. On file: University of Maryland, Archaeology in Annapolis Laboratory, College Park.

Bates, Wiley H. 1928. *Researches, Sayings and Life of Wiley H. Bates.* Annapolis, Md.: City Printing Co.

Beadenkopf, Kristopher M., Emily Brown, Michelle Clements, and Hillery Pous. 2002. The Power of Place Settings: Ceramic Variation within Households as a Measure of Participation within the Capitalist Socio-Economy of Annapolis, Maryland. Paper produced for the Department of Anthropology, University of Maryland. On file: University of Maryland, Archaeology in Annapolis Laboratory, College Park.

Beaudry, Mary C., Lauren J. Cook, and Stephen A. Mrozowski. 1991. Artifacts and Active Voices: Material Culture as Social Discourse. In *The Archaeology of Inequality,* ed. Randall H. McGuire and Robert Paynter, 150–91. Oxford: Basil Blackwell.

Beauregard, Alan D., and Marian Davis. 1995. Phase I Cultural Resources Identification Survey: U.S. Naval Academy Golf Course, U.S. Naval Academy
North Severn, Annapolis, Anne Arundel County, Md. On file: Maryland Historical Trust Library, Crownsville, Md.

Beavan, Michelle. 1988. Bottle Glass Analysis, 193 Main Street, Feature 12
(Privy). Report prepared by Archaeology in Annapolis. On file: University of
Maryland, Archaeology in Annapolis Laboratory, College Park.

Beirne, Francis F. 1957. *Baltimore: A Picture History.* New York: Hasting House.

Beisaw, April M. 2000. Phase II Archaeological Site Examination of the Dunn
Site (18AP84), 44 West Street, Annapolis, Maryland. On file: Maryland Historical Trust Library, Crownsville, Md.

Bellion, Wendy. 2004. "Extend the Sphere": Charles Willson Peale's Panorama
of Annapolis. *Art Bulletin,* 86.3 (September): 529–49.

Bentham, Jeremy. 1962. *The Works of Jeremy Bentham.* Edited by John Bowring.
Vol. 4. New York: Russell & Russell.

Bernal, Martin. 1987. *Black Athena: The Afroasiatic Roots of Classical Civilization.* New Brunswick, N.J.: Rutgers University Press.

Bhabha, Homi. 2002 [1994]. *The Location of Culture.* New York: Routledge.

Binford, Lewis R. 1982. Objectivity—Explanation—Archaeology. In *Theory and
Explanation in Archaeology,* ed. Colin Renfrew, Michael J. Rowlands, and
Barbara A. Seagreaves, 125–38. New York: Academic Press.

———. 1983a. *In Pursuit of the Past: Decoding the Archaeological Record.* New
York: Thames & Hudson.

———. 1983b. *Working at Archaeology.* New York: Academic Press.

———. 1987. Researching Archaeology: Frames of Reference and Site Structure.
In *Method and Theory for Activity Area Research—An Ethnoarchaeological
Approach,* ed. Susan Kent, 449–512. New York: Columbia University Press.

Blakey, Michael L. 1983. Sociopolitical Bias and Ideological Production in Historical Archaeology. In *The Sociopolitics of Archaeology,* ed. Joan Gero, D. M.
Lacy, and M. L. Blakey, 5–16. Research Reports No. 23. Amherst: Department of Anthropology, University of Massachusetts.

———. 1989. American Nationality and Ethnicity in the Depicted Past. In *The
Politics of the Past,* ed. P. Gathercole and D. Lowenthal, 38–48. London: Unwin
Hyman.

Bodor, Thomas W. 1992. Archaeological Excavations at the Retallick-Brewer
House Site in Annapolis, Maryland, 18AP37. Report prepared by Archaeology in Annapolis. On file: University of Maryland, Archaeology in Annapolis Laboratory, College Park.

Bodor, Thomas W., Gilda M. Anroman, Jean B. Russo, Hannah Jopling, and
Kevin M. Etherton. 1993. Cultural Resource Survey at the United States
Naval Academy in Annapolis, Maryland. Report prepared by the University of Maryland Archaeology in Annapolis Project, submitted to the Chesapeake Division, Naval Facilities Command, United States Naval Academy.
On file: University of Maryland, Archaeology in Annapolis Laboratory, College Park.

Bourdieu, Pierre. 1977. *Outline of a Theory of Practice.* Translated by Richard
Nice. Cambridge: Cambridge University Press.

Braudel, Fernand. 1979. *The Wheels of Commerce: Civilization and Capitalism, 15th–18th Century.* Vol. 2. New York: Harper & Row.

Breslaw, Elaine G. 1975. Wit, Whimsy, and Politics: The Uses of Satire by the Tuesday Club of Annapolis, 1744–1756. *William and Mary Quarterly,* 3d ser., 32: 295–97.

———, ed. 1988. *Records of the Tuesday Club of Annapolis, 1745–1756.* Urbana: University of Illinois Press.

Brown, Joan Seyers. 1977. William Faris Sr., His Sons and Journeymen— Annapolis Silversmiths. *Antiques,* January–February, 378–85.

Brown, Kenneth L., and D. C. Cooper. 1990. Structural Continuity in an African American Slave and Tenant Community. *Historical Archaeology* 24.4: 7–19.

Brugger, Robert J. 1988. *Maryland: A Middle Temperament, 1634–1980.* Baltimore: Johns Hopkins University Press.

Burlaga, Anna-Marie. 1995. Baroque Influence in Maryland's Capital. Senior thesis, Department of Anthropology, University of Maryland. On file: University of Maryland, Archaeology in Annapolis Laboratory, College Park.

Burton, Sarah Ruhl. 1995. Appendix L—Albemarle Site Report and Catalogue. In Lisa DeLeonardis, *A Phase II Archaeological Investigation of the Cultural Resources Associated with the Carroll-Caton House Courtyard, 18BC6, Baltimore, Maryland.* Baltimore Center for Urban Archaeology Research Series Report No. 47.

Campbell, Lex. 1997. Historic Preservation Plan: United States Naval Academy, Annapolis, Maryland. On file: Maryland Historical Trust Library, Crownsville, Md.

Carroll, Charles [of Annapolis], and Charles Carroll [of Carrollton]. 2001. *Dear Papa, Dear Charley: The Peregrinations of a Revolutionary Aristocrat, as Told by Charles Carroll of Carrollton and His Father, Charles Carroll of Annapolis, with Sundry Observations on Bastardy, Child-Rearing, Romance, Matrimony, Commerce, Tobacco, Slavery, and the Politics of Revolutionary America, 1748–1782.* Edited by Ronald Hoffman, Sally D. Mason, and Eleanor S. Darcy. 3 vols. Chapel Hill: University of North Carolina Press for the Omohundro Institute of Early American History and Culture, Williamsburg, Virginia, the Maryland Historical Society, Baltimore, and the Maryland State Archives, Annapolis.

Castañeda, Quetzil E. 1996. *In the Museum of Maya Culture: Touring Chichén Itzá.* Minnesota: University of Minnesota Press.

Chisholm, Amelia G. 2004. Finders' Guide to Archaeology in Annapolis Collections, Both Artifacts and Records. On file: University of Maryland, Archaeology in Annapolis Laboratory, College Park.

Cochran, Matthew D. 1999. Hoodoo's Fire: Interpreting Nineteenth Century African-American Material Culture at the Brice House, Annapolis, Maryland. *Maryland Archaeology* 35.1: 25–33.

Coleman, Simon, and Matthew Johnson. 1985. Exploratory Analysis of the Layout of the *Maryland Gazette.* Paper produced for the Department of Anthropology, University of Maryland. On file: University of Maryland, Archaeology in Annapolis Laboratory, College Park.

Comer, Elizabeth Anderson, and L. L. Baker. 1987. Baltimore's Magnificent

Media Machine. In *Captivating the Public through the Media while Digging the Past,* ed. Kristen S. Peters, Elizabeth Anderson Comer, and R. E. Kelly, 14–20. Technical Series No. 1. Baltimore: Center for Urban Archaeology.

Conrad, Earl. 1947. *Jim Crow America.* New York: Duell, Sloan & Pearce.

Cosans, Betty. 1972. Upton Scott House. Archaeological Feasibility Study. On file: Maryland Historical Trust Library, Crownsville, Md.

Cox, C. Jane, and John J. Buckler. 1995. A Summary of Archaeological Excavations from 1983–1986 at the Green Family Print Shop, 18AP29, Annapolis, Maryland. Report prepared by Archaeology in Annapolis. On file: University of Maryland, Archaeology in Annapolis Laboratory, College Park.

Cox, C. Jane, John L. Seidel, Carey O'Reilly, and Gilda Anroman. 1994. Catalog of Historic Maps for Cultural Resource Management, United States Naval Academy. Legacy Resource Management Program Archaeological Reconnaissance Survey. Report prepared by Archaeology in Annapolis and U.S. Naval Academy. On file: University of Maryland, Archaeology in Annapolis Laboratory, College Park.

Creel, Margaret Washington. 1988. *A Peculiar People: Slave Religion and Community—Culture among the Gullahs.* New York: New York University Press.

Cressey, Pamela J. 1985a. The Alexandria, Virginia City-Site: Archaeology in an Afro American Neighborhood, 1830–1910. Ph.D. diss., Department of Anthropology, University of Iowa. Ann Arbor, Mich.: University Microfilms.

———. 1985b. *The Archaeology of Free Blacks in Alexandria, Virginia.* Alexandria Archaeology Publications No. 19. City of Alexandria, Va.

———. 1989. *The Nineteenth Century Transformation and Development of Alexandria, Virginia.* Alexandria Archaeology Publication No. 1. City of Alexandria, Va.

Crosby, Constance. 1984. A Preliminary Site Report for the Victualling Warehouse, Annapolis, Md. Report prepared by Archaeology in Annapolis. On file: University of Maryland, Archaeology in Annapolis Laboratory, College Park.

Cuddy, Thomas W. 2005. Phase II Archaeological Excavations at 99 Main Street 18AP21 (Sign of the Whale), Annapolis, Maryland. On file: University of Maryland, Archaeology in Annapolis Laboratory, College Park.

Deagan, Kathleen A., and Darcie A. MacMahon. 1995. *Fort Mose: Colonial America's Black Fortress of Freedom.* Gainesville: University Press of Florida.

Deagan, Kathleen A., and Joan K. Koch. 1983. *Spanish St. Augustine: The Archaeology of a Colonial Creole Community.* New York: Academic Press.

De Cunzo, Lu Anne. 1995. Reform, Respite, Ritual: An Archaeology of Institutions. The Magdalen Society of Philadelphia, 1800–1850. *Historical Archaeology* 29.3: 1–164.

Deetz, James F. 1977. *In Small Things Forgotten: The Archaeology of Early American Life.* Garden City, N.Y.: Anchor Press/Doubleday. Rev. ed. 1996.

DeLeonardis, Lisa. 1995. *A Phase II Archaeological Investigation of the Cultural Resources Associated with the Carroll-Caton House Courtyard, 18BC6, Baltimore, Maryland.* Baltimore Center for Urban Archaeology Research Series Report No. 47.

Dent, Richard J. 1985. Archaeological Excavations at the Hammond-Harwood

House, Annapolis, Md. Report prepared by Archaeology in Annapolis. On file: University of Maryland, Archaeology in Annapolis Laboratory, College Park.

Dent, Richard J., and S. Elizabeth Ford. 1983. Interim Report on Reynolds Tavern Excavation. Report prepared by Archaeology in Annapolis. On file: University of Maryland, Archaeology in Annapolis Laboratory, College Park.

Dent, Richard J., S. Elizabeth Ford, and Richard Hughes. 1984. Archaeological Excavations at the Carroll Family Tomb in St. Anne's Church Yard, Annapolis, Maryland. Report prepared by Archaeology in Annapolis. On file: University of Maryland, Archaeology in Annapolis Laboratory, College Park.

Derrida, Jacques. 1986. Declarations of Independence. *New Political Science* 15 (Summer): 7–15.

Dézallier d'Argenville, Antoine-Joseph [Alexander Le Blond, pseud.]. 1722 [1709]. *La Théorie et la pratique du jardinage* . . . Paris: Chez Jean Marielle.

———. 1728 [1712]. *The Theory and Practice of Gardening. . . . By le sieur Alexander Le Blond* [Dézallier d'Argenville]. Translated by John James. London: Bernard Lintot.

Dolgin, Janet L. 1977. *Jewish Identity and the JDL*. Princeton, N.J.: Princeton University Press.

Douglass, Frederick. 1986 [1845]. *Narrative of the Life of Frederick Douglass, an American Slave*. New York: Penguin Books.

Du Bois, W. E. B. 1969 [1903]. *The Souls of Black Folk*. New York: Dodd, Mead.

Edwards, Ywonne. 1990. Master-Slave Relations: A Williamsburg Perspective. MA thesis, College of William and Mary.

———. 2001. African American Medicine and the Social Relations of Slavery. In *Race and the Archaeology of Identity*, ed. C. E. Orser Jr., 34–53. Salt Lake City: University of Utah Press.

Eisenstein, Elizabeth L. 1979. *The Printing Press as an Agent of Change: Communications and Cultural Transformations in Early Modern Europe*. New York: Cambridge University Press.

———. 1983. *The Printing Revolution in Early Modern Europe*. New York: Cambridge University Press, 1983.

Elias, Norbert. 1978–82. *The Civilizing Process*. Translated by Edmund Jephcott. Vol. 1: *The Development of Manners*. New York: Horizen Books. Vol. 2: *Power and Civility*. New York: Pantheon Books.

Epperson, Terrence W. 1990. To Fix a Perpetual Brand: The Social Construction of Race in Virginia, 1675–1750. Ph.D. diss., Temple University. Ann Arbor, Mich.: University Microfilms.

———. 1999 Constructing Difference: The Social and Spatial Order of the Chesapeake Plantation. In *"I, too, am America": Archaeological Studies of African American Life,* ed. Theresa Singleton, 159–72. Charlottesville: University Press of Virginia.

Ernstein, Julie H. 1990a. Archaeological Testing at the John Brice II (Jennings-Brice) House, 18AP53, 195 Prince George Street, Annapolis, Maryland. Report prepared by Archaeology in Annapolis. On file: University of Maryland, Archaeology in Annapolis Laboratory, College Park.

———. 1990b. Limited Excavations at the Gassaway-Feldmeyer House, 18AP49,

194 Prince George Street, Annapolis, Maryland. Report prepared Archaeology in Annapolis. On file: University of Maryland, Archaeology in Annapolis Laboratory, College Park.

———. 1994. Continuity and Change on an Urban Houselot: Archaeological Excavations at the 22 West Street Back Lot (18AP51) of the Annapolis National Historic District, Anne Arundel County, Maryland. Report prepared by Archaeology in Annapolis. On file: University of Maryland, Archaeology in Annapolis Laboratory, College Park.

———. 2004. Constructing Context: Historical Archaeology and the Pleasure Garden in Prince George's County, Maryland 1740–1790. Ph.D. diss., Boston University. Ann Arbor: University Microfilms International (UMI) Dissertation Services.

Etherton, Kevin. 1994. *An Archival Investigation of Cultural Resources Associated with "Captain Wells' House" and the "London Coffee House," Fells Point, Baltimore, Maryland.* Baltimore Center for Urban Archaeology Research Series Report No. 48.

Fagan, Brian M. 1995. *Ancient North America.* 2d ed. New York: Thames & Hudson.

Faris, William. 2003. *The Diary of William Faris: The Daily Life of an Annapolis Silversmith.* Edited by Mark Letzer and Jean B. Russo. Baltimore: Maryland Historical Society Press.

Fairbanks, Charles H. 1972. The Kingsley Slave Cabins in Duval County, Florida, 1968. *Conference on Historic Site Archaeology Papers,* 1971, 7: 62–93.

———. 1984, The Plantation Archaeology of the Southeastern Coast. *Historical Archaeology* 18.1: 1–14.

Fehr, April L. 1997. Cultural Resources Management Investigations for the Main Street Reconstruction Project, Annapolis, Anne Arundel Co., MD. On file: Maryland Historical Trust Library. Crownsville, Md.

Fennel, Christopher. 2000. Conjuring Boundaries: Inferring Past Identities from Religious Artifacts. *International Journal of Historical Archaeology* 4.4: 281–313.

———. 2003. Group Identity, Individual Creativity, and Symbolic Generation in a Bakongo Diaspora. *International Journal of Historical Archaeology* 7.1: 1–31.

Ferguson, Leland G. 1992. *Uncommon Ground: Archaeology and Early African America, 1650–1800.* Washington, D.C.: Smithsonian Institution Press.

Fleming, Kevin. 1988. *Annapolis, the Spirit of Chesapeake Bay.* Foreword by St. Claire Wright; text by Patricia B. Kohlhepp. Annapolis, Md.: Portfolio Press.

Foucault, Michel. 1973. *The Order of Things: An Archaeology of the Human Sciences.* New York: Vintage Books.

———. 1979. *Discipline and Punish.* New York: Random House.

Franklin, Maria. 1997. Out of Site, Out of Mind: The Archaeology of an Enslaved Virginian Household, c. 1740–1778. Ph.D. diss., University of California, Berkeley. Ann Arbor, Mich.: University Microfilms.

———. 2001. The Archaeological Dimensions of Soul Food: Interpreting Race, Culture, and Afro-Virginian Identity. In *Race and the Archaeology of Identity,* ed. C. E. Orser Jr., 88–107. Salt Lake City: University of Utah Press.

Frey, Jacob. 1893. *Reminiscences of Baltimore*. Baltimore: Maryland Book Concern.

Fry, Gladys-Marie. 1990. *Stitched From the Soul: Slave Quilts from the Ante-Bellum South*. New York: Dutton.

———. 2001 [1975]. *Night Riders in Black Folk History*. Chapel Hill: University of North Carolina Press.

Gadsby, David A. 2002. Industrial Re-use of Domestic Ceramics at the Swan Cove Site. (18AN 934). *Maryland Archaeology* 38.1: 19–26.

Galke, Laura J. 1990. Paca Garden Archaeological Testing, 18AP01, 186 Prince George Street, Annapolis, Maryland. Report prepared by Archaeology in Annapolis. On file: University of Maryland, Archaeology in Annapolis Laboratory, College Park.

———. 1992. *Cultural Resources Survey and Inventory of a War-Torn Landscape: The Stuart's Hill Manassas National Battlefield*. Regional Archaeology Program, National Capital Region, Occasional Report No. 7. Washington D.C.: National Park Service.

———. 1995. A Quantitative Appraisal of the Green Family Print Site in Annapolis, Maryland. MA thesis, Arizona State University.

———. 2000. Did the Gods of Africa Die? A Reexamination of a Carroll House Crystal Assemblage. *North American Archaeologist* 21.1: 19–33.

Galke, Laura J., and Lynn D. Jones. 1993. Archaeological Testing at 10 Francis Street, Annapolis, Maryland, 18AP55. Report prepared by Archaeology in Annapolis. On file: University of Maryland, Archaeology in Annapolis Laboratory, College Park.

Gero, Joan M., David M. Lacy, and Michael L. Blakey. 1983. *The Sociopolitics of Archaeology*. Research Reports No. 23. Amherst: Department of Anthropology, University of Massachusetts.

Gibb, James G. 1999. *A Layperson's Guide to Historical Archaeology in Maryland*. Myersville, Md.: Archaeological Society of Maryland.

Gomez, Michael A. 1998. *Exchanging Our County Marks: The Transformation of African Identities in the Colonial and Antebellum South*. Chapel Hill: University of North Carolina Press.

Graham, Willie, Edward Chappell, Carl Lounsbury, and Orlando Ridout, IV. 1998. An Architectural Investigation of the Slayton House at Ridout Row. On file: University of Maryland, Archaeology in Annapolis Laboratory, College Park.

Greengrass, Mara R. 1991. Glass Analysis Made Difficult: Preliminary Analysis of a Bottle Glass Sample from 163 Duke of Gloucester Street, Annapolis, MD. Report prepared by Archaeology in Annapolis. On file: University of Maryland, Archaeology in Annapolis Laboratory, College Park.

Gundaker, Grey. 1993. Tradition and Innovation in African-American Yards. *African Arts*. April, 58–71, 91–96.

———. 1998a. Introduction: Home Ground. In *Keep Your Head to the Sky*, ed. id., 3–23. Charlottesville: University Press of Virginia.

———. 1998b. *Signs of Diaspora, Diaspora of Signs*. New York: Oxford University Press.

Habermas, Jürgen. 1975. *Legitimation Crisis*. Translated by Thomas McCarthy. Boston: Beacon Press.

————. 1984–87. *The Theory of Communicative Action*. Vol. 1, *Reason and the Rationalization of Society*. Vol. 2, *Lifeworld and System: A Critique of Functionalist Reason*. Translated by Thomas McCarthy. Boston: Beacon Press.

Haley, Alex. 1976. *Roots*. Garden City, N.J.: Doubleday.

Hall, Gwendolyn Midlo. 1971. *Social Control in Slave Plantation Societies: A Comparison of St. Dominigue and Cuba*. Baltimore: Johns Hopkins Press.

————. 1992. *Africans in Colonial Louisiana: The Development of Afro-Creole Culture in the Eighteenth Century*. Baton Rouge: Louisiana State University Press.

Hamilton, Alexander. 1948 [1744]. *Gentleman's Progress: The Itinerarium of Dr. Alexander Hamilton, 1744*. Edited by Carl Bridenbaugh. Chapel Hill: University of North Carolina Press.

————. 1988. *Records of the Tuesday Club of Annapolis, 1745–1756*. Edited by Elaine C. Breslaw. Urbana: University of Illinois Press.

————. 1990. *The History of the Ancient and Honorable Tuesday Club*. Edited by Robert Micklus. 3 vols. Chapel Hill: University of North Carolina Press.

Handler, Jerome S. 1974. *The Unappropriated People: Freedmen in the Slave Society of Barbados*. Baltimore: Johns Hopkins University Press.

————. 1991. *Supplement to a Guide to Source Materials for the Study of Barbados History, 1627–1834*. Providence, R.I.: John Carter Brown Library and Barbados Museum and Historical Society.

Handler, Jerome S., Michael D. Conner, and Keith P. Jacobi. 1989. *Searching for a Slave Cemetery in Barbados, West Indies: A Bioarchaeological and Ethnohistorical Investigation*. Carbondale: Center for Archaeological Investigations, Southern Illinois University at Carbondale.

Handler, Jerome S., Ronnie Huges, and Ernest M. Wiltshire. 1999. *Freedmen of Barbados: Names and Notes for Genealogical and Family History Research*. Charlottesville, Va.: Published for the Friends of the Barbados Archives by the Virginia Foundation for the Humanities and Public Policy.

Handler, Jerome S., and Frederick Lange. 1978. *Plantation Slavery in Barbados: An Archaeological and Historical Investigation*. Cambridge, Mass.: Harvard University Press.

Handler, Richard. 1986. Authenticity. *Anthropology Today* 2.1: 2–4; 2.2: 3: 24.

————. 1988. *Nationalism and the Politics of Culture in Quebec*. Madison: University of Wisconsin Press.

————. 1991. Who Owns the Past? In *The Politics of Culture*, ed. Brett Williams, 63–74. Washington, D.C.: Smithsonian Institution Press.

Handler, Richard, and William Saxton. 1988. Dyssimulation: Reflexivity, Narrative, and the Quest for Authenticity in "Living History." *Cultural Anthropology* 3.3: 242–65.

Harmon, James M., and Jessica L. Neuwirth. 2000. Archaeological Investigations at the James Brice House (18AP38), A National Historic Landmark Site: 42 East Street, City of Annapolis, Anne Arundel County, Maryland. Report prepared by Archaeology in Annapolis. On file: University of Maryland, Archaeology in Annapolis Laboratory, College Park.

Harrington, J. C. 1955. Archaeology as Auxiliary Science to American History. *American Anthropologist* 57.6: 112–30.

Harris, Teresa D. 1986. Grammar and the *Maryland Gazette* as Reflections of the Georgian Mindset in Eighteenth- and Early Nineteenth-Century Annapolis. Paper produced for the Department of Anthropology, University of Maryland. On file: University of Maryland, Archaeology in Annapolis Laboratory, College Park.

Hermann, Nadja. 1999. Habermas and Philosophy of Education. *Encyclopedia of Philosophy of Education*. www.vusst.hr/ENCYCLOPEDIA/habermasenglish .htm. Accessed May 26, 2004.

Herskovits, Melville J. 1958 [1941]. *The Myth of the Negro Past*. Boston: Beacon Press.

Hodder, Ian. 1986. *Reading the Past: Current Approaches to Interpretation in Archaeology*. Cambridge: Cambridge University Press.

Hoepfner, Christine, and Parker B. Potter Jr. 1987. The Preserved is Political. *ICOMOS Information*, July–September, 10–16.

Hoffman, Ronald. 2000. *Princes of Ireland, Planters of Maryland: A Carroll Saga, 1500–1788*. Chapel Hill: University of North Carolina Press for the Omohundro Institute of Early American History and Culture.

Hopkins, Joseph W., III. 1984. A Map of the Ridout Garden. Made with assistance from Nigel Holman. Annapolis, Md.: Historic Annapolis Foundation.

———. 1985. Preliminary Report: Archaeological Site Excavations at the Newman Street Site, Annapolis, Maryland. Report prepared by Archaeology in Annapolis. On file: University of Maryland, Archaeology in Annapolis Laboratory, College Park.

———. 1986a. Church Circle, Annapolis, 1986 Monitoring of Public Works Excavation. On file: University of Maryland, Archaeology in Annapolis Laboratory, College Park.

———. 1986b. Preliminary Report on Excavations at the State House Inn, Annapolis, Maryland, 1985. Report prepared by Archaeology in Annapolis. On file: University of Maryland, Archaeology in Annapolis Laboratory, College Park.

Hyatt, Harry M. 1970–78 [1935]. *Hoodoo–Conjuration–Witchcraft–Rootwork: Beliefs Accepted by Many Negroes and White Persons, These Being Orally Recorded among Blacks and Whites*. 5 vols. Hannibal, Mo.: Western Publishing.

Isaac, Rhys. 1982. *The Transformation of Virginia, 1740–1790*. Chapel Hill: University of North Carolina Press.

Jones, Lynn D. 1995. The Material Culture of Slavery from an Annapolis Household. Paper presented at the annual meeting of the Society for Historical Archaeology, Washington, D.C., January 1995. On file: University of Maryland, Archaeology in Annapolis Laboratory, College Park.

———. 1999. Crystals and Conjuring in an Annapolis Household. *Maryland Archaeology* 35.2: 1–8.

———. 2000. Archaeological Investigations at Slayton House (18AP74), Annapolis, Maryland. Report prepared by Archaeology in Annapolis. On file: University of Maryland, Archaeology in Annapolis Laboratory, College Park.

———. 2001. Archaeological Monitoring and Excavation in St. Anne's Churchyard 18AP43, Annapolis, Maryland. Report prepared by Archaeology in Annapolis. On file: University of Maryland, Archaeology in Annapolis Laboratory, College Park.

Jopling, Hannah. 1991. Interview Transcripts from Archaeology in Annapolis African-American Archaeological Project. On file: University of Maryland, Archaeology in Annapolis Laboratory, College Park.

———. 1992. Interview Transcripts from Focus Group Interviews with Gott's Court Residents. Transcript. On file: University of Maryland, Archaeology in Annapolis Laboratory, College Park.

Joyner, Charles. 1984. *Down by the Riverside: A South Carolina Slave Community.* Urbana: University of Illinois Press.

———. 1999 *Shared Traditions: Southern History and Folk Culture.* Urbana: University of Illinois Press.

Kearns, Richard. 1977a. Urban Design. *Antiques,* January–February, 158–59.

———. 1977b. The Annapolis Cityscape. *Antiques,* January–February, 194–200.

Kenyon, Jeff. 1972. Archaeological Investigations of 43 Pinkney Street. On file: University of Maryland, Archaeology in Annapolis Laboratory, College Park.

Klingelhofer, Eric. 1987. Aspects of Afro-American Material Culture: Artifacts from the Slave Quarters at Garrison Plantation, Maryland. *Historical Archaeology* 21.2: 112–19.

Kryder-Reid, Elizabeth B. 1991. Landscape as Myth: the Contextual Archaeology of an Annapolis Landscape. Ph.D. diss., Department of Anthropology, Brown University.

Langley, Batty. 1726. *New Principles of Gardening.* London: A. Bettesworth and J. Batley.

———. 1967 [1740]. *The City and the Country Builder's and Workman's Treasury of Designs.* New York: Benjamin Blom.

LaRoche, Cheryl J. 1994. Beads from the African Burial Ground, New York City: A Preliminary Assessment. *Beads: Journal of the Society of Bead Researchers* 6.3: 20.

LaRoche, Cheryl J., and Michael J. Blakey. 1997. Seizing the Intellectual Power: the Dialogue at the New York African Burial Ground. *Historical Archaeology* 31.3: 84–106.

Larsen, Eric L. 2001. Phase I/II Report for the Banneker-Douglass Museum Expansion: The Courthouse Site (18AP63), 86–90 Franklin Street, Annapolis, Maryland, 2000. Report prepared by Archaeology in Annapolis. On file: University of Maryland, Archaeology in Annapolis Laboratory, College Park.

———. 2002. Phase III Archaeological Investigations for the Banneker-Douglass Museum Expansion: The Courthouse Site (18AP63), 86–90 Franklin Street, Annapolis, Maryland. Report prepared by Archaeology in Annapolis. On file: University of Maryland, Archaeology in Annapolis Laboratory, College Park.

Le Blond. See Dézallier d'Argenville.

Lefkowitz, Mary R., and Guy MacLean Rogers, eds. 1996. *Black Athena Revisited.* Chapel Hill: University of North Carolina Press.

Leone, Mark P. N.d. *Annapolis: Reflections from the Age of Reason.* 25-minute video production. Telesis Productions of Baltimore. On file: University of Maryland, Archaeology in Annapolis Laboratory, College Park.

———. 1981a. Archaeology's Relationship to the Present and the Past. In *Mod-*

ern Material Culture, ed. R. A. Gould and M. B. Shiffer, 5–13. New York: Academic Press.

———. 1981b. The Relationship between Artifacts and the Public in Outdoor History Museums. In *The Research Potential of Anthropological Collections,* ed. Anne-Marie Cantwell, J. B. Griffin, and N. Rothchild, 301–313. New York: New York Academy of Sciences.

———. 1984. Interpreting Ideology in Historical Archaeology: Using the Rules of Perspective in the William Paca Garden in Annapolis, Maryland. In *Ideology, Representation and Power in Prehistory,* ed. C. Tilley and D. Miller, 25–35. Cambridge: Cambridge University Press.

———. 1987. Rule by Ostentation: The Relationship between Space and Sight in Eighteenth-Century Landscape Architecture in the Chesapeake Region of Maryland. In *Method and Theory for Activity Area Research: An Ethnoarchaeological Approach,* ed. Susan Kent, 604–33. New York: Columbia University Press.

———. 1988. The Georgian Order as the Order of Merchant Capitalism in Annapolis, Maryland. In *The Recovery of Meaning: Historical Archaeology in the Eastern United States,* ed. M. P. Leone and Parker B. Potter Jr., 235–61. Washington, D.C.: Smithsonian Institution Press.

———. 1995. A Historical Archaeology of Capitalism. *American Anthropologist* 97.2: 251–68.

Leone, Mark P., with assistance from Marian Creveling and Christopher Nagle. 1999. Ceramics from Annapolis, Maryland: A Measure of Time Routines and Work Discipline. In *Historical Archaeologies of Capitalism,* ed. M. P. Leone and Parker B. Potter Jr., 195–216. New York: Kluwer Academic / Plenum Publishers.

Leone, Mark P., Julie H. Ernstein, Elizabeth Kryder-Reid, and Paul A. Shackel. 1989. Power Gardens of Annapolis. *Archaeology* 42.2: 34–37, 74–75.

Leone, Mark P., and Gladys-Marie Fry. 1999. Conjuring in the Big House Kitchen. *Journal of American Folklore* 112.445: 372–403.

Leone, Mark P., and Gladys-Marie Fry, with assistance from Timothy Ruppel. 2001. Spirit Management among Americans of African Descent. In *Race and the Archaeology of Identity,* ed. Charles E. Orser Jr., 143–57. Salt Lake City: University of Utah Press.

Leone, Mark P., and Russel G. Handsman. 1989. Living History and Critical Archaeology and the Reconstructed Past. In *Critical Traditions in Contemporary Archaeology,* ed. Valerie Pinsky and Alison Wylie, 117–35. Cambridge: Cambridge University Press.

Leone, Mark P., James M. Harmon, and Jessica L. Neuwirth. 2005. Perspective and Surveillance in Eighteenth-Century Maryland Gardens, Including William Paca's on Wye Island. *Historical Archaeology* 39.4:131–50.

Leone, Mark P., and Silas D. Hurry. 1998. Seeing: The Power of Town Planning in the Chesapeake. *Historical Archaeology* 34.4: 34–62.

Leone, Mark P., Paul R. Mullins, Marian C. Creveling, Laurence Hurst, Barbara Jackson Nash, Lynn D. Jones, Hannah Jopling Kaiser, George C. Logan, and Mark S. Warner. 1995. Can an African American Archaeology be an Alternative Voice? In *Interpretive Archaeologies,* ed. Ian Hodder, Michael Shanks,

Alexandra Alexandri, Victor Buchli, John Carman, Jonathan Last, and Gavin Lucas, 110–24. London: Routledge.

Leone, Mark P., and Parker B. Potter Jr. 1996. Archaeological Annapolis: A Guide to Seeing and Understanding Three Centuries of Change. Reprinted in *Contemporary Archaeology in Theory,* ed. Ian Hodder and Robert W. Preucel, 570–98. Oxford: Blackwell.

Leone, Mark P., Parker B. Potter Jr., and Paul A. Shackel. 1987. Toward a Critical Archaeology. *Current Anthropology* 28.3: 283–302.

Leone, Mark P., and Paul A. Shackel. 1987. Forks, Clocks, and Power. In *Mirror and Metaphor,* ed. Daniel Ingersoll and Gordon Bronitsky, 45–61. Lanham, Md.: University Press of America.

———. 1990. Plane and Solid Geometry in Colonial Gardens in Annapolis, Maryland. In *Earth Patterns,* ed. William Kelso and Rachel Most, 153–67. Charlottesville: University Press of Virginia.

Leone, Mark P., Jennifer Stabler, and Anna-Marie Burlaga. 1998. A Street Plan for Hierarchy in Annapolis: An Analysis of State Circle as a Geometric Form. In *Annapolis Pasts,* ed. Paul A. Shackel, Paul R. Mullins, and Mark S. Warner, 291–306. Knoxville: University of Tennessee Press.

Liggett, Barbara. 1976. Excavations at 43 Pinkney Street (1974–1975). On file: University of Maryland, Archaeology in Annapolis Laboratory, College Park.

Lindauer, Anthony D. 1997. *From Paths to Plats, the Development of Annapolis, 1651–1718.* Annapolis, Md.: Maryland State Archives and the Maryland Historical Trust.

Little, Barbara J. 1987. Ideology and Media: Historical Archaeology of Printing in Eighteenth-Century Annapolis, Maryland. Ph.D. diss., Department of Anthropology, State University of New York, Buffalo. Ann Arbor, Mich.: University Microfilms International.

———. 1988. Craft and Culture Change in the Eighteenth-Century Chesapeake. In *The Recovery of Meaning: Historical Archaeology in the Eastern United States,* ed. Mark P. Leone and Parker B. Potter Jr., 263–92. Washington, D.C.: Smithsonian Institution Press.

———. 1992. Explicit and Implicit Meanings in Material Culture and Print Culture. *Historical Archaeology.* 26.3: 85–94.

———. 1994. "She Was . . . an Example to Her Sex": Possibilities for a Feminist Historical Archaeology. In *Historical Archaeology of the Chesapeake,* ed. Paul A Shackel and Barbara J. Little, 189–204. Washington, D.C.: Smithsonian Institution Press.

———. 1998. Cultural Landscapes of Printers and the "Heav'n Taught Art" in Annapolis, Maryland. In *Annapolis Pasts: Historical Archaeology in Annapolis, Maryland,* ed. Paul A. Shackel, Paul R. Mullins, and Mark S. Warner, 225–43. Knoxville: University of Tennessee Press.

Little, Glenn J., II. 1967–68. Letters. Re: Archaeological Research on Paca Garden. November 8, 1967, May 24, 1968. On file: Historic Annapolis Foundation, Annapolis, Md.

———. N.d. Blueprints of Trenches of the Lower William Paca Garden. Annapolis, Md.: On file: Historic Annapolis Foundation, Annapolis, Md.

Lockwood, A. B. 1934. *Gardens of Colony and State: Gardens and Gardeners of the American Colonies and of the Republic before 1840*. 2 vols. New York: Scribner.

Logan, George C., Thomas W. Bodor, Lynn D. Jones, and Marian C. Creveling. 1992. 1991 Archaeological Excavations at the Charles Carroll House in Annapolis, Maryland, 18AP45. Report prepared by Archaeology in Annapolis. On file: University of Maryland, Archaeology in Annapolis Laboratory, College Park.

Luckenbach, A. 1995. *Providence—1949*. Studies in Local History. Crownsville, Md.: Maryland Historical Trust and Maryland State Archives.

Luckenbach, A., C. Jane Cox, and John Kille. 2002. *The Clay Tobacco-Pipe in Anne Arundel County*. Annapolis, Md.: Anne Arundel County Trust for Preservation.

Lukács, Georg. 1971. Reification and the Consciousness of the Proletariat. In id., *History and Class Consciousness: Studies in Marxist Dialectics*. Translated by Rodney Livingstone, 83–222. Cambridge, Mass.: MIT Press.

Macpherson, C. B. 1962. *The Political Theory of Possessive Individualism: Hobbes to Locke*. Oxford: Oxford University Press.

Magdoff, JoAnn M. 1977. The Tillage of His Husbandry: A Symbolic Analysis of Change in Male Female Identity in an Industrializing Town in Central Italy. Ph.D. diss., Princeton University. Ann Arbor, Mich.: University Microfilms International.

Martin, Peter. 1984. "Long and Assiduous Endeavours:" Gardening in Early Eighteenth-Century Virginia. In *British and American Gardens in the Eighteenth Century*, ed. Robert P. Maccubbin and Peter Martin, 107–16. Williamsburg, Va.: Colonial Williamsburg Foundation.

Marx, Karl. 1970 [1843–44]. *Critique of Hegel's "Philosophy of Right."* Translated by Annette Jolin and Joseph O'Malley. Edited by Joseph O'Malley. Cambridge: Cambridge University Press.

———. 2002. *Marx on Religion*. Edited by John Raines. Philadelphia: Temple University Press.

Maryland. General Assembly. House of Delegates. 1783. Assessment Record. AA [Anne Arundel County]. Annapolis Hundred. MSA [Maryland State Archives] S 1161-1.

———. State Planning Commission. 1934–35. *Population of Maryland, 1790–1930*. Baltimore: Maryland State Department of Health.

Matthews, Christopher N. 1996. "It is quietly chaotic. It confuses time": Final Report of Excavations at the Bordley-Randall Site in Annapolis, Maryland, 1993–1995. Report prepared by Archaeology in Annapolis. On file: University of Maryland, Archaeology in Annapolis Laboratory, College Park.

———. 2002. *An Archaeology and History of Tradition*. New York: Kluwer Acaemic/Plenum Publishers.

———. 2004. Public Significance and Imagined Archaeologists: Authoring Pasts in Context. *International Journal of Historical Archaeology* 8.1: 1–25.

———. 2005. Public Dialectics: Marxist Reflection in/of Archaeology. *Historical Archaeology* 39.4: 18–36.

———. N.d. The Location of Archaeology: Postcolonial Methods and Public

Practice. Unpublished manuscript. Hempstead, N.Y.: Department of Anthropology, Hofstra University.

Matthews, Christopher N., and Matthew M. Palus. N.d. Archaeologists with Faces: Heritage and Social Power in Public. In *Ethnographies and Archaeologies: Iterations of 'Heritage' and the Archaeological Past,* eds. Lena Mortensen and Julie Zimmer. London: Routledge.

McDougall, Harold A. 1993. *Black Baltimore: A New Theory of Community.* Philadelphia: Temple University Press.

McGuire, Randall H. 1988. Dialogues with the Dead: Ideology and the Cemetery. In *The Recovery of Meaning,* ed. M. P. Leone and P. B. Potter Jr.,435–80. Washington, D.C.: Smithsonian Institution Press.

———. 1992a. Archaeology and the First Americans. *American Anthropologist* 94.4: 816–36.

———. 1992b. *A Marxist Archaeology.* New York: Academic Press.

McKee, Larry W. 1992. The Ideals and Realities Behind the Design and Use of Nineteenth-Century Virginia Slave Cabins. In *The Art and Mystery of Historical Archaeology: Essays in Honor of James Deetz,* ed. A. E. Yentsch and M. C. Beaudry, 195–213. Boca Raton, Fla.: C.R.C. Press.

———. 1995. Food Supply and Plantation Social Order: An Anthropological Perspective. In *"I, too, am America": Studies in African American Archaeology,* ed. Theresa Singleton, 218–39. Charlottesville: University Press of Virginia.

McLuhan, Marshall. 1994 [1964]. *Understanding Media: The Extensions of Man.* New York: McGraw-Hill.

Mennell, Stephen. 1989. *Norbert Elias: Civilization and the Human Self-Image.* Oxford: Basil Blackwell.

Micklus, Robert. 1983. "History of the Tuesday Club": A Mock Jeremiad of the Colonial South. *William and Mary Quarterly,* 3d ser., 4.1: 42–61.

Miller, David. 1972. Ideology and the Problem of False Consciousness. *Political Science* 20.4: 432–47.

Miller, Henry M. 1986. *Discovering Maryland's First City: A Summary Report on the 1981–1984 Archaeological Excavations in St. Mary's City, Maryland.* St. Mary's City Archaeology Series No. 2. St. Mary's City, Md.

———. 1988a. Baroque Cities in the Wilderness: Archaeology and Urban Development in the Colonial Chesapeake. *Historical Archaeology* 22.2: 57–73.

Miller, Naomi F. 1987. Analysis of Plant Remains from the Calvert Site. Calvert Interim Report No. 7. Report prepared by Archaeology in Annapolis. On file: University of Maryland, Archaeology in Annapolis Laboratory, College Park.

———. 1988b. Calvert Site, Annapolis, Maryland Seed Remains. Report prepared by Archaeology in Annapolis. On file: Maryland Historical Trust, Crownsville, Md.

Miller, Philip. 1731–39. *The Gardeners Dictionary.* 2 vols. London: Printed for the Author.

Morgan, Edmund S. 1975. *American Slavery, American Freedom: The Ordeal of Colonial Virginia.* New York: Norton. Reprinted 2003.

Moxon, Joseph. 1978 [1683]. *Mechanick Exercises on the Whole Art of Printing.* New York: Dover.

Moyer, Matthew L. 1997. Notes to Mark Leone. Department of Anthropology,

University of Maryland. On file: University of Maryland, Archaeology in Annapolis Laboratory, College Park.

Mukerji, Chandra. 1993. Reading and Writing with Nature: A Materialist Approach to French Formal Gardens. In *Consumption and the World of Goods*, ed. John Brewer and Roy Porter, 439–61. London: Routledge.

———. 1997. *Territorial Ambitions and the Gardens of Versailles*. Cambridge: Cambridge University Press.

Mullin, Michael. 1976. *American Negro Slavery: A Documentary History*. Columbia: University of South Carolina Press.

———. 1999. *Africa in America: Slave Acculturation and Resistance in the American South and the British Caribbean, 1736–1831*. Urbana: University of Illinois Press.

Mullins, Paul R. 1999. *Race and Affluence: An Archaeology of African America and Consumer Culture*. New York: Kluwer Academic / Plenum Publishers.

Mullins, Paul R., and Mark S. Warner. 1993a. Final Archaeological Investigations at the Maynard-Burgess House (18AP64), an 1850–1980 African American Household in Annapolis, Maryland. Report prepared by Archaeology in Annapolis. On file: University of Maryland, Archaeology in Annapolis Laboratory, College Park.

———. 1993b. Phase I–II Archaeological Investigations on the Courthouse Site: An 1850–1970 African American Household in Annapolis, Maryland. On file: University of Maryland, Archaeological Laboratory, College Park.

Neuwirth, Jessica L., and Matthew D. Cochran. 1999. In My Father's Kingdom There Are Many Houses: Interior Space and Contested Meanings in Nineteenth-Century African-American Annapolis. Paper prepared for Archaeology in Annapolis. On file: University of Maryland, Archaeology in Annapolis Laboratory, College Park.

Noël Hume, Ivor. 1963. *Here Lies Virginia: An Archaeologist's View of Colonial Life and History*. New York: Knopf.

———. 1969. *Historical Archaeology*. New York: Knopf.

———. 1974. *All the Best Rubbish: Being an Antiquary's Account of the Pleasures and Perils of Studying Everyday Objects from the Past*. New York: Harper & Row.

———. 1982. *Martin's Hundred*. New York: Knopf.

Olson, Sherry H. 1997. *Baltimore: The Building of an American City*. Baltimore: Johns Hopkins University Press.

O'Reilly, Carey. 1994a. Archaeological Excavations at 18AP44: 193 Main Street, Annapolis, Maryland, 1985–1987. Report prepared by Archaeology in Annapolis. On file: University of Maryland, Archaeology in Annapolis Laboratory, College Park.

———. 1994b. Archaeological Excavations at the Sands House (18AP47), Annapolis, Maryland. Report prepared by Archaeology in Annapolis. On file: University of Maryland, Archaeology in Annapolis Laboratory, College Park.

Orr, Kenneth. 1975a. The Archaeological Situation at the William Paca Garden (Spring House and Presumed Pavilion House). On file: University of Maryland, Archaeology in Annapolis Laboratory, College Park.

———. 1975b. Preliminary Field Report on the Archaeological Excavation of the 99 Main Street Site, Annapolis, Maryland, November 1974–February 1975. On file: University of Maryland, Archaeology in Annapolis Laboratory, College Park.

Orr, Kenneth, and Ronald G. Orr. 1978. Archaeological Investigations at Reynolds Tavern, 4 Church Circle, Annapolis, Maryland. On file: University of Maryland, Archaeology in Annapolis Laboratory, College Park.

Orser, Charles E., Jr. 1988a. The Archaeological Analysis of Plantation Society: Replacing Status and Class with Economics and Power. *American Antiquity* 53: 735–51.

———. 1988b. *The Material Basis of the Postbellum Tenant Plantation: Historical Archaeology in the South Carolina Piedmont.* Athens: University of Georgia Press.

———. 1992. Beneath the Material Surface of Things: Commodities, Artifacts and Slave Plantations. *Historical Archaeology* 26.3: 95–104.

———. 1994. The Archaeology of African American Slave Religion in the Antebellum South. *Cambridge Archaeological Journal* 4: 33–45.

———. 1996. *A Historical Archaeology of the Modern World.* New York: Plenum Press.

———. 2004. *Race and Practice in Archaeological Interpretation.* Philadelphia: University of Pennsylvania Press.

Orser, Charles E., Jr., and Brian Fagan. 1995. *Historical Archaeology.* New York: HarperCollins.

Paca, Barbara. 1983. The William Paca Gardens, Annapolis, Maryland. Master plan (map). Historic Annapolis Foundation, Annapolis, Md.

Paca-Steele, Barbara, with the assistance of St. Clair Wright. 1987. The Mathematics of an Eighteenth-Century Wilderness Garden. *Journal of Garden History* 6.4: 299–20.

Palus, Matthew M. 2003. Preliminary Report on Archaeological Investigations in the Eastport Neighborhood of the City of Annapolis, Anne Arundel County, Maryland: 119 Chester Avenue (18AP93) and 110 Chesapeake Avenue (18AP94). Prepared by Archaeology in Annapolis. On file: University of Maryland, Archaeology in Annapolis Laboratory, College Park.

———. 2005. Final Report on Archaeological Investigations in the Eastport Neighborhood of Annapolis, Anne Arundel County, Maryland: 2001–2004. Report prepared for Archaeology in Annapolis. On file: University of Maryland, Archaelogy in Annapolis Laboratory, College Park.

———. N.d. "Building an Architecture of Power: Electricity in Annapolis, Maryland in the Nineteenth and Twentieth Centuries." In *Archaeologies of Materiality,* ed. Lynn M. Meskell. London: Blackwell.

Palus, Matthew M., and Elizabeth Kryder-Reid. 2002. Report on Archaeological Investigations Conducted at the St. Mary's Site (18AP45), 107 Duke of Gloucester Street, Annapolis, Maryland 1987–1990. Report prepared for Archaeology in Annapolis. On file: University of Maryland, Archaeology in Annapolis Laboratory, College Park.

Papenfuse, Edward C. 1975. *In Pursuit of Profit: The Annapolis Merchants in the Era of the American Revolution, 1763–1805.* Baltimore: Johns Hopkins University Press.

————. 1995. *"Doing Good to Posterity."* Annapolis: Maryland State Archives and Maryland Historical Trust.

Papenfuse, Edward C., and Joseph M. Coale III, eds. *The Hammond–Harwood House Atlas of Historical Maps of Maryland, 1608–1908.* Baltimore: Johns Hopkins University Press, 1982.

Papenfuse, Edward C., and Jane McWilliams. 1971. Southern Urban Society after the Revolution. Annapolis, Maryland 1782–1786. Appendix F. Lot Histories and Maps. Final Report: National Endowment for the Humanities Grant #H69–0–178. 2 vols. Typescript. Annapolis, Md.: Maryland State Archives.

Patten, Drake. 1992. Mankala and Minkisis: Possible Evidence of African American Folk Beliefs and Practices. *African American Archaeology* 6: 5–7.

Patterson, Thomas C. 1985. Culture and Ideology: Distinct Concepts or Alternative Metaphors? Paper presented at the annual meeting of the Radical Archaeology Theory Symposium, November 16, Binghamton, N.Y.

————. 1986. The Last Sixty Years: Toward a Social History of Americanist Archaeology in the United States. *American Anthropologist* 88.1: 7–26.

————. 1989. History and the Postprocessual Archaeologies. *Man* 24.4: 555–66.

————. 1999. *Change and Development in the Twentieth Century.* Oxford: Berg Publishers.

————. 2003. *Marx's Ghost: Conversations with Archaeologists.* Oxford: Berg Publishers.

Paynter, Robert. 1985. Surplus Flow between Frontiers and Homelands. In *The Archaeology of Frontiers and Boundaries,* ed. S. W. Green and S. Perlman, 163–211. Orlando, Fla.: Academic Press.

————. 1988. Steps to an Archaeology of Capitalism. In *The Recovery of Meaning in the Eastern United States,* ed. M. P. Leone and P. B. Potter Jr., 407–33. Washington, D.C.: Smithsonian Institution Press.

————. 1990. Afro-Americans in the Massachusetts Historical Landscape. In *Politics of the Past,* ed. D. Lowenthal and P. Gathercole, 49–62. London: Unwin Hyman.

Pearson, Marlys J. 1991. Archaeological Excavations at 18AP14: The Victualling Warehouse Site, 77 Main Street, Annapolis, Maryland. Report prepared by Archaeology in Annapolis. On file: University of Maryland, Archaeology in Annapolis Laboratory, College Park.

Perdue, Charles L., Jr., Thomas E. Barden, and Robert K. Phillips. 1976. *Weevils in the Wheat.* Charlottesville: University of Virginia Press.

Peterson, Karin E. 1981. Summary of Archaeological Excavation Data from the Wm. Paca House. On file: Maryland Historical Trust Library, Crownsville, Md.

Pinsky, Valerie, and Alison Wylie, ed. 1989. *Critical Traditions in Contemporary Archaeology: Essays in the Philosophy, History, and Socio-politics of Archaeology.* New York: Cambridge University Press.

Popernack, Paul. 1989. An Examination of Eighteenth-Century Land Records in Annapolis, Maryland. Paper produced for the Department of Anthropology, University of Maryland. On file: University of Maryland, Archaeology in Annapolis Laboratory, College Park.

Potter, Parker B., Jr. 1994. *Public Archaeology in Annapolis, A Critical Approach* to *History in Maryland's Capital City.* Washington, D.C.: Smithsonian Institution Press.

Potter, Parker B., Jr., and Mark P. Leone. 1986. Liberation Not Replication: Archaeology in Annapolis Analyzed. *Journal of the Washington Academy of Sciences* 76.2: 97–105.

Powell, B. Bruce. 1966. Archaeological Investigation of the Paca House Garden, Annapolis, Maryland. November 16, 1966. Typescript. Historic Annapolis Foundation, Annapolis, Md.

Price, Richard. 1990. *Alabi's World.* Baltimore: Johns Hopkins University Press.

Price, Richard, and Sally Price. 1999. *Maroon Arts: Cultural Vitality in the African Diaspora.* Boston: Beacon Press.

Rabinow, Paul, ed. 1984. *Foucault Reader.* New York: Pantheon Books.

Raboteau, Albert J. 1978. *Slave Religion: The "Invisible Institution" in the Antebellum South.* New York: Oxford University Press. Reprinted 2004.

Radoff, Morris L. 1972. *The State House at Annapolis.* Publication No. 17. Annapolis, Md.: Department of General Services.

Randolph, A. Philip. 1919. Lynching: Capitalism Its Cause; Socialism Its Cure. *The Messenger* 2.7: 9–12.

Rawick, George, ed. 1972. *The American Slave: A Composite Autobiography.* Vols. 1–19. Westport, Conn.: Greenwood Press.

———. 1977. *The American Slave: A Composite Autobiography.* Supplement, series 1. Vols. 1–12. Westport, Conn.: Greenwood Press.

———. 1979. *The American Slave: A Composite Autobiography.* Supplement, series 2. Vols. 1–10. Westport, Conn.: Greenwood Press.

R. Christopher Goodwin & Associates. 1993. Phase II/III Archaeological Investigations of the Gott's Court Parking Facility, Annapolis, Maryland, Final Report. Report prepared by R. Christopher Goodwin & Associates. On file: University of Maryland, Archaeology in Annapolis Laboratory, College Park.

Read, Esther Doyle, Mark Leone, Barbara J. Little, Jean B. Russo, George C. Logan, and Brett Burk. 1990. Archaeological Investigations around State Circle in Annapolis, Maryland. Report prepared for Archaeology in Annapolis. On file: University of Maryland, Archaeology in Annapolis Laboratory, College Park.

Reeves, Matthew B. 1997. By Their Own Labor: Enslaved Africans' Survival Strategies on Two Jamaican Plantations. Ph.D. diss., Syracuse University. Ann Arbor, Mich.: University Microfilms International.

———. 2004. Asking the "Right" Questions. In *Places in Mind,* ed. P. A. Shackel and E. J. Chambers, 71–81. London: Routledge.

Reitz, Elizabeth J. 1987. Preliminary Analysis of Vertebrate Remains from the Calvert Site in Annapolis, Maryland and a Comparison with Vertebrate Remains from Sites in South Carolina, Georgia, and Jamaica. Calvert Interim Report No. 6. On file: University of Maryland, Archaeology in Annapolis Laboratory, College Park.

Reps, John W. 1965. *The Making of Urban America.* Princeton, N.J.: Princeton University Press.

———. 1972. *Tidewater Towns: City Planning in Colonial Virginia and Maryland.* Williamsburg, Va.: Colonial Williamsburg Foundation.

Richardson, Edgar P., Brooke Hindle, and Lillian B. Miller. 1983. *Charles Willson Peale and His World.* New York: Abrams.

Ridout, Orlando, IV. 1978. The James Brice House Annapolis, Maryland. On file: University of Maryland, Archaeology in Annapolis Laboratory, College Park.

Ridgely, David. 1841. *Annals of Annapolis.* Baltimore: Cushing & Brother.

Riley, Elihu. 1887. *"The Ancient City": A History of Annapolis in Maryland, 1649–1887.* Annapolis, Md.: Record Printing Office. Reprinted by Anne Arundel County–Annapolis Bicentennial Committee.

———. 1897. *Souvenir Volume of the State Conference of Firemen.* Annapolis, Md.

———. 1901. *Annapolis, "Ye Ancient Capital of Maryland," 1649–1901.* Annapolis, Md.: Annapolis Publishing Co.

Riordan, Timothy B., Silas D. Hurry, and Henry M. Miller. 1995. A Good Brick Chappell: The Archaeology of the 1667 Catholic Chapel at St. Mary's City. Manuscript. St. Mary's City, Md.: Historic St. Mary's City.

Rothstein, Edward. 1997. Cursive, Foiled Again: Mourning the Demise of Penmanship. *New York Times,* April 7, B1, B6.

Roulette, Billy Ray, and Eileen Williams. 1986. *A Topographic Survey of the Charles Carroll of Carrollton Garden.* Annapolis, Md.: Historic Annapolis Foundation.

Ruppel, Timothy, Jessica Neuwirth, Mark P. Leone, and Gladys-Marie Fry. 2003. Hidden in View: African Spiritual Spaces in North American Landscapes. *Antiquity* 77.296: 321–35.

Russo, Jean B. 1983. The Structure of the Anne Arundel County Economy. In Annapolis and Anne Arundel County, Maryland: A Study of Urban Development in a Tobacco Economy, 1649–1776, principal investigator, Lorena Walsh. Manuscript. NEH Grant R S 20199–81–1955. Historic Annapolis Foundation, Annapolis, Md.

———. 1990. William Paca House and Garden. Historic Annapolis Foundation, Annapolis, Md.

Samford, Patricia. 1996. The Archaeology of African-American Slavery and Material Culture. *William and Mary Quarterly,* 3d ser., 53: 87–114.

———. 2000. Power Runs in Many Channels: Subfloor Pits and West African-based Spiritual Traditions in Colonial Virginia. Ph.D. diss., University of North Carolina, Chapel Hill. Ann Arbor, Mich.: University Microfilms.

Sarudy, Barbara Wells. 1989. Eighteenth-Century Gardens of the Chesapeake. *Journal of Garden History* 9.3: 104–59.

Schrire, Carmel. 1988. The Historical Archaeology of the Impact of Colonialism in Seventeenth-century South Africa. *Antiquity* 62: 214–25.

———. 1995. *Digging through Darkness: Chronicles of an Archaeologist.* Charlottesville: University Press of Virginia.

Schuyler, Robert L. 1970. Historical and Historic Sites Archaeology and Anthropology: Basic Definitions. *Historical Archaeology* 4: 83–89.

———. 1978. *Historical Archaeology: A Guide to Substantive and Theoretical Contributions.* Farmingdale, N.Y.: Baywood Publishing Co.

————. 1980. Sandy Ground: Archaeology of a Nineteenth-Century Oyster-ing Village. In *Archaeological Perspectives on Ethnicity in America: Afro-American and Asian American Cultural History*, ed. id., 48–59. Farmingdale, N.Y.: Baywood Publishing Co.

Scientists Find Slaves Kept African Culture. 1991. *New York Times*, September 15, Campus Life section 1, pt. 2, 43.

Seidel, John L. 1996. Intensive Level Reconnaissance at the United States Naval Academy: The Main Campus, NSWC Annapolis Housing, USNA North Sev-ern, and the Naval Academy Dairy Farm, Annapolis and Anne Arundel Co., MD. On file: Maryland Historical Trust Library, Crownsville, Md.

Shackel, Paul A. 1986. Archaeological Testing at the Main Street Site, 18AP44, Annapolis, Maryland. Report prepared by Archaeology in Annapolis. On file: University of Maryland, Archaeology in Annapolis Laboratory, College Park.

————. 1988. Excavations at the State House Inn Site, 18AP42, 15 State Circle. Report prepared for Archaeology in Annapolis. On file: University of Mary-land, Archaeology in Annapolis Laboratory, College Park.

————. 1993. *Personal Discipline and Material Culture, an Archaeology of An-napolis, Maryland, 1695–1870*. Knoxville: University of Tennessee Press.

————. 1996. *Culture Change and the New Technology, An Archaeology of the Early American Industrial Era*. New York: Plenum Press.

Shackel, Paul A., and Laura J. Galke. 1988. Excavations at the St. Anne's Church-yard, 18AP43, Church Circle, Annapolis, Maryland. Report prepared by Ar-chaeology in Annapolis. On file: University of Maryland, Archaeology in An-napolis Laboratory, College Park.

Shackel, Paul A., Joseph W. Hopkins, III, and Eileen Williams. 1988. Excava-tions at the State House Inn Site, 18AP42, 15 State Circle, Annapolis, Mary-land. Report prepared by Archaeology in Annapolis. On file: University of Maryland, Archaeology in Annapolis Laboratory, College Park.

Sheehan, Nora B. 1998. Phase I Archaeological and Architectural Investigations and Phase II Evaluation of Site 18AP80, Related to the MD 450–Gateway Circle Project, Annapolis, MD. On file: Maryland Historical Trust Library, Crownsville, Md.

————. 1999. Phase I–III Archaeological Investigations for the Chilled Water Line Upgrade (p-165), Including Site 18AP83, U.S. Naval Academy, Annapolis, Maryland. On file: Maryland Historical Trust Library, Crownsville, Md.

Sheehan, Nora B., and Martha R. Williams. 1998. Phase I Archaeological In-vestigation, Phase II Evaluation, and Phase III Mitigation Studies Related to the Replacement of the HTW Piping, United States Naval Academy, An-napolis, MD. On file: Maryland Historical Trust Library, Crownsville, Md.

Shellenhamer, Jason 2004. The Archaeology and Restoration of the William Paca Garden, Annapolis, Maryland, 1966–1990. Report prepared for Archaeol-ogy in Annapolis. On file: University of Maryland, Archaeology in Annapo-lis Laboratory, College Park. See also www.bsos.umd.edu/anth/arch/Paca Garden/index.htm (accessed October 20, 2004).

Shephard, Steven J. 1987. Status Variation in Antebellum Alexandria: An Archaeological Study of Ceramic Tableware. In *Consumer Choice in Historical Archaeology,* ed. Suzanne M. Spencer-Wood, 163–98. New York: Plenum Press.

Simmons, Scott E. 1990. *An Investigation of the Archaeological Resources Associated with Piers 5 and 6 and the Harrison's at Pier 5 Complex (18BC62 & 18BC63), Baltimore, Maryland.* Baltimore Center for Urban Archaeology Research Series Report No. 29.

Singleton, Theresa A. 1985. *The Archaeology of Slavery and Plantation Life.* Orlando, Fla.: Academic Press.

———. 1988. An Archaeological Framework for Slavery and Emancipation, 1740–1880. In *The Recovery of Meaning: Historical Archaeology in the Eastern United States,* ed. M. P. Leone and P. B. Potter Jr., 345–70. Washington, D.C.: Smithsonian Institution Press.

———. 1995. *"I, too, am America": Studies in African American Archaeology.* Charlottesville: University Press of Virginia.

Singleton, Theresa A., and Mark D. Bograd. 1995. *The Archaeology of the African Diaspora in the Americas.* Guides to the Archaeological Literature of the Immigrant Experience in America No. 2. Glassboro, N.J.: Society for Historical Archaeology.

Smith, J. 1965 [1755]. *The Printer's Grammer.* London: Greig Press.

Smith, Theophus. 1994. *Conjuring Culture: Biblical Formations of Black America.* New York: Oxford University Press.

Sonderman, Robert C. 1988. Archaeological Excavations at the Retallick-Brewer House, Annapolis, Maryland. Report prepared by Archaeology in Annapolis. On file: University of Maryland, Archaeology in Annapolis Laboratory, College Park.

South, Stanley. 1967. The Paca House, Annapolis, Maryland. MS. Historic Annapolis Foundation, Annapolis, Md.

Stabler, Jennifer A. 1990. Emergency Excavations at the Bordley-Randall House 18AP5O, 9 Randall Court, Annapolis, Maryland. Report prepared by Archaeology in Annapolis. On file: University of Maryland, Archaeology in Annapolis Laboratory, College Park.

Stevens, William O. 1937. *Annapolis: Anne Arundel's Town.* New York: Dodd, Mead.

Stiverson, Gregory A., and Phebe R. Jacobsen. 1976. *William Paca, A Biography.* Baltimore: Maryland Historical Society.

Stone, Garry Wheeler. 1974. St. John's: Archaeological Questions and Answers. *Maryland Historical Magazine* 69.2: 146–68.

Stower, C. 1965 [1808]. *The Printer's Grammar.* London: Greig Press.

Stover, John F. 1987. *History of the Baltimore and Ohio Railroad.* West Lafayette, Ind.: Purdue University Press.

Tatum, George B. 1977. Great Houses from the Golden Age of Annapolis. *Antiques,* January–February, 174–85.

Taylor, Owen. 1872. *History of Annapolis.* Baltimore: Turnbull.

Thom, Alexander. 1978. *Megalithic Remains in Britain and Brittany.* Oxford: Oxford University Press.

Thomas, Isaiah. 1975. *The History of Printing in America.* New York: Weathervane Books.

Thompson, E. P. 1967. Time, Work-Discipline, and Industrial Capitalism. *Past and Present* 38: 56–97.

———. 1974. Patrician Society, Plebeian Culture. *Journal of Social History* 7: 382–405.

Thompson, Robert F. 1983. *Flash of the Spirit: African and Afro-American Art and Philosophy.* New York: Random House.

———. 1991. *Dancing between Two Worlds: Kongo-Angola Culture and the Americas.* New York: Caribbean Cultural Center.

———. 1993. *Face of the Gods: Art and Altars of Africa and the African Americas.* New York: Museum of African Art.

Thornton, Tamara Plakins. 1997. Handwriting as an Act of Self-Definition. *Chronicle of Higher Education,* August 15, B7.

Trollope, Frances. 1997 [1832]. *Domestic Manners of the Americans.* London: Penguin Classics.

United States. Bureau of the Census. 1800–20. Anne Arundel County, Enumeration District #6 (Annapolis). MSA [Maryland State Archives] M2054 (1800), MSA M2059 (1810), and MSA M2063 (1820).

———. 1832. Fifth Census of the United States, 1830. Anne Arundel County, City of Annapolis. MSA SM 61–82, reel # M65–2 (1830).

———. 1841. Sixth Census of the United States, 1840. Population Schedules. Anne Arundel County, City of Annapolis. National Archives Microfilm Publications (1840).

———. 1853. Seventh Census of the United States, 1850. Population Schedules. Anne Arundel County, City of Annapolis. National Archives Microfilm Publications (1850).

———. 1864. Eighth Census of the United States. 1860. Population Schedules. Anne Arundel County, City of Annapolis. National Archives Microfilm Publications (1860).

Van Horne, John. 1986. *The Correspondence and Miscellaneous Papers of Benjamin Henry Latrobe,* vol. 2: *1805–1810.* New Haven, Conn.: Yale University Press.

Van Horne, John, and Lee W. Formwalt, ed. 1984. *The Correspondence and Miscellaneous Papers of Benjamin Henry Latrobe,* vol. 1: *1784–1804.* New Haven, Conn.: Yale University Press.

Van Winkle, Cornelius. 1981 [1818]. *The Printer's Guide, or an Introduction to the Art of Printing.* New York: Garland Publishing.

Vlach, John M. 1978. *The Afro-American Tradition in the Decorative Arts.* Cleveland: Cleveland Museum of Art.

———. 1987. Afro-American Domestic Artifacts in Eighteenth-Century Virginia. *Material Culture* 19:1: 3–23.

———. 1991. Plantation Landscapes of the Antebellum South. In *Before Freedom Came: African American Life in the Antebellum South,* ed. E. D. C. Campbell III, 21–49. Charlottesville: University Press of Virginia.

———. 1993. *Back of the Big House: The Architecture of Plantation Slavery.* Chapel Hill: University of North Carolina Press.

Walsh, Lorena S., principal investigator. 1983. Annapolis and Anne Arundel County, Maryland: A Study of Urban Development in a Tobacco Economy,

1649–1776. Manuscript with articles by Nancy Baker, Lois Green Carr, Jean B. Russo, Lorena S. Walsh, and M. G. Harris. NEH Grant RS 20199–81–1955. Historic Annapolis Foundation, Annapolis, Md.

————. 1997. *From Calabar to Carter's Grove: The History of a Virginia Slave Community.* Charlottesville: University Press of Virginia.

Ward, Jeanne A. 2000. Phase I Archaeology Survey of the Proposed Park Place Development, City of Annapolis, Anne Arundel County, Maryland. On file: Maryland Historical Trust Library, Crownsville, Md.

Ward, Jeanne A., and John McCarthy. 2001. Phase IB/II Archaeological Investigation of Selected Portions of the Proposed Park Place Development, City of Annapolis, Anne Arundel County, Maryland. On file: Maryland Historical Trust Library, Crownsville, Md.

Warner, Mark S. 1990. Ground Penetrating Radar Testing of the Franklin Street Site. Report prepared by Archaeology in Annapolis. On file: University of Maryland, Archaeology in Annapolis Laboratory, College Park.

————. 1991. Faunal Remains from Feature 82 (18AP45). Report prepared by Archaeology in Annapolis. On file: University of Maryland, Archaeology in Annapolis Laboratory, College Park.

————. 1992. Test Excavations at Gott's Court 18AP52. Report prepared by Archaeology in Annapolis. On file: University of Maryland, Archaeology in Annapolis Laboratory, College Park.

————. 1998. Food and the Negotiation of African American Identities in Annapolis, Maryland and the Chesapeake. Ph.D. diss., Department of Anthropology, University of Virginia. Ann Arbor, Mich.: University Microfilms International.

————. 2001. Ham Hocks on Your Corn Flakes. *Archaeology,* November–December, 48–52.

Warner, Mark S., and Paul R. Mullins. 1993. Archaeological Investigations on the Courthouse Site (18AP63), A Historic African American Neighborhood in Annapolis, Maryland. Report prepared by Archaeology in Annapolis. On file: University of Maryland, Archaeology in Annapolis Laboratory, College Park.

Weekley, Carolyn J. 1977. Portrait Painting in Eighteenth-Century Annapolis. *Antiques,* January–February, 345–53.

Weidman, Gregory R. 1977. Furnishing the Museum Rooms of the William Paca House. *Antiques,* January–February, 163–71.

Wilkie, Laurie A. 1997. Secret and Sacred: Contextualizing the Artifacts of African-American Magic and Religion. *Historical Archaeology* 31.4: 81–106.

————. 2000. *Creating Freedom: Material Culture and African American Identity at Oakley Plantation, Louisiana, 1840–1950.* Baton Rouge: Louisiana State University Press.

————. 2001. Race, Identity and Habermas's Lifeworld. In *Race and the Archaeology of Identity,* ed. C. E. Orser Jr., 108–24. Salt Lake City: University of Utah Press.

Williams, Eileen. 1988. Excavations at 178 Prince George's Street, the Back of the Brice House, 18AP38, Annapolis, Maryland. Report prepared by Archaeology in Annapolis. On file: University of Maryland, Archaeology in Annapolis Laboratory, College Park.

Williams, Eileen, Julie H. Ernstein, and Paul A. Shackel. 1987. A Cultural Resource Survey of the College Creek Area, Annapolis, Maryland. Report prepared by Archaeology in Annapolis. On file: University of Maryland, Archaeology in Annapolis Laboratory, College Park.

Worden, Robert. 2004. Transcriptions of Letters between Charles Carroll of Annapolis and Charles Carroll of Carrollton, April 3, 1773, September 28, 1774, September 29–30, 1774, October 6, 1774. Annapolis, Md.: Robert Worden.

Wright, Henry T. 1963. Report on 4 Possible Archaeological Sites in Annapolis. On file: University of Maryland, Archaeology in Annapolis Laboratory, College Park.

———. 1970. Field Notes on Maryland Archaeology. On file: Maryland Historical Trust Library, Crownsville, Md.

———. 1973. An Archaeology Sequence in the Middle Chesapeake Region, Maryland. Report prepared for Historic Annapolis Foundation. On file: Maryland Historical Trust Library, Crownsville, Md.

Wright, Russell J. 1977. The Town Plan of Annapolis. Antiques, January–February, 148–51.

Wright, St. Clair. 1977a. The Paca House Garden Restored. Antiques, January–February, 172–73.

———. 1977b. Saving the William Paca House. Antiques, January–February, 160–61.

———. 1977c. Historic Preservation in Annapolis. Antiques, January–February, 152–59.

Wylie, Alison. 2002. Thinking from Things: Essays in the Philosophy of Archaeology. Berkeley: University of California Press.

Yentsch, Anne E. 1985. Archaeological Testing at the Patrick Creagh House, 18AP34. Report prepared by Archaeology in Annapolis. On file: University of Maryland, Archaeology in Annapolis Laboratory, College Park.

———. 1986. Preliminary Analysis of Features from Period 1 Associated with Posthole Buildings at the Calvert Site, Annapolis, MD. Calvert Interim Report No. 1. Report prepared by Archaeology in Annapolis. On file: University of Maryland, Archaeology in Annapolis Laboratory, College Park.

———. 1987. Summary of Excavations at the Calvert Site. Calvert Interim Report No. 3. Report prepared by Archaeology in Annapolis. On file: University of Maryland, Archaeology in Annapolis Laboratory, College Park.

———. 1988. Preliminary Report on Bordley-Randall Site in Annapolis, Maryland. Report prepared by Archaeology in Annapolis. On file: University of Maryland, Archaeology in Annapolis Laboratory, College Park.

———. 1991a. Engendering Visible and Invisible Ceramic Artifacts, Especially Dairy Vessels. Historical Archaeology 25.4: 132–55.

———. 1991b. The Symbolic Division of Pottery: Sex-related Attributes of English and Anglo-American Household Pots. In The Archaeology of Inequality, ed. Randall H. McGuire and Robert Paynter, 192–230. Oxford: Basil Blackwell.

————. 1993. *A Chesapeake Family and Their Slaves.* Cambridge: Cambridge University Press.

Yentsch, Anne E., Karen Bescherer, and Stephen E. Patrick. 1990. The Calvert Ceramic Collection. Calvert Interim Report IV. On file: University of Maryland, Archaeology in Annapolis Laboratory, College Park, Maryland.

Yronwode, Catherine. 2002. *Hoodoo, Herb, and Root Magic: A Materia Medica of African-American Conjure, Traditional Formulary Giving the Spiritual Uses of Natural Herbs, Roots, Minerals and Zoological Curios.* Forestville, Calif.: Lucky Mojo Curio Co.

————. N.d. *Lucky Mojo.* www.luckymojo.com. Accessed June 24, 2004.

Young, Amy L. 1996. Archaeological Evidence of African-Style Ritual and Healing Practices in the Upland South. *Tennessee Anthropologist* 21: 139–55.

Index

Abercrombie, Nicholas, 24
Acuff, Lysbeth, xii
Adams-Kilty House, 5
aesthetics, 257; Georgian, 9; and popular opinion, 163–64; and preservation, 30; Victorian, 175. *See* architecture; decorative arts
Africa, 22, 192, 203, 208, 214; debate as to whether or not parts of Africa survive in America, 214, 247; not a monolithic cultural presence, 223, 234; as origin of the West, 260, 262; presence of BaKongo, Fan, Ifa, and Yoruba traditions in Annapolis, 214; religion, 259; as symbol of community, 247, 265; West African religions, 203, 208, 214–15, 224, 236. *See also* African Americans; African descent; Herskovits, Melville J.; spirit practices
African America, xi, xiii; culture, 195, 214, 218, 245. *See also* African Americans; caches; Kunte Kinte Festival; James Brice House site; St. Mary's site; Slayton House site; spirit practices
African Americans, 4, 19, 21–23, 29, 31, 37, 40, 56–57, 59, 192; and African-inspired traditions, 193, 197, 199–200, 202–4, 208, 213–14, 232, 234; as alternative to European rationality, 58, 189, 237, 243–44; and archae-

ology, 187–89, 192–95, 207, 213, 244, 247, 261–62; acquisition of goods from street vendors, 195, 198; Aunt Jemima images, 175; backyards, 195; buttons, 195; bric-a-brac, 195; within capitalism, 192–94, 199, 211–12, 237, 245–46, 256–57, 260; communities as opposed to monolithic group, 199, 234, 246; and concept of lifeworld, 187–88, 190, 192–93, 236, 243–44, 247, 257, 260, 262; concern with coopting of their traditions, 193, 213–14, 219; and critique of history, 58, 188–90, 193, 255, 266; culture, xix, 245; and current conditions, 190, 245, 257; debate as to whether or not parts of Africa survive in America, 214, 247; and dominant ideology, xxi, 58, 107–8, 110, 150, 176–77, 193, 243–46, 256–57, 260; and double-consciousness, 176, 196, 246–47, 262; emphasize community over individualism, 265; as entrepreneurs, 245, 256; foodways, 159–60, 175, 194, 199, 258; fresh approach to community collaboration, 189, 213; genealogy, 199; hierarchy within, 246; integration into mainstream via ownership and consumption of goods, 58, 61–62, 174, 194, 198; life histories, 194; manumis-

African Americans *(continued)*
  sion, 108; and market economy, 161,
  195; material possessions distinct
  from those of European American
  households, 194, 207, 257; middle-
  class aspirations, 196, 256–57;
  neighborhoods 193, 195–96, 198,
  245; opportunities to market, 107,
  194; oral histories, 175, 194–96;
  ownership of own past, 195, 246;
  rejection of possessive individualism,
  58, 108–09, 192–93, 212, 256–57,
  260, 265; religion, xxi, 58, 193,
  199–203, 208, 211, 213–18, 223–
  24, 235–36, 260, 262; resistance,
  110, 175–76, 189, 192–94, 197,
  212, 231, 262; segregation, 196–
  97; stereotypes in service to market
  interests, 198; and symbolic violence, 231; undercapitalized business
  ventures, 245; as Union soldiers in
  Civil War, 254; West and Central
  African connections, 203, 208, 214–
  17, 222, 224, 236; and yard work,
  106, 232. *See also* caches; Federal
  Writers' Project; free blacks; gardens;
  Jürgen Habermas; ideology; oral
  histories; oystermen; slavery; spirit
  practices; watermen/waterwomen
African descent: people of, xx, 22, 29,
  40, 56, 61–62, 105, 188, 194–95,
  198–99, 203, 207, 212–13, 232,
  234–35, 243, 245, 248, 255; inden-
  tured servants, 214. *See also* Africa;
  African Americans; slavery; spirit
  practices
African Diaspora, xix, xx, 61, 106–7,
  199, 203, 235
Africanisms. *See* African Americans:
  African-inspired traditions
African Methodist Episcopal (A.M.E.)
  Church, 193, 258
African spirit tradition. *See* spirit practices
Afrocentrism, 262. *See also* Bernal,
  Martin; Thompson, Robert Ferris;
  Washington, Maisha
Afro-Christianity, 236, 259–60. *See also*
  African Americans; spiritual practices
agricultural improvement, 168. *See also*
  horticulture
Alexander, Brian, xii
Alexandria Archaeology program (Alex-
  andria, VA), xx
alienation, 34; and crisis of legitimacy,
  264; of labor, 34. *See also* ideology
alleyways, 84, 94
Althusser, Louis, xix, 24–26, 29, 31, 35,

41, 45, 55, 59, 67, 109, 144–45, 148,
  151, 179–81, 185–87, 192, 212, 247,
  256, 263, 265–66. *See also* ideology
America. *See* United States of America
American history, 199
American Revolution, 1, 2, 15, 18, 21,
  23, 34, 48–49; tied to ideology, 58,
  100, 108, 138, 212, 264–65
*The American Slave: A Composite Auto-
  biography. See* Federal Writers'
  Project
American Studies, 199
"Ancient City," *See* Annapolis
analogy, 78
ancestors, 61. *See also* spirit practices
Anderson, Benedict, 48–49, 51, 53, 98,
  100; 114, 138, 141–42. *See also*
  imagined community; popular
  opinion; print culture
Anglican Church, 83
Annapolis, 1–7, 10–12, 14–15, 18–19, 22,
  29–30, 49, 77, 99, 108, 111, 253,
  265–66; absence of seventeenth-
  century African-inspired spirit practices in Annapolis's
archaeological record; ambiguity toward
  black independence, 198; African
  American churches, xiii; as African
  city, 61, 199–200, 234; as "the
  Ancient City," 1; Arundel Town,
  11; boating capital, 4, 15; as commercial city, 154, 186; design, 5–
  6; eighteenth-century, 4–5, 22, 29,
  36–37, 40, 63, 66, 80, 85–86, 88,
  92, 95, 97, 108, 113–14, 151, 162,
  165, 172, 264; gardens, 38, 42–43,
  66; as historic district, 155; illusion
  as metaphor, 80; and Ku Klux Klan,
  256; landscapes, 12, 42, 81; as
  Maryland capital, 1, 18–19, 57, 64,
  114; Mayor and City Council, xiii;
  as microcosm of America and both
  African and European, 266; as
  museum, 29–30, 38; nineteenth-
  century, 4, 5, 21, 36, 41, 47, 86,
  89, 174, 193, 257; and penetration
  of ideology of individualism, 55,
  99, 186–87; as port, 3, 11; post-
  Revolutionary, 3, 36–37; as racially
  torn, 232, 236, 251; as reflection and
  enaction of national truths and realities, 266; and seafood industry, 4;
  as setting for critical alternative history, 188–89, 237, 244; seventeenth-
  century, 5, 9, 15, 41, 83, 85, 92; as
  southern city, 2, 23; suburbs, 253;
  its topography, 3, 83, 93; as tourist

destination, 4, 11; twentieth-century,
4, 87, 194, 257; as U.S. capital, 2,
95, 97; waterfront, 3–4; watermen/
waterwomen, 4. *See also* African
Americans; American Revolution;
archaeology; Archaeology in Annapolis; baroque design; Catholicism;
discipline; freedom; gardens; historic preservation; ideology; individualism; landscapes; panopticism;
panopticon; town planning; population; research design; wealth
Annapolis, Charles Carroll of (father of
Charles Carroll of Carrollton), 205
*Annapolis: Reflections from the Age of
Reason* (film). *See* Archaeology in
Public in Annapolis
Anne Arundel County Courthouse site,
xiv, 193–95, 274
Anne Arundel County, MD, 19, 23, 108,
252. *See also* population
Anroman, Gilda, xii
anthropology, 28, 34, 187, 203
Antonellis, Joseph, xviii
apartheid, 188
Archaeological Annapolis (guidebook). *See*
Archaeology in Public in Annapolis
archaeology, 2, 6, 10, 11, 64, 77, 82, 95;
of African America, 60, 192–244,
258, 260–62; critical archaeology,
185; as critique, 33, 258, 260–61,
266; Cultural Resource Management
(CRM), 220–21; and Foucault's
technologies of the self, 36–37, 56,
153; historical archaeology, 27–28,
55, 78, 214; and identity, 188–89,
199; and interpretation, 182; linking
past and present, 188–89, 213, 258;
as means for investigating the effects
of capitalism, 187, 266; as means for
protecting freedom, 262; as means
for social action, 189, 257, 260, 265;
as method of historical discovery,
255, 258; and post-colonialism in
South Africa, 188–89; prehistory,
180, 215; as process, 193; self-
consciousness, 58; as site of struggle
in Africa, 59–60, 188. *See also*
Archaeology in Annapolis; Foucault;
ideology; theory
Archaeology in Annapolis, xi–xv, xx,
24, 30–31, 179–80, 188, 259; and
cultural anthropology, 194; field
school participants, xxii–xxv; scale
of analysis, 157; use of natural
stratigraphy, 157; vis á vis historic
preservation, 189, 258; widespread

recognition, 258. *See also* historic
preservation; research design
Archaeology in Public in Annapolis,
179–80, 258; and African American
congregations, 195; audiovisual
production, 184–85; awareness of
ideology of individualism and its
history as original interpretive goal,
181–82, 186–88; Black Entertainment Television (BET), 258; challenging interpretation as liberating
for site visitors, 182, 261; cited
in most introductory archaeology
textbooks, 258; class relations, 188;
emphasis on methods, 181, 260; and
exhibits, 183, 195; failure to engage
public debate and change, 183–
86, 188–89; film, 183; guidebook/
pamphlets, 182–84; promotion via
Smithsonian Institution's Anacostia
Museum, 258; redefined goal as
elucidation of the African American
lifeworld, 187–89, 243, 247, 255;
race relations, 188; sample tours,
181–83; streaming video, 184,
255, 258; successes, 185; themes/
messages, 181–87; as top-down
interpretations, 186; visitor feedback, 185. *See also* ideology; living
history; research design; theory
architecture: and balance/symmetry, 39;
federal, 14, 197; Georgian, 6, 8, 57,
215; vernacular, 5, 30; Victorian,
86, 193, 197. *See also* aesthetics;
Enlightenment philosophy; panopticism; panopticon; surveillance
Arias, Angela, 137. See also *Maryland
Gazette;* printer's type
Armstrong, Douglas, xx
Arnoult, Philip, xv, 181. *See also* Archaeology in Public in Annapolis
art history, 79, 157
Arundel Town, 83. *See also* Arundel Town
Arundel Town, 11. *See also* Arundelton
Aten, Gary, 184
Austin, Heather, xvii
Austin, Stephen P., xii, 127
authenticity, 29, 63–64, 72, 75, 213;
purity as illusion, 266
authority. *See* social control
authorship. *See* Declaration of Independence; *Maryland Gazette;* popular
opinion; print; culture
autobiographies. *See* Federal Writers'
Project
autoCAD, 93. *See also* geographic information systems (GIS)

Babiarz, Jennifer, xi, xvii
bags. *See* spirit practices
Bailey-Goldschmidt, Janice, 147
BaKongo. *See* spirit practices
Baltimore Center for Urban Archaeology
    (Baltimore, MD), 183
Baltimore, MD, 5, 12, 14, 21, 252;
    domed buildings, 12–13, 47, 97;
    as federal city, 12, 47, 98; gardens,
    104–5; and industrialization, 3, 5,
    12; nineteenth-century, 12, 97–99;
    pre-Revolutionary 12; slaves, 104,
    252; slave market, 252; tooth-
    brushes, 183. *See also* Latrobe;
    panopticism; panopticon; town
    planning
Baltimore Museum of Art, 202–3
Baltimore & Ohio Railroad, 3
Baltimore Theatre Project, xv
Banneker-Douglass Museum, xiii, 60,
    192–95, 258, 274
Barnett, Steve, 24, 180
baroque design, 7, 8, 10, 11, 43, 64–
    65, 80, 83, 85; acts of show, 80,
    82; and nationhood, 41, 114; and
    optical illusions, 41, 77, 94; as
    theory of power, 8–10, 80–82, 84,
    94, 182; use of focal points, 84. *See
    also* Annapolis; Braudel, Fernand;
    Nicholson plan; Rome; St. Mary's
    City; theory; town planning;
    Williamsburg, VA
Bates, Wylie, 196, 245, 247, 256–57,
    265; Bates's autobiography, 196,
    246, 255
Bayly, Susan, xvi
Beadenkopf, Kristopher, xii, 158. *See
    also* ceramics
beads. *See* caches
Beavan, Michelle, 272
Beaven, Colin, 215–16
Beaudry, Mary C., 24, 45, 59, 186
Bellis Court site, 156, 159; changing
    racial demographics, 195
Bentham, Jeremy, 13–14, 96–98; influ-
    ence on Latrobe, 98. *See also* panop-
    ticism; panopticon; surveillance
Bernal, Martin, 259
Bescherer, Karen, 272
Bhabha, Homi, 33, 261–62, 266; and
    notion of history as hybrid, 190;
    and parody, 262, 266
Bill of Rights. *See* Constitution
Binford, Lewis R., 78. *See also* theory
Bishop, William, 196
Blackshear, Leonard, xiii
Blakey, Michael, xx–xxi

Bodor, Thomas, xiv, 271, 275
Bograd, Mark, 199
Bolsheviks, 187
Bordley-Randall House, xiv. *See also*
    Bordley-Randall site
Bordley-Randall site, 156, 273
Boston, MA, 2, 4, 7, 29, 152, 157
bottle. *See* caches
Bowen, Lynell, xii
Bradshaw, Omar, 188
Braudel, Fernand, 8, 80, 82
Brainerd, Samuel, 127
bric-a-brac, 195
Brigham, Laurence S., 64, 71. *See also*
    William Paca Garden
Brown, Ken, xxi
Brown, Lancelot "Capability," 81.
    See also gardens
Brown, Capt. and Mrs. Randall, xiv
Buckler, John J., xiv–xv, 120, 270
bundles. *See* spirit practices
Burgess, Willard, 197. *See also* Maynard-
    Burgess site
Burlaga, Anna-Marie, 87–90, 94
Burlaga, Leonard F., 93
buttons, 195, 203, 224–26, 232–33.
    See also caches; spirit practices

Cabral, Judith, xiii
caches, 59, 201–08, 210–11, 213, 215–
    16, 219–21, 224, 232, 234, 236;
    loci of recovery as reported in CRM
    reports in Maryland and Virginia,
    221–22, 225, 230, 239; loci of recov-
    ery as reported in Federal Writers'
    Project, 231; misinterpretation,
    209, 215; necessary for inflicting
    malign results, 231; purpose, 234;
    as rejection of dominant ideology,
    59; search for diagnostic archaeolog-
    ical signature, 220, 224, 230, 234;
    span slavery to post Emancipation
    contexts, 213–14, 222; as unique
    response to racism, 222; widespread
    across American South, 208, 213.
    See also spirit practices
California, 213
Callahan, Dennis, xiii
Callahan, Dorothy, xii
Calvert family (Lords Baltimore), 8, 11,
    18, 83
Calvert House Hotel, xiv. *See also*
    Calvert House site
Calvert House site, 270; hypocaust, 43;
    public well, 86
Calvinism, 11, 236; and predestination,
    153

Campbell, Glenn, xii
Camp Parole (Anne Arundel Co., MD), 253
Cape Town (South Africa), 188. *See also* University of Cape Town
capitalism, 24, 36, 60, 212, 257; amelioration of capitalist practices, 28, 32, 186, 193, 211–12, 257; Georgian Order as capitalism, 57, 187; and ideology, 25–27, 177, 186, 193, 199, 245, 247; and the lifeworld, 187, 193, 243, 247, 266. *See also* Jürgen Habermas
Caribbean ethnography, 106, 233
Carr, Lois Green, 14. *See also* Chesapeake historians
Carroll, Charles. *See* Carroll family; Charles Carroll of Carrollton; Charles Carroll of Carrollton Garden; Charles Carroll House
Carroll, Dr. Charles, 165–66
Carroll family, 18, 23. *See also* Charles Carroll of Carrollton; slavery
Carroll House site, xiv, 5, 200–206, 219, 231; cache contents: 204. *See also* spirit practices, St. Mary's site
Carrollton, Charles Carroll of (son of Charles Carroll of Annapolis), 3, 12, 14, 17, 82, 86, 101, 182, 197, 201, 205; African cook, 204–5; education of, 81
Carvel Hall Hotel, 70–71. *See also* William Paca House
Catholicism: in Baltimore, 12; Redemptorist Order, 256; Roman Catholic church in Annapolis, 3, 166, 197, 204; in St. Mary's City, 83; and voting in colonial era, 3. *See also* Carroll family; Charles Carroll of Carrollton; St. Mary's Church; St. Mary's City
census, 19–22, 30, 194. *See also* population
centering. *See* spirit practices
ceramics, 35, 55–56, 120, 154, 177; adoption as function of wage labor and not emulation, 163; and African American foodways, 159–60, 175; archaeological assemblages juxtaposed against probate assemblages, 163; in Carroll House (St. Mary's site) cache, 204; colonoware, 208; homogeneous vs. heterogeneous table settings, 159; increase in sets of matched tablewares, 158; increasing number of types of tableware, 155–56, 159; at Maynard-Burgess site,

174–76; in middling and lower-wealth assemblages, 162; as place settings, 166, 183–84; as resistance to market forces, 158; in Slayton House caches, 207; use in spirit practices, 199; variation in form and decoration, 158–59; uniformity as measure of penetration of possessive individualism, 56–57, 158; variability index scores, 156, 159. *See also* etiquette; individualism; separation and segmentation; technologies of the self
ceramic variability index. *See* ceramics
challenge. *See* reform
Chambers, Erve, xvi
Charles Carroll of Carrollton Garden, 68, 73–75, 77, 79–80, 201; and absence of power, 82, 182; date of construction, 81. *See also* garden; geometry; landscape
Charles Carroll House, xiv, 5, 200–205; cache contents: 204. *See also* St. Mary's site
Charleston, SC, 3
charms, 224, 230, 235–37. *See also* caches; spirit practices
Chase-Lloyd House, 4, 6, 39, 275
Chernela, Janet, xvi
Chesapeake Bay, 1–4, 11, 21, 46, 77, 84
Chesapeake & Ohio Canal, 3
Chesapeake historians: study of changing wealth, 14. *See also* Carr, Lois Green; Papenfuse, Edward C.; Russo, Jean B.; Walsh, Lorena
Chestertown, MD, 173
Chidester, Robert, xii
children, 40; childrearing, 174; as lacking in discipline, 166–67
Chisholm, Amelia G., xii, 267
Christianity, 61, 223, 235–37, 247, 260; possible African influences upon (e.g., magic left within), 259–60
chronometer. *See* clocks
Church Circle, 9–10, 44, 84, 94–95, 143; as egg, 90
Church of England. *See* Anglican Church
circles. *See* baroque design; Church Circle; State Circle
citizen: as basis for newly formed community, 98, 138–39, 153,; as individual, 51, 57, 96, 143. *See also* citizenship; freedom
citizenship: as foundation of republics, 97, 100, 114, 139, 153; and opinion, 144; and print, 141–42; and race, 196, 212, 264; and routines of daily

citizenship *(continued)*
    life, 55, 168, 179; as routinized
    people, 167, 172; and rules, 100,
    108; vote empowers state, 49, 58,
    97, 99, 141, 263–64; watchful, 26,
    36–37, 39, 47, 57–58., 96–97, 99–
    100, 109, 114, 143–44, 150–51,
    182, 212, 264. *See also* Foucault,
    Michel; ideology; imagined com-
    munity; Maryland State House;
    panopticism; panopticon; popular
    opinion; print culture; property;
    state; surveillance
city, definition: 22
Civil War, 18
Clark, Joseph, 98
Clark, Wayne, xv
class, 14–15, 26, 31, 145, 155, 174,
    177, 179, 186; 188, 190, 263, 265.
    See also social hierarchy; wealth
clocks, 46, 165, 168. *See also* measure-
    ment of nature; technologies of the
    self
Coale, Joseph M. III, xii
Cochran, Matthew D., xii, xxi, 215–16,
    232
Coggin, Lucy Dos Passos, xii
coins. *See* spirit practices
Cole, Charles, 145–46, 148. *See also*
    Tuesday Club of Annapolis
Coleman, Simon, 127
Colonial Williamsburg. *See* Williams-
    burg, VA
Comer, Elizabeth Anderson, xviii,
    183–84
Communists, 187
composite autobiographies. *See* Federal
    Writers' Project
conjure (a.k.a. malign conjure conjura-
    tion), 232–35, 247, 251, 253, 260;
    defined, 214; involves harm, 231;
    persons to whom it may have been
    directed, 232–34. *See also* Federal
    Writers' Project; hands; mojos; James
    Brice House; Slayton House; spirit
    practices; Yronwode, Catherine
Conrad, Earl, 176
conscience. *See* discipline
consciousness, 28, 31, 61, 108, 232, 251;
    despite absorption into capitalism,
    247, 260, 263, 266; as emancipa-
    tory, 31, 37, 58, 178, 185, 191, 247,
    265–66; and resistance, 61, 187,
    189, 199, 231. *See also* Habermas,
    Jürgen
Constitution, 2, 67, 95, 100, 264; as
    authorless document, 142–43; Bill of

Rights, 67, 150. *See also* Derrida,
    Jacques; Paca, William; popular
    opinion
consumer revolution, 27
consumption: as measure of penetration
    of ideology of individualism and not
    aspirations toward fashion, 162; as
    form of resistance, 175. *See also*
    material culture
contradictions. *See* ideology
control. *See* power
Cook, Lauren J., 24, 45, 59, 186
Cooper, Doreen, xxi
Corey, Mary, xii
Cornhill Street, 94, 98
correctional system, 96. *See also* Jeremy
    Bentham; panopticism; panopticon;
    surveillance; technologies of the self
Cosans, Betty J., 269
cosmograms, 203, 208, 211, 217–19, 222,
    231, 233–34, 242; definition, 203,
    218; purpose, 234, 241; use-life,
    234. *See also* James Brice House
Cox, C. Jane, xiv, xxi, 120, 221–22, 224,
    270, 275
Creel, Margaret Washington, 200
Cressey, Pamela, xx
Creveling, Donald K., xiv, 118
Creveling, Marian, xiii
critical theory. *See* theory
Crosby, Constance, xiv, 118–19, 269
crystals: in Carroll House (St. Mary's
    site) cache, 204; used by Native
    Americans as well as people of
    African descent, 202. *See also* spirit
    practices
Cuddy, Thomas, xiii, 269
Cummings, Steven M., xviii

Daley, Matthew, xviii
Davenport, Joan, xviii
Deagan, Kathleen, xv, xx
Declaration of Independence, 264; as
    authorless document, 140–42; and
    panopticism, 150; and race, 150;
    signers, 2, 67, 82. *See also* Charles
    Carroll of Carrollton; Franklin,
    Benjamin; Jefferson, Thomas; Paca,
    William; panopticism; popular
    opinion
decorative arts, 8
Deetz, James, xv, 35, 48–49, 53, 55–57,
    79–80, 115, 121, 127, 138, 140,
    143, 152–55, 157–58, 161, 165,
    175, 263–64; *In Small Things For-
    gotten* as an early inspiration for
    Archaeology in Annapolis, 53, 148,

154, 164; New England as foil for
Chesapeake, 49, 53, 55–57, 80, 154,
161, 166; New England material
traditions as extension of English
traditions, 152. *See also* Georgian
Order; individualism; Renaissance
degradation. *See* exploitation
democracy, 24, 26, 30, 37, 64, 187, 199,
211–12, 254, 261; coexists with
hierarchy, 266. *See also* hierarchy;
ideology demographics. *See* census;
population
demystification, 182–83, 186, 261–62.
See also Archaeology in Public in
Annapolis
Dent, Richard J., xiv, 30, 267, 270, 272
Derrida, Jacques, 50–51; signatures and
anonymity, 140–42
design. *See* Annapolis; architecture;
decorative arts; landscape design;
town planning
devil, 248
diaries, 101. *See also* documents
diasporic communities, xx, 61, 106–7,
199, 203, 223, 235–36, 260; and
rejection of ideology of possessive
individualism, 109, 265
Dicke, Karen, xiii
difference. *See* exploitation
dining, 55–56, 154; internalized rules
for proper behavior, 96, 153. 161,
163, 165, 174. *See also* ceramics;
etiquette; individualism; separation
and segmentation; technologies of
the self
discipline: and eating, 154, 166, 174;
as measure of efficiency, 170; and
penmanship, 142; personal discipline, 35, 54, 103, 161, 168, 183;
as precision, 169; and reading and
writing, 48, 53, 58; and time, 104–
5, 153, 165, 168; and work, 153,
161, 165. *See also* baroque design;
etiquette; Foucault, Michel; print
culture; surveillance; technologies
of the self; Thompson, E. P.
discs. *See* spirit practices
dishes. *See* ceramics. *See also* etiquette;
individualism; separation and segmentation technologies of the self
Disneyland, 30
Disneyworld, 30
documents, 14, 22, 30, 77–78; as independent grids in relation to archaeology, 78, 80. *See also* census;
Chesapeake historians; diaries; land
records; maps; *Maryland Gazette;*

newspaper; photographs; probate
inventories; tax assessments
Dodds, Susan and Philip, xiv
Dolgin, Janet, 24, 180
doll parts. *See* caches
dome. *See* Maryland State House
domination. *See* inequality; power
Douglass, Frederick, 61, 107
Dowsett, Margaret, xiv
Dreyer, Peter, xviii
Du Bois, W. E. B., 58, 61, 176, 198,
246–47
Dulaney, Ed, xviii
Dutch colonial experience, 187–89. *See
also* apartheid; archaeology; Archae-
ology in Public in Annapolis; voices

East Street, 94
Edelstein, Stewart, xvi
Edgar, Blake, xviii
Edwards, Ywonne, xxi
Egypt, 259, 261
Eisenstein, Elizabeth, 117
Elias, Norbert, 161
Emancipation, 18, 22, 58, 105, 176, 210.
See also Enlightenment; slavery
emotion, 103–4
emulation: rejection of, 163, 265. *See
also* ceramics
Enlightenment: and architecture, 50;
assumptions, 39; and business/
trade training, 167; and gardens,
45; philosophy, 10–11, 38–40, 54,
64, 106, 144, 166; rationality and
modernity, 167, 170; reason and
experience, 170; as self-awareness/
emancipation, 32, 245; and science,
144–45. *See also* William Paca
Garden
Epperson, Terrence, xviii
Erenfeld, Howard, xviii, 184
Ernstein, Julie H., xiii–xiv, xvi–xvii, 269,
272–73
equality. *See* ideology
equity. *See* ideology
Ersts, Heather, xii
etiquette, 35–36, 53, 56, 97, 174; modernizing, 163, 183; and separations at
table, 48, 55, 153, 155, 161, 163,
165. *See also* ceramics; dining; Foucault, Michel; individualism; separation and segmentation; technologies
of the self
European descent: people of, 196
Evelyn, John, 11
exchange, 169. *See also* discipline, and
time

exploitation, 24, 186, 245; in form of
  racism, 58, 174–77, 190–91, 193,
  196–98, 212, 235, 245–46, 252,
  257, 260; sexism, 172, 262. See also
  ideology

Fahr, George, xv
falls. See gardens
Fairbanks, Charles, xx
Fan. See spiritual practices
Faris, William, 45, 102, 109, 176–77,
  245; artisan gardener, 101; plant
  exchanges, 46. See also gardens;
  William Faris's Garden
farming: tobacco, 21
Fascists, 187
Federal architecture. See architecture; panopticism; panopticon;
  surveillance
Federal era, 12, 40, 70, 81, 96, 100
Federal Writers' Project, xvi xix, 41, 60–
  61, 209–10, 213, 222, 224, 231–37,
  247–48, 251, 260–61; and Anne
  Arundel County, 251, 253–55; break
  with evidence noted in archaeological record, 231; descriptions of conditions in Annapolis, 251, 253–54,
  257; items commonly used in African spirit practices, 226–29; intersection with archaeological record,
  223–24, 229–30, 244, 260; interview protocol, 210–11; level of
  descriptive detail that archaeology
  rarely provides, 251; limitations,
  233–34; narratives as critique of the
  business of capitalism, 61, 212, 247,
  250, 265–66; regions covered, 211;
  as source for preparation of modern-
  day mojos and hands, 213–14, 223;
  and spirit world, 105–06, 223–24;
  underutilized by those studying
  Maryland slavery and history, 251.
  See also Fry, Gladys-Marie; gardens;
  Ruppel, Timothy
Feldmeyer-Gassaway House site, 273
Fennel, Christopher, 223
Fennie, William, xvii
Ferguson, Leland, 208
Fife, Julie, xii
Figueroa, Laura, 137–38. See also
  Maryland Gazette; printer's type
fixing. See conjure
Fligsten, Ann, xii
folkore, 199, 203
force. See power
Fort Mose (Florida), xx
Foucault, Michel, 35–37, 48, 97, 100,

122, 138, 141–42, 144, 153, 155,
  157, 165. See also citizenship; panop-
  ticism; panopticon; surveillance;
  technologies of the self
Founding Fathers, 143, 168. See also
  Franklin, Benjamin; Jefferson,
  Thomas; popular opinion; Washington, George
Ford, Beth, xii, 270, 272
France, 97, 152
Frankfurt School. See theory
Franklin, Benjamin, 140–42. See also
  Green, Jonas; Jefferson, Thomas;
  popular opinion
Franklin, Maria, xxi
Franklin Street neighborhood, 196;
  archaeology, 197; Wylie Bates's
  store, 196; William Bishop's properties, 196. See also oral history
free blacks, 19, 21–23, 40, 58, 60, 105,
  174, 197–98, 213, 245; purchase of
  freedom, 105–06, 108, 110. See also
  African Americans; African descent;
  caches; spirit practices
freedom: and African Americans, 175,
  177, 196–97, 199, 212, 245, 247,
  254; in Annapolis, 12, 23, 64, 192;
  and ideology, 25, 29, 34–36, 46–47,
  49, 51, 53, 59, 83, 95, 105, 108,
  138, 143–44, 150, 153, 165, 167,
  182, 186, 263; as perpetually incomplete, 157, 212–13; and revolutionaries, 162, 264. See also American
  Revolution; democracy; individualism; personal liberty; print culture
Freidenberg, Judith N., xvi
Freud, Sigmund, 31, 180
Fry, Gladys-Marie, xix, 60, 105, 207–
  09, 211, 213, 220–21, 223–24, 230,
  237, 255; on symbols in quilts, 258

Gaarder, Syd, xiii
Galke, Laura J., xiii–xiv, xx, 267, 272–73
garden history, 66–67, 70. See also
  gardens; geometry; landscape design;
  landscapes
gardeners: cross-section of social classes,
  104. See also Carrollton, Charles
  Carroll of; Faris, William; Paca,
  William; Ridout, John
gardens, 38, 41–42, 73, 78–79; as
  baroque, 43, 80, 143; beds, 77; and
  botany, 104; broadening terrace
  widths, 77; classical/mythological
  references, 79; dates of construction,
  80, 82; descent/falling, 54, 64, 68,
  70, 81–82, 84, 102; as didactic

devices, 79, 83; diminishing terrace widths, 68, 73; flat gardens, 104; focal point within, 69; and harmony, 42; horticulture, 79; hydrology, 79; as ideology, 67, 81; as illusions, 42, 63, 67–68, 79–80, 182–83; interrelationship of parts, 79; manuals, 66, 68–69, 78–83, 90, 101, 104; Maryland, xvii; mixture of ornament, pleasure, and home use, 101; as ostentatious display, 81–82; and their paths, 64, 69, 71; and political instability, 81; prevalence of gardens associated with Annapolis houses, 104; as quests for power, 80, 82, 182; ramps, 77; in relationship to house, 70, 72, 79; and scientific information, 66; and scientific instruments, 46, 104–5, 165, 184; shared rules with town planning, 42–44, 64, 77, 93, 101, 182; slave gardens, 105–09, 151; slave labor in other people's gardens, 105; and stylistic time-lag, 81; surveying and control of nature, 46, 182; terracing, 64–66, 68–70, 75, 77, 80, 104; and time, 104, 165; topographic mapping, 66, 69, 71, 73–77, 79; vernacular design, 45, 101; to whom views were addressed, 154; wilderness, 71, 81. See also Brown, Lancelot "Capability"; Charles Carroll of Carrollton Garden; geometry; Ridout Garden; William Faris's Garden; William Paca Garden
geographic information systems (GIS), xiv–xv, 88–91. See also geometry
geometry: converging lines of perspective, 69, 75, 94; curvilinear, 71; diverging lines of perspective, 94; ground planes, 70; and GIS, 88; illusions and proportions, 8, 42, 64, 68–69, 77, 79–81, 93–95; manipulation of lines of sight, 85, 94–95; net of squares, 72–73, 77; optics, 44, 79, 82; plane geometry, 64, 72–73, 80, 87, 91–92; and plants, 63–64, 69; rectilinear, 71–72; solid geometry, 63, 75, 87, 91, 96, 99, 182; use of color, 69–71; use of perspective, 68–69, 73–75, 77, 79, 82, 99. See also Charles Carroll of Carrollton Garden; gardens; Paca, Barbara; Ridout Garden; rules; Shackel, Paul A.; William Paca Garden; Wright, St. Clair
George Washington University, 203

Georgian architecture. See architecture
Georgian mindset. See Georgian Order; Deetz, James
Georgian Order, 9, 57, 152, 157, 175
God, 236
Godefroy, Maximilian, 99
Goldstein, Irwin, xvi
Gomez, Michael, 199, 223
Gott's Court site, 156, 159, 273
Grasshopper Pueblo (Arizona), 202
Green, Anne Catherine, 51–52, 113, 118, 139–41, 154
Green family print shop, xiv, 28, 48, 111, 118, 156, 270; cellar, 120; changes to domestic structure in relation to print shop, 120; excavation, 113–19, 129; fire, 120; foundation, 118; stratigraphic contexts, 119–20, 132, 137. See also Creveling, Donald K.; Crosby, Constance; Little, Barbara J.; Maryland Gazette; popular opinion; print culture; printer's type; segmentation and separation
Green, Frederick, 139, 141
Green, Jim, xviii
Green, Jonas, 51–52, 55, 111, 113, 126, 139–41, 151, 154, 245; former apprentice to Benjamin Franklin, 142; member of Tuesday Club of Annapolis, 113
Green, Samuel, 141
Greengrass, Mara, 275
grid: as metaphor for interpreting points of intersection between landscapes, power, and politics, 78, 80–82, 170. See also gardens; geometry; ideology
Gundaker, Grey, 106, 223

Habermas, Jürgen, xix, 27, 31–32, 179, 186, 244, 258, 265; absorptive capability of capitalism, 27, 32, 36, 187, 247; and alternative lifeworlds, 262; on democracy, 32; exemption from disfranchisement, 27, 261, 265; and history, 33, 190; and notion of the lifeworld, 187, 190, 193, 236, 243, 247
Haitian Revolution of 1793, 212. See also slavery
Hale, Cynthia, xvi
Haley, Alex, 4, 251. See also Roots; slavery
Hall, Charles, xv
Hall, Gwendolyn Midlo, 200
Hall, Robert, xiii
Hall, William, xiii
Hamilton, Alexander, 12

Hamilton, Dr. Alexander (of Annapolis),
    14, 39, 41, 54, 146, 150–51, 163–
    64, 184, 262. *See also* Tuesday Club
    of Annapolis
Hammond-Harwood House, 4, 50, 267
Handler, Jerome, xx
Handler, Richard, 34, 155, 157
hands, 207, 213, 215, 218, 224, 231,
    234, 237; contents of modern-day
    hands, 213–15. *See also* caches;
    spirit practices
Hanson, Alexander Contee, 102
Harmon, James, xvii, 81, 215, 271
Harrington, J. C., xviii
Harris, Page, 253; time in Annapolis,
    253–54. *See also* Federal Writers'
    Project
Harris, Teresa D., 121, 123–24, 127
Haury, Emil, xx
Herman, Stanley, xvii
Herskovits, Melville J., 214
hierarchy: and ancestry, 235; disguised
    as republic, 38, 83, 102, 143, 150,
    184, 261, 266; and gender, 172; of
    knowledge, 38; social, 2, 10, 14–15,
    17–18, 22–23, 25, 37, 41–42, 45,
    81–82, 94, 103, 104–5, 109, 113,
    150, 154–55, 212; and race, 197;
    social hierarchy disguised as natural,
    163, 167, 172, 182, 266; spatial, 55,
    104. *See also* ceramics; ideology;
    social control
Hill, Anna, 137, 139. See also *Maryland
    Gazette;* printer's type
Hill, Stephen, 24
Hillman, Richard, xiii
Historic Annapolis Foundation, xii, 3,
    24, 29–30, 43, 45, 63, 65–66, 70,
    85, 118, 180, 195, 197, 205, 251,
    267, 269–78
Historic Annapolis, Incorporated. *See*
    Historic Annapolis Foundation
historical archaeology. *See* archaeology;
    research design; theory
historic preservation, 3–4, 7, 29–30, 197;
    as homogenizing process, 184; and
    power, 189. *See also* Annapolis
    Historic Annapolis Foundation
Historic St. Mary's City, 120, 180. *See
    also* St. Mary's City, MD
Hobbes, Thomas, 34, 36, 162, 263–64
Hodder, Ian, 24, 45, 59, 186
Hoepfner, Christine, 183
Holy Ghost, 248
homogeneity, 7, 192. *See also* ideology
Hoodoo, xvi, defined, 214. *See also*
    hands; James Brice House; mojos;

    Slayton House; spirit practices;
    Yronwode, Catherine
Hopkins, Alfred, xiii
Hopkins, Joseph W. III, xiv, 271–72
horticulture: as nineteenth-century
    outgrowth of eighteenth-century
    interest in landscapes as loci for
    observing and perfecting nature,
    163, 168, 182
Hughes, Richard, xv, 272
Hurst, Lawrence, xiii
Hyatt, Harry, 237; description of spirit
    practices, 237–43
Hyde/Thompson site, 156, 270
hygiene: as measure of penetration of
    personal discipline, 56, 164, 183.
    See also discipline; etiquette; indi-
    vidualism; separation and segmenta-
    tion; technologies of the self

ideology, 24–25, 28, 45, 100, 104–5,
    109, 179, 197; and archaeology, 36,
    41, 179–91, 199, 213; and behavior,
    39, 55, 143–44; and class, 177–79;
    constructed so as to appear unassail-
    able, 212; critique, 24–26, 45, 109,
    185, 212, 247 , 266; definition, 24;
    dominant, 37, 41, 106, 108, 110,
    186; as equivalent of presentism and
    projection, 180; of equality, 175;
    escape from, 28, 58, 60, 82, 199,
    255; as false, 178; group cohesion,
    192; harmony, 93–94; and the indi-
    vidual, 34–35, 45–47, 53, 58, 62,
    104–5, 108, 113, 150–51, 162, 179,
    181, 184, 186, 193, 245–46, 256,
    263–64; and industrialism, 264; and
    instrumentation, 46, 165, 167–68;
    limitations, 26, 62; masks contradic-
    tions, 25, 29, 35, 102, 110, 118,
    150–51, 154, 162, 212, 245, 247,
    260, 266; naturalizing ideology, 25,
    38, 44–45, 59, 79, 81, 99, 102, 106,
    144, 150–51, 162–63, 165, 167,
    170, 172–73, 181, 254; as nearly
    inescapable, 256; and order, 38, 46,
    53, 104–5, 153, 163; origins, 179,
    181, 258; and patriotism, 180, 186;
    piercing, 27–29, 59, 145, 150–51,
    186, 191, 212, 245, 256, 265; and
    power, 41, 67, 80, 182, 191, 212;
    and precedent/origins, 144–46, 148,
    150, 188; and pre-Revolutionary
    Annapolis, 26, 67, 212–13; and pub-
    lic program, 32–33, 179–91, 261;
    purpose, 25; and race, 150, 199,
    212–13, 248, 252; and religion, 190,

223, 248; and resistance, 45, 62,
150, 187, 189, 193, 231; as social
construct and therefore mutable,
181, 236; and social inequality, 26,
185; and social reproduction, 109,
165, 167, 184; stylistic, 81; and
technology, 67, 165, 245; as timeless, 181; as transparent, 25. *See
also* Althusser, Louis; American
liberty; critical theory; freedom;
Habermas, Jürgen; individualism;
Marx, Karl; material culture; measurement; popular opinion; technologies of the self
Ifa. *See* religious practices
illumination. *See* demystification
illusions. *See* gardens. *See also* geometry
imagined community, 51, 98, 100; and
archaeology, 52; and citizenship,
141; and the printed page, 127, 139;
and unity, 142. *See also* Anderson,
Benedict; literacy; *Maryland Gazette;*
popular opinion; print culture
inclusion, 186. *See also* voice
indentured servitude, 22
independence. *See* ideology
Independence Hall, 146. *See also* Peale
Museum; Philadelphia, PA
Indian descent: people of, 188
individualism: and acquisition of skills
and possessions, 154, 157, 162,
165–68, 170–71, 264; central characteristics, 34, 144; and European
capitalism, 154; and laws of nature,
154, 165, 182; as learned, 155, 170,
182; and movement into wage-labor
market, 163; masks contradictions,
154, 245, 260; and material culture,
153, 155, 165; as material expression of ideology, 155, 161, 165, 182,
184, 186, 212; and personhood,
153, 165, 170, 179, 181, 190, 260;
possessive, 25–26, 34–37, 41, 46,
48, 51, 56–58, 83, 95, 99, 102,
104–5, 109–10, 138, 143–44, 150–
51, 155, 162, 169, 183–84, 190,
193, 196, 243, 245, 256, 263–64;
possessive individualism as basis
for government, 264; possessive
individualism defined, 154; and production line, 157; and purchase of
freedom by slaves, 105, 108, 110,
154; and slavery, 154, 245–57, 260–
61; and space, 153. *See also* freedom; ideology; Macpherson, C. B.;
state; surveillance
Industrial Revolution, 39

industrialization. *See* Baltimore
inequality, 31–32, 109, 183, 185, 190,
193, 265. *See also* class; race; social
hierarchy; wealth
inspection stations: in form of schools,
churches, libraries, hospitals, and
private homes, 97. *See also* panopticism; panopticon
International Masonry Institute, xiv, 215
Italy, 152

Jackson, Barbara, xiii, 60, 192–94, 199,
203, 258
Jackson, Fatimah L. C., xvi
James Brice House, xiv, 4, 32, 214–
20, 271, 273; African-American
presence, 215–20; caches, 215–20,
230–31; contents of Brice House
caches, 215–17, 219–20, 222, 233;
interpretive disagreement among
excavators, 215–20; loci of recovery,
215–18
Jefferson, Thomas, 2, 3, 12, 66, 145,
168; correspondence with Charles
Willson Peale, 144; and signature,
140–42; visit to Maryland State
House, 98
Jensen, Anne, xiv
Jesuits. *See* Catholicism
Jesus, 236, 260
Johannesburg (South Africa), 188
John Brice II House (Jennings-Brice), 273
Johnson, Dean, xiii
Johnson, Matthew, 127
Jonas Green print shop. *See* Green family
print shop
Jones, Lynn D., xiii, xx, 207, 223, 272–
73, 276. *See also* cache; Slayton
House; spirit practices
Jopling, Hannah, xi, 194
Jordan, Dempsey, 248–51. *See also*
Federal Writers' Project
Joyner, Charles, 200

kalunga line, 203; defined, 242. *See also*
cosmograms; spirit practices
kinship: as explanatory matrix for
African spiritual practices, 235
Kinte, Kunte, 4, 251. *See also* Alex
Haley; Kunte Kinte Festival; *Roots*
Kirwan, William, xvi
Klingelhofer, Eric, xxi
Knower, Stewart, xiv
knowledge: as a possession, 83; system-
atizing, 38–39. *See also* ideology
Kohlhepp, Patricia, xii
Kraus, Lisa, xi

Kryder-Reid, Elizabeth, xi, xiii, 6, 147, 272
Ku Klux Klan, 256–57
Kunte Kinte Festival, xiii, 195
Kwass, Stephen, xviii

Lamp, Frederick, xix–xx, 202–3
landowners, 17, 23, 57. *See also* Charles Carroll of Carrollton
land records, 104
landscape design, 8, 42, 45, 77. *See also* gardens; geometry; landscapes; town planning
landscapes, 12, 35, 41–42, as didactic devices, 79, 83; as encyclopedic array of; as environments for scientific observation, 162, 167, 169–70; as ideology, 67, 100, 109, 182–83, 186; knowledge, 42; and perspective, 68, 77, 83, 99, 182; planned, 45, 66, 81–83, 91–93, 98–99, 162–63; and their public interpretation, 182; swept yards, 232. *See also* baroque design; Charles Carroll of Carrollton Garden; gardens; landscape design; Ridout Garden; town planning; William Faris's Garden; William Paca Garden
landscape studies, xx
Larsen, Eric, xi, 274
Latin American descent: people of, 61. *See also* spirit practices
Latrobe, Benjamin, 3, 12, 97–99; Baltimore design projects, 13, 97, 99
laws: as systematized knowledge, 38, 79. *See also* gardens; ideology
Lawyer's Alley, 94
layout. *See* Annapolis; baroque design; Nicholson, Francis; Nicholson plan; town planning; Williamsburg, VA
Lee, Ann, 177
Leone, Joanne, xviii
Leone, Veronika, xvii
leisure. *See* Archaeology in Public in Annapolis
liberty: American, 26, 41; attempted exclusion of poor whites and those of African descent, 109, 197–99, 263–65; and ideology, 186–87, 212–13, 247; personal, 18, 23, 25, 29, 37, 49, 51, 58, 64, 83, 100, 105, 143, 150, 157, 184, 264; and rights, 264. *See also* freedom; ideology; individualism
life histories, 194, 209. *See also* Federal Writers' Project; oral history
lifeworld: defined, 187; as critique of

capitalism, 247, 250, 266; as means for identifying alternatives, 187–90, 237, 243–44, 247, 255. *See also* African Americans; Habermas, Jürgen
Liggett, Barbara, 269
Lindauer, Anthony, 17
lines of sight. *See* geometry. *See also* gardens
literacy, 51; aural and visual literacy, 51, 55; reading and citizenship, 114, 138–39, 141–42. *See also* citizen; citizenship; *Maryland Gazette;* popular opinion; print culture; Tuesday Club of Annapolis
literature, 199
Little, Barbara J., xi, 6, 40, 52, 111, 113–21, 129, 132, 138, 140; dissertation, 118. *See also* Green family print shop; *Maryland Gazette;* print culture; printer's type
Little, Glenn, 71. *See also* William Paca Garden
Lindauer, Tony, xiv
living history, 180. *See also* Archaeology in Public; Historic St. Mary's City; Williamsburg, VA
Locke, John, 34, 162, 263–64
Lockwood, Alice B., 68
Logan, George C., 272
London (England), 8, 49, 77, 81, 143, 168
Londontown, 22
Longacre, William, xx
Luckenbach, Al, xiv
Lucas, Michael, xii
Lukács, Georg, xix, 31–32, 258; and historical knowledge, 179–81, 186, 190; and origins of conditions leading to inequality, 31, 179–91. *See also* consciousness
Lutheranism, 11

Macpherson, C. B., 34, 37, 155, 162, 263, 265; his definition of liberal democratic government, 263–64. *See also* possessive individualism
Madison, James, 98
Magdoff, JoAnn, 24, 180
magic, 202, 235, 260. See also *Maryland Gazette;* spiritual practices
Malone, Timothy, xviii
manners. *See* discipline, and time; discipline, personal; etiquette
Mansbach, Steven, xv–xvi
manuals. *See* gardens. *See also* Langley, Batty; Miller, Philip
maps: Sanborn Fire Insurance Maps, 90.

See measurement as locus of control.
See also geographic information
systems (GIS)
Martin, Paul S., xx
Marx, Karl, xix, 24–26, 31, 35–37, 247,
263; and history: 31, 180–81
Marxism: as challenge to capitalism, 187.
See also theory
Maryland, 11–12, 238–39, 264; as
planned society, 11; seventeenth-
century, 11–12, 21; southern, 107.
See also social hierarchy
Maryland Archaeological Conservation
(MAC) Laboratory, 267, 276–77
Maryland Avenue, 94
Maryland Gazette, xvii, 30, 48–51, 111,
113, 115–17, 125–26, 165–67; advertisements, 49, 51, 126–27, 138–39,
165, 169–70, 264; content, 48–51,
53, 113, 117, 121, 144; disappearance of signature (increasingly
anonymity), 51–52, 112, 123, 129,
139–41; geographic reach, 51;
grammar, 49, 113, 123–24; as
imagined description of daily life,
51, 113, 117; increased visual homogeneity, 121–22, 127, 131, 140;
increasing emphasis on Maryland
news, 121; layout of paper, 48–49,
51–52, 116, 122, 137–38; likened to
separation at dining table, 138, 164;
as means for internalizing society's
lessons/rules, 114, 123, 143, 150,
164–65, 170, 172; organization
and increased segmentation and
uniformity of page, 49, 52, 112,
115–17, 121–22, 127, 129–30, 132,
136, 138, 140; political news, 49,
116; presented as classless, 112;
production requirements, 132; as
promoter of etiquette and other
technologies of the self, 97, 111,
113–14, 142–44, 164–65, 170; reor-
ganization in relation to American
Revolution, 138; rules of grammar
and syntax, 122–24, 141; science
replaces magic, 145, 168; segmentation by subject, 121; shape of
printed words, 48–49; and shared
information, 50, 53, 139; vehicle
for controversy and propaganda,
117, 143–44. *See also* Arias, Angela;
Austin, Stephen P.; Brainerd, Samuel;
Coleman, Simon; Derrida, Jacques;
Figueroa, Laura Green family print
shop; Green, Anne Catherine; Green,
Frederick; Green, Jonas; Green,

Samuel; Harris, Teresa D.; Hill,
Anna; Johnson, Matthew; Little,
Barbara J.; Moyer, Matthew; Parks,
William; Pearson, Marlys; popular
opinion; print culture; printer's type
Maryland Historical Trust, xv
Maryland Humanities Council, xv–xvi,
195
Maryland Legislature, 147
Maryland State Archives (Hall of Records), 111, 125–26, 128, 130–31,
136
Maryland State House, 2, 4, 8, 10, 13,
83–85, 87, 93–97, 182; dome: 14,
47, 90, 95–98, 183, 269; lawn, 90;
as painted by Peale, 97–98. *See also*
panopticism; panopticon; Shipper,
Thomas Lee; state; surveillance
mass-production: of individuals, 36,
105, 116, 153, 167; via printed
word, 114; who are also workers,
174. *See also* etiquette; individualism
material culture, 152–53, 174, 193–94;
and the color line, 199; as conscious
exercise in power, 56, 153, 182,
186, 206–7; luxury items, 165; as
vehicle of ideology, 59, 104, 143,
148, 152, 165, 184, 186, 264. *See
also* caches; ceramics; discipline;
individualism; national brands; technologies of the self; tin cans; toothbrushes; spirit practices
Matthews, Christopher N., xi, 6, 273
Maynard-Burgess site, 156, 174, 197–99,
275, 254, 256; archaeology corrects
received wisdom about site, 197–98;
consumption of goods as resistance
to racism, 198–99; as exclusively occupied by persons of African descent,
197; proposed museum interpretation, 254, 257
Maynard, John, 175, 197–98. *See also*
Maynard-Burgess site
Maynard, Maria, 175
McCarthy, John P., 278
McGuire, Randall, xvii–xviii, 186
McKee, Larry, xxi
McKinney, Kirby, xiii
McLuhan, Marshall, 54
measurement: as locus of control, 46,
104, 165, 168. *See also* gardens
medicine, 170
Meyerhoff, Sayra and Neil, xviii
middle class, 100–102, 112–13, 129,
150, 175–76, 179, 193, 199, 245,
247, 256, 265. *See also* class; Tuesday Club of Annapolis

middle range theory. *See* theory
Miller, Henry M., 11. *See also* baroque
    design; St. Mary's City; town
    planning
Miller, Naomi F., 270
Mills, Robert, 99
modernity: critique of, 62, 212, 250,
    255, 266; origins of modern con-
    ditions: 31, 179–91, 245, 258
mojos, 207, 213, 218, 231; contents of
    modern-day mojos, 213–14. *See also*
    caches; hands; spirit practices; tobys
Morgan, Edmund, 18. *See also* personal
    liberty; slavery
Moses, 236, 260
Mote, Daniel, xvi
Moxon, Joseph, 124. *See also* printer's
    manuals
Moyer, Ellen, xiii
Moyer, Matthew, 119, 129, 132–35,
    137–38. *See also* printer's type
Mrozowski, Stephen A., 24, 45, 59, 186
Mueller, Joseph, xiv
Mukerji, Chandra, 67, 81. *See also*
    Versailles
mulatto, 23. *See also* population; race
Mullin, Michael, 199
Mullins, Paul R., xi, 6, 58, 61–62, 163,
    174–77, 194, 197–99, 246, 257,
    274–75
music, 163, 165, 199. *See also* ideology;
    separation and segmentation
musical instruments, 46, 184. *See also*
    nature; separation and segmentation
muted groups, 27; women, 173. *See also*
    voices

Nagle, Christopher, 158
national brands, 194; consumption as
    form of resistance to racism, 197–
    98
nation-building, 38, 41, 52. *See also*
    Anderson, Benedict; imagined
    communities
National Endowment for the Humani-
    ties, xv; Fellowship for Independent
    Study and Research, xvi
Native American: religious practice, 202,
    214
nature: comprised of rules, laws, and
    principles, 162, 164, 182; control
    of, 38, 42, 182; measurement of,
    46, 167–70. *See also* ideology
    naturalizing
Naval Academy. *See* United States Naval
    Academy
Nazis, 187

negotiation: between past and present, 4,
    30, 184, 189, 213
Neuwirth, Jessica L., xiii, xix, 81, 105–6,
    216, 271
Newburg, NY, 146. *See also* Charles
    Willson Peale
New Orleans , LA, 248
newspaper. *See Maryland Gazette;* print
    culture; *Washington Bee*
Newton, Isaac, 79. *See also* Enlighten-
    ment
New York, NY, 3–4, 7, 29, 213
New York Times, 202
Nicholson, Francis, 7–11, 17, 83–84, 92,
    94–96. *See also* Annapolis; baroque
    design; Nicholson plan; town
    planning; Williamsburg, VA
Nicholson plan (of Annapolis), 43–44,
    84, 87, 99; flaws, 84–85, 94;
    imposed on pre-existing plan, 92.
    See also baroque design; geometry;
    Nicholson, Francis; Reps, John;
    Stoddert plan of Annapolis; town
    planning
Nick, Bertina, xiii
Noël Hume, Ivor, xviii
North Carolina, 245
Northeast Street, 94

observation. *See* surveillance
Old Treasury Building, 183
opinion: written opinion as social
    construct, 54, 138, 145. *See also*
    imagined
communities; popular opinion; print
    culture
oppression. *See* exploitation
oral histories, 175, 194–96, 258
order. *See also* gardens; ideology;
    spiritual practices
O'Reilly, Carey, 272
origins. *See* ideology
Orr, Kenneth, 267, 269
Orr, Ronald, G., 270
Orser, Charles E., xviii, xxi
ostentation. *See* Braudel, Fernand;
    gardens
oystermen. *See* African Americans;
    African descent; Annapolis;
    watermen/waterwomen; working
    class

Paca, Barbara, 72–74, 77. *See also*
    gardens; geometry; William Paca
    Garden
Paca, William, xi, 17, 23, 67, 70, 81–82,
    96, 101; education, 66, 81; portrait,

71, 73, 81. *See also* William Paca
  Garden; William Paca House; Peale,
  Charles Willson; slavery
Palus, Matthew, xi, 6, 272, 278–79
panopticism, as reciprocal watching, 47,
  96–98; and the state, 47, 96, 150.
  See also Jeremy Bentham; citizen-
  ship; Foucault, Michel; panopticon;
  state; surveillance
panopticon, 14, 96; defined, 96–99. *See
  also* Bentham, Jeremy; surveillance
Paolisso, Michael, xvi
Papenfuse, Edward C., 14. *See also* Chesa-
  peake historians
Park Place #1 site, 277
Park Place #2 site, 278
Park Place #3 site, 278
Parker, Alecia, xii
Parks, William, 116, 125, 127, 167–68
Paris (France), 9
parody, as means for piercing ideology,
  263, 266. *See also* Tuesday Club of
  Annapolis
parterres. *See* gardens
Patrick, Stephen A., 272
patriotism, 82, 186, 257; as post hoc
  social achievement, 83
Patterson, Richelle, xvii
Patterson, Thomas, xvii–xviii
Paynter, Robert, xviii, xxi
Peale, Charles Willson, 71, 73, 97–98;
  and natural history, 144, 146. *See
  also* William Paca Garden; William
  Paca House; Peale Museum
Peale Museum (Philadelphia, PA), 144,
  146
Pearson, Marlys, xvii, 165, 269
Pearson, Paul, xiv
Perry, Warren, xx
Perry, Wendy, xiii
personal discipline. *See* discipline
personal liberty. *See* liberty. *See also*
  freedom; ideology; individualism
Philadelphia, PA, 2–3, 29, 171
photographs, xviii, 77, 184; aerial, 77
pins. *See* spirit practices
plantation, 21–22, 68, 107, 168; Contee
  plantation (Prince George's Co.,
  MD), 252. *See also* Maryland
politics. *See* hierarchy; ideology; power;
  wealth
Popernack, Paul, 104
popular opinion: as authorless, 51, 140–
  43; as basis for citizenship, 51–52,
  114, 138, 141–42, 144; definition,
  114; as illusion, 141, 148; and
  parody, 55, 148; related to posses-

sive individualism, 51, 138–43; and
  standardization of rules, 52, 140–
  41, 144–45, 163, 183; as widely
  held, 51, 144–45, 264. *See also*
  Anderson, Benedict; citizenship;
  Constitution; Declaration of Independence; *Maryland Gazette;* print
  culture; Tuesday Club of Annapolis
population, 2, 18–23. *See also* census
Port of Annapolis, 197
possessions. *See* material culture; property
possessive individualism. *See* individualism
post-colonialism. *See* archaeology;
  Bhabha, Homi; South Africa
Potter, Parker B., Jr., xi, 6
poverty, 23, 39–41, 49; and individualism, 153, 190. *See also* exploitation
power: claiming of power through spirit
  practices, 231, 234, 243; face-to-face
  knowledge as key to social control,
  235; maintenance, 41, 97, 103, 105,
  265. *See also* baroque design; Charles
  Carroll of Carrollton Garden; class;
  Foucault, Michel; gardens; ideology;
  landscape; material culture; social
  hierarchy; technologies of the self;
  town planning; wealth; William Paca
  Garden
Powell, B. Bruce, 267
Pretoria (South Africa), 188
precedent. *See* ideology
prehistoric archaeology. *See* archaeology;
  research design; theory
prehistory. *See* archaeology; research
  design; theory
presentism, 180. *See also* Archaeology in
  Public in Annapolis; Freud, Sigmund;
  living history; ideology; projection
Prince George's County, MD, 252
Princeton University (Princeton, NJ), 180
print culture, 35; and capitalism, 118;
  democratization of text, 117; and
  the formation of
popular opinion, 48–49, 51, 114, 138–
  39; and the individual, 127–29, 154;
  products of the press, 50; separation
  and segmentation, 49, 53, 118, 154;
  standardization of vernacular language, 117, 124, 139, 145. *See also*
  Anderson, Benedict; citizenship;
  ideology; *Maryland Gazette;* mass
  production; popular opinion; separation and segmentation
printers. *See* Green, Anne Catherine;
  Green, Frederick; Green, Jonas;
  Green, Samuel; Parks, William; print
  culture

printer's manuals, 49, 115, 123–24.
     See also *Maryland Gazette;* print
     culture
printer's type, 48–49, 52, 111–14, 116,
     129, 141; archaeological data set,
     116, 118–19, 129; capital letters,
     122; cataloguing, 118, 129; chronol-
     ogy, 119–20; compared against pages
     of *Maryland Gazette,* 119, 128–
     29, 132, 137; decreasing homo-
     geneity, 52, 132; distribution of type
     size through time, 121, 132, 137;
     fonts, 117, 120, 124, 129; increase
     in fonts as page became authorless/
     anonymous, 52; and increased visual
     homogeneity, 121–22, 132, 141;
     manufacture, 116; point sizes, 132,
     136–37; questions generated by
     type, 117, 132; quotation marks,
     122; separation into fonts, 119;
     standardization of elements, 117;
     typefaces used by Green family
     printers, 129, 131–35; and typeset-
     ting, 124; typology, 119. See also
     Maryland Gazette; print culture;
     printing
printing: American colonial, 140, 143;
     importance in Western civilization,
     111
prison. See Bentham, Jeremy; panopti-
     cism; panopticon; surveillance; tech-
     nologies of the self
probate inventories, 15, 30, 41, 46, 104,
     157, 163, 199. See also Chesapeake
     historians; class; property; Shackel,
     Paul A.; social hierarchy; wealth
profit, 58, 170, supreme over self and
     freedom, 265
projection, 180. See also Archaeology in
     Public in Annapolis; Freud, Sigmund;
     ideology; living history, presentism
proletariat. See working class
property, 35, 49, 55, 143; as means for
     restricting access to democratic
     process, 212, 264–65
prophets, 237
Protestantism, 236, in Maryland, 83
Providence, 22
public archaeology, xv. See also Althusser,
     Louis; Archaeology in Public in An-
     napolis; Habermas, Jürgen; ideology;
     living history; Lucács, Georg; Marx,
     Karl; research design; theory
Public Circle. See State Circle
public program. See Archaeology in
     Public in Annapolis; critical theory
Puritanism. See Calvinism

Quinan, John, xiii

Raboteau, Albert, 223, 248
race, 22, 257
race relations, 188. See also African
     Americans; Archaeology in Public
     in Annapolis; population; power
     racism. See exploitation
Randolph, A. Philip, 246–47, 250
rationalism. See Enlightenment
rationality. See Enlightenment
Rawick, George, 237
Read, Esther Doyle, xiv, 273–74
reading: newspaper, 48, 53, 114, 129,
     142, 144, 154. See popular opinion;
     print culture; technologies of the self
Reconstruction, 257
reform, 96, 151; within capitalism, 109,
     179, 186–87, 189. See also disci-
     pline; panopticism; panopticon;
     surveillance
Reitz, Elizabeth, 270
Renaissance, 79–80, 83; and celebration
     of self, 148, 152–53, 157
Reps, John, 84–85, 94–95. See also
     baroque; town planning
repression, 190
research design, 2, 31, 35
Retallick-Brewer House site, 271
Reyes, Daniel, xv
Reynolds Tavern site, xiv, 270
Richmond, VA, 221
Ridout Garden, 68, 73–77, 80, 271; beds,
     75, 77, 79; central ramp, 75; date of
     construction, 80; excavation, 75. See
     also garden; geometry; landscape
Ridout House, 271
rings. See spirit practices
Ringgold, Thomas, 173
ritual bundles. See spirit practices
Roach, Terrance, xvi
Rockefeller, John D., Jr. See Williams-
     burg, VA
Rome: as baroque design, 8–9, 11, 77,
     81, 143
Roots. See Alex Haley
root work, 214, 231, 247, 260; defined,
     214. See also hands; James Brice
     House; mojos; Slayton House; spirit
     practices; Yronwode, Catherine
rotundas: as representative of equality
     of access, hearing, instruction, and
     visibility, 99
routines. See etiquette, modernizing
Royce, Lisa, xvii
rules: behavior and dining, 163, 166,
     183; for childrearing, 166; gardens,

68, 72, 74, 77, 99, 142; and gender, 172; print, 41–42, 113, 141; and trades/professions, 167. *See also* ceramics; etiquette; hygiene; ideology; popular opinion; surveillance
Ruppel, Timothy, xix, 60, 105–06, 224, 230–31, 237
Russo, Jean B., xvii, 14, 45. *See also* Chesapeake historians

saints of the Gospels, 236–37, 260
Samford, Patricia, xxi
Sands House site, xiv, 272
Sandy Ground (Staten Island, NY), xx
Sarudy, Barbara Wells, xvii, 45, 81, 101, 104–5
Satan. 260. *See also* devil
Saulsgiver, Priscilla, 186
Schmidt, Kimberly, xvii
Schrire, Carmel, xviii
Schuyler, Robert, xix–xx
science: as means for revealing natural rules, laws, and principles, 162. *See also* Enlightenment; ideology
Scott, Upton, 102
School Street, 94
Seidel, Elizabeth A., xiv, 274–75
Seidel, John L., xiv–xv, 88, 274–75, 277
segregation: residential, 188
self-inspection. *See* surveillance
separation and segmentation, 49, 53, 55–56, 115, 117, 165, 181, 183–84. *See also* Archaeology in Public in Annapolis; ceramics; *Maryland Gazette;* material culture; possessive individualism; print culture; technologies of the self
sexism. *See* exploitation
Shackel, Paul A., xi, 6, 153, 158, 163–65, 183, 269, 272
Shaw, Richard, xii
Shellenhammer, Jason, xii, 71. *See also* William Paca Garden
Shephard, Stephen, xx
Shiplap House site, 270
Shippen, Thomas Lee, 98
signage: removal from streetscape, 85
signature: as authenticating symbol, 142. *See also* citizenship; *Maryland Gazette;* popular opinion; print culture
Silverman, Martin, 24
Simms, Dennis, 251. *See also* Federal Writers' Project
Singleton, Teresa A., xx, 199
site tours. *See* Archaeology in Public in Annapolis; living history

slave autobiographies. *See* Federal Writers' Project
slave gardens. *See* gardens
slave narratives. *See* Federal Writers' Project
slavery, 4, 18, 22–24, 37, 40–41, 46, 49, 55, 58, 61, 67, 77, 82, 104–5, 143, 154, 174, 192, 196, 245, 253; auctions, 248, 251–52; and democracy, 212, 265; descriptions of conditions in Annapolis, 251, 253–54; documentation of slaves' lives, 209; invisible/unacknowledged heritage, 251, 253; legacy continues in Maryland to this day, 251; not the explanatory matrix for African spirit practices, 223; physical violence against, 205, 248, 253, 256, 260; resistance, 212, 231, 255; slaves as property, 212; terror, 253, 256. *See also* African Americans; caches; exploitation; Federal Writers' Project; Kunte Kinte; Kunte Kinte Festival; spirit practices
Slayton House site, 59, 276; African presence, 206, 213; caches in basement workrooms, 206, 213, 219; caches span slavery to post-emancipation contexts, 213–14, 222; contents of seven caches, 207–10; excavations, 205–07; garden, 206. *See also* cache; spirit practices
Smith, John, 124, 168. *See also* printer's manuals
Smith, Joseph, 177
Smith, Robert, xvi
Smith, Theophus, 223, 234, 236–37
Snider, Jeffrey, xvii
social control, 12, 36, 82; sources, 36, 45, 143. *See also* hierarchy
society: as natural entity. *See also* naturalizing ideology; science
Society for American Archaeology, 259
Society for Historical Archaeology, xix
Sonderman, Robert, xii, 271
South Africa, xvii, 59, 188–89
South, Stanley, xv, 267
spirit practices, xix. 58, 60–61, 203, 214–15, 258–62; absence of contradiction between African-inspired spirit practices and Christianity, 236–37, 260; absence of seventeenth-century African-inspired spirit practices in Annapolis's archaeological record, 214; absence of seventeenth-century African-inspired spirit prac-

spirit practices *(continued)*
tices in Virginia's archaeological
record, 222; as alternative set of
actions and understandings to
dominant ideology promoted by
whites in Annapolis, 237, 244–45,
255, 265–66; archaeology's unique
contributions to understanding,
222, 229, 231, 234, 244; associated
practices, 211; bags, 231, 234, 237;
BaKongo traditions, 203, 214, 223,
258; better represented in Virginia's
archaeological literature than in
Maryland's, 221; bundles, xxi, 202–
3, 206, 208, 215, 219, 221, 231–
34, 236–37; centering, 234–35;
and Christianity, 223, 235–39, 247;
chronology, 222; closed to whites in
eighteenth- and nineteenth-century
Annapolis, 237, 247; coins, 204,
210, 225, 227, 230; comparative
study, 60, 211, 220–24, 230–31,
234, 237; Congo traditions, 223;
conjure/conjuration, 214, 231–35,
254; cosmograms, 203, 208, 211,
217–19, 222, 231, 233–34, 241–42;
crystals, 200–203, 215; Condomblé,
60, 223, 235–36, 260; and danger,
232–33; debate as to whether they
are syncretic/creole traditions or
remain wholly African in origin,
214, 235, 238–, 243, 248; devoid
of a large practitioner class, 237;
difficulties in specifying their African
origins, xxi, 207; discs, 209, 225,
242–43; and disease, 230–31; Fan
traditions, 214; as exempt from lure
of possessive individualism, 244–45,
253–54; fostered but not created
within institution of slavery, 223;
Hoodoo, xvi, 214, 231; Ifa traditions,
214; interpretive disagreement surrounding, 201, 203, 215–20; kinship
as likely explanatory matrix, 235;
loci of recovery, 203, 216–17; and
maintenance of order, 235; malign
uses, 231; as means for preserving
African identity, 61, 190; and Native
American religions, 223; oyster and
tortoise shells in caches, 215; Palo
Mayombe, 61, 223, 236; pins, 210,
220, 225, 228, 230, 234; purposes,
60, 204–5, 224, 230–31, 237, 243;
rings in caches, 216; root work,
214; Shango, 260; Santeria, 61, 223,
235–36, 260; shiny and/or reflective
objects as metonyms, 215, 234; span

slavery and post-Emancipation
contexts, 213–14, 222, 237; and
swept yards, 232; in twentieth-
century contexts, 213–14; underex-
plored avenues in study of, 223,
237; Voodoo, 61, 223, 235–36;
worn or carried vs. buried items,
224–30; Yoruba traditions, 214.
See also African Americans; African
descent; James Brice House site;
cache; diasporic communities; Federal Writers' Project; kalunga line;
Latin American descent; St. Mary's
site; Slayton House site; Yronwode,
Catherine
spirits of the dead, 206–7, 248, 260;
ability to shape shift, 230; in Caribbean, 233; control of, 106, 203,
206–7, 215, 218, 229–30, 232–34,
236–37, 240–41, 243; points of
access, 206–7, 215, 218, 232–33;
travel, 203. *See also* cosmogram;
spirit practices
St. Anne's Church, 10, 84, 271
St. Augustine archaeology project (St.
Augustine, FL), xx
St. John's College (of Annapolis), 19
St. Mary's Catholic Church, xiv
St. Mary's City, MD, 11, 14; seventeenth-
century, 11, 83–84. *See also* baroque
design; Chesapeake historians; His-
toric St. Mary's City; living history;
Miller, Henry M.; town planning
St. Mary's Colored School (Annapolis,
MD), 256
St. Mary's site, 156, 200–201, 271;
African presence at site, 204, 213.
See also cache; spirit practices
Stabler, Jennifer, xiv, 87, 90, 94, 273
Stapleton, Jennifer, xiii
Stamp Act, 28, 151
standardization. *See* mass production;
separation and segmentation
Stanton Center, xiii
state: crisis of legitimacy, 264–65; and
individuals, 34, 186, 190, 263–
65; as police-like apparatus, 36,
153, 188; as new republic, 47, 138.
See also Foucault
State Circle, 8, 10, 44, 83–86, 88–90,
93–95, 98, 143, 183, 273; changes
to, 84–90, 95; as egg, 44, 86–93,
95; excavation, 84–88, 95; features,
87; stratigraphy, 85, 87; terraces, 90
State House. *See* Maryland State House
State House Inn, xiv, 86, 271
Stein, Nancy, xiii

Stewart, Elizabeth, xiii
Stiverson, Gregory, xii
Stoddert plan (of Annapolis), 84, 90–92,
94–95. *See also* Nicholson plan of
Annapolis; town planning
Stone, Garry Wheeler, 120
Stower, Caleb, 124. *See also* printer's
manuals
stratification. *See* social hierarchy
street pattern. *See* baroque design; town
planning
streets: as funnels to monuments, 85, 94
Strausbaugh, John, xv
Streuver, Stuart, xv, xx
Stuart, William T., xvi
subordination. *See* exploitation; social
hierarchy
surveillance, 13–14, 39, 60–61, 96–
97, 153, 169; and the creation of
subjects, 48, 143; as mutual inspection, 97, 99–100, 114, 142–44, 183;
as self-inspection, 97, 114, 153, 171,
173–74, 182, 212, 245. *See also*
Bentham, Jeremy; citizenship; discipline; Foucault, Michel; panopticism; panopticon; power; state
survivals. *See* African Americans
Sweeney, Judith, xii
swept yards. *See* landscapes; spirits
of the dead
symbolic violence, 232
Symonds, Pringle, xii–xiii, 85

table settings. *See* ceramics; etiquette;
individualism; separation and
segmentation; technologies of the
self
tableware. *See* ceramics; etiquette; ideology; individualism; separation and
segmentation; technologies of the
self
taste. *See* aesthetics
tax assessments, 22, 30. *See also* documents; population
technologies of the self, 35, 37, 53, 57–58,
97, 153, 165, 167, 179, 184, 186,
211; anger control, 36, 166; ceramics, 55–56; clothing, 36; dining,
155, 165; deodorants, 36; driving
tests, 36; as equivalent of Deetz's
Georgian mindset, 97, 138, 154,
165; forks, 36; as form of social
capital, 97; gardening, 97, 109, 165,
184; glasses, 36; knives, 36; literacy,
numeracy, and writing, 97, 166; politeness, 36, 97; and reading, 53, 97,
100, 111, 138, 166; as source of

power in new governments, 97,
138; toothbrushes, 36, 56, 165, 183;
voice modulation, 36. *See also* Foucault, Michel; hygiene; ideology;
panopticism; panopticon; power;
surveillance
Tetrault, Tara, xii
Texas: caches, 208
theory: archaeological, 31, 185; baroque,
8, 143, 153; critical, 31, 33, 182,
185, 187–88, 190, 193, 260; cultural ecology, 180; cultural evolution, xix; economic determinism,
xix; Frankfurt School, 187; function-
alism: rejection of, 57; Marxian,
xviii; Marxist, xv, xviii, 157, 179–
80, 185–87; materialist, 180; middle
range, 78; social theory and ideology, 23, 141–43. *See also* consciousness; landscapes; town planning
Thom, Alexander, 87. *See also* State
Circle
Thomas, David Hurst, xx–xxi
Thompson, E. P., 165–66
Thompson, Raymond H., xx, 202
Thompson, Robert Ferris, 199–200, 202,
215, 223, 260
time discipline. *See* discipline
tin cans, 194; dating of deposits containing them, 194
tobacco. *See* farming
Tobacco Prise site, 267
tobys, 207, 224, 231. *See also* spirit
practices
Toll, John, xvi
toothbrushes, 36, 56, 165, 183. *See also*
etiquette; hygiene; ideology; individualism; separation and segmentation; technologies of the self
tourism, 4, 11; heritage tourism, 30.
See also Annapolis; Archaeology in
Public in Annapolis; living history;
St. Mary's City
town planning, 1; in Annapolis, 1, 5, 7,
9, 12, 14, 30, 64–65, 83–91; in
Baltimore, 5, 12, 14; baroque, 7–
9, 41, 77, 84; and calculus, 92;
central planning, 12; and egg, 92;
and freedom/liberty, 12, 83; and
quest for power, 94; relationship
to garden design, 85, 94; and social
control, 12, 41, 94; in Williamsburg,
VA, 29. *See also* geometry; landscapes; State Circle
tradition, African American: 4. *See also*
gardens; landscape; material culture;
spirit practices

Tuesday Club of Annapolis, 14, 37, 54–
55, 113, 147–50; parody as means
for claiming equality with agents of
power, 262–63; rules and protocol,
146–47, 150, 165; satire of public
opinion, 55, 113, 145, 148–49, 151,
163, 179, 266; as social commentary, 14, 54–55, 145, 147–48, 265.
See also Cole, Charles; Green, Jonas;
Hamilton, Dr. Alexander
Tulip Hill, 73
Turner, Brian 24
Turpin, Bill, xiii

United Nations, 188
United States of America, 95, 97: as
both African and European, 266;
as imagined community, 51; larger
implications of Annapolis-specific
work for, 258, 266. See also Anderson, Benedict; citizen; citizenship;
democracy; Derrida, Jacques; freedom; imagined community; liberty;
nation-building; popular opinion;
state
United States Naval Academy, xiv, 1, 3,
19, 195, 275–77
unity. See ideology; imagined community;
popular opinion
University of Arizona, xix, 202
University of Cape Town (South Africa),
59, 192; visiting faculty experience
as leading to redirection in Annapolis public program, 188. See also
Archaeology in Public in Annapolis
University of Maryland (at College Park),
xi–xiii, xvi, 24, 30, 60, 207, 213,
251
upper class, 112–13
Upton Scott House, 4–5, 269
urban design. See town planning
urban renewal, 195
utilities: burial, 85
utopian communities: as critiques of
capitalism, 212
utopian socialists: Eddy, Mary Baker,
62; Lee, Mother Ann, 62; Smith,
Joseph, 62
Uunila, Kirsti, xii

Van Winkle, Cornelius, 124. See also
printer's manuals
vernacular architecture. See architecture
vernacular garden. See garden
Versailles: gardens, 67, 81, 143. See also
Mukerji, Chandra
Victualling Warehouse site, 156, 269

views. See geometry
Virginia, 60, 82, 264; caches, 208, 221,
225, 230. See also spirit practices;
Williamsburg,
VA visibility, 99. See also Bentham,
Jeremy; gardens; geometry; landscapes; Latrobe, Benjamin; panopticism; panopticon; surveillance;
technologies of the self; town
planning
vista. See geometry
Vlach, John Michael, xx, 203
voice: alternative, 27, 59, 237, 244, 258,
266; American historical archaeology and the search for alternative
voices, 27, 187–89. See also African
Americans; ideology; muted groups

wage earners, 167, 174
Walsh, Lorena, 199. See also Chesapeake
historians
War of 1812, 2, 12
Ward, Jeanne A., 277–78
Waring, Sarah, xvii
Warner, Mark S., xi, 6, 58, 62, 174–77,
194, 197–98, 256–57, 272–75
Washington Bee, 256
Washington, Booker T., 196, 246–47
Washington, DC, 12
Washington, George, 2, 31, 99, 168
Washington, Maisha, xiii, 255, 258–62;
African sources for many western
concepts, 259, 261; archaeology-
based educational outreach, 258–
63. See also Bernal, Martin
watching. See discipline; ideology; panop-
ticism; panopticon; power; state;
surveillance
wealth, 14–17, 25, 67, 78, 80, 82, 212;
hierarchy of, 18, 35–37, 49, 104, 109,
141, 197, 199, 212, 257; unequal
concentration, 57. See also class;
power; probate inventories; property;
social hierarchy
Wedgewood, Josiah, 166
Wells, Nan, xvii
White, Leslie, xix
Whitehead, Tony L., xvi
Wiggins, James, 255. See also Federal
Writers' Project
Wilkie, Laurie, xxi
William Faris's Garden, 45, 101–03; com-
pared and contrasted with Charles
Carroll of Carrollton Garden and
William Paca Garden, 102. See also
Faris, William; garden; landscape
William Paca Garden, xii, 2, 43–45,

63–68, 70–71, 73–75, 77, 80, 84,
113, 155, 259, 261,
267; and absence of power, 63, 67, 82;
canal, 71; Chippendale bridge, 71;
and conjecture, 71; date of construction, 80; diminishing terrace width,
68; excavation, 70–71; pavilion, 45,
64, 71; planned, 65, 73; and political aspirations of its planner, 67, 81;
pond, 71; purpose, 63; restoration,
64; as unique, 66, 74, 77; wall, 70–
71. *See also* authenticity; Brigham,
Laurence; garden; geometry; ideology; landscape; Paca, Barbara; Paca,
William; Peale, Charles Willson;
William Paca House; Wright, St.
Clair
William Paca House, 2, 5, 9, 63, 70, 155,
267
Williams, Aubrey, xvi
Williams, Eileen, 269, 272
Williamsburg, VA, xix, 2, 7, 19, 29, 155,
180, 221; eighteenth-century, 7, 101;
nineteenth-century, 7; twentieth-
century, 7. *See also* authenticity;
living history; population women,
40
Williams, "Parson" Resin, 252. *See also*
Federal Writers' Project

witchcraft, 214, 236
Worden, Robert, xiv, 200–201, 203
work discipline. *See* discipline
working class, 31, 36, 100, 167, 195;
exploitation of, 18. *See also* class
Wren, Christopher, 8, 11
Wright, Henry T., 267–71
Wright, Ruffin, xii
Wright, St. Clair, xii–xiii, 24, 30, 64,
66–67, 70, 73, 75, 85, 118. *See also*
geometry; Historic Annapolis Foundation; historic preservation; Paca,
Barbara; William Paca Garden
writing. *See* discipline; ideology; imagined communities; literacy; popular
opinion; print culture; technologies
of the self
Wye Island, xi, 81; Paca's garden and
property at Wye, xvii, 81. *See also*
Paca, William
Wylie, Alison, xviii

Yale University, 215
Yentsch, Anne E., xiv, 6, 30, 40, 270–73
Yoruba. *See* spirit practices
Yronwode, Catherine, 213–15. *See also*
spirit practices

Zaretsky, Irving, xviii

Compositor: Integrated Composition Systems
Text: 10/13 Sabon
Display: Sabon
Printer and binder: Maple-Vail Manufacturing Group

DATE DUE
